The Laws of War

The

Constraints

Laws

on Warfare in

of

the Western

World # War

Edited by

Michael Howard,

George J. Andreopoulos, and

Mark R. Shulman

Yale University Press

New Haven and London

Published with the assistance of the Frederick W. Hilles Publications Fund of Yale University.

Designed by James J. Johnson and set in Times Roman type by The Composing Room of
Michigan, Inc., Grand Rapids, Michigan. Printed in the United States of America by Vail-Ballou
Press, Binghamton, New York.

Library of Congress Cataloging-in-Publication Data

Howard, M. (Michael)
    The laws of war : constraints on warfare in the Western world / edited by Michael Howard,
George J. Andreopoulos, and Mark R. Shulman.
        p.   cm.
    Includes bibliographical references and index.
    ISBN 0-300-05899-3

    1. War (International law)   I. Andreopoulos, George J.   II. Shulman, Mark R.   III. Title.
JX4521.H77   1994

341.6—dc20   94-18818

A catalogue record for this book is available from the British Library.

The paper in this book meets the guidelines for permanence and durability of the Committee on
Production Guidelines for Book Longevity of the Council on Library Resources.

10   9   8   7   6   5   4   3   2   1

Contents

CONTENTS

Preface

The purpose of the essays included in this volume is to examine both formal constraints on the conduct of war from classical antiquity to our own time and unwritten conventions as to what was "done" or "not done" in the course of military operations. In this context the essays consider the relations of such practices to the common culture of the time and the extent to which they were affected by the development of weapons technology. As the reader would note, each era had its own peculiarities, but common to all, and especially in land war, were issues like belligerent rights, treatment of prisoners and civilians, observation of truces and immunities, the acceptability or otherwise of particular weapons or weapon systems, the distinction between the treatment of "civilized" and "uncivilized" combatants, codes of honor, and war crimes in general. Although the volume deals primarily with *jus in bello* rather than *jus ad bellum* issues, the latter are included when critical junctures in the evolution of perceptions of the just war are discussed.

This study has also a contemporary dimension. As recent debates on the nature and extent of the international community's involvement in places like the Persian Gulf, Bosnia-Herzegovina, and Somalia have demonstrated, there are strong parallels with certain concerns exhibited during earlier periods—among others, the extent to which the traditional distinction between international and noninternational conflicts is becoming unsustainable and the extent to which the staying power of notions like exemplary violence and military necessity will be affected by the continuing calls for enforceable humanitarian norms.

Thus, in a concluding chapter, some of the key elements of the preceding case studies are highlighted and reflections are offered on the challenges facing the quest for humanitarian norms in warfare on the eve of the twenty-first century.

MICHAEL HOWARD
GEORGE J. ANDREOPOULOS
MARK R. SHULMAN

Michael Howard   I

Constraints on Warfare

.

The subject of this volume is the limitations that Western
societies have imposed on themselves in their conduct of
war: not just the laws of war as expressed in such positive enactments as the Hague
and Geneva Conventions, but rather what has sometimes been termed the "cultural
regulation of violence"; what was, in the old-fashioned phrase, "done" and "not
done" in war; constraints of which formal laws were only expressions, or which did
not necessarily coincide with formal laws at all. Our contributors describe these
constraints as they applied in classical antiquity, in the High Middle Ages when war in
Western Europe was specifically constrained by codes of chivalry and the dictates of
Christendom, in the Europe of the Renaissance and Napoleonic eras, and in the
frontier wars in North America. They discuss their application to war at sea, and the
attempts of international lawyers to control the increasing destructiveness of warfare
in the first half of the twentieth century. Finally they consider the two peculiar
phenomena of the second half of this century: planning for nuclear war, and national
liberation struggles in which one of the participants was not an organized state but
was treated by at least part of the international community as if it were.

Constraints of our own have unfortunately compelled us to confine our study to
the Western world. We would certainly have learned much from comparing Western
practices with those of China or Islam or such African cultures as those of the Ashanti
or the Zulus. But within the limits we have set ourselves we hope to learn something
about the way in which not only warfare but moral standards have evolved in the West;
to determine whether there has been a constant improvement in civilized standards,
and if not, why not. We can learn a great deal about a people's culture and the manner
in which it develops by observing how they fight.

There is a crude assumption that in war societies act as if all is fair, that all normal
moral constraints are suspended, and that they consider themselves entitled to do any

damage necessary to destroy the enemy. Clausewitz gave currency to this view when he wrote: "War is an act of force to compel our enemy to do our will. . . . [A]ttached to force are certain self-imposed, imperceptible limitations hardly worth mentioning, known as international law and custom, but they scarcely weaken it."[1] He knew very well, however, that the conduct of war was subject to considerably greater and more perceptible limitations in his own time than it had been in the days of, say, Genghis Khan. He explained this by saying that "if wars between civilized nations are far less cruel and destructive than wars between savages, the reason lies in the social conditions of the states themselves and in their relationship to one another."[2] Restraints on war grew out of the cultures of the war-making societies, rather than being imposed on them by some transcendent moral order.

In fact, "savages," as Clausewitz described them (a word habitually employed during the era of the Enlightenment), are not more cruel and destructive in war than civilized peoples.[3] Anthropological studies show that although war in some form was endemic in most primitive societies, it was often highly ritualized and sometimes almost bloodless. It could be a *rite de passage* for adolescents, a quasi-religious ceremonial substituting for legal process, or a legitimized form of violent competition comparable to team sports in contemporary societies. Clausewitz's definition of war as an instrument of *Staatspolitik* was one that would not have been widely accepted, or indeed understood, in Europe before the fifteenth century, and perhaps even less in the rest of the world. There is no contribution in this volume on primitive warfare, and we would probably need a great many to cover it adequately. But our Western classical and medieval examples show the extent to which wars even in those societies were ritual or agonistic and, as such, subject to strict and generally recognized regulation.[4]

Constraints on war as we have experienced them in our own societies have been largely shaped by Christian ethic defined by leading teachers in the Catholic church of the Middle Ages and the Renaissance, an ethic transformed in the seventeenth and eighteenth centuries into something more rationalistic and utilitarian by such early international lawyers as the Dutchman Hugo Grotius and the Swiss Emerich de Vattel, and made increasingly specific by international agreements such as the Hague and Geneva Conventions in the nineteenth and twentieth centuries. The Christian doctors, from Augustine to Aquinas in the Middle Ages, followed by Francisco Suárez, Alberico Gentili, and Francisco de Vitoria in the sixteenth century, were above all concerned with defining the just war, *jus ad bellum:* wars in which Christians might fight with a clear conscience. They laid down principles which still hold fairly good today. The war must be waged by a legitimate authority, for a cause itself just—to make reparation for an injury or to restore what had been wrongly seized— and in general with the intention of advancing good or avoiding evil. There had to be a reasonable prospect of victory, and every attempt should have been made to reconcile the differences by peaceful means. Attempts were made to ensure that holy days were not profaned. Immunity was, in principle, enjoyed by noncombatants, especially priests and pilgrims; war, it was accepted, should be monopolized so far as possible by the war-making classes and lesser breeds should be spared less out of humanity than out of contempt as not being worth powder and shot—or rather cold steel. But the principle of the immunity of noncombatants was mitigated by the countervailing principle, as it was called, of double effect, which is often used to justify what today we would call collateral damage. That lays down that although innocent bystanders should not be deliberately targeted, it is permissible to inflict hurt upon them if it occurs simply as a by-product of an attack on a legitimate military target. Finally, it was laid down that the amount of force used should not be disproportionate to the object to be achieved—a moral imperative translated by military specialists into the principle of economy of force. This principle, incidentally, is one that has never enjoyed a very high priority in the American way of warfare.[5]

The relationship between these principles and the actual conduct of war in the Middle Ages is covered in this volume by Professor Stacey. He makes the essential point that, whereas the theologians concentrated on *jus ad bellum*, the right to go to war, the laws for the conduct of war, *jus in bello*, were an entirely secular creation developed to suit the needs of a rigidly stratified social order in which the right to bear arms was a jealously guarded privilege. Much the same has applied, as Professor Ober shows us, in classical Greece. But in medieval Europe, war was also a highly organized industry. Its laws were primarily concerned with such mundane questions as the regulation of plunder and the ransoming of prisoners. This kind of warfare, *bellum hostile*, was the norm within Western Christendom. But in wars against outsiders, infidels, or barbarians, the West had inherited a brutal legacy from the Romans which they termed *bellum romanum*, or *guerre mortelle*, a conflict in which no holds were barred and all those designated as enemy, whether bearing arms or not, could be indiscriminately slaughtered. This was initially to be the case when Christian warriors first encountered the "savages" of the New World, until the Spanish theologians Suárez and Vitoria introduced the principle of the universality of civil society, a principle however far longer honored in the breach than in the observance.[6]

Perhaps the most significant of all the developments that occurred in the early modern period, that era when Europe emerged from the chaos of the wars of religion and which international-relations specialists associate with the name of Hugo Grotius, was the virtual abandonment of the concept of the just war. War became accepted as a natural, if not indeed a necessary, element in international politics, and its conduct was molded by pragmatic necessities rather than by abstract principles. If the seventeenth and eighteenth centuries were the heyday of what later came to be called limited war, those "temperate and indecisive contests" of which Edward Gibbon wrote so complacently, it was not because the moral standards of that epoch were higher than those which preceded or succeeded them, but because it suited everyone that it should be so. Wars were conflicts over political power rather than ideology: no party regarded defeat as an ultimate catastrophe. They were conducted by small and expensive professional armies whose expense kept them small. Unless trade continued to bring money into state treasuries, war would not be possible at all, so economic activity was, so far as possible, left undisturbed (except of course at sea, which, as Professor Hattendorf shows us, was a very different story).

The armies consisted partly of a supranational or international aristocracy, who were likely to have as many cousins on the opposing side as on their own; partly by tough professionals prepared to sell their services to the highest bidder; and partly by luckless conscripts likely to desert at the first opportunity. They had no great incentive to kill one another, and the short range of their weapons gave them limited opportunity to do so. So the chivalric constraints developed during the later Middle Ages became generalized as the conduct of warfare extended beyond the narrow aristocratic group that had originally developed them. There was every incentive to take unwounded prisoners; officers brought a lucrative ransom, and other ranks could be recruited into one's own forces. Battle, when joined, was unavoidably and indescribably bloody, which was a good reason for avoiding it whenever possible. Campaigns revolved around sieges rather than battles, and siegecraft had been reduced to a fine art which had strong ritualistic and agonistic elements, as the Gobelin tapestries that depict them indicate very strongly. Nonetheless, sieges could be as bloody as battles, and Professor Parker shows how the sacking of conquered cities continued to be deliberately and demonstratively brutal, from the time of the Dutch War of Independence to that of the Peninsular War.

In general, noncombatants within the battle zone had no rights or immunities as such, and indeed were not to have any until the twentieth century. But there were beginning to creep into the conduct of war not only prudential but ethical constraints on their treatment. The nightmare days of the Thirty Years War when troops, themselves desperate and starving, tortured, slaughtered, and burned their way across Europe were not prolonged into the following century. There was still looting and burning and rape, but the wearing of a uniform was no longer regarded as a license to do such things. Rather the contrary: the goodwill of the local population was seen as a necessary prerequisite to the subsistence of the armies in their midst, and requisitions were carried out in orderly and temperate fashion. When, exceptionally, the French armies systematically ravaged the Rhenish Palatinate in 1688, it was regarded as an outrage comparable almost to the Holocaust in our own time.

The Wars of the French Revolution are generally considered by historians to indicate the end of limited and the beginning of total war. But Professor Rothenberg shows how little, if at all, the behavior of the revolutionary and Napoleonic armies differed from that of the armies of the ancien régime. The early examples of revolutionary extremism were brief. It is true that the members of these revolutionary armies were no longer drawn exclusively from the old, transnational military classes, but their officers were as often as not old professionals, and Napoleon was the most professional of them all. The concept of military self-interest still guided their treatment of opposing forces. Certainly the enormous size of the Napoleonic armies and their more casual attitude toward logistics made their exactions on the civil population both more arbitrary and less predictable, but examples of deliberate cruelty and savagery were rare. In spite of what Clausewitz had to say on the matter, Napoleonic warfare remained a great deal more limited in its conduct than that of the seventeenth century, let alone the centuries that succeeded it.

But there was, as Professor Parker also points out, a massive and gruesome exception to the humanization of warfare that was occurring in the seventeenth and eighteenth centuries. The concept of *bellum romanum,* of total war, was still flourishing, especially with respect to three categories of adversary: rebels, infidels, and "savages." For the English, the Irish were all three. The ruthlessness with which the English "pacified" Ireland was to be carried over, as Professor Selesky makes clear, into the treatment accorded by the early settlers in North America to the indigenous inhabitants that they encountered there; a ruthlessness compounded by the fear natural to a minority far from home, in an alien environment and fearing for their very survival. The contrast between the manner in which French and English soldiers treated each other, even though they were enemies, and the way they treated the Indians, provides textbook examples of the two kinds of war. The contrast was to reappear a little later under rather different circumstances during the War of Independence. On the one hand there were the standards laid down by George Washington, himself a regular soldier, who was at pains to show, by the professional behavior of the American armies, that the United States had the right to be treated as a sovereign state. On the other was the ferocious banditry into which the war degenerated at the fringes, as it is always liable to do when irregular belligerents escape professional control.

When we reach the nineteenth century we find two contradictory developments taking place in Western societies. On the one hand, the growth of wealth and education was producing a bourgeois culture whose members were increasingly ill at ease if not with war itself, then certainly with the brutalities of war—brutalities which the development of communication could now bring to the attention of the entire literate world.[7] Before 1850 few people outside the military profession knew what a battlefield was really like; though it is arguable that pain, disease, mutilation, and sudden death were so much part of everyday life before the nineteenth century that they would not have been too upset if they had. But the dispatches of William Howard Russell from the Crimea, and the photographs of Roger Fenton and his colleagues in the American Civil War brought the realities of mass military slaughter to the attention of a generation that hoped and believed that mankind was emancipating itself from such barbarities. The experience in 1859 of the first two major European battles since Waterloo, Magenta and Solferino, was so horrific that it led the royal commanders of the two armies, the Emperors Franz Joseph and Napoleon III, to conclude an armistice as quickly as possible. Further, it resulted in the foundation, by the Swiss Henri Dunant, of the International Red Cross Society to alleviate the sufferings of belligerents in future wars, and the signing in 1864 of the first Geneva Convention for the protection and care of the sick and wounded in war. A consensus was growing that, although war might still be a necessary element in international politics—indeed all the more so as new nations such as Germany and Italy were fighting for their freedom—it should be waged, so far as possible, with humanity: especially since, after 1870, armies consisted increasingly of conscripts who shared the value systems of their societies. This was the generation that produced the first comprehensive codification of the regulations for the conduct of war by land: the United States Army General Order No. 100, *Instructions for the Government of Armies of the United States in the Field,* known after its author, Dr. Francis Lieber of Columbia University, as the Lieber code, a formulation that determined the practice of armies not only in the United States but in many other countries for years to come.[8]

Such constraint was of course all the more desirable as the weapons of war became increasingly destructive; and this was the second development that I have noted. It was precisely at this time, the latter half of the nineteenth century, that the growing range and destructive power of weapons were beginning exponentially to increase the lethality of warfare, both on the battlefield and beyond it. There had been occasional attempts in the Middle Ages to prevent the introduction of weapons regarded as unfair or inhumane: the crossbow had been singled out in the twelfth century, and there had been a lot of grumbling about the introduction of firearms from the *chevaleresque* aristocracy, although nothing had been done about it. The developing technology of the industrial age, however, opened a Pandora's box of horrors that we have been trying ever since to close.

The first attempt was the Saint Petersburg Declaration of 1868 which prohibited the use of explosive bullets under 400 grams in weight: a nasty little weapon, one must agree, though arguably no nastier than explosive shells over 400 grams in weight, to say nothing of such devices as napalm, to which we have gone on almost without blinking. But more interesting than the prohibition itself was the rationale given for it, which opens a window into the mentality of the era:

> Considering that the progress of civilisation should have the effect of alleviating as much as possible the calamities of war;
> That the only legitimate object which States should endeavour to accomplish during war is to weaken the military forces of society;

That for this purpose it is sufficient to disable the greatest possible number of men;

That this object would be exceeded by the employment of arms which uselessly aggravate the sufferings of disabled men, or render their death inevitable;

That the employment of such arms would, therefore, be contrary to the laws of humanity.[9]

These were the principles that guided Western statesmen in their attempts to codify the laws of war during what we may call the Hague era, the period examined by Professor Roberts in his contribution to this volume. It takes its name from the two Hague peace conferences of 1899 and 1907; a third, scheduled for 1915, never took place, but there still survives the palace that was built to host it. The era really began, however, in 1856 with the Congress of Paris, which attempted to set limits to naval warfare—attempts charted in his chapter by Professor Hattendorf. And arguably it continues still, so long as the various Hague and Geneva conventions continue to be debated and updated.

Perhaps the most notable successes of this era have been in the field of international law, especially the creation of the International Court of Justice and the development of international arbitration; but these lie beyond our frame of reference here. In controlling weapon use and development, its record has been almost totally negative. All attempts to control or limit air bombardment have failed, as Professor Biddle shows in her chapter, apart from a brief agreement not to throw explosive substances out of air balloons. Professor Rosenberg makes clear, further, that the control of nuclear weapons use has not even been attempted except on a unilateral basis. Only in the field of chemical and biological warfare was a limited success chalked up with the Protocol of 1925 (though it took the United States fifty years to ratify it). The most fruitful area of Hague activities has been in dealing with casualties of war rather than with the conduct of war itself, particularly the treatment of prisoners. This achievement is not to be underrated. In Western Europe at least, throughout both world wars, the Geneva Conventions respecting prisoners of war were observed by both sides. But even so, on the Russian front and in the Pacific theater, the situation was horrifyingly different.

The two world wars saw the beginning of the end of what we have called the Grotian era. That era had been marked, as we have seen, by two characteristics. First, the concept of the just war, *jus ad bellum,* had virtually disappeared from European warfare. No one called in question the right of states to go to war if their interests seemed to demand it. Second, and associated with this, was an assumption of common values that would govern the conduct of those wars, whether or not these values were codified. Their existence was proclaimed most notably by the Russian jurist

Feodor Martens in his famous preamble to the Hague Convention of 1907, which declared:

> These provisions, the drafting of which has been inspired by the desire to diminish the evils of war, so far as military requirements permit, are intended as a general rule of conduct for the belligerents in their own mutual relations and in relation to the inhabitants. . . . In cases not included in the Regulations adopted . . . the inhabitants and the belligerents remain under the protection and the rule *of the principles of the laws of nations, derived from the usage, established among civilized peoples, from the laws of humanity, and the dictates of the public conscience* (emphasis added).[10]

The assumption of a common code of conduct among the peoples of all Western nations had a certain validity during the first two decades of the twentieth century. Even so, this was not necessarily identical in other cultures. Whatever agreements the political leaders of Japan might enter into, they could not speak for a military caste whose beliefs as to what was and what was not licit in war and, more important, what was and was not honorable derived from a totally different cultural tradition and one all too little understood in the West. But more sinister still was the way in which members of the European family itself were quite deliberately renouncing their traditional cultural values. The moral code that enabled the Soviet leadership, on the one hand, to carry out the deliberate massacre of Polish officers at Katyn, and the German army, on the other, to shoot Soviet political commissars on sight and work or starve millions of Soviet prisoners of war to death had been formulated in deliberate contradiction to the bourgeois ideals set out in the Martens preamble. In the elimination of enemies of the proletariat or the establishment of a racial hegemony there was no room for "the laws of humanity" or "dictates of the public conscience." This was total war of a kind that had been barely seen in Europe since the Dark Ages, though it had not been unknown in the New World: war, not just for the overthrow of the adversary's political power, but for the physical destruction of his entire society.

At the root of the Christian-humanist attempts to constrain war has been the recognition of the adversary as a human being possessing certain fundamental rights. It was justifiable to kill him so long as he bore arms and so had accepted the risks inherent in that activity. But once he was disarmed he regained all the rights due to him as a child of God or a member of civil society. If he was seen not as a human being, however, but as a member of an inferior but still menacing race, it made no difference whether he was wearing a uniform and bearing arms or not—whether indeed he was man, woman, or child. He had no more rights than a wild animal or an insect. In consequence the Nuremberg tribunals had to take account of war crimes of a kind, and on a scale of which Martens had never conceived.

Simultaneously, if paradoxically, there was ending the long-held view that war was a natural and value-free element in relations between states. The trauma of the First World War strengthened the belief, among sections of Western society whose views were still influential if waning, that war as such was now impermissible. In 1928, during that tragically brief period between the wars when it looked as if stable peace might be possible, the nations of the world under the guidance of Secretary of State Frank B. Kellogg of the United States and French foreign minister Aristide Briand signed an agreement whereby they solemnly renounced war "as an instrument of policy," except in self-defense. "Planning aggressive war" itself became a crime, and both German and Japanese leaders were arraigned for it in 1946.

Whether such a renunciation of war has had any real value is a matter for legitimate doubt. Certainly it has not reduced the general incidence of war: nations simply no longer declare it. The Italians invaded Abyssinia in 1935, the Japanese China in 1937, without such formalities, and the Second World War was virtually the last time they were observed. American troops fought in Korea, Vietnam, Grenada, Panama, and the Gulf without any formal declaration of war. The British and the French invaded Egypt in 1956 without formal declaration of war. The Soviet Union invaded Hungary in 1956 and Afghanistan in 1979 without formal declaration of war, and so did Saddam Hussein when he occupied Kuwait in 1990. As for planning aggressive war, I am afraid that the archives of the defense departments even of the most peace-loving countries contain contingency plans that would provide pretty damning evidence if those states were ever to lose a war and their leaders had to face trial. Sadly, the renunciation of war as a distinct relationship between states, to be entered into with only considerable forethought and solemnity and conducted according to certain well-defined conventions, has only made the use of armed forces as an instrument of policy perhaps more acceptable and certainly no less frequent.

But there is another way in which the constraints on war observed during the Grotian era have been dissolved. The lawyers of that period inherited and preserved from their medieval predecessors the belief that war was permissible only if waged by legitimate authority: a very necessary distinction was made between public wars waged by Christian princes, and the private wars, vendettas, and *chevauchées* conducted in medieval Europe by local warlords or bands of unemployed and indigent knights. By the seventeenth century the legitimate authorities had crystallized into finite and recognized states that had the right both to make war on their neighbors and to suppress rebellion within their own realms. It was further assumed that both activities would be carried out by regular, professional armed forces, and the laws of war, written or unwritten, were based on that assumption. The status of civilians who joined in the defense of their own territory against an invader was anomalous: before the nineteenth century it did not happen very often. The status of civilians who rose against the authority of their rightful sovereign was, however, perfectly clear: they had no rights at all, and if they lost their activities were judged, and judged very severely, by the criminal law.

The first serious example in Western Europe of civilians joining unasked in the defense of their territory was probably that of the Spaniards in the Peninsular War of 1808–14. Although that resulted in the reciprocal horrors so movingly depicted by Goya, I am not aware that it led to any change in the formal laws of war. Much more influential was the far less ferocious resistance put up to the German invaders of 1870 by the French *francs-tireurs:* resistance, however, sufficiently effective to impel the draftsmen of the Hague Convention on Land Warfare in 1907 to devote several paragraphs to defining and limiting the legitimacy of such action and, more important, to lead the German army to write into its own war book instructions for the most ruthless suppression, mainly by way of reprisals, of such civilian activities. These instructions were to be put into effect when Germany invaded Belgium in 1914, with results that can only be described as counterproductive. They were used again on a far wider scale in the Second World War, when the German armies faced large-scale guerrilla resistance in the Soviet Union and Yugoslavia and on a smaller scale in France, in suppression of which they committed some of the most notorious atrocities for which their leaders were tried and condemned after the war. The experience of that war resulted in the far more comprehensive regulations for the protection of civilians in warfare that were embodied in the Geneva Conventions of 1949.

This is indeed the field where such regulation is most necessary. It is not too difficult for soldiers to treat their professional adversaries with respect and humanity, especially after they have disarmed them. But when they are surrounded by a civilian population which has every reason for detesting them, whose language they do not understand, and whose every movement they suspect—it is then that there occur the kind of atrocities committed by the Germans at Oradour or, I am afraid it must be said, by the Americans at My Lai.

What, finally, about that other area of civilian irruption into war—rebellion, or as it is termed if one approves of it, war of national liberation? Professor Andreopoulos deals fully with this in his chapter. Here a distinction has to be made between the legitimacy of the cause, and the conventions and constraints observed by those involved in the conflict. Traditionally in such rebellions legitimacy could only be determined by the outcome of the struggle itself. The American Revolution was successful, so its instigators ceased to be rebels; the War of Secession was not, so the cause of the Confederacy was never legitimized. If the British forces treated the American colonists, and the forces of the Union treated those of the Confederacy as de facto belligerents rather than as civilian conspirators, it was because in both cases the insurgents were organized in regular armies which were themselves capable of observing the laws of war—and undertaking reprisals against their adversaries if the latter did not.

But in the twentieth century a new phenomenon appeared—insurgency movements which obtained widespread international recognition, even if they showed little hope of military success, because of what was widely seen as being the intrinsic justice of their cause: national liberation movements struggling against colonial or ethnic oppression. By the first Geneva Protocol of 1977, the full rights and protection granted to the forces of sovereign states by the Geneva Conventions of 1949 were extended to "armed conflicts in which people are fighting against colonial domination and alien occupation and against racist regimes in the exercise of their right of self-determination."[11]

Professors Andreopoulos and Kennedy deal with the implications of this protocol, which not only placed the forces of the insurgent movements and those of incumbent authorities in a position of virtual equality before the law, but imposed upon the former the obligation to observe the Geneva Conventions in full, something that could present considerable problems to an incipient guerrilla movement. I will only observe that it marks a further step away from the clarity of Grotian law, not only by abandoning the traditional definition of just authority but by reintroducing an older concept of *jus ad bellum,* legitimizing the conflict not in terms of the authorities fighting it or the methods they use but in terms of the cause for which it is fought. Most of us would probably at least have some sympathy with this development, Americans perhaps more than the old imperialist British. But that sympathy is likely to find its limits with the insurgents' readiness and capacity to observe those constraints which have characterized wars between sovereign states—and which states were called to account for if they did not observe.

I have dealt in this introduction more than I would have wished with formal laws of war rather than with what belligerents do in war, laws or no laws. But to see what the laws have been provides us with at least a starting point. They show us, in the first place, the standards of behavior to which armed forces in the past have aspired; and secondly they indicate where those armies were conscious of shortcomings, of activities that needed to be prevented by positive prohibitions. Both of these are matters that will be further explored in the body of this volume.

Josiah Ober   2

Classical Greek Times

When approaching the subject of agreements regulating the conduct of interstate warfare it is important to separate the relatively informal, socially mandated and enforced rules of war from legally enacted laws of war.[1] Here my emphasis will be on the former, since there is little evidence that the archaic and classical Greeks enacted internationally recognized laws governing the practice of warfare. There are only two real candidates for long-term, formal, sworn agreements intended to control the form taken by armed conflict among the mainland Greek states. First, a tradition reported by the geographer Strabo (10.448) claims that in the course of the War of the Lelantine Plain on the island of Euboea in about 700 B.C., the contending parties (including most of the big states) agreed to ban the use of projectile missiles. A second tradition, mentioned by the orator Aeschines (oration 2, *On the Embassy* 115), suggests that after the so-called First Sacred War (fought over control of the oracle of Delphi) of about 600 B.C. the victorious states swore never again to cut off besieged fellow Greeks from food or water. Upon examination both traditions look very dubious—the supposed covenants are reported only by relatively late sources and they were certainly not always honored in practice.[2] Moreover, despite the existence of the Amphictyonic League (an "international" organization of Greek peoples which regulated the affairs of Delphi), there is no evidence for the Greek development of what H. L. Hart called "first order rules" regarding military conduct—that is, no organized procedure for enacting the laws that might govern interstate warfare.[3] In the absence of securely attested and formal "second order" laws (actual sworn covenants), and without evidence for first order rules by which such covenants might have been devised, there is not much to say about classical Greek laws regarding general military conduct.

On the other hand, Greek combatants did recognize a number of rules of engagement, and these rules do seem to have been generally regarded as normative in that their breach could occasion indignant comments in our sources. The rules of war, which in the late fifth century B.C. were sometimes referred to as the "common customs (*koina nomima*) of the Hellenes" (Thucydides 3.59.1, 6.4.5; cf. Euripides *Heraclidae* 1010), range from what might be called neoformal rules to practices conditioned largely by practicality. There was in antiquity no canonical list of the rules. But the following, in descending order of formality, seem to me to sum up the most important of the unwritten conventions governing interstate conflict:[4]

1. The state of war should be officially declared before commencing hostilities against an appropriate foe; sworn treaties and alliances should be regarded as binding.
2. Hostilities are sometimes inappropriate: sacred truces, especially those declared for the celebration of the Olympic games, should be observed.
3. Hostilities against certain persons and in certain places are inappropriate: the inviolability of sacred places and persons under protection of the gods, especially heralds and suppliants, should be respected.
4. Erecting a battlefield trophy indicates victory; such trophies should be respected.
5. After a battle it is right to return enemy dead when asked; to request the return of one's dead is tantamount to admitting defeat.
6. A battle is properly prefaced by a ritual challenge and acceptance of the challenge.
7. Prisoners of war should be offered for ransom rather than being summarily executed or mutilated.
8. Punishment of surrendered opponents should be restrained.
9. War is an affair of warriors, thus noncombatants should not be primary targets of attack.
10. Battles should be fought during the usual (summer) campaigning season.
11. Use of nonhoplite arms should be limited.
12. Pursuit of defeated and retreating opponents should be limited in duration.

I will risk asserting, as a broad generalization, that most of these informal rules were followed, most of the time, in intra-Greek warfare of 700 to 450 B.C. The main problem in proving this assertion is the very lacunar nature of our sources for the practice of intra-Greek warfare in the seventh and sixth centuries. But when the evidence is assembled, as it has been by W. Kendrick Pritchett and Victor Hanson, the impression of a relatively clear set of rules is strong. There is more evidence to back up my next two assertions. First, rules of war pertained primarily in intra-Hellenic conflicts (rather than in wars between Greeks and non-Hellenes). And second, these rules, and especially numbers 5 through 12, tended to break down in the period 450 to 300 B.C.[5] The bulk of this article is devoted to investigating the implications of the premise that the three assertions are correct: that the informal rules of war listed above did in fact pertain among Greeks before the mid-fifth century, that they were developed in the context of intra-Greek warfare, and that war by the rules was considerably less common after the mid-fifth century.

If we assume that the rules of war listed above did once pertain in mainland Greece, we may ask in whose interest the rules were developed and maintained. Raising the question of interest seems valid, in that any argument which assumes that a universal sense of fair play and decency was an innate part of early Greek military culture is easily falsified. Even a casual reading of the *Iliad* makes it clear that some of the rules of war I have listed were not deeply rooted in Homeric society. The warriors of the *Iliad* do indeed show some respect for sworn truces and for the sacrosanctity of heralds, but otherwise the conventions of Homeric warfare are quite different. Achilles' brutal treatment of his fallen enemy, Hector, may be an extreme, but one can cite, for example, the night raid of Odysseus and Diomedes, culminating in Diomedes' cold-blooded execution of the war prisoner Dolon and slaughter of sleeping men (10.454–97). Use of projectile weapons (spears, arrows, rocks) is key to the action in the *Iliad;* pursuit of retreating enemies is vigorous and savage. There is no campaigning season and no formal distinction between Hellene and barbarian. Homeric society is at least partly a poetic fiction, but I think that one can safely assume that most of the Hellenic rules of war with which we are concerned crystallized in a historical era after the Homeric epics were written down, that is, after the mid to late eighth century B.C. If this is right, then the Greek rules regarding the proper conduct of warfare were presumably formulated in the course of the seventh century—the age in which Greek warfare came to be dominated by the highly organized formation of massed heavy infantry known as the hoplite phalanx. And thus it is reasonable to seek an answer to the cui bono question among the ranks of the hoplites themselves.[6]

Who were the hoplites? Or, more precisely: who could be a hoplite and how was the class of the hoplites defined? The answer varied somewhat over time and from polis to polis. But the simple answer is that an adult free male could be a hoplite if he could afford the capital investment in the appropriate arms and armor, and could afford to spend a good part of the summer marching about the countryside and fighting when called upon to do so. The typical hoplite was an independent subsistence farmer: a man who owned enough land—perhaps ten or fifteen acres—to support himself and his big family without the need for family members to work for wages on a regular basis. At Athens, the polis for which our evidence is best, in 594 B.C. the reformer Solon distributed political privileges hierarchically among four economic classes. Membership in each class was determined on the basis of annual agricultural production. Those in the top class had to be able to demonstrate that their farms could generate 500 standard units of produce. Membership in the second class of cavalrymen required 300 units. The third class, requiring a minimum of 200 units, was dubbed the *zeugitai,* or yokemen. The fourth class was composed of laborers (*thetes*). The third census group is the Athenian equivalent of the hoplite class—its members were probably called yokemen either because they were metaphorically yoked together in the phalanx or because they could afford a yoke of oxen. Both etymologies (whether right or wrong) are appropriate: the hoplites were in essence yoked together when they marched in the phalanx, since each hoplite soldier depended upon the men next to him in the line as surely as an ox depended upon its yokemate. And the minimum size of a moderately successful independent farm was probably about the size of holding at which keeping a yoke of oxen for plowing and other hard labor was economically feasible—roughly ten to eleven acres.[7]

How large was the hoplite class as a percentage of the total free (male) population? The simple answer would usually be a "substantial minority." Basic infantryman's equipment was not outrageously expensive.[8] Given the frequency of conflict in Greece and the dominance of phalanx tactics, every Greek state had a vested interest in maximizing the pool of heavy infantrymen, and hence it was counterproductive to deny those who could afford hoplite armor and weapons the opportunity to use them. In the period of the battles of Marathon and Plataea (490 and 479 B.C., respectively), Athens could field some nine thousand hoplites, which represented perhaps a fifth to a third of free adult males.[9] Assuming that the sociological distribution of the preimperial era population of Athens was not radically atypical of central and southern Greek norms, we may suppose that in the period 700 to 450 B.C. hoplites typically represented roughly 20 to 40 percent of the free adult males of a Greek polis. The hoplite class (including here the families of the hoplites themselves) would thus have represented a minority of a Greek city-state's total population: an elite indeed, but not a tiny or particularly exclusive elite. Moreover, when speaking of hoplites, we must use the term *class* with some care: the heavy infantry did not represent an economically homogeneous group, and the relationship of individual hoplites to the economic mode of production will have varied. Although in some poleis (for example, Athens) the very wealthiest citizens served in the cavalry, in every polis some hoplites were considerably wealthier than others.[10] Rich hoplites in many poleis undoubtedly employed slaves in working their estates. Others depended on occasional employment of wage laborers. Those at the bottom of the group depended primarily on the labor of draught animals and family members. Only a very few of the richest hoplites would have avoided the necessity of working their land with their own hands.

Phalanx warfare evolved rapidly in the early seventh century B.C. and it was soon fully institutionalized as the dominant mode of violent dispute resolution between the Greek poleis. And it was the hoplites themselves, as a relatively broad-based social elite, who benefited most from the rules of warfare which had evolved in the course of the seventh century. These informal rules ensured that it was the heavy infantrymen who dominated intra-Greek military encounters (rather than the wealthier cavalry-men, poorer light-armed skirmishers, or more specialized archers and slingers). During the archaic and classical periods the Greek way of war, which placed the heavy infantry in the center of the action, supported and reinforced the privileged social position of the hoplite class vis-à-vis the very rich and the poor. Because their arms determined the outcome of military encounters, the hoplite class occupied a clearly defined middle ground between the small elite of leisured aristocrats and the majority of males who were unable to afford hoplite equipment. Although it is dangerously anachronistic to speak of a self-conscious Greek middle class, the hoplites, as a well-defined social group, staked out a broad and central position in polis society and their social centrality had clear political ramifications.

If we view the world from the perspective of the hoplite class, we can see how the practice of warfare limited the influence of both the very rich and the poor. The rich men who served in the cavalry gained thereby an opportunity to display their wealth in a conspicuous fashion—but their role in battle was limited to scouting and protecting the flanks of the phalanx. The free poor and the unfree (whether slaves or helots) were relegated to a largely logistical role in times of war: they could carry the gear of the fighters, but were not effective fighters themselves. Because traditional Greek ideology strongly linked social and political status with the ability to fight in defense of family and community, the leisure class often found it difficult to impose a political order exclusively dominated by the very rich. By the same token, the poor and unfree could effectively be excluded from political participation and various social privileges. In short, the practice of hoplite warfare tended to define the limits of, but also to undergird, the social and political hierarchies of the Greek polis.[11]

On the other hand, the experience of the phalanx helped to promote an egalitarian ethos within the ranks of the hoplites themselves. The rich hoplite might have prettier armor, a fancier crest, and a more highly decorated shield than the struggling farmer of ten acres who stood next to him in the line, but the two men used offensive weapons that were virtually identical and each was utterly dependent upon the other in matters of defense. Steadfastness was the primary virtue of the hoplite warrior. In times of combat, leaping out in front of the line or flinching back from it were equally disruptive to the all-important cohesion of the phalanx. The goal of the phalanx was complete homogeneity of effort. Men who were economic unequals were thus equalized in combat, and this egalitarian habit translated from battlefield to polis life. Hoplite egalitarianism reached its apogee in classical Sparta, where the educational, sociocultural, economic, and political systems all emphasized the complete homogenization of a hoplite class that was coextensive with the citizenry.[12]

Although few Greek poleis took either hierarchy or egalitarianism to Spartan extremes, hoplite warfare was an important structural element in archaic and early classical Greek society in that it reified existing lines of social distinction (especially between independent farmers and poor laborers) at the same time that it promoted social and political equality within the ranks of the upper third or so of polis society. The socially constructed and socially maintained rules of war buttressed this social system. Each of the rules numbered five through twelve, above, helped to maintain the long-term practical workability of the hoplite-dominated socio-military system: since to request one's dead was to admit defeat, and that request could not legitimately be refused by the victors, the outcome of a single battle was generally regarded by both sides as decisive, at least for a season. Thus wars tended to be brief affairs which could be fought effectively by amateur farmer-soldiers. The rituals of challenge to battle and acceptance of the challenge, the limitation of combat to a short campaigning season, and the limited use of nonhoplite arms lessened the impact of war on farmlands and ensured that only appropriate players took key roles on the field of battle. Generally lenient treatment of defeated enemies, the ransoming of prisoners of war, and the lack of determined pursuit of retreating soldiers kept casualties within an acceptable range. The ideologically significant ritual of the battle could thus be performed quite frequently (and thus its social impact could be maximized) without risking demographic catastrophe for the participants.[13]

It is perhaps in the relative uninvolvement of noncombatants in archaic and early classical Greek warfare that the social bases of the rules of hoplite combat are manifested most clearly. Traditional hoplite war is in essence warfare without strategy: the aim of each phalanx was to engage the other phalanx head-on. This ritualized (although genuinely violent and bloody) form of conflict was efficient in that it determined which side was superior quickly and decisively. Although tactical maneuvering, or even trickery, might be employed in the attempt to fight from the most advantageous position, the goal of each side remained simple: to meet the enemy soldiers in an open battle. This was not the only way the Greeks could have chosen to fight. The hierarchical society of the polis offered a seemingly obvious target for a strategy based on sociopolitical subversion. Those who were disadvantaged by the Greek social system (the unfree and subhoplite populations) represented a potential Achilles' heel for many poleis; revolts by Sparta's helot population demonstrated just how willing the oppressed might be to turn against their masters. Invaders who persuaded the poor and unfree to fight their oppressors, or simply to withhold their labor inputs (most obviously by running away), would severely hamper their opponents' war effort. Yet until well into the Peloponnesian War, the strategy of encouraging discontent among the enemy's lower social strata was not employed. It is hardly necessary to point out that Greeks were both inventive and capable of serious analytical thought. But in Greece, as in other human societies, innovation was channeled by social priorities. Until the last third of the fifth century B.C., strategies based on attacking the enemy's social and economic system were effectively banned by the informal rules of war—rules which thereby further reinforced the existing social order.[14]

From about 700 to 450 B.C. intra-Greek wars were fought by fellow participants in what we might fairly call the hoplite-centered social order. Because of constraints imposed by the rules of war, these conflicts rarely became a matter of a polis's national survival. It was a very different matter when Greeks fought non-Greeks. In the best documented series of Greek-barbarian conflicts, the Persian Wars of 490–478 B.C., the issue for many poleis was national survival and the Persian invaders were not participants in the socio-military system I have sketched out above. Although the Greek defenders at Marathon and Plataea used hoplite formations against the numerically superior Persian forces, they did not employ the ordinary norms of intra-Greek combat. In their conflict with the Persians the Greeks summarily executed heralds (Herodotus 7.133) and offered no formal challenge to battle or exchange of war dead. Retreating Persian soldiers were pursued relentlessly and slaughtered in the thousands at Marathon, and most of the Persian survivors of the battle of Plataea were massacred after the Athenians successfully stormed their camp. Greek conduct during the Persian Wars demonstrates clearly the essentially voluntary nature of the rules of intra-Greek conflict and points to the possibility of a voluntary defection from those rules.[15]

In the century after about 450 B.C.—and especially during the Peloponnesian War of 431–404 B.C.—the informal Greek rules of war broke down. Thucydides' history of the Peloponnesian War demonstrates how the rules listed above were violated in the course of the long and drawn-out conflict—for example, in executions of enemy ambassadors, seamen, and allied troops (by both Athens and Sparta); and in massacres of captured prisoners of war: Thebans by Plataeans in 431, Plataeans by Thebans and Spartans in 427, Melians by Athenians in 415, Athenians by Syracusans in 413. The last of these atrocities was set up by a sustained strategic pursuit of the Athenian army by Syracusan forces. But perhaps the most striking departure from previous practice was the conscious employment of systematic pressure on the enemy's social system: in 425 the Athenians threatened the internal stability of Sparta by constructing a military base at Pylos in Messenia, from which they encouraged helot insurrection. The Spartans eventually responded with a permanent base at Decelea in Attica, precipitating the flight of over twenty thousand Athenian slaves. Although hoplite phalanx battles were still being fought and some of the old rules honored in specific circumstances, the general structure of war by the rules was shattered in the late fifth century B.C. and never effectively reconstructed thereafter.[16]

The question that confronts us, then, is why the socially stabilizing system of war by the rules fell apart. Although prodromic symptoms of the breakdown can be detected well before 431 B.C., the great Peloponnesian War fought by the hegemonic alliances led by Sparta and Athens is clearly implicated. As Thucydides points out in the introduction to his *History* (1.1, 1.23.1–3), this was a war unlike any that had been fought on Greek soil. Thucydides implies that at the outbreak of the war, Sparta (with its agricultural, helot-based economy) was the quintessential hoplite power and Athens was a very nontraditional naval power. The Spartans entered the war expecting a typical conflict that would be decided by phalanx battles fought according to the usual rules. The Athenians had something rather different in mind. Thus it is to Athens that we must turn in attempting to understand why it was that the system of war by the rules failed to survive the fifth century B.C.[17]

In the mid-fifth century the polis of Athens was exceptional in several ways: very big by mainland Greek standards at about one thousand square miles and with an adult male citizen population of at least forty to fifty thousand, Athens was a preeminent naval power and controlled a great Aegean empire. Moreover, Athens was a democracy. A series of revolutionary political reforms, initiated in the sixth century and largely complete by 450 B.C., had resulted in the evolution of a startlingly original form of direct government by the people. Key political decisions in Athens— including all matters of state finance and foreign policy—were made in open and frequent assemblies at which every citizen had an equal vote. Legal matters were decided by people's courts staffed by large juries of ordinary citizens. Most government officials were chosen by lot; a few—including the generals—were elected to renewable annual terms of office. Leaders, including the redoubtable Pericles, maintained their positions by demonstrating ability in handling financial and military affairs and by rhetorical skill in public debates. The existence at Athens of the political system of democracy had important social ramifications. In Athens all citizens, regardless of their property holdings, regardless of whether or not they could afford hoplite armor, were political equals in that each Athenian's vote in assembly and lawcourt was of equal weight. Because the relatively poor (those who could not afford hoplite arms) were in the majority and had developed a sophisticated consciousness of their own place in Athenian politics, the political center of gravity at Athens was lower than in nondemocratic poleis. And this low center of political gravity gave Athens remarkable stability.[18]

The democratic political culture of Athens meant that the implicit social contract between economic classes of natives—foreign-born slaves were another matter—was based on premises very different from those assumed in the typical hoplite-centered polis. Social inequality as a result of differential access to economic assets certainly remained, but Athenian native male society was much less hierarchical than that of other poleis. The formal equality of citizens, along with the practice of democratic politics in assembly and courtroom, served to unify the Athenian native male citizenry across the boundaries of economic class—in much the same way that the mutual interdependence of the hoplites in the phalanx unified the hoplite class elsewhere. The difference, of course, is that the Athenian citizen population (native males and their families) was a much larger percentage of the total population.

In part as a direct consequence of democratic ideology, the hoplites of Athens were considerably less self-consciously a class than they were in other, nondemocratic poleis and Athenian society was not dependent for its stability on maintenance of a stable hoplite ideology. This blurring of the lines between the hoplites and the poorer citizens of Athens can be traced in the aftermath of the oligarchic coup of 411 B.C. The Athenian hoplites played a key role in overthrowing the narrow oligarchy of the Four Hundred and they participated in the establishment of a new government in which full citizenship would be limited to the hoplite class. This so-called Constitution of the Five Thousand earned Thucydides' praise (8.97.2), but it never jelled into a stable government. Within a few months Athens had evolved back into a full democracy—the Athenian hoplites simply did not have an adequate sense of themselves as a distinct group to sustain a form of government based on hoplite identity. The role of the hoplite class in the maintenance of social stability at Athens was further undercut in the early- to mid-fifth century by the burgeoning importance of the Athenian navy. The rise of the navy was roughly contemporary with the flowering of Athenian democracy. The creation of a major naval force in the mid-480s, at the behest of the politician and general Themistocles, allowed Athens to play a central role in the defeat of the Persians at Salamis in 480 B.C., and subsequently led to the hegemony of Athens over the Delian League—a coalition of Aegean coastal and island states which coalesced after the defeat of the Persians. With the evolution of the Delian League into an Athenian empire in the second quarter of the fifth century, the navy became the key arm of Athenian military forces. As Aristotle later recognized, the growth of Athenian naval power was linked to the development of democratic political institutions because traditional Greek ideology linked the value of the citizen to his role in the defense of the state. The trireme warships of Athens were rowed largely by citizens who could not afford hoplite armor—as the navy's role became more and more decisive to the exercise of Athenian power in the Greek world, the poorer citizens took a larger and more direct role in the day-to-day governance of the state.[19]

I suggested above that in many Greek poleis the informal rules of warfare aided in the survival of the hoplite class and abetted its social and political dominance. In terms of military conventions, a key result of the conjoined growth of democratic political culture and the navy at Athens was the social and political displacement of the Athenian hoplites. The mass of ordinary citizens rather than the hoplite class now defined the political and military center of gravity of Athens. As a result, Athenian social structure was no longer fundamentally dependent on a continued adherence to the hoplite ideology—nor to the rules of war which sustained that ideology. The interests of the hoplite class no longer determined either the general direction or the specific decisions of Athenian internal and foreign policy. And so by the mid-fifth century B.C. the Athenians could afford to break the rules of war. Their unique social system meant that the Athenians need not fear social instability as a result of this breach of convention, and their unique political system meant that men with a primary stake in maintaining the rules were no longer in charge.

Democratic government at Athens led to the formation of an implicit social contract that integrated the interests of middling and poorer citizens and so allowed the extraordinarily large manpower resources of Athens to be safely and efficiently deployed in naval operations. This factor proved to be of key importance in the creation and the maintenance of the Athenian overseas empire. By 450 B.C. Athens was a major imperial power, controlling some one hundred sixty subject states—this was the first and only really successful empire run by a Greek polis. Whatever the subjects of the empire may have thought about their position, the empire was run for the profit of Athens, and the financial resources which accrued to Athens as a result of hegemony were enormous by Greek standards.[20] By the date of the outbreak of the Peloponnesian War, Athens had amassed a large strategic financial reserve—and as Thucydides points out (1.141.2–1.142.1), that cash reserve had a decided bearing on how Athens chose to fight the war with Sparta. Traditionally, Greek wars were decided quickly, usually by a single battle. No Greek state dominated by the hoplite class would desire or could afford a long, indecisive conflict.[21] But democratic, imperial Athens could. Once again, unique circumstances, linked to the existence of the democracy, naval power, and empire rendered the traditional rules of war irrelevant to the Athenians.

So far, I have laid out the structural factors which made it possible for Athens to ignore the rules of war. But I do not suppose that just because this approach had become possible it was in any sense inevitable. Before the possibility could become an actuality someone had to see that recent developments had enabled a new approach to war, had to come up with a concrete operational plan, and had to persuade the Athenians to go along with the plan. That someone was Pericles. The two Periclean assembly speeches in Thucydides' *History,* along with Thucydides' own comments, make it clear that Pericles had in fact devised a strategic plan for fighting the Peloponnesian War.[22]

The conflict Pericles foresaw was that of a land power against a sea power and on the face of it the land power seemed to hold the advantage. In a traditional war by the rules Sparta and its allies would march into Athenian territory; the smaller, less highly trained Athenian phalanx would meet the invader's challenge by marching out into the open fields and would be defeated. The Athenian navy would never become a factor in the conflict, and Athens would have lost the war in the first year. Not liking the implications of this scenario, Pericles determined to change it. His plan was simple and radical. Since the Spartans would win a war that was fought according to the traditional Hellenic rules of engagement, Pericles reasoned that Athens might be able to win by opting out of the rules. This was a key moment in the history of Greek warfare in that it was the beginning of truly sophisticated long-term strategic analysis. Rather than worrying about the tactical problem of how to win a particular battle, Pericles thought through the interplay of a variety of forces—military, financial, political, and psychological—over the course of a war that he knew would take several years at least. He had, in essence, invented grand strategy.

The key to success in Pericles' plan was for the Athenian land army to avoid engagement with the Peloponnesian army: when Sparta invaded Attica, the Athenian hoplites must refuse the ritual challenge to battle and remain barricaded behind the city's walls. Without an army of defenders to fight, the Spartan-Peloponnesian phalanx would be rendered impotent. The invaders would not risk assaulting the walls. Nor was Sparta likely to attempt a siege of the city-Piraeus complex; this would require a huge counterwall and the Peloponnesians could not spare the manpower to hold it. Finally, the Spartans could not hope to starve the Athenians out; the empire of Athens provided the revenues and its Long Walls and its warships security. Athenian merchantmen would resupply the city fortress from grain markets in Egypt and south Russia. Given the clear naval superiority of Athens, its deep financial reserves, and its independence from the hoplite ideology, the defensive side of Pericles' strategy was thoroughly rational.[23]

But how was Athens to defeat Sparta? The Spartan center of gravity—in military, social, and political terms alike—was the hoplite citizenry of the Peloponnesus and the Athenian navy could not threaten these men directly. An indirect approach might be more productive. Sparta's hoplite class lived from the surplus generated by the oppressed and potentially restive helots of Laconia and Messenia. With Sparta distracted by helot revolts, the Peloponnesians would be stymied. In the event, although a series of naval raids were launched against the Peloponnesian coasts, Athens established no base in Spartan territory during the first six years of the war. It seems likely that despite his radical decision to ignore some of the traditional conventions of engagement, Pericles foresaw no need for a wholesale abandonment of the rules of war. His initial offensive goal was probably a limited one: control of Megara, a small city-state whose territory lay north of the Isthmus of Corinth and west of Attica. Megara was strategically located across the land routes from the Peloponnesus into central Greece. The passes through the Megarian mountains were defensible: the Athenians had set up the battle of Tanagra by occupying the Megarian passes in 458 B.C. If Athens could permanently control the Megarian passes, the Spartans would be bottled up in the Peloponnese and Athens would have a free hand in central and northern Greece. Thus, rather than overthrow, Pericles aimed at containment of Sparta: an extension to the mainland of the operational plan that had worked well in the Aegean against the Persians since 478. And containment of Sparta, he believed, could be achieved by a limited withdrawal from the conventions of hoplite warfare.[24]

When the Peloponnesian army arrived in Attica late in the summer of 431 B.C., Pericles' war plan was put into effect: the Athenians evacuated the country districts, took up residence in the city, and refused battle with the Peloponnesian army. The invaders were stymied and left Attica a few weeks later, having accomplished virtually nothing. Once the Spartans and their allies were safely back in the Peloponnesus, Pericles sent the Athenian land army into Megarian territory where it ravaged Megara's small agricultural plain. If this pattern had kept up for a few years, all might have gone as Pericles had planned. Eventually the Spartans would have become frustrated with their meaningless incursions; eventually the Megarians, excluded from Aegean trade by the Athenian fleet and with their agriculture disrupted annually, would have submitted to Athens.[25]

But of course that was not the way it actually worked out. A devastating plague reduced Athenian manpower, imperial subjects became restless, Athenian generals turned to the strategy of social disruption, and their Spartan counterparts proved equally capable of employing innovative strategies of social subversion and economic coercion. In the end the Athenians lost because the Spartans realized that the war could be won by expanding the theater of operations and their own resource base. Persian subsidies allowed Spartan admirals to launch attacks on the states of Athens's empire, to threaten the overseas grain routes, and to challenge the navy that guarded the empire and the sea lanes. By the end of the war the Spartans had proved just as willing to ignore the customs of engagement as their opponents, and the old regime of war by the rules was a dead letter.[26]

Cut free from traditional constraints, warfare rapidly developed a new style in the fourth century B.C. Although hoplite phalanx battles were still fought (witness, for example, the battles of Nemea, Leuctra, and Mantinea), intra-Greek conflicts were no longer limited in duration, there was no fixed campaigning season, and the combatants were less frequently citizen hoplites. The employment of mercenaries, often highly specialized light-armed fighters, meant that pursuit and annihilation of defeated enemies became more common. Noncombatants were increasingly the targets and victims of strategies based on social disruption and destruction of economic resources.[27]

The new style of combat had considerable impact on Greek society. The practice of war now tended to undermine rather than support the existing social order of many poleis. With the abandonment of the rules of conflict that had undergirded it the old hoplite ideology lost its coherence; the center could no longer hold. Without the mediating factor of the political and social dominance of the hoplite class, the underlying conflicts between rich and poor escalated more easily into bloody internecine conflicts. Moreover, the strategies of economic coercion employed by fourth-century armies produced serious economic dislocations and widespread impoverishment. And thus the new warfare contributed materially to the wave of civil wars that wracked so many Greek poleis in the late fifth and fourth centuries—the conditions that Thucydides (3.69–85) described as pertaining in Corcyra in 427 B.C. became a recurrent theme in the history of many Greek states.

Paradoxically, Athens, the state whose policies appear to have done most to precipitate the breakdown of the traditional rules of war, exhibited extraordinary social and political stability in the decades after the end of the Peloponnesian War.[28] Once again the explanation can be sought in the well-developed and resilient democratic political culture of Athens. Since Athens did not depend on the hoplite ideology for the maintenance of social order, the collapse of that ideology had few directly adverse effects on the polis. Just as in the second half of the fifth century the existence of the democracy had made a break with the traditional rules conceivable, so too in the fourth century the democracy allowed Athens to weather the social storms generated by war without rules. And so, despite the traumatic loss of the Peloponnesian War, by the mid-fourth century the Athenians found themselves in much better shape than their victorious rivals, Sparta and Thebes—poleis whose social and political regimes were intimately bound up in what I have been calling the hoplite ideology.

Finally, what of the relationship of the Greek rules of war and military technology? When compared to modern society the ancient Greek world was notoriously nontechnological. There is, however, one area in which the Greeks did demonstrate considerable technological inventiveness: siege weaponry and its defensive corollary, military architecture. The link of military technology with the rules of war is quite clear. During the period in which hoplite warfare dominated the Greek scene there was little advance in siegecraft. Hoplite equipment and training were ill-adapted to the conduct of efficient siege operations, and relatively simple walls were sufficient to deter most assaults. But with the breakdown of hoplite warfare and the rules that had sustained it, siegecraft and defense against siege became more serious issues. And so, not surprisingly, the period from 400 to 300 B.C. saw rapid advance in both military architecture and siege technique.

Because warfare in the age after the Peloponnesian War tended to be destructive to state economies and civilian populations, Greek poleis expended considerable efforts to exclude enemy forces from economic and population centers. City walls were built and rebuilt: at Athens, for example, major work was undertaken on the city circuit in the period 395 to 385 B.C., and again in 337, 307, and in the third century. Perhaps even more impressive were efforts to exclude enemy troops from economically vital rural areas. The Thebans constructed a stockade around their central agricultural districts in the 370s. And in the middle decades of the fourth century, Athens, Thebes, and probably other poleis as well constructed elaborate systems of border fortifications intended to preclude enemy forces from entering and ravaging the interior.[29]

By the mid-fourth century B.C. both besiegers and defenders were typically utilizing catapult artillery. Originally invented as a siege weapon by arms makers employed by the tyrant Dionysios I of Syracuse in 399 B.C., the nontorsion (crossbow-type) catapult was a frightening antipersonnel weapon. But early catapults were not strong enough to endanger well-built stone walls, and so for a time the expenditure of polis assets for perimeter defense seemed the most logical course of action. But not for long: by about 340 B.C. engineers in the employ of Philip II, king of Macedon, had developed the first true torsion (hair or sinew spring) catapults. Torsion machines, which threw large stone balls, proved their worth by smashing city walls at Alexander's epic siege of Tyre in 322 B.C.[30]

It is hardly an accident that the first version of catapult artillery was developed in the workshops of an imperialist Sicilian tyrant, the second phase in imperial Macedonia. Technological development and rearmament with the new machines required financial assets that much exceeded the means of ordinary Greek poleis. By the late fourth century B.C. few individual poleis could hope to win conflicts against the great dynasts who controlled the money and manpower generated by Macedonian expansionism. As we have seen, border defense strategies were a primary response of several Greek poleis to the military situation precipitated by the collapse of the traditional conventions governing the conduct of intra-Hellenic warfare. But the new artillery technology developed by Philip's engineers helped to render border defense strategies obsolete. Rural forts proved unable to hold off Hellenistic generals in the late fourth and third centuries.[31] The dynastic successors of Alexander with their highly trained mercenary armies and with their superior artillery dominated the military landscape. The upshot was that polis citizens were left with no very effective military response to the threat offered by hostile forces deployed by the several new great powers. The city-states of Greece with their limited economic and manpower resources could not compete in the new military climate and therefore the age of the truly independent polis drew to a close.

In conclusion, the relationship between the Greek sociopolitical order and the rules of war that I have attempted to trace above leads to a paradox—and one that quite frankly gives me pause. Archaic and early classical Greek social mores and political culture supported a form of warfare that was highly, if informally, rule oriented. The rules of early intra-Greek warfare successfully constrained the horrors of war while supporting an overtly hierarchical social order. In the fifth century B.C. the polis of Athens discovered in democratic politics a way to broaden the base of the social order and, as a result, Greek culture blossomed as never before. Classical Athens witnessed the apogee of polis culture, marked by bold innovations in many spheres: literature, visual arts, philosophy—and military strategy. Unfettered by the need to maintain a rigid social hierarchy, Athenian leaders were free to experiment with military strategies that ignored some of the constraints imposed by the traditional rules of war. This initial period of experimentation, while not intended to overthrow the rules, precipitated an unprecedented series of innovations in military strategy, personnel, and technology. And these innovations in turn did overthrow the rules of war and in the process undermined the social and political order on which independent polis culture depended. Thus Athenian democracy was, in a sense, the condition of its own impossibility. This is, I believe, a profoundly disturbing conclusion for any citizen of a democratic state. On the other hand, fourth-century Athenian history may suggest that more democracy is the most appropriate response to crises precipitated by the new options presented by democracy. It is perhaps in forcing historians of politics, culture, and society to confront paradoxes such as this one that the study of international security finds some part of its justification.

Robert C. Stacey 3

The Age of Chivalry

To those who lived during them, of course, the Middle Ages, as such, did not exist. If they lived in the middle of anything, most medieval people saw themselves as living between the Incarnation of God in Jesus and the end of time when He would come again; their own age was thus a continuation of the era that began in the reign of Caesar Augustus with his decree that all the world should be taxed. The Age of Chivalry, however, some men of the time— mostly knights, the *chevaliers,* from whose name we derive the English word "chivalry"—would have recognized as an appropriate label for the years between roughly 1100 and 1500. Even the Age of Chivalry, however, began in Rome. In the *chansons de geste* and vernacular histories of the thirteenth and fourteenth centuries, Hector, Alexander, Scipio, and Julius Caesar appear as the quintessential exemplars of ideal knighthood, while the late fourth or mid-fifth century Roman military writer Vegetius remained far and away the most important single authority on the strategy and tactics of battle, his book *On Military Matters (De re militari)* passing in translation as *The Book of Chivalry* from the thirteenth century on.[1] The Middle Ages, then, began with Rome; and so must we if we are to study the laws of war as these developed during the Age of Chivalry.

In Roman eyes, "every war needed justification. The best reason for going to war was defence of the frontiers, and, almost as good, pacification of barbarians living beyond the frontiers. Outside these reasons one risked an unjust war, and emperors had to be careful." But within these limits, the conduct of war was essentially unrestrained. Prisoners could be enslaved or massacred; plunder was general; and no distinction was recognized between combatants and noncombatants. Classical Latin, indeed, lacked even a word for a civilian. The merciless savagery of Roman war in this sense carried on into the invasion period of the fifth and sixth centuries. When the Ostrogoths under Theodoric captured Italy from the Huns in the late fifth century, they annihilated the Huns so completely that all trace of the Hunnish presence in Italy disappeared.[2]

In practice Roman war was not always so savage. But such was the understanding of Roman war with which medieval theorists of war worked, and they erected *bellum Romanum* in this sense into a category of warfare which permitted the indiscriminate slaughter or enslavement of entire populations without distinctions between combatant and noncombatant status. This was a style of warfare appropriate only against a non-Roman enemy, and in the Middle Ages this came to mean that Christians ought only employ it against pagans, like the Muslims in the Holy Land or, in the sixteenth century, the aboriginal peoples of the New World. By identifying *Romanitas* (literally, "Romanness") with adherence to Roman Christianity, however, the early Middle Ages added to this tradition of bellum Romanum a wholly un-Roman celebration of war by God's people for God's own purposes, chief amongst which were to protect and extend the Christian faith of Rome. As Professor Wallace-Hadrill has remarked, "One may sense in this a driving-force, perhaps also an absence of brakes, that could make Christian warfare something more formidable than its pagan imperial counterpart."[3] And so, I would suggest, it did.

Augustine had insisted, and most churchmen agreed, that the ultimate end of war was peace; but it was war, not peace, that early medieval churchmen celebrated. And so long as it was fought for pious ends, such warfare knew no effective limits. The wars of conquest which Charlemagne waged against the pagan Saxons during the eighth century thus qualified perfectly as a Roman war. After thirty years of plunder, massacre, enslavement, and mass deportations the Saxons finally saw the reasonableness of Christianity and agreed to accept baptism at the hands of the Franks, "and so to become one people with them," as the chronicler Einhard remarked[4]—a Christian people and hence a Roman people, who in the next century would in turn wage Roman war against their own pagan neighbors to the east, the Slavs.

In the midst of all this, early medieval penitentials continued to insist that killing, even in war, was murder nonetheless. But this was a perfectionist ethic which few took seriously before the ninth century.[5] Even then, when the church did begin to make concerted attempts to restrain violence, its efforts were prompted not by any opposition to war per se, but by the fact that warfare had now become civil and internal and was therefore misdirected. Most ninth- and tenth-century ecclesiastical writers on war were actually trying to increase the bellicosity of contemporary kings and their people, while redirecting it away from Christian neighbors and toward the pagan invaders—the Vikings, the Hungarians, and the Muslims.[6] Carl Erdmann has made it fashionable to see in the militarization of the church during these centuries the origins of the crusade as a Christian holy war.[7] With all respect to a very great scholar, I think the view mistaken. Warfare had been integrated into the Christian mission long before. What was new in the tenth and eleventh centuries was that the church could no longer appeal with any effect to secular authorities in its efforts to restrain and direct Christian warfare away from Christian targets. The First Crusade was in this respect a counsel of despair.

Ecclesiastical efforts to restrain intra-Christian violence during the tenth and eleventh centuries did bear some fruit, however, and it is with them that we begin to see the outlines of the laws of war as these would emerge in the Age of Chivalry. Carolingian church councils issued a number of decrees which demanded that noble miscreants give up their belt of knighthood, their *cingulum militare,* as part of the punishment for their crimes. We see in these measures our first evidence that the bearing of arms was seen as a noble dignity connected with a code of conduct, the violation of which might cost a man his status as a warrior. We also see a more concerted effort to impose penances on warriors who fought against other Christians, in 1066 even in a campaign that was sanctioned by the papacy itself. And in the Peace and Truce of God movements of the tenth and eleventh centuries we see the first systematic attempts to define and protect the status of noncombatants, and to prohibit violence altogether on the holiest days of the Christian year.[8] It is easy to mock these efforts. In practice the noncombatant immunity guaranteed by the Peace of God to all clergy, women, children, the aged, agricultural workers, and the poor was no more effective than the Truce of God's declarations that Christians could only attack other Christians between Monday morning and Thursday evening except during Advent and Lent, when they could not attack them at all. But I would insist nonetheless that by defining for the first time a reasonably consistent set of noncombatant immunities, and by clearly reiterating the principle that the conduct of war between Christians ought to be fundamentally different from the conduct of war between Christians and non-Christians, the Peace and Truce of God movements made a very significant contribution to the formulation of the laws of war in western Europe.

These efforts corresponded with important social, economic, and military changes in European society. "The intensification of warfare," especially during the eleventh century, "went hand in hand with dramatic developments in the methods, techniques and equipment for fighting on horseback."[9] The development of the massed cavalry charge with couched lance between 1050 and 1100 increased both the demand for and the costs of maintaining large numbers of trained knights. Settlement patterns changed more gradually, but by the end of the eleventh century heavily armored knights were exercising direct lordship over nucleated peasant villages across much of Europe. Manorial structures had also hardened, with consequent reductions in status for many free peasants. All these changes contributed to the emergence of a social order which drew an increasingly sharp division between the armed *nobilis,* noble by virtue of his horses and arms, and the *inerme vulgus,* the unarmed, vulgar herd of common humanity.[10]

With respect to the laws of war, two consequences followed from these developments. First, long-established but only dimly perceptible codes of noble conduct on the battlefield began to be applied to the knights as well. A greater number of fighters were now covered by these standards of honorable conduct. In 1066, for example, William the Conqueror expelled from his *militia* a knight who struck at the dead Harold's body on the battlefield with his sword.[11] Whether this meant that the Conqueror expelled him from his household troop or stripped him instead of his very knighthood we cannot now determine. In either event, knighthood had clearly emerged by 1100 as an indissoluble amalgam of military profession and social rank that prescribed specific standards of behavior to its adherents in peace and war. The laws of war would develop in the Age of Chivalry as a codification of these noble, knightly customs on the battlefield.

Second, however, the sharp division which this knightly elite now drew between itself as an order of *bellatores* and the rest of society made up of *oratores* or *laboratores* meant that the laws of war themselves applied only to other nobles. In theory, peasants and townsmen ought not to fight at all; it was the job of knights to protect (and exploit) these noncombatant *pauperes*.[12] If such common men did fight, however—and in practice they did, regularly—then no mercy was owed them on the battlefield or off. In the ordinary circumstances of battle a knight ought not kill another knight if it was possible instead to capture him for ransom. Armed peasants and townsmen, however, could be massacred at will.

This was not the church's view, of course, but the laws of war in the Age of Chivalry were an almost entirely secular creation.[13] Theology prior to the sixteenth century concentrated almost exclusively on the right to declare war, the *jus ad bellum,* insisting that war could only be fought if declared by a competent authority, fought for a just cause, with proper intent and a proportionality between provocation and response, and toward the end of reestablishing peace. The question with which theologians and canon lawyers dealt was whether a Christian could, without sin, participate in a given war at all. Theology was much less concerned with what a soldier was permitted to do in prosecuting a war once it was sanctioned as a just and legitimate conflict. The church did show some minor concern with particular weaponry. Several efforts were made in the twelfth century, for example, to ban bows of all sort, especially crossbows. But these efforts were entirely ignored by practicing soldiers and even by the papacy itself, which hired hundreds of crossbowmen for its wars against the emperor Frederick II. By the fourteenth century, when gunpowder was introduced into European warfare, the church had abandoned altogether the effort to discriminate between weaponry, not to revive it until the twentieth century and the advent of the nuclear age.[14]

To the laws governing the actual conduct of war—what theorists call *jus in bello*—theology therefore contributed little beyond the elementary notions of noncombatancy enunciated by the Peace of God. Even these were progressively whittled down by the canon lawyers. As an enforceable body of defined military custom, the laws of war as we are discussing them emerged instead out of the interplay of knightly custom with Roman law as this was studied and applied in court from the twelfth century on. By the fourteenth century this combination of knightly practice and legal theory had given rise to a formal system of military law, *jus militare,* the law of the *milites,* the Latin word for knights. The enforceability of this law, at least in the context of the Hundred Years War, needs to be stressed.[15] Charges brought under the laws of arms were assigned to special military or royal courts—the Court of Chivalry in England, the Parlement of Paris in France—where lawyers refined and clarified its precepts in formal pleadings. Knights and, of course, heralds remained the experts in the laws of arms. Their testimony was sought both in defining the law and in applying it to specific cases, a reflection of the status of *jus militare* as a body of international knightly custom. From the fourteenth century on several attempts were made to record these customs in writing, the most famous being Honoré Bouvet's *Tree of Battles.*[16] Like all medieval lawbooks these were partial and tendentious with a bias toward kings. The real history of the laws of war in the Age of Chivalry is buried in the hundreds of court cases brought under it and in the scores of chroniclers' accounts of the conduct of actual war, and it is from these sources that Maurice Keen has reconstructed them.[17] I should not wish to hold Dr. Keen responsible for the views which follow, but I must acknowledge the extent of my indebtedness to his research.

The laws of war in the later Middle Ages were constructed on two fundamental propositions. First, that "soldiering in the age of chivalry was regarded as a Christian profession, not a public service. Though he took up arms in a public quarrel, a soldier still fought as an individual, and rights were acquired by and against him personally, and not against the side for which he fought." Every knight supplied his own equipment, at his own risk, although horses lost in action were sometimes replaced by his lord. But a knight supported his own squires, grooms, and other servants, and if captured, arranged his own release and paid his own ransom. Although nominally in receipt of wages from his king or captain, these wages did not begin to meet his expenses in war. Rather, he fought because his honor as a knight obliged him to fight, because his lord required his service, and because the profits of successful war might, with luck, make it worth his while to do so. He fought, however, on his own. He did not fight as a salaried servant of the public interest.[18]

The second proposition, which follows from the first, was that the laws of war were essentially contractual. Late medieval armies, especially in England, were most commonly recruited by indentures, written contracts sealed first between a prince and his captains, and then between a captain and his soldiers. These contracts set rates of pay, length of service, and other conditions of employment. But the analogy between the laws of war and the laws of contract went far beyond the mechanics of recruitment. War was conceived in law as a kind of joint-stock operation; by serving in the war a soldier acquired a legally enforceable right to a share of its profits, gained chiefly through plunder and ransom. The majority of the cases decided under the law of arms turned on the proper division of booty between a soldier, his captain, and the prince under whom they served and for whom they ostensibly fought.

I say ostensibly because in the extraordinary confusion which characterized the Hundred Years War, it was sometimes extremely difficult to tell who the prince was in whose name the various free companies, local lords, and wandering gangs of outright extortionists were in fact fighting. That they fought in the name of some prince mattered: without princely sanction their war was not a public one, and so by the law of arms they acquired no legally enforceable title to the ransoms and booty they captured.[19] A common man could not simply declare war off his own bat, help himself to his neighbor's cattle herd, and declare them his by the laws of war. In theory, at least, only a sovereign lord could act in this manner.

Sometimes, of course, such niceties mattered to no one. The mercenary companies who held the papal court to ransom at Avignon in the 1360s sought no public authority for their actions and lost nothing by its absence. But the principle that legal title could only be established in a public war mattered enough that in 1365, a period of truce between the kings of England and France, we find one freelancing English captain, John Verney, "levying open war as the official lieutenant of a lunatic who believed himself to be the rightful king of France," so as to continue fighting with at least a patina of legality about it. As Keen remarks, "Few, no doubt, and least of all the victims of his depredations, were much impressed by John Verney's claim, but it is significant that he should have troubled to make it at all."[20]

Public authority mattered; to this extent the law of arms did indeed build on the learned traditions of the just war, which required that war be declared only by a competent authority. In the Middle Ages, however, who was a competent authority to declare war? Was it only the pope, or perhaps the Roman emperor? Was it only kings, as kings themselves liked to suggest? What then about the duke of Burgundy, who held his lands from a king and an emperor, but who was in practice a sovereign lord independent of both? And what too about all the other feudal lords of western Europe, whose right to resort to violence to settle their quarrels was an ancient privilege attaching to their noble rank? No fully coherent answers were worked out to these questions during the Age of Chivalry, but in practice the late Middle Ages witnessed a growing de facto monopoly of war-making power being gathered into the hands of kings and of a few great lords, all of whom could plausibly claim effective sovereignty within their lands. Public authority mattered, and by 1500 sovereignty itself was a far better defined notion than it had been in 1300. But the Age of Chivalry could never recognize in practice any absolute polarity between public and private warfare. The realities of power were simply too complex.

Instead, the laws of war distinguished between four basic types of war.[21] The first, *guerre mortelle,* also known as Roman war, was "fought by the rules which in antiquity had applied in the wars of the Roman people. There was no privilege of ransom; the conquered could be slain or enslaved." Prisoners could be massacred, and no distinctions between combatants and noncombatants applied. The most common examples of guerre mortelle were the wars against the Muslims in Spain and the Holy Land. Between Christians guerre mortelle was rare. Only in exceptional circumstances would knights agree to fight other knights under such conditions. It was too dangerous for all involved and not very profitable either, since ransoms were disallowed. But it did happen: the French at Crécy and Poitiers were under orders to give no quarter, as were Joan of Arc's forces at Orléans. But essentially, guerre mortelle assigned to war between Christians the nature of a crusade against infidels. It was common enough among Christians, however, for its sign to be universally known: the display of a red banner or flag by a force meant that it would give no quarter, take no prisoners, and accept no ransom.[22]

Interestingly, this form of war was more common in civil conflicts, where it merges with a private legal condition known as "mortal enmity." Two individuals in a state of mortal enmity were permitted in law to kill each other on sight, if they could; and in theory, at least, no feud was to follow from the resulting murder so long as the relationship between the two had been publicly declared by visible signs well beforehand.[23]

Similar principles operated with respect to guerre mortelle when it was fought between a man and his lord. It was presumably on this basis that the French army at Crécy flew its bloodred banners against the English: Edward III of England was the vassal of King Philip VI of France for Gascony, and yet he had declared himself the rightful king of France, rupturing the bonds of fidelity which bound him to his lord. The most dramatic example I know of guerre mortelle in a civil conflict, however, is the conduct of the battles of Lewes and Evesham in 1264 and 1265, respectively, fought between the forces of King Henry III of England and his brother-in-law, Simon de Montfort, earl of Leicester.[24] Open conflict between the two men had erupted in 1258, when de Montfort participated in a political reform movement that reduced the king to a figurehead in his own kingdom. By 1264 their relationship had degenerated into open warfare. De Montfort began a harrying campaign against the king's supporters; a truce broke down, the dispute was submitted to the arbitration of the king of France, but de Montfort then refused to accept the king of France's verdict, and the harrying resumed again. Finally, on May 12, 1264, the two sides found themselves drawn up against each other near Lewes. Negotiators passed between them for several days; de Montfort's forces were badly outnumbered and he sought such terms as he could get from the king. But Henry refused all terms and at this point formally broke the bonds of homage and fealty which bound him and de Montfort. This formal defiance (*diffidatio*) established a state of open and total war between a lord and his man. De Montfort responded by dressing his army in crusader crosses—a significant gesture in many respects,[25] but significant in our context because it symbolized his army's recognition that it could expect no quarter from the royalists, as a state of guerre mortelle now existed between them. This fact was emphasized on the morning of May 14, when the king's forces advanced onto the battlefield, "preceded by the banner of the red dragon which portended general death to their enemies."[26]

Remarkably, de Montfort's forces triumphed. They were not fighting under conditions of mortal war and so took many prisoners for ransom. To the king and his eldest son, Edward, however, de Montfort immediately renewed his oaths of homage and fealty. Their enmity was thus ended, and de Montfort began to rule England with the king as his puppet. Edward, however, escaped from de Montfort's custody in the spring of 1265 and gathered an army. A second battle followed at Evesham between Edward's forces on the one side, de Montfort and the captive king on the other. As they had at Lewes, Edward's forces fought under the conventions of guerre mortelle, but this time they were victorious. De Montfort was killed and his body hideously mutilated. Many of his supporters also were killed on the battlefield, and the king, now freed from captivity, declared the lands of all survivors to be forfeit. He eventually relented and permitted the Montfortians to ransom their lands from the royalists to whom Henry had initially granted them.[27] The consequences of the battle of Evesham were thus, in the end, somewhat less than they might have been. Under the laws of war, however, there is no doubt that the king's initial intentions were just under the conventions of guerre mortelle. Politically, however, they were inadvisable because they would have made a lasting peace impossible.

Such savagery made a mockery of the international brotherhood of knighthood; and insofar as guerre mortelle could admit of no lasting resolution short of the unconditional elimination of one force or the other, it was also a deeply unsatisfactory way for an individual soldier to pursue the business of war. Far more palatable to all concerned was the *bellum hostile,* the open, public war fought between two Christian sovereigns. Such war was declared by the display of the prince's regular banner (not his red one) before his forces, which committed him on his honor to do battle. "From this moment on, the laws of war were in force," and "the common law . . . suspended." Spoil and plunder were the order of the day, and soldiers had an absolute right to share in all booty taken. To preserve discipline and guarantee a fair distribution, the booty was usually gathered centrally and then distributed after the battle to each soldier in accordance with his rank and merit. The precise customs governing the division of spoil varied from country to country, but everywhere this distribution created a legally recognized, heritable, and assignable right of property in the captured objects.[28] Military historians have long admired the close coordination between English naval forces patrolling along the coast of northern France and the English land armies pillaging the interior of the country. The admiration is not misplaced; but it is worth remarking that this fleet not only provided food and supplies to the army. It also acted as a kind of floating safe-deposit box for the troops, who could be sure that their loot would get back to their families in England even if they did not survive the campaign.[29] In terms of keeping up the morale of his troops, this may not have been quite as important to Edward III as maintaining a steady supply of beer. But it must have run a close second; and it points quite clearly to the central importance of plunder in the conduct of bellum hostile.

Theorists of the law of arms continued to insist on the immunity of noncombatants from pillage. In keeping with the theological traditions established by the Peace of God, agricultural workers, women, children, the elderly, and the clergy were all supposed to be protected from looting. In practice, however, neither soldiers nor the lawyers and judges who adjudicated the resulting disputes over plunder paid the slightest attention to such immunities. In enemy territory a soldier could plunder a peasant or a merchant just as freely as he could an enemy soldier on the claim that all such men gave aid and countenance to the opposing army. In the circumstances of the Hundred Years War this was not an entirely specious argument. The war did indeed turn to a large degree on the capacity of each side to mobilize the financial and military support of its populace in the war effort. Moreover, the effectiveness of the French military effort was unquestionably reduced by the enormous destruction wrought by the armies that pillaged its territory for the better part of a century.[30]

Not all the pillagers were invaders, however. Medieval soldiers were badly paid when they were paid at all; for most, the booty they acquired and the protection money they extorted were the most reliable means of support they had while on campaign. As such, medieval soldiers frequently extorted protection money from friendly territory as well as hostile. This was doubly grievous for the peasantry of the area. Not only were they forced to pay protection money to one army, but these payments then laid them open to pillage by the other side on the grounds that such payments rendered aid and countenance to the opposition. The laws of war in the Age of Chivalry knew something about the immunity of noncombatants, though what they knew they usually ignored. But they knew virtually nothing of the concept of neutrality.[31]

With rare exceptions combatants in a bellum hostile sought to avoid the uncertain verdict of a pitched battle. God was a just judge, and where battle could not be avoided He would render a just verdict. But it was best not to tempt Him or rush Him to a hasty decision. For both sides it was usually better to wait. For an invader it was more profitable to lay waste the countryside, while for a defender it was usually safer to stand out of the way and wait until one's opponent had tired himself out or fallen victim to disease, and so went home.

There were circumstances, however, where different calculations might apply. In a civil war the countryside both armies were laying waste was, after all, their own, and in England particularly this fact forced both sides toward a rapid resolution of the conflict. As Philippe de Commynes remarked with some astonishment, "If a conflict breaks out in England one or other of the rivals is master in ten days or less. . . . [I]t is a custom in England that the victors in battle kill nobody, especially none of the ordinary soldiers, because everyone wants to please them. . . . Even King Edward [IV] told me that, in all the battles he had won, as soon as he could sense victory, he rode round ordering the saving of the common soldiers."[32]

In France, however, English armies sought to avoid pitched battles where they could. It was generally the French forces that provoked the major battles which occurred. At Crécy, Edward III's devastation of the countryside, carried out in pursuit of his claim to be the rightful king of France, had by 1346 brought the legitimacy of Philip VI's own kingship into serious question, compelling Philip to give battle, with disastrous results. At Crécy as later at Poitiers and Agincourt, the overwhelming numerical advantage enjoyed by the French host over the English forces also encouraged the French to force a battle. In all three cases, however, the strategy backfired and a crushing defeat resulted. No French king would try it again until Francis I met the emperor Charles V at the battle of Pavia in 1525, where, once again, the French army was destroyed and their king captured. Pitched battles were dramatic, but drama was a poor substitute for policy.

The laws of war governing pitched battles were quite detailed, but they applied only to knights and squires, in the later Middle Ages the only two groups capable of bearing heraldic insignia. Foot soldiers, archers, miners, engineers, gunners, urban militiamen, peasant levies, and local volunteers were almost always also present on a battlefield, but none of these gave any quarter or were given any by the knights. At Crécy, the French knights literally rode down their own crossbowmen in their charge against the English line. At Lewes, the battle was lost in part because Prince Edward allowed his section of the royal army to chase and massacre the London militiamen for hours after they fled the field in revenge for the Londoners' having hurled manure on Edward's mother some months before. Common men like the Londoners could not hold prisoners for ransom under the laws of war, and they were not wealthy enough to be made prisoners themselves by the knights. Since they could draw no profit from them, nonnoble soldiers therefore had few compunctions about killing their prisoners, as they did at Agincourt and at Aljubarrota. Such conduct was expected of them and was rarely if ever criticized. Some forces, like the Swiss pikemen and the Flemish militias, became notorious for their refusal to take prisoners even when they fought under captains who could legally do so.[33]

Knights, however, were not supposed to kill other knights in a bellum hostile unless it was absolutely necessary. Instead, they took their noble opponents prisoner and held them for ransom. No chivalric reproach attached to being captured: captivity was, rather, an honorable relationship which established immediate bonds of obligatory service by a captive toward his master.[34] This was part of the reason why great noblemen, and especially princes, were so careful to surrender to an opponent of equal or superior rank if at all possible. The Black Prince, that paragon of chivalric courtesy, acknowledged such expectations by seating his captive, King John II of France, in a place of honor above himself at the banquet he gave for his noble prisoners on the evening after the battle of Poitiers.[35]

Captivity was also, however, a form of contract, established orally on the battle-field at the moment a victor accepted his opponent's gauntlet or badge, but quickly recorded in writing when the battle was over. In the language of the law, the captor's actionable interest in the contract was acquired by the service he performed in saving his captive's life; the prisoner's body, in turn, became the pledge for his ransom. "On this principle, the captor could do anything to a prisoner which might in reason seem necessary to obtain due payment [of the ransom]. He could keep him under lock and key, or even in irons, but he could not threaten him with death, or demand that he do anything contrary to law or his honour." Nor could he knock out his teeth with a hammer, as a subsequent court ruling established. A prisoner dishonorably treated could defy his captor if he escaped. If recaptured, he would then belong to his new master and not to his previous one. Similarly, a prisoner who agreed to an excessive ransom under threat of death, or who was kept in degrading or dangerous captivity, like the knight who counted "eighteen serpents and other reptiles" in his prison cell, could contest the validity of his agreement in the court of his master's lord, provided that he survived the mistreatment.[36] It is a mark of the extent to which the international laws of chivalry were acknowledged by the medieval nobility that a mistreated prisoner could expect to get such a case heard at all.

A prisoner *en parole* gave his word that, if released, he would pay his ransom—this is, indeed, the origin of our English word *parole*—and it was on his word alone, and the sealed contract of ransom he left behind, that he was released. Until his ransom was paid, a paroled prisoner remained a noncombatant with the same immunities as other noncombatants. He also remained bound to return to his captor if summoned, his personal obligations to his captor's service overriding all other allegiances, including those to his king or captain. If a paroled prisoner defaulted on his obligations or failed to pay his promised ransom, his captor had two alternatives. He could bring suit in the appropriate court of chivalry, usually that of his captive's lord, as he would for any other breach of contract; or he could formally dishonor the defaulter's arms by suspending them publicly from his horse's tail, for example, or hanging them upside down at a tournament or court. "Such an insult was deadly," and could be used also to punish other breaches of knightly faith, such as the sacking of churches, flight from battle, rape, arson, or the breaking of a solemn pledge.[37] Until the reproach was removed, a knight publicly dishonored in this way was banned from association in any knightly endeavor. In the international world of late medieval chivalry, news of such reproaches traveled quickly. Not every defaulter was thus brought to justice, but of what legal system can it be said that it was invariably effective?

Such were the rules of war pertaining to bellum hostile between knights. Rarely, however, did the fortunes of war turn decisively on the outcome of a pitched battle. The English won all four of the pitched, decisive battles of the Hundred Years' War, at Crécy, Poitiers, Nájera, and Agincourt. B·it they lost the war, which turned instead on the outcome of hundreds of individual sieges. The laws of war governed sieges, too, but they were completely different from those which applied to open battle.[38] A siege began when a herald went forward to demand that a town or castle admit the besieging lord. If the town agreed, this constituted a surrender, and the lives and property of the townspeople would be protected. If the town refused to surrender, however, this was regarded by the besieging lord as treason, and from the moment the besieger's guns were fired, the lives and property of all the town's inhabitants were therefore forfeit. "Women could be raped, and men killed out of hand. All the goods of the inhabitants were regarded as forfeit. If any lives were spared, this was only through the clemency of the victorious captain; and spoliation was systematic." Strictly speaking, the resulting siege was not an act of war but the enforcement of a judicial sentence against traitors who had disobeyed their prince's lawful command. In strict law, therefore, the town and all its goods belonged to the king, who granted them to his troops.

These laws of siege presented the captain of a besieged garrison with a terrible dilemma. If he resisted, he was sentencing the entire population of the town to death; but if he surrendered without resisting, the lord from whom he held the town would treat this too as treason, and the lives and property of the townspeople would be similarly forfeit to him. Careful captains of garrisons therefore often made written contracts with their lords specifying exactly how long they were obliged to hold out under siege. With the besieging force a captain could then seek to negotiate a conditional surrender: if relief from his lord had not arrived by the time specified in his contract, the garrison commander would surrender the town, and the lives and property of the townspeople would be protected. Heroic captains held out anyway, but the risks they ran were enormous. When Edward III finally captured Calais in 1347, he spared the lives of the townspeople who survived the siege, but he expelled the entire population of the town. Henry V did the same at Harfleur.

Siege warfare was thus something of a special case, and I have therefore categorized it as a third form of warfare, neither guerre mortelle nor bellum hostile. There was also a fourth form of war, *guerre couverte,* "covert war," the private war between two feudal lords who held their lands from the same sovereign.[39] By the law of arms one could kill one's enemies in such a war, but plunder, ransom, and burning were all, in theory, prohibited. Nor could one fly one's banner, a sign restricted to public war. Only a battle cry established allegiance in a guerre couverte, and no legal rights could be established to any captured property. The attraction of attaching one's private disputes to a public cause was therefore enormous. So long as war lasted between the kings of England and France, all a local lord had to do to turn his private war into a public one was to substitute the king of England's battle cry for his own. The king himself would in all likelihood know nothing at all about his new allies. They received no wages or other formal recognition from him; they wore no uniform and adopted no distinctive livery beyond their own. In no sense did they fight for England. But they did fight for the king of England, and that was enough to give their private war the public character which rendered ransom, arson, and plunder legitimate.

It is no wonder that in such a world the suppression of private warfare should have been difficult and that atrocities should have been common. The law of arms was an international law, but not in the sense that it regulated the conduct of warring nations. Rather, it was designed to protect the rights of the individual soldiers who joined the fighting wherever they might choose to fight. But "the principle . . . that any sort of hostile act requires sovereign authority" to sanction it slowly gained ground during the fifteenth century, and by the sixteenth century it had triumphed across most of Europe.[40] To share in plunder a soldier now had to have his name enrolled on the official muster lists of an army; and as the costs of war rose ever higher, only kings and a few other great lords could afford to maintain such a force. The growing military irrelevance of heavily armored cavalry also contributed to the declining importance of *jus militare* in its medieval sense. The knights did not disappear, however, anymore than did the nobility. Instead, they became officers in the new national armies of the late fifteenth century, and what had been a chivalric code of military conduct was thereby transformed into a code of conduct for officers toward other officers—which in some sense, of course, it had always been. In this regard the laws of war in the Age of Chivalry are the direct ancestors of the Geneva Conventions on the treatment of prisoners, not least in the distinctions drawn at Geneva between the treatment of captive officers versus enlisted men. We may count this as one of their successes. Their failures are also instructive: their complete ineffectiveness in protecting non-combatants, in limiting weaponry, and in protecting the common soldier from indiscriminate slaughter. On the failures of the laws of war in the Age of Chivalry, however, we should not be too harsh. For in the very areas in which chivalry failed to limit war, all succeeding systems of international law have also failed to limit effectively the conduct of war by soldiers and nations. I am prepared to believe in the prospect of a better system than the one described here. But I have not yet seen it in practice.

Geoffrey Parker 4

Early Modern Europe

In a provocative article entitled "The Gulf Crisis and the Rules of War," published recently in *Military History Quarterly,* Martin van Creveld highlighted numerous contrasts between the ancient and modern laws of war. On the one hand he noted a transformation in the *jus ad bello* (rules concerning the legitimacy of war), since the use of force to alter national boundaries is now prohibited by the United Nations Charter, whereas formerly it was the commonest single cause of conflict. On the other van Creveld pointed to significant changes in the *jus in bello* (rules concerning the conduct of war), with widespread condemnation of Iraq's use, or threatened use, of hostages, terrorism, and prohibited weapons during the Gulf War of 1991, despite the fact that all of them had long formed a part of the West's military repertoire. On the basis of these continuities he concluded that "what is and is not considered acceptable behavior in war is historically determined, neither self-evident nor unalterable."[1]

Van Creveld's argument is misleading in two respects, however. First, many of his contrasts are more apparent than real since they juxtapose principle, which always tries to set standards, however exalted, and practice, which often, for one reason or another, falls short of the ideal. Thus, despite the United Nations Charter, Israel, Korea, Vietnam, and Iraq have in fact used force with varying success to extend their national boundaries since 1945. Second, some of the greater restraint in the conduct of war stems from changes in technology, logistics, and the power of the state rather than from improved morality on the part of troops. Thus the fate of the civilians killed or mutilated by the aerial bombardment of Dresden or Hiroshima in 1945 or of Baghdad and Basra in 1990 was no more humane than that of the equally defenseless victims of My Lai or Bosnia who actually saw, however briefly, the soldiers who terminated or ruined their lives. Yet, in general, only those who kill or maim innocent civilians face-to-face risk citation before a war crimes tribunal; those who act from a distance, although they do far more damage, rarely go to trial. On the positive side, the growing power of the state in most parts of Europe notably reduced military mistreatment of the civilian population by removing one of its underlying causes: with regular pay and food, soldiers no longer needed to plunder in order to survive.[2]

This is not to deny that important changes have occurred over time in Europe's prevailing laws of war. Thus in the mid-sixteenth century hostages were regularly taken from hostile, or potentially hostile, communities and were frequently executed if need arose; at least twenty attempts were made by Catholic fanatics sponsored by foreign powers to assassinate Queen Elizabeth I of England in the 1570s and 1580s, while the queen herself made widespread use of hired assassins in Ireland to rid herself of tiresome opponents; and in 1566 enemies of Philip II of Spain allegedly entered areas through which his army was about to pass "with ointments to spread the plague."[3] All of these practices would now, as van Creveld correctly observed, be condemned as contrary to the current laws of war, yet at the time they were almost universally accepted as legitimate. But when did this critical change occur? It is the argument of this chapter that most of the modern conventions concerning restraint in war appeared in Europe between 1550 and 1700, both in theory and, rather more slowly, in practice.

In fact the laws of war in Europe have rested since the Middle Ages upon the same five foundations. First come a series of prescriptive texts: the Bible (above all Deut. 20:10–20), Roman law, canon law (especially the *Decretum* of Gratian), the writings of Augustine, and the *Summae* of Thomas Aquinas. All these works laid down the permissions and prohibitions that should obtain in war, and as time passed their findings were collected, codified, and developed by writers interested in the law of nature and, later, the law of nations.[4] Second, from the eleventh century in France, and slightly later elsewhere, the Peace of God movement pioneered by the Roman church laid down the principle that the weak who could do no harm should not themselves be harmed, while the Truce of God simultaneously attempted to restrict armed conflict between Christians to certain days of the week.[5] Third, at much the same time armies began to enact their own legal codes, the articles of war, that determined the rules of tolerable and intolerable conduct for all troops: duty to God, obedience to all superiors, vigilance and loyalty in camp and in action, humanity toward civilians (unless ordered otherwise), and so on. Most codes consciously emulated earlier ones, creating an impressive continuity and leaving any offenses not specifically mentioned to "be punished according to the general customs and laws of war."[6] These customs—the fourth foundation of Western military practice— consisted largely of precedents created by the conduct of war itself, to which both theorists and practitioners referred when considering or justifying their military choices. "The general sense and practice in all Wars," in the phrase of Sir Thomas Fairfax, parliamentary commander during the English civil wars, was already the touchstone of acceptable and unacceptable behavior by the 1640s.[7] Fifth and finally, participants in armed conflict almost always came to appreciate, sooner or later, the advantages of mutual restraint. Honoring surrenders, sparing the wounded, and respecting flags of truce reduced the danger and chaos of conflict for all combatants because creating a contractual etiquette of belligerence provided each party with a vital framework of expectations concerning the conduct of others. However, this powerful combination of natural and divine law, ecclesiastical precept, military law, common custom, and self-interest only coalesced to impart a new and enduring consistency to both the *jus ad bellum* and the *jus in bello* in the period between 1550 and 1700.

Jus ad Bellum: The Lawful Initiation of War

Few Europeans before the eighteenth century seem to have questioned the legitimacy of war itself. Although most Anabaptists, and later most Quakers, argued that violence was incompatible with the teaching of Christ, their numbers were few. The majority of Christians, Protestant as well as Catholic, saw their God as the Lord of Battles and had little time for pacifism. Instead, they concentrated on establishing whether a war was just or not. In the Middle Ages, cities, nobles, and even ordinary knights exercised the same freedom as their rulers to redress a grievance or avenge a wrong by declaring war on an enemy and seeking to inflict maximum damage on his or her dependents and property. However, the combined pressure of continued church censure, the spread of Roman law, and the growing power of the state gradually redefined the issue so that by the sixteenth century wars were only deemed just when waged by a legitimate government. Of course, in some parts of Europe the earlier norms survived: thus the memoirs of Götz von Berlichingen "of the iron claw" (dictated in the 1540s and entitled, significantly, *My Feuds and Disputes*) boasted of the thirty private wars he had waged in Germany since the turn of the century, either in his own name or by proxy; while in Scotland the blood feud long continued to be big business (at least in Scottish terms) with almost four hundred feuds recorded between 1573 and 1625.[8] But by then, in most parts of Europe, ordinary subjects—whether knights, nobles, or cities—who went to war without government warrant faced condemnation as rebels, traitors, or enemies of the public peace and, when defeated, suffered draconian penalties.

Conversely, few now questioned the absolute right of sovereigns to wage war—with the brief and remarkable exception of Britain in the mid-seventeenth century when King Charles I was tried and executed for war crimes. In April 1648, after a three-day marathon of fasting and prayer, the assembled officer corps of England's New Model Army declared that after they had defeated the royalists they would call

"Charles Stuart, that man of blood, to an account for that blood he had shed, and mischief he had done . . . against the Lord's cause and [the] people in these poor nations." In November of that year the council of officers agreed to put this demand to Parliament and, when that body proved recalcitrant, the following month they purged its members (Pride's Purge) until a majority in favor of trial was secured. A high court of justice was then set up, with 135 commissioners, 57 of whom agreed to sign the king's death warrant. He was beheaded in London on January 30, 1649.[9]

But Charles I was unlucky. Almost all of his contemporaries accepted the absolute right of legitimate rulers to use war as an instrument of policy, as and when they chose. The debate on the *jus ad bellum* from the sixteenth century onward focused not on who had the right to make war, but on the conditions upon which sovereigns (and only sovereigns) might justly do so. The formula laid down in the treatise *De iure et officiis bellicis,* published in the Netherlands in 1582 by Balthasar Ayala, represented the prevailing orthodoxy on this question. Ayala acknowledged several grounds for a just war: "for defense of ourselves or our allies"; "to regain from the enemy something which he is forcibly and unjustly detaining"; "to take vengeance for some wrong which has been unjustifiably inflicted"; when a neighbor denies to our forces permission to cross his territory peacefully; and to repress heresy and rebellion.[10]

Scarcely surprisingly, since he wrote in the midst of Spain's bitter struggle to suppress the Protestant-led revolt of the Netherlands, Ayala devoted much space to his last category. Heresy, he argued, should be met according to God's direct command in Deut. 20 with "wars of fire and blood" in which no quarter was to be either given or expected. Survivors, if any, should be deprived of all their possessions and enslaved. It is true that other writers of the day (such as Matthew Sutcliffe, Richard Bernard, and William Gouge) condoned only wars in defense of a given faith, while others still (Francisco de Vitoria, Francisco Suárez, and Francis Bacon) denied the legitimacy of any religious war among Christians; but in practice many European statesmen (like Ayala's sovereign, Philip II of Spain) proclaimed with pride that they fought principally to advance the cause of their church.[11] Thus in 1586 King Philip welcomed a papal suggestion that he undertake either the invasion of Protestant England or the conquest of Muslim Algiers, because "the destruction of the infidels and heretics, extending the bounds of Christendom, is also the desire of His Majesty." Having consulted (as was his custom) a team of theologians concerning the legitimacy of the two ventures, the king opted for the enterprise of England. Somewhat later, when the pope rather unfairly accused Philip of wishing to attack England solely for political reasons, the king retorted that there were many other ways for him to solve his differences with Elizabeth Tudor (negotiation, for example), and that "I was only persuaded to listen to His Holiness's proposal for the sake of God's service."[12] A similar "messianic imperialism" colored the political rhetoric of many Protestant countries—particularly England, Sweden, and the Dutch Republic—whose leaders between 1550 and 1650, despite the censure of the theorists, were usually prepared to wage war for the Protestant cause.[13]

Ayala likewise argued that "disobedience in the part of subjects and rebellion against the prince is treated as a heinous offense and put on a par with heresy."[14] He denied rebels the right to make war, however intolerable their situation, and claimed that if they did so they "ought not to be classed as enemies, the two being quite distinct, and so it is more correct to term the armed contention with rebel subjects execution of legal process, or prosecution, not war. . . . For the same reason the laws of war, and of captivity, and of postliminy, which apply to enemies, do not apply to rebels." It followed that "a war waged by a prince with rebels is a most just one, and that all measures allowed in war are available against them, such as killing them as enemies, enslaving them as prisoners, and, much more, confiscating their property as booty."[15]

Alberico Gentili proved tragically right when he wrote in 1589 that the "chief incentive to cruelty [in war] is rebellion." Thus during the Spanish campaign to annex the Azores in 1582 Philip II's commander justified the summary execution of all his captured opponents because he did not consider it a war but rather a police action against rebels. Later revolts such as the Jacobite rising in Britain (1745) were repressed with exemplary brutality. In 1774–75 some British officers viewed the American colonists' defiance in the same light as the Jacobite insurrection and advocated the same treatment; while in 1777 the Howe brothers received orders from the British government to consider the systematic destruction of the New England ports used by American cruisers attacking Britain's maritime communications.[16] Even the repression of more recent rebellions confirms Gentili's dictum, with levels of brutality rarely replicated in conventional wars: the Paris Commune (1871), Warsaw (1944), and Hungary (1956) in Europe; the Congo and Biafra in Africa during the 1960s; Nicaragua and El Salvador in Central America during the 1980s; and so on.

Jus in Bello: The Lawful Conduct of War

A certain amount of brutality is inevitable in all conflicts, given that the business of the military in war is killing people and breaking things; or, to quote Francisco de Valdés, a prominent Spanish soldier of the sixteenth century, "The day a man picks up his pike to become a soldier is the day he ceases to be a Christian."[17] Moreover, many atrocities take place in situations that have produced similar results in almost all societies: when the sudden collapse of an enemy force turns one army into a cowardly mob and the other into a murderous crowd. This could easily happen after an adversary was completely broken in battle; for whereas in close combat, in the midst of a press of men, it might be difficult to deal deadly blows, it was very different when the victors could ride down individual fugitives. In 1586, reporting the massacre of a Scottish expeditionary force in Ireland, Captain Thomas Woodhouse wrote, "Truly I was never, since I was a man of war, so weary with killing of men, for I protest to God, . . . as fast as I could I did but hough [hew] at them and paunch [stab] them, sometimes on horseback, because they did run as we did break them, and sometimes on foot." Some two thousand men were slain. And in 1643, after the rout of the parliamentary infantry at the battle of Torrington, the royalist cavalry pursued them "until their swords were blunted with the slaughter" and, of the survivors, there was "scarce a man without a cut over the head or face."[18]

Carnage was even more common when a town was taken by storm, for sieges have always been treated as total war. Soldiers who sought a civilian shelter and civilians who militarized their homes by accepting a garrison in effect presented an undifferentiated target to the besiegers: military and civilian personnel and property were hard to distinguish during the battery, the assault, or the sack that normally followed a successful storm.[19] Moreover, the catharsis of passing through the killing ground of the breach and emerging unscathed spurred many victors on to indiscriminate violence, while the panic and even paralysis which often gripped defeated defenders seems to have whipped up a blood lust, much as a frightened and cornered animal may provoke rather than pacify its hunters. Thus, during the English Civil War, when Cirencester fell to the royalists in 1643 the parliamentary garrison "were at their wits' end and stood like men amazed, fear bereft them of understanding and memory" as they were cut down; while at the storm of Lincoln, the following year, the royalists within threw down their arms and "cried out for quarter, saying they were poor Array Men [conscripts]. We slew fifty of them."[20]

Similar examples of brutality can be found in almost any conflict. At Jericho around 1350 B.C. Joshua and the Israelites "utterly destroyed all that was in the city, both man and woman, young and old, and ox, and sheep, and ass, with the edge of the sword. . . . And they burnt the city with fire, and all that was therein."[21] Much the same fate befell captured cities on the European eastern front during World War II, and the intervening 3,300 years bristle with similar instances of barbarism. But did such terrible examples of blood lust occur more frequently in certain periods? At first sight the sixteenth and seventeenth centuries stand out. On the one hand a rapid growth in army size—tenfold in some states—created logistical problems that few governments seemed able to solve directly. Plunder and wanton exploitation of civilian resources took place more frequently in part because, until the emergence of an adequate tax base and administrative structure, the larger armies could not be fed in any other way. Thus, although they deprecated unrestrained looting (which had been central to the feud), most early modern writers accepted that it was lawful to take away from innocent parties goods that an enemy could also use (for example, their weapons and their ships), and to destroy any assets (crops, merchandise, and so on) that might nourish enemy forces. On the other hand the fragmentation of religious unity in the West in the wake of the Reformation weakened some other restraints on war derived from the Middle Ages: although women and children were still normally spared (except during a sack), and mutilation of the dead and wounded remained rare, the protection of priests and pilgrims now usually extended only to those of the same creed, while foreigners, merchants, and the poor (formerly covered by the Peace of God) became fair game.[22]

Nevertheless, some striking examples of restraint still occurred during this period. Thus in 1574 during Spain's desperate struggle to crush the revolt of the Netherlands following the failure of the Spanish army's siege of Leiden serious consideration was given to the systematic inundation of the rebel provinces. The opportunity seemed perfect: the fact that most of Holland and Zeeland lay below sea level was self-evident—everyone could see the drainage mills on the dikes, ceaselessly keeping the water at bay; and memories of previous catastrophes which had inundated large areas of the province remained vivid. Furthermore, the rebels themselves had broken several dikes, first in order to blockade the royalist garrison in Middelburg (1572) and then to impede the Spanish siege of Alkmaar in North Holland (1573).[23] More dramatically, in August 1574 they began to break the dikes and open the sluices along the rivers to the south of Leiden. It was a controlled operation, designed to let in only enough water for a fleet of flat-bottomed barges to sail provisions into Leiden and thus raise the siege; but it gave the frustrated Spaniards in the trenches pause. As Francisco de Valdés, the Spanish commander before Leiden, wrote to his commander in chief:

> When I first entered Holland with the army, I intercepted a letter written by the prince of Orange [the Dutch leader] in his own hand [to one of his officials] . . . in which he wrote the following words: "I had given orders that you should break the sluice at Maaslandsluis in order to flood the area, but we have gathered together here . . . some learned men, and they find that if these sluices are broken, the whole countryside will be flooded without it being possible ever to reclaim it. So it would be better not to break them." I thought I should let Your Excellency know this [Valdés continued] so that you will be aware that if at any time you might wish to flood this country, it is in your power. And since our enemies have taken the initiative in doing so, if they continue in their obstinate rebellion they indeed deserve to be flooded out.[24]

This suggestion, which bears a striking resemblance to the proposed United States air strikes against the dams and dikes of the Red River delta during the Vietnam War (the Rolling Thunder and Linebacker campaigns), was duly approved by the high command in Brussels and forwarded to the king for authorization. But, to the disgust of all the military men, Philip II—like President Johnson four hundred years later in remarkably similar terms—forbade the operation:[25]

It is very clear [the king wrote] that the severity, wickedness and obstinacy of the rebels has reached the level where no one can doubt that they are worthy of a harsh and exemplary punishment. . . . And [we know that] we can easily flood Holland by breaking the dikes. But this strategy would give rise to a great disadvantage: that once broken, the province would be lost and ruined for ever, to the evident detriment of the neighboring provinces which would have to build new dikes of their own. . . . So that, in effect, it would not be wise to adopt this strategy, nor must we do so because (apart from the disadvantages already mentioned, great and manifest as they are) we should also recognize that it would earn for us a reputation for cruelty which would be better avoided, especially against our vassals, even though their guilt is notorious and the punishment justified.[26]

However, such restraint by a sovereign against rebellious subjects, especially when many of them professed a different faith, was rare in the century following 1550. François de La Noue, like other military writers of the later sixteenth century, believed that war had grown far more brutal during his own lifetime, with virtually no holds barred in conflict; and he ascribed this development to the prevalence of both rebellion and religious schism which multiplied the number of those to whom no quarter should be given.[27] The argument is highly plausible: both political and social uprisings, many of them aiming at religious change, occurred with remarkable frequency in early modern Europe, with peaks in the 1560s, the 1590s, and the 1640s.[28] Moreover, some of the worst recorded excesses involved soldiers of one creed butchering those of another: the massacres perpetrated by the Catholic forces of Spain in the Netherlands during the 1570s; the destruction of Protestant Magdeburg in Germany by the Catholic imperial army in 1631; or the sack of Drogheda in Ireland by the Protestant New Model Army in 1649. Moreover, the victors normally justified these and other similar deeds with the rhetoric of messianic imperialism buttressed by the examples of severe chastisement of unbelievers to be found in the Old Testament. Thus a sermon preached in 1645 to the parliamentary forces just before they stormed Basing House (the stronghold of a Catholic peer) condemned those within as "open enemies of God," "bloody papists," and "vermin" and called for their extermination. Not surprisingly, few of the defeated defenders received quarter.[29]

But there is less to all this than meets the eye. In the first place, it may well be that atrocities seemed more numerous simply because wars were more numerous: scarcely a year in the period 1520–1650 saw the Continent entirely at peace. Second, the age abounded in brutality: the soldiers themselves were normally subjected to draconian and sometimes arbitrary penalties by their officers. The articles of war promulgated for the English parliamentary army in 1642 contained forty-five offenses punishable by death. Collective misdemeanors in most armies were castigated by drawing lots or by decimation to determine who was to be shot; several mutinies by the Spanish Army of Flanders in the 1570s were provoked by punishments deemed by the soldiers to be arbitrary or degrading.[30] Third and most important, in most parts of Europe battles became relatively rare and sieges constituted the hinge of success and failure.

According to the laws of war, a town which rejected a summons to surrender from someone who claimed it as a right offered an insult to his authority which he was honor bound to avenge; and the longer it held out, the worse the penalty. In the early stages this might merely be pecuniary. Thus in 1650 during the English conquest of Scotland the city of Saint Andrews in Fife surrendered only at the second summons and therefore had to pay five hundred pounds to the soldiery.[31] Far more serious was refusal to surrender until the battery was brought up, for then the inhabitants had no right to quarter if the town were taken by storm. Henry V's brutal speech to the besieged burghers of Harfleur, written by William Shakespeare in the 1590s, reflected the contemporary situation well:

> If I begin the batt'ry once again,
> I will not leave the half-achieved Harfleur
> Till in her ashes she lie buried.
> The gates of mercy shall be all shut up
> And the flesh'd soldier, rough and hard of heart,
> In liberty of bloody hand shall range
> With conscience wide as hell, mowing like grass
> Your fresh fair virgins and your flow'ring infants.
> What is't then to me if impious war,
> Array'd in flames, like to the prince of fiends,
> Do, with his smirch'd complexion, all fell feats
> Enlink'd to waste and desolation?

Attitudes remained the same throughout the eighteenth century, of which the duke of Wellington later wrote: "I believe that it has always been understood that the defenders of a fortress stormed have no claim to quarter."[32]

Even so, the degree of violence permitted during a sack was limited. Public opinion normally tolerated actions committed in the sudden flush of total victory when, as Lucy Hutchinson observed in her memoirs of the English Civil War, "the brave turn cowards, fear unnerves the most mighty, [and] makes the generous base, and great men do those things that they blush to think on."[33] Later on it was different. Thus when Mechelen in the Netherlands fell by storm in 1580 a group of nuns begged the Protestant soldiers who had invaded their convent for a swift death, but the troops rather surprisingly spared them on the grounds that "the fury was over and they no longer had license"; while in 1644 an English royalist preacher enjoined the king's soldiers that "you neither do, nor . . . suffer to be done, in coole blood, to the most impious rebells [viz., supporters of Parliament], any thing that savours of immodesty, barbarousnesse, or inhumanity."[34]

Nevertheless, even armchair theorists of this period, while calling in general terms for restraint, acknowledged that sound military reasons might justify unbridled brutality. Thus Francisco de Vitoria, in his seminal work on international law composed in the 1540s, recognized three reasons for the exemplary punishment of an obdurate town and its population: first, on grounds of overall strategy (for example, to prevent the provision of assistance to the enemy at a later stage); second, to keep up the morale of one's own army (especially if pay had been in short supply during the siege); and third, to scare other enemy towns into surrender.[35] These considerations became particularly important when the towns concerned were engaged in rebellion for, as the duke of Alba (commander of the government's forces in the Netherlands) acutely observed soon after the outbreak of the Dutch revolt in 1572, not all towns that fell into an enemy's hands were equally guilty: they should therefore not all be treated alike. He discerned six distinct types. First, those that had been taken by the enemy after a siege; second, those that had held out until the enemy brought up its artillery and could therefore resist with impunity no longer; third, those that had admitted the enemy because they had no alternative; and fourth, those that had requested a royalist garrison but had been threatened by the enemy before help could arrive. All such towns, according to Alba, deserved leniency when recaptured. Quite different were his fifth category—those that had surrendered before need arose—and his sixth—those that had refused government troops when offered them, choosing instead to admit the enemy.[36]

An analysis of the conduct of the Spanish army in the Netherlands during the first stage of the Dutch revolt shows that the duke adhered meticulously to his own formula. Thus the first town to be sacked in 1572 was Mechelen (Malines), which undoubtedly belonged to Alba's sixth category. It had refused his offer of a garrison in June but had freely admitted—and had paid—the troops sent by the prince of Orange in August. To make matters worse, as the Spanish troops approached, the Orangist garrison fired warning shots (before abandoning the town at midnight).[37] Mechelen nevertheless refused the duke's demand for unconditional surrender and was taken by storm almost immediately: the ensuing orgy of sack and plunder lasted three entire days, with the duke and his senior commanders grimly looking on. According to an eyewitness, "the soldiers behaved as if this religious capital of the country were a Muslim city and all the inhabitants barbarians. The desolation was so complete that not a nail was left in a wall." Even four years later another eyewitness remained unable to describe what he had seen: "One could say a lot more," he wrote to a friend, "if the horror of it did not make one's hair stand on end—not at recounting it but at remembering it!"[38] But these men were civilians: most soldiers recognized that Francisco de Vitoria's three justifications for exemplary punishment all came into play at Mechelen. First, as already noted, the town was unquestionably guilty, yet it refused to surrender when summoned: therefore a full sack was entirely legitimate. Second, the Spanish army was suffering from chronic lack of pay: the Spaniards themselves were owed eighteen months' wage arrears and the Walloon troops almost three, while the German regiments had received nothing at all since they enlisted.[39] Alba may well have felt that he could not afford clemency for fear his unpaid troops would mutiny unless they were allowed some plunder.[40] Third, and no less important, the duke calculated that exemplary brutality against one town in revolt would persuade others to surrender swiftly.[41] And so it proved: the sack of Mechelen seems to have satisfied the victorious troops both psychologically and financially; and it provoked within a matter of days the submission of the other rebellious towns in Flanders and Brabant.[42] All of them received an immediate pardon. Alba and his troops thus did no more than put Francisco de Vitoria's stern views on the *jus in bello* into practice: it was a classic hard war combination of terror and discipline.

A similar explanation can be advanced for the sack of Magdeburg in 1631, an event condemned by Protestants at the time as a "memorable catastrophe" to be ranked alongside the fall of Troy and Noah's flood.[43] Yet the city had refused to admit an imperial garrison since the summer of 1629; it made an alliance with Gustavus Adolphus of Sweden, a declared enemy of the emperor, in the summer of 1630; and it repeatedly rejected the demands for surrender received from an imperial siege army commanded by Count Tilly. Even after some of the outer defenses fell, trusting in Gustavus's rash promises of immediate assistance, the city nevertheless repudiated a final ultimatum on May 18, 1631. Tilly, fearing the arrival of a Swedish relief column, launched a general storm at dawn two days later. His forces burst through the walls in three places and vented their fury on all who crossed their path. Thousands perished but, contrary to the assertions of Protestant polemicists, not through sectarian passion but according to the laws of war reinforced by strategic necessity.[44]

Much the same story can be told of the equally reviled sack of Drogheda in 1649. A relatively small English army commanded by Oliver Cromwell brought up a powerful siege train on September 9 and summoned the town the following day but was rebuffed. Thereupon battery began in earnest and by the afternoon of the eleventh two breaches had been made and a general assault took place. It is true that Cromwell later claimed that he was moved by a spirit of confessional vengeance: "I am persuaded that this is a righteous judgment of God upon these barbarous [Catholic] wretches, who have imbrued their hands in so much innocent [Protestant] blood"; and that accordingly, "in the heat of the action" he forbade his troops "to spare any that were in arms in the town." But that statement scarcely does justice to events. First, the defenders of Drogheda included English Catholics, English Protestants, and Irish Protestants as well as Irish Catholics; second, English and French Catholics previously encountered by Cromwell's army had been decently treated; third, a number of noncombatants in the town (including all Catholic clergy) were also killed; and fourth, much of the slaughter took place some time after the heat of the action was past. Thus several parties of defenders (including the one-legged governor, Sir Arthur

Aston, and his entourage) were first allowed to surrender and then butchered an hour after quarter was given them. Indeed, according to one source, Aston's brains were beaten out with his own wooden leg, and what remained of his head was then sent to Dublin along with those of fifteen other senior officers to be set on poles. In all, perhaps one thousand civilians and twenty-five hundred soldiers were killed by the New Model Army at Drogheda on or immediately after September 11, 1649.[45]

As at Mechelen and Magdeburg, however, this appalling brutality was intended to secure important strategic goals. According to Cromwell's lieutenants, sometimes less addicted to religious rhetoric than their leader, "the extraordinary severity was designed to discourage others from making opposition" and thus "tend to prevent the effusion of blood for the future." In this it succeeded splendidly. According to the marquis of Ormond, the leader of the Irish forces, "It is not to be imagined how great the terror is that those successes and the power of the rebels [Cromwell and his troops] have struck into this people, who though they know themselves resigned, at best, to the loss of all they have and to irrecoverable slavery, and have yet numbers enough and other competent means to oppose . . . are yet so stupefied that it is with great difficulty I can persuade them to act anything like men towards their own preservation."[46] Sure enough, news of the sack of Drogheda swiftly produced the surrender of other neighboring garrisons. Its fate, like the others discussed above, was thus no sectarian massacre—let us recall once more that many of the defenders and townsfolk were Protestant—but an action carried out for strategic (not confessional) reasons and, as such, largely sanctioned by the contemporary laws of war.

Extending the Laws of War

Before long, moreover, such orgies of destruction began to seem exceptional. On the one hand, fewer places chose to resist until an assault became inevitable, thus permitting a negotiated surrender: in the concise formula of Alberico Gentili, "Cities are sacked when taken; they are not sacked when surrendered." Admittedly the terms might be harsh, even unconditional, which could lead to the execution of some of the defenders; but the loss of life and property was still less.[47] On the other hand, as time passed, the range of military misconduct condoned by military authorities and by public opinion steadily narrowed. Taking and killing hostages or perpetrating exemplary atrocities, which Vitoria and Gentili had tolerated in the sixteenth century, came to be execrated by writers such as Johann Justus Moser and Emerich de Vattel in the eighteenth; while today some theorists condemn even sieges and economic blockades as a species of terrorism because they intentionally inflict harm on innocent civilians in order to force governments to capitulate.

Moreover, in most of the wars waged in Europe since the sixteenth century, breaches of the norms for military conduct laid down in treatises (and more recently in treaties) have been condemned and chastised with increasing rigor. Individual soldiers faced trial and punishment by special military tribunals for crimes committed against either fellow soldiers or civilians.[48] Thus in 1574 Philip II ordered a judicial enquiry into accusations that the duke of Alba had used disproportionate force in his conduct of the war against the Dutch rebels, and although Alba himself was acquitted, several of his senior officials were banished from court.[49] After the brutal sack of Antwerp by the Spanish army in 1576, a full judicial enquiry was held to determine responsibility for the atrocities which left eight thousand citizens dead and one thousand houses destroyed; and in Ireland after the trauma of the civil war and the Cromwellian occupation, a court of claims was established in 1662 specifically to examine charges against those accused of war crimes.[50]

This development constituted a significant and lasting extension in the application of the laws of war and it was paralleled by another: conventions previously applied selectively during the early modern period gradually came to be enforced almost universally. In a sense this process merely represented a stage in a longer evolution. Many tribal societies equated mankind with members of their own tribe and regarded all others as nonhumans to be treated—or, rather, mistreated—as animals. Even in medieval Europe the laws of war only governed "the conduct of men who fought to settle by arms quarrels which were in nature private, and whose importance was judged by the social status of the principals involved." They therefore affected only equals.[51] In the sixteenth century, however, starting in Spain's war against the Dutch, the same rules began to be applied to all combatants, whatever their social status.

Even as Balthasar Ayala composed his uncompromising treatise on the need to wage a war to the death against all rebels, his commanding officer (Alessandro Farnese, duke of Parma) negotiated generous terms for the return of rebellious cities to the king's obedience and for the exchange and ransom of captured soldiers in enemy hands.[52] Soon afterward the regular exchange of prisoners of war became standard practice: by 1599, if not before, Spain and the Dutch Republic had concluded a formal convention—the *cuartel general*—stipulating that every captain should ransom all his captured men within twenty-five days. First, prisoners of equal rank on each side were to be exchanged free of charge; thereafter, a ransom appropriate to the soldier's rank (usually the equivalent of one month's pay) was due, plus an agreed per diem "entertainment" for time spent in captivity. The convention was reissued every few years, with the schedule of payments revised upward to take account of inflation. In 1637 and again in 1643 the Dutch-Spanish protocol was translated and published in English; and from 1639 the same system was introduced into the war between Spain and France.[53] Likewise, agreement was reached that sick and injured soldiers who fell into enemy hands should be placed under a special safeguard and repatriated with a minimum of formality.[54] Thus matters which had previously been subject to private contract now came under state regulation; and the available evidence suggests that exchanges were effected fairly and fast—even if the prisoners were released "from the most remote parts, as usual, so that they will not find it easy to return home."[55]

Simultaneously, new regulations began to limit the violence and plunder of unpaid soldiery at the expense of noncombatants. Both sides in the Low Countries' Wars began to accept prearranged sums of protection money from individual communities based on mutual guarantees that they would neither engage in hostilities nor be subjected to further extortions from those whom they paid. Parties of troops took up station specifically to enforce the agreements. Once again, the idea was not new: during the Hundred Years' War most local commanders had issued letters of protection to a community in return for financial contributions, but each safeguard only bound the party that issued it—a community was still liable to depredations from the troops of other commanders even when they were on the same side. In the Low Countries' Wars, however, the growing power of the state made the system binding on all troops, and its effectiveness may be judged from a letter written by a Spanish field officer to his superiors in 1640: "The majority of the villages [near the enemy frontier] . . . contain enemy 'protection troops.' . . . [This] gives rise to many inconveniences for His Majesty's service. One is that our own men cannot go there to collect information about the enemy, because they are immediately arrested as spies by the protection troops. And, thanks to their presence, the peasants are able to bring in their crops safely and provide full aid and assistance to the enemy."[56]

Four factors explain the new restraint in war. First, the composition of armies underwent a major change: the contingents hired and maintained via military contractors gave way to units raised and sustained directly by the state. The significance of this transition for the conduct of war was illuminated by an exchange between two royalists—Lord Glamorgan, an aristocrat, and Lord Ruthven, a professional soldier—during the English Civil War. Glamorgan (admittedly a very rich man) had kept his own troops under tight control at the siege of Gloucester in 1643, "without so much as making use of free quarter, but all uppon the penny." Ruthven (a veteran of the Thirty Years' War) objected that this created problems for other commanders who lacked the money to pay their troops, and complained to King Charles I; but Glamorgan boldly replied that "I yielded to His Excellencie to be a better soldier, but still to be a soldier of fortune, here today and God knows where tomorrow, and therefore needed not care for the love of the people; but though I were killed myselfe I should leave my posteritie behind me, towards whom I would not leave a grudge in the people, but whilst I could serve His Majestie upon my owne purse and creditt I would readdyly doe it, and afterward leave it to such as his Lordship."[57] As the seventeenth century advanced, less and less was left "to such as his Lordship" and troops raised by private contractors. Instead, governments created supply magazines, fortified frontiers, and centrally controlled contributions systems which gradually reduced the need for looting as a survival strategy for the individual soldier. Of course, excesses still occurred and the penalties imposed for failing to provide the stores required could be draconian; but the new methods nevertheless reduced the occasions for friction between soldiers and civilians that had so often produced atrocities in the past.[58]

A second reason favoring greater restraint in the conduct of war in the West was a steady process of deconfessionalization. By 1650 the religious frontiers of Europe had largely stabilized, for the religious rebels had either succeeded in gaining recognition as a state (as with the Dutch Republic) or had been forced either to conform or leave (as in the Spanish Netherlands). Furthermore, the calamitous changes of fortune experienced by each creed during the period seem to have dented the absolute certainty of many participants that they served as agents of God's purpose: a sense of resignation often replaced the dynamic providentialism that had led men to fight to the death with a clear conscience.[59] Almost simultaneously, after the Peace of Westphalia in 1648 religion ceased to be an issue for which most states were prepared to go to war. Thus at the turn of the eighteenth century Louis XIV's bid for European mastery met defeat at the hands of a coalition led by the staunchly Calvinist William of Orange, whose most important ally was the Catholic Prince Eugene of Savoy, a minister of the no less Catholic Austrian Habsburgs; while in the Great Northern War, Lutheran Sweden was eventually laid low by an alliance of Lutheran Denmark, Calvinist Brandenburg, Catholic Poland, and Orthodox Russia. Of course atrocities still occurred, such as the devastation of the Palatinate by the forces of Louis XIV in 1688–89; but religion played no part in the process and the chorus of condemnation was all but universal. As time passed, deconfessionalization became reinforced by Enlightenment values which enjoined ever greater restraint upon soldiers.[60]

Alongside this gradual intellectual process lay another: a general feeling that in the wars of the mid-seventeenth century Europe had come perilously close to self-destruction. "Oh, come on!" ran one of the German pastor Paul Gerhardt's hymns, "Wake up, wake up, you hard world, open your eyes before terror comes upon you in swift, sudden surprise." A desperate entry in a Swabian peasant family's Bible from 1647 reads: "We live like animals, eating bark and grass. No one could imagine that anything like this could happen to us. Many people say that there is no God." A little later in England, writing a few months after the end of the civil war, John Locke regretted "all those flames that have made such havoc and desolation in Europe and have not been quenched but with the blood of so many millions."[61] Political leaders, as well as writers, artists, and ordinary people, felt a revulsion toward the excesses of the preceding period and harbored a fervent hope that it should never happen again. As in the aftermath of World War I, the slaughter had been so great, the specter of chaos so terrifying, that "no more war" attitudes became common. Some have detected in these sentiments a climate favorable to the development of absolute states; certainly they created a climate favorable to greater restraint in the conduct of war.[62]

A fourth and final explanation for the growth of restraint in early modern European warfare lay in the steady spread of reciprocity. During the Middle Ages honor and reputation had to some extent ensured observance of the conventions, but they were always reinforced by the threat of vengeance: the kin of a knight slain by treachery would normally seek revenge, creating a blood feud. And where this sanction was lacking, restraint diminished. Thus encounters between knights and members of the lower social orders normally turned into bloodbaths, whoever won: witness the carnage after the various victories of the Swiss or after the defeat of peasant armies. Restraint only appeared in such unequal conflicts when they became protracted: barbarous behavior by one side, confident of the righteousness of its own cause and its own invulnerability, changed dramatically when the other side acquired the capacity to retaliate. Thus in the early stages of the Dutch revolt, according to the duke of Alba himself, it was Spain's strict policy to hang all prisoners.[63] But this changed abruptly in the autumn of 1573 when the Dutch captured one of Alba's most capable subordinates, the count of Bossu. The Dutch leaders made it clear that, unless the systematic execution of Dutch prisoners ceased, Bossu would be hanged. The Spaniards reluctantly agreed, and negotiations began for the release of Bossu and other Spaniards in exchange for certain rebels in Spanish hands.[64] Enemy troops came to be accepted as soldiers first and rebels second. Likewise, during the civil war in England, although the king's provost marshal initially treated captured parliamentarians as rebels and traitors, Parliament's threats to hang all their royalist prisoners in retaliation caused a notable reduction in severity.[65]

Parallel developments occurred at the local level. Where garrisons from opposing sides existed in close proximity, conventions emerged that anticipated the live and let live system on relatively quiet sectors of the trenches on the western front during World War I: tacit and sometimes even formal treaties of neutrality were concluded between belligerents. In order to remove the intolerable tension of living on permanent alert, rival garrison commanders or neighboring (but opposed) communities would agree not to attack each other. There was even a ratchet effect, as cooperation on such basic matters led to deals in other areas, such as where each side might safely forage.[66] It took a little longer for the same principle to be accepted in the war at sea. As late as 1622–25 the crews of Flemish privateers were either hanged or thrown overboard ("foot watering" as it was known) when captured by their Dutch adversaries; but when the Dunkirkers captured no fewer than fifteen hundred Dutch prisoners the foot watering abruptly ceased.[67]

The Limits of Restraint

The spread of reciprocity was not universal, however, and appalling atrocities continued to occur, often with the full support of the state—witness the policy of the German army on hostages throughout World War II, the conduct of the Red Army in 1944–45 as it invaded Germany, and the ethnic cleansing and systematic rape that accompanied the Yugoslav war in 1991–93. Perhaps we should not be surprised, for an important aim of state-sponsored propaganda before and during war is specifically to destroy any sense of identification with the enemy by dehumanizing all adversaries so that they can be killed, mutilated, and otherwise mistreated with a clear conscience. Evidence of subhuman traits and racial inferiority, as well as alleged atrocities and supposedly implacable malice, all play their part in this process. Thus Nazi Germany prepared its troops for the invasion of the Soviet Union in 1941 by portraying the soldiers of the Red Army as *keine Kameraden* to whom one could do anything, anywhere, at any time, without scruple. "We must remove any feeling of military comradeship" from our troops, Hitler instructed his generals before Barbarossa. "The Communist has never been, and will never be, a comrade. We are engaged in a war of extermination." Soviet Russia replied in kind. An order distributed to the troops besieging Danzig in March 1945 ended: "Soldiers of the Red Army, kill the Germans! Kill all Germans! Kill! Kill! Kill!"[68]

In the early modern period the category of keine Kameraden applied in Europe to the native Irish, who were killed and enslaved and whose property was destroyed or confiscated with little or no pause for thought. According to his approving biographer, whenever in the 1570s Sir Humphrey Gilbert invaded "the enemies countrie, he killed manne, woman and child; and spoiled, wasted and burned, by the grounde, all that he might, leavyng nothing of the enemies in saffetie, which he could possiblie waste or consume"; and the way to his headquarters whenever he campaigned in Gaelic Ireland was flanked by a line of severed heads.[69]

Overseas, such conduct was already the norm. Most Europeans saw their African and Native American adversaries as keine Kameraden to whom the laws of war did not apply. Several justifications were adduced. To begin with, they were pagans. Admittedly, from 1512 onward a special text (known as the *Requerimiento* and based on Deut. 20:10–16) was read out before each Spanish advance in the Americas, requiring the native peoples of the New World to accept immediately both the authority of the Spanish crown and the tenets of Christianity or face the consequences. Failure to submit instantly legitimized for most Spaniards a war of fire and blood, culminating in the expropriation of all possessions and the enslavement of all persons. Many Westerners further justified this appalling behavior on the grounds that their overseas opponents corresponded to the peoples described by Aristotle as born to be slaves, to whom few rights under the law remained. It is true that the legitimacy of such conduct was sometimes queried, and that a number of full-dress debates took place around the year 1550 concerning the Europeans' right to enslave the Indians, but little changed. Alleged cases of cannibalism, the mass slaughter of sacrificial victims by the Aztec priests, or the mass production of pottery depicting fellatio, sodomy, and group sex by some Pre-Columbian peoples all served to justify the Spaniards' view that the Native American peoples were incapable of reading the book of nature implanted in all true men by God and therefore stood in need of education—both for their own good and for the good of the whole human community whose integrity could be endangered by cannibalism or unnatural sex even in remote areas like America. Any opposition to the process of education was accordingly viewed as unjust war and the perpetrators therefore received no mercy.[70]

Another reason for the continuing harshness of colonial wars lay in the fact that, to some extent, a measure of brutality was probably essential if the (initially) extremely small numbers of invaders were to retain control several thousand miles from their home base. The point was well put by one of the last of the conquistadores, Richard Meinertzhagen, whose account of the subjugation of Kenya between 1902 and 1906 is strewn with dead bodies. When he prepared his diaries for publication in the 1950s, Meinertzhagen himself was slightly shaken. "On reading through . . . this record I am shocked by the account of taking human life," he wrote. "I do not pretend to excuse it, but perhaps I may explain it. I have no belief in the sanctity of human life or in the dignity of the human race. Human life has never been sacred; nor has man, except in a few exceptional cases, been dignified. Moreover in Kenya fifty years ago, when stationed with 100 soldiers amid an African population of 300,000, in cases of emergency where local government was threatened we had to act, and act quickly." No doubt Hernán Cortés, commanding only five hundred Europeans in his campaign against the Aztecs in 1519–21, or Francisco Pizarro with less than two hundred Europeans when he destroyed the Inca empire in 1532–33, would have heartily endorsed this rude philosophy.[71]

Yet despite their numerical superiority, the conquerors' victims failed to establish reciprocity. Cooperation between enemies requires neither rationality (for if it works, it will continue), nor trust (thanks to the penalties of defection), nor mutual communication (because deeds speak louder than words). Only durability is essential: some recognition of adversaries from earlier encounters and some certainty that the two sides will meet again.[72] The absence of this vital precondition helps to explain not only the brutality of colonial wars but also the hard war policies followed by Sherman's army on its march through Georgia during the American Civil War, by the army of Morocco on its advance from Seville during the Spanish Civil War, by the German army against Soviet soldiers and civilians during the Second World War, and by the Red Army during its conquest of Germany in 1944–45, just as it had played its part in the destruction of native America. There was no time for reciprocity to develop.

The rules of war followed by most European societies both at home and abroad have thus displayed a remarkable continuity since the sixteenth century. This stems in part from the relative stability of human nature—the advantages of cooperation and the dangers of total collapse were as apparent to Renaissance soldiers as they are today—in part from the lasting influence of the Bible, the church fathers, and Roman law on Western civilization. But both of these considerations received reinforcement from the weight of practice and precedent by the frequent appeals to custom in assessing military conduct. It is true that the theoretical restrictions of the *jus in bello* have multiplied; it is also true that those restrictions have been breached at regular intervals. But almost every excess, from the sixteenth century onward, has been subjected by contemporaries to detailed scrutiny: had the troops been provoked beforehand (for instance, by the previous mutilation of their captured comrades); had they been starved of pay; had the enemy reneged on a previous oath not to fight again? And if no excuses were available, moral condemnation and then legal sanctions ensued. Most of the actions today outlawed by the Geneva Conventions have been condemned in the West for at least four centuries; only the degree and the extent of enforcement have changed over time. Thus every generation of playgoers has understood (despite the bogus Welsh accent) Fluellen's outrage in Shakespeare's *Henry V* upon hearing of the massacre of the unarmed camp followers after the battle of Agincourt:

> Kill the poys and the luggage! 'Tis expressly against the law of arms; 'tis as arrant a piece of knavery, mark you now, as can be offert; in your conscience, now, is it not?[73]

Yes, it was against the law of arms in the 1590s, when the play was first performed, as it still is today, constituting just one of the numerous "self-evident and unalterable" features of the laws of war that crystallized in early modern Europe and survived virtually intact down to our own day, counterbalancing the contrasts detected by Martin van Creveld.

Harold E.
Selesky

5
Colonial America

To render the enormous subject of constraints on war in colonial America more manageable, this chapter is divided into three sections, according to the nature of the military situation encountered by the people living in English (later British) America in the sixteenth, seventeenth, and eighteenth centuries. The first section examines the expectations and experience the early settlers brought with them to their new homes, in particular how experience in the Elizabethan conquest of Ireland was reflected in their first encounters with Native Americans in Virginia and New England. The second section deals with how colonial Englishmen responded to dangers on the frontier with French Canada during the seventy years of the imperial wars for control of North America from 1690 through 1760. Again the problem was largely how to counter the threat posed by Native Americans, but now with the important admixture of the fact that the colonists believed the Indians were instigated and led by other Europeans, men who were otherwise presumed to share at least some of the culture and civility of Englishmen themselves. The final section examines what colonial Americans thought about proper conduct, especially by the British, in their war for independence, and concludes by focusing on how each side waged a partisan war in 1778 in the no-man's-land around the principal British base at Manhattan, in which small units operating between the main armies continually probed and jostled each other for control of resources and information.

The prerequisite in dealing with this subject is suspending moral judgment about the actions of people who did not shrink from doing what they thought they had to do. People in colonial America surely knew the difference between kindness and cruelty, and most probably would have chosen kindness most of the time, all other things being equal. But so often other things were not equal, and men acted without hesitation to do the things they thought were necessary to achieve their goals and worried only afterward about their consciences and other men's opinions. This description of conduct is obviously not limited to colonial America. Men in all ages have used concepts like necessity, raison d'état, and just following orders to justify their conduct and assuage their consciences. In all ages, too, limits on what is considered fair in war seem to have been set more by what one side thinks it can get away with than by some abstract and arbitrary set of moral standards. While recognizing the pragmatic character of military action, it is nonetheless important to understand why men thought certain forms of violence were more effective and socially acceptable than others. Moreover, it must be recognized that not all of their actions were the products of a rational calculus of advantage. Men do things in war that they have a hard time explaining thereafter to themselves, to contemporaries, and to posterity. The best course for the historian is to evaluate their actions in light of their own hopes and fears, see if they did the best with what they had, and not condemn them too quickly for what might appear in retrospect to have been overly harsh behavior.

How, then, did the first English settlers in North America apply their expectations and experience to the problem of self-defense in a land inhabited by a people whose culture was, by their standards, pagan, heathen, and barbarian? The fact that Englishmen were encountering in North America a people so thoroughly unlike themselves was crucial to the way in which they perceived the threat those people posed and what they believed was appropriate military action in response. Attempts to subdue Ireland, which began in the mid-1560s and involved some of the same men who twenty years later undertook the first settlement in what is now North Carolina, provide a working model of English attitudes about war, not so much because of the direct transfer of tactics and methods to North America as for the light they throw on how Englishmen dealt with people they considered to be their inferiors.

To the Englishmen of the Elizabethan age, the Irish were an uncivilized, un-Christian, and unworthy race. According to a modern historian, the conduct of the Elizabethans makes it clear that they "believed that in dealing with the native Irish population they were absolved from all normal ethical restraints." The dirty, treacherous, priest-ridden, bog-bred Irish had to be treated severely: according to one Englishman, "nothing but fear and force can teach dutie and obedience" to this "rebellious people." "Englishmen argued that it was their duty and responsibility to hold . . . down [the Irish] by force so that through subjection they could achieve liberty," by which they meant the liberty to labor for the Englishmen who had been so beneficent as to teach them right from wrong.[1]

How did these theoretical propositions translate into military action? When Englishmen in Ireland dehumanized an enemy who did not meet their standards of culture, true religion, and civil behavior, they concluded that all stratagems and cruelties were reasonable if that was what was required to defeat a foe who was not worthy of civilized treatment. Take for example the way in which Sir Humphrey

Gilbert undertook to conquer and pacify the province of Munster in the remote southwestern tip of Ireland. When Gilbert was appointed military governor in October 1569, "war in Munster became total war." "The pamphleteer, Thomas Churchyard, who accompanied Gilbert to Munster," later tried to justify "the slaughter of noncombatants on the grounds of expediency." Because the efforts of noncombatants were "essential to sustain the rebels," Churchyard argued, "the killing of them by the sword was the way to kill the men of war by famine." Gilbert engaged with energetic ruthlessness in some extremely brutal measures to terrorize the inhabitants, and it is worth quoting Churchyard at length to appreciate the depths to which the conqueror went to erode the popular will to continue to fight against his troops. Gilbert ordered that

> the heads of all those (of what sort soever they were) which were killed in the day, should be cut off from their bodies and brought to the place where he encamped at night, and should there be laid on the ground by each side of the way leading to his own tent, so that none [especially no Irishman] could come into his tent . . . but . . . he must pass through a lane of heads which he [Gilbert] used ad terrorem, the dead feeling nothing more the pains thereby; and yet did it bring great terror to the people when they saw the heads of their dead fathers, brothers, children, kinfolk, and friends, lie on the ground before their faces.

The principal argument Churchyard used to justify such atrocities was expediency: "through the terror which the people conceived thereby, it made short wars."[2]

This last point is worth emphasizing. Embedded in their contempt of the enemy, be he Irishman or Native American, was a strong practical strain often understated by contemporary observers and therefore underappreciated by modern historians. A short war was a good thing because it was less costly in terms of manpower and money for the English and also, they could argue, better for the Irish or the Indians because the terror sown by cruelty to a few would break resistance sooner and leave more of them alive at the end of a short, sharp terrorization than would be the case after a campaign of attrition directed against their food supplies. Englishmen demonstrated in Ireland that they clearly understood how to use deliberate terror to speed the conquest of an unworthy foe.

There is a second point here, one which Churchyard's cultural arrogance would never have allowed him to state openly, but which is crucial when considering the attitudes Englishmen brought to the New World. Relatively conventional ways of waging war, what one might use against, say, Spanish or French troops on the Continent, might have limited success in subduing people who had neither the means nor the training to stand and fight with similar weapons and equivalent tactics. Irishmen and Native Americans could be intractable, and dangerous, foes simply because they did not fight, indeed could not fight, in standard ways. If they proved difficult to subdue using the techniques of "civilized" war, a frustrated English commander might decide to use any means at his disposal to reduce his opponents' ability to resist. Another motive, one which does not support notions of English military superiority, may also have played a role. Conventional methods might not only fail to secure victory quickly, but might also allow an enemy greater scope for his own unconventional methods and create a situation which might actually endanger the English position. While Churchyard clearly believed that using the severed heads of Irish enemies to terrorize their relatives was a shrewd calculation by Gilbert, it is certainly possible that in Ireland, as later would be the case in North America, such cruelty was the expedient of the frustrated and anxious commander of a relatively small force who sought ways to crush a determined, dogged, and desperate foe with the greatest speed and the lowest casualties to his own troops.

Englishmen brought to North America a cruelly practical view of war, and this was the case regardless of whether or not they had had any actual experience of war in Ireland or on the Continent. North America added the final ingredient to the mix of attitudes about how war could and should be waged. I have yet to read an account of the settlement of Virginia and New England which clearly and unabashedly admits that the settlers were afraid of the natives, but that is the most likely conclusion one can reach from a consideration of how the settlers responded when they thought they were being threatened by Native Americans. From the outset Englishmen viewed Native Americans as an alien people, and realized that the Indians' knowledge of the land and how to move across it would make them a formidable opponent if hostilities should break out. Although some Englishmen did make sincere attempts to include Indians in the new societies they were trying to create in North America, nearly all of them seem to have realized that competition for control of resources, principally land, would generate considerable friction between two such different cultures. Conflict was inevitable, probably sooner rather than later. The English settlers were so rigidly ethnocentric that they had no intention of accepting Native American culture as a valid alternate lifestyle, and they offered the Indians no real reason to want to become second-class Englishmen with red skins.

Yet the newcomers had no easy solution to the threat the natives could pose to the survival of their settlements. As the settlers continually explained to anxious relatives across the Atlantic, all the Indians had to do to destroy the newcomers was refuse to sell them food, ambush them as they tried to sow, tend, and harvest crops of their own, and kill their cattle. The settlers had to face the paradox that, at the same time that they held Native American culture in contempt, they were not certain they possessed the military ability to protect their homes and families from destruction by those otherwise inferior natives. They feared Native American warriors because Indians fought in ways the settlers could not counter directly with the tactics and technology they brought from England. The settlers understood that native warriors feared European firearms, but probably did not fully comprehend that this was probably more because the natives were unfamiliar with gunpowder technology than because they were impressed by the settlers' own very modest level of skill in hitting a moving target with a musket ball. Still, in the words of one Virginia settler, the newcomers considered the natives a "naked and cowardly" people because they would "dare not stand the presentment of a staff in manner of a piece [a musket], nor an uncharged piece in the hands of a woman, from which they fly as so many hares."[3] But mistaking prudence for cowardice did not solve the problem. They could do little about the fact that, because the natives lacked the requisite technology—muskets, pistols, pikes, and armor—to defeat the settlers in formal, European-style contests, Indian warriors generally refused to offer battle in ways which would lead only to their own destruction.

Advice from England on how to fight the natives in the European manner reminded the settlers of the defensive advantages of pikes and muskets, but it could not suggest ways of imposing the will of the settlers on Indians who did not wish to fight decisive battles. In 1624 the father of the governor of Virginia offered his son some sound tactical advice. When the natives "should be perceived to incline to a resolution to venture to charge up close breast to breast," the first rank of musketeers should fire once and then retire into the spaces between the men in the second rank, whereupon the men in the second rank could fire at the charging warriors "with fresh and more effectual volleys in their bosom." The men of the first rank might then "wheel about and charge the enemy in the flank," which would be "to good effect" if it is "the more unexpected." The father failed, however, to indicate how his son might induce Indian warriors to advance into range of the English muskets, the prerequisite on which the rest of his plan was based, and then to stay there while Englishmen wearing bulky wool clothing and stiff leather shoes outflanked them.[4]

Unfortunately for the newcomers, any scenario which depended for its decisiveness on the willingness of Indian warriors to attack unbroken English defensive formations was extremely unlikely to occur. True, Englishmen in Virginia and New England did find that by sticking together in a loosely packed, alert group they could use their firearms to defeat attacks on their formations.[5] But if they left the security of their hedgehog to move through the woods in pursuit of the natives, most of them knew that they would be extremely vulnerable to ambush by the much more mobile warriors, who, if they could get close enough, could readily kill them with their relatively primitive bows and arrows. Cultural arrogance and lack of familiarity with Indian weapons occasionally led a few Englishmen astray, but those who saw the military abilities of the Indians at first hand were under no illusion of how deadly an enemy they could be. In 1635 Lion Gardener, commander of the small outpost at Saybrook at the mouth of the Connecticut River, sent to Boston as proof of the deadliness of Indian technology an arrow he had pulled, with much difficulty, from the corpse of one of his soldiers. The arrow had penetrated the man's rib cage on one side with such force that the arrowhead stuck out between two ribs on the other side. Already by 1635 men living in Boston were so insulated from the reality of life on the frontier that some Massachusetts leaders had claimed "that the arrows of the Indians were of no force."[6]

Most settlers in Virginia and Connecticut were under no such illusions. They clearly understood that the natives could use stealth, cunning, and deception to frighten, frustrate, and kill the English. Fear and frustration in turn led to desperation. Because the settlers did not have the military skills to force the natives to fight a decisive battle, they commonly adopted a strategy the Virginians in the aftermath of the Indian assault of 1622 called a "feedfight," that is, a strategy aimed at destroying the enemy's food supplies and thus, as in Gilbert's campaign in Ireland, to use famine to sap the will and the strength of the enemy to continue the contest.[7]

The results of the first confrontation between natives and newcomers in what is now Connecticut amply demonstrated that a strategy of indirect pressure through destruction of the enemy's resources was often the only military option available to the settlers. In August 1636 the arrogant leaders of the Massachusetts Bay Colony sent an expedition to chastise and intimidate the Pequots, a tribe with a reputation for ferocity that lived along the banks of the Pequot (now Thames) River in what would become southeastern Connecticut. But the Pequots refused to fight the Massachusetts settlers, who were drawn up in rank and file on the shore of the river, and the settlers, in turn, refused to go marching through the woods into which they had seen the Pequots retire. All the Englishmen could do was ravage the Pequots' dwellings and food supplies, get back aboard their ships, and sail back to Boston. They had struck the Pequots a hard blow, but it was not decisive. Indeed, the expedition's principal— and predictable—result was to enrage the Pequots to the point that they struck back at the closest Englishmen, skirmishing around Saybrook over the winter, and then in early April 1637 sent perhaps a hundred warriors to raid the three upriver towns of Connecticut. But the Pequots too did not strike hard enough to do decisive damage. Although they killed nine settlers and took two women as captives, they returned home immediately thereafter; hostile Indians marauding in the neighborhood for a few weeks would have been far more damaging to the settlers. We do not know why the Pequots did not use more force; perhaps lack of food and shelter over the winter had diminished their strength, or perhaps either for reasons imbedded in Indian culture or because of a cautious appraisal of the balance of forces they deliberately chose to limit their response.

Despite its relatively limited character, the Pequot raid sparked an explosive response. The Connecticut settlers, united in the belief that they faced a crucial crossroad, unhesitatingly decided in May 1637 to strike back with all the force they could muster. Their leaders sent eighty men, probably all the able-bodied men in a population of two hundred fifty souls, to try to eliminate the Pequot threat. While it is relatively easy to understand why the settlers thought that their only option was to fight, it is harder to appreciate that they also knew they had neither the military skill nor the material resources to fight a lengthy, indecisive, and wasting guerrilla war. When they succeeded in obliterating the Pequots, an outcome beyond their wildest expectations, they attributed it, with a thoroughly ex post facto certitude, to God's protection of His people. It actually was the result of their willingness to run the risk of relying on the loyalty of local Indian allies.[8]

Several aspects of the Connecticut expedition against the Pequots have interest in the context of this essay. First, the Connecticut settlers responded to Pequot hostility with everything they had, no holding back, no holds barred, keeping nearly nothing in reserve, a sure sign that they at least thought their survival was at stake. Second, the expedition would never have had a chance of achieving decisive results without the help of Indian allies. The Connecticut commander, John Mason, aware that the Massachusetts farmers had failed to come to grips with the Pequots the previous August, gambled on the fact that other tribes, particularly the Mohegans and the Narragansetts, hated the Pequots so much that they would provide the settlers with the crucial tactical element in their success. By accompanying the English through the woods and thus diminishing the settlers' fear of ambush, Indian allies restored mobility to the English and created the conditions which allowed the newcomers to corner the Pequots into fighting a decisive battle.

The third point, and the one most important here, is the fact that when the settlers did manage to surprise and trap a large part of the Pequot tribe in one of its fortified towns—an almost unbelievable combination of luck and circumstance which they characteristically attributed to divine intervention—they exploded in a spasm of destruction that swept away Indian men, women, and children. The chance to damage, and if possible destroy, a tribe which they thought was preparing to ravage their homes and families was too precious to throw away. When they saw how well the Pequot warriors were fighting to defend their own homes and families, the English-men wasted no sympathy on the Indians. In a clear case of kill or be killed, the settlers burned the Pequot enclosure, destroying the men, women, and children trapped inside, and shot down anyone who tried to escape. The settlers fought with a ber-serker frenzy, the memory of which, in the aftermath of their success, did not sit well with all of them. One man who participated in the destruction of the Pequots, John Underhill, one of Mason's subordinate officers, showed something of a guilty con-science that the battle had been so bloody, but as he explained in an account published in London in 1636, "every [English]man . . . fell upon the work without compas-sion, considering the blood they [the Pequots] had shed of our native countrymen, and how barbarously they had dealt with them." To Underhill it was clear that "severe justice must now and then take place."[9]

What are we to conclude from the attitudes and behavior of the Englishmen who settled in Virginia after 1607 and in New England after 1620? They were probably no more cruel, vicious, or careless of the lives of people unlike themselves than any Europeans of their time. They took the actions they thought they needed to take, and knew that not all of their countrymen back home would understand the particular circumstances which prompted them to act with more ferocity and ruthlessness than what they might have thought was appropriate for Christian and civilized Englishmen. But if they tended to view military action through the lens of expediency, it was because they found themselves on a frontier where their survival was difficult to assure. Neither the Virginians who survived the Indian uprising of 1622, when the natives waged a coordinated campaign to destroy the intruders by deceit, treachery, and every other means within their power, nor the Connecticut settlers who believed their destruction of the Pequots was convincing evidence that their God would preserve them from the overwhelming perils around them had the luxury to seek anything but the utter extirpation of their foes. The frontier was not an environment in which the settlers could relax their vigilance or eschew opportunities to destroy Indians they believed were trying to destroy them. They knew that nothing and no one was safe from the hideous violence directed at them by a people who lived interspersed among them, those naked, heathen, and barbarous savages who would have to be eliminated if they did not have the good sense to subordinate themselves to the culture, and for the benefit, of Englishmen. All in all this was a very different physical and psychological reality from the more stable and ordered society they had left behind in England, where relationships among men of various social and economic distinctions were understood and where there were no utterly alien elements like the Indians with whom they were forced to deal.

As the colonies survived and managed to grow beyond their precarious early years, the frontier moved inland. People in the relatively longer settled towns along the Atlantic seaboard began to lose some of the sense of danger still present along the frontier, where newly encountered Indian tribes continued to present a threat to the survival of the colonists. Indians continued to be the main villains shaping the way the English colonists—now increasingly native-born Americans themselves—viewed war and went about organizing and justifying the military actions they took. The new element in the mix after 1689 was that fellow Europeans, the perfidious French, were condoning, and in some cases inciting and leading, enemy Indians in some exceedingly stomach-churning and revolting behavior.

Various Indian cultures surrounded their war making with rituals of torture and cannibalism which all Europeans wanted to believe were far more calculatingly brutal and cruel than anything their own civilized societies would ever inflict. English colonists sitting safely, they hoped, in communities along the coast shuddered when regaled with tales of what was happening on the frontier. They were stunned and sickened by reports of how tribes in league with the French applied to Englishmen the same torments those savages had refined in wars with other Indians, and were especially outraged at the role Frenchmen played in encouraging, allowing, and even emulating these barbarities. Unlike modern historians, they could muster little sympathy for Frenchmen who might be caught between conflicting objectives, like the missionaries who were compelled to watch in silence while the Indians they were trying to convert to Christianity tied an enemy warrior to a tree and eviscerated him while he sang his death song, his tormentors commenting with studied interest on how many times they could wrap his small intestine around the tree before he cried out in pain. The issue here is to understand how the English colonists responded when threatened by these devil-driven fiends who were now directed and led in the French interest by fellow European colonists.[10]

Events along the frontier with French Canada were never remote from the minds of English colonists, however many miles away those events were from their own firesides. The northern colonies, the region most exposed to the ravishment of French-led raiders based in Canada and Nova Scotia, did not lack for authors eager to describe, interpret, and moralize about the torments through which frontier settlements were passing. In 1699 Cotton Mather, a Harvard-educated minister famous for his erudition, his florid prose, and his relentless and neurotic moralizing, published one of the most noted accounts, which he entitled *Decennium Luctuosum [the sorrowful decade, 1688–1698]: An History of Remarkable Occurrences in the Long War, which New-England hath had with the Indian Salvages [sic]*, the details of which he claimed to have "faithfully composed and improved," that is, used for the moral edification of his readership.[11] In 1726 Samuel Penhallow, the chief justice of the Massachusetts Superior Court, published *The History of the Wars of New-England with the Eastern Indians, or a Narrative of their Continued Perfidy and Cruelty*, which covered in annalistic detail the next round of the conflict, from 1703 through 1726. It is from this latter work, more straightforward in its narrative style than Mather's, that I select my illustrations of what war was like along the Anglo-French imperial frontier.[12]

The outlying settlements in Maine, then legally part of Massachusetts, were especially hard hit by French and Indian raiders with a numbing and relentless cruelty that Penhallow's readers must have found all too shocking. Every page tells of loss and suffering, but one example must suffice here. Because there was no garrison house in the small settlement of nine families directly across the Fore River from what is now Portland, Maine, there was no fortified place to which the inhabitants could retire and defend themselves when raiders struck in August 1703. The raiders made captive the members of eight families, and—here quoting Penhallow—"inhumanly butchered twenty-five [people], among whom was the wife of Michael Webber, who being big with child, they knocked her on the head, and ript open her womb, cutting one part of the child out; a spectacle of horrid barbarity."[13]

Faced with this kind of behavior from fiends who could appear in an instant seemingly out of nowhere, devastate your world, and slink back into the shadows just as quickly, taking with them into a devilish captivity your wife, children, and neighbors, what was a New Englander to do? I would suggest that New Englanders responded in the only way they could: be as vigilant as possible to reduce the risk of a devastating surprise attack, and try when possible to take the war to the enemy. Given the fear and danger preoccupying the frontier, it is clearly unreasonable to have expected them to have behaved with less ruthlessness than the foe they were fighting. These frontiersmen, like the early settlers of Virginia and Connecticut, clearly believed that all was fair when they were fighting for their survival. When they got their hands on an enemy, they would destroy him without a second thought and, moreover, bring home the evidence of their triumph in the form of the scalps of Indian men and, not so rarely as to be called uncommon, of Indian women and children too.

Penhallow's account of one such counterraid illustrates how spasms of individual violence had become a casual and acceptable part of this bloody frontier war.[14] In May 1704 Caleb Lyman, then of Northampton but who by 1726 had become a respected "elder of a church in Boston," led a six-man expedition to raid a settlement of enemy Indians at a place called Cowassuck on the extreme upper reaches of the Connecticut River. Lyman was the only white man in the party, the other five being what he called "friend Indians," thus emphasizing again the typical situation in which most colonial Indian fighters continued to depend on Indian allies to be tactically effective in the woods of eastern North America; very few English colonists ever possessed much skill at tracking and fighting in the wilderness.[15]

After a series of events filled with the danger of discovery and proof sufficient for Lyman of the miraculous way in which God preserved the party from being observed, the six men came upon the wigwam of some enemy Indians sometime before daybreak:

Being unwilling to lose any time, we crept on our hands and knees till we were within three or four rods . . . [of the wigwam]. Then we arose, and ran to the side of the wigwam, and fired in upon them; and flinging down our guns, we surrounded them with our clubs and hatchets, and knocked down several we met with. But after all our diligence, two of their number made their escape. . . . When we came to look over the slain, we found seven dead upon the spot, six of whom we scalped, and left the other unscalped. (Our Indians saying, they would give one to the country, since we had each of us one, and so concluded we should be rich enough.) When the action was thus over, we took our scalps and plunder, such as guns, skins, etc, and the enemy's canoes, in which we came down the [Connecticut] river about twelve miles by break of day, and then thought it prudence to dismiss and break the canoes, knowing there were some of the enemy betwixt us and home.

After more adventures Lyman and his companions eventually reached Northampton on June 20.[16]

Later that summer Lyman petitioned the Massachusetts General Assembly for a reward for the exploits of his party, and the assembly saw fit to grant them thirty-one pounds, substantially less than the forty pounds the leaders had earlier offered to pay for each enemy scalp. Twenty-two years later Penhallow was astonished at "how poorly this bold action and great service was rewarded. No doubt, they looked for and well deserved, eight times as much; and now [in 1726] the province would readily pay eight hundred pounds in the like case. But a gracious God has recompensed to the Elder [Lyman], I trust, both in the blessings of his providence and grace." And He may also have assuaged Lyman's conscience with the knowledge that killing and mutilating the hated and feared enemy was the righteous and appropriate thing to do.[17]

Lyman's account raises two important issues. First, despite what some modern Indian apologists never tire of asserting, removing the scalp of a dead or dying enemy was a Native American cultural ritual. Despite Humphrey Gilbert's penchant for collecting Irish heads, Europeans did not have to teach Indians how to take scalps because they already knew how to do it. Some Indian tribes, like some representatives of the European nations, took heads as well; scalping seems to have come into vogue among Indian tribes long before contact with Europeans, because it was easier than taking heads and provided just as tangible proof that a man had triumphed over his enemy. (It was, however, possible to survive a scalping, especially if the scalper's knife was sharp and his, or her, hands and teeth were skillful.) The act of scalping your enemy and the vocabulary associated with the ritual were imbedded in Native American culture and were incorporated by European settlers into the ways in which they made war in North America. Closer contact with, and greater reliance on, Indian allies seems to have made scalping more prevalent among the French and French Canadians, or at least the English colonists thought so. But there is no shadow of a doubt that Englishmen engaged enthusiastically in this borrowing from Indian culture at the same time as they utterly rejected and refused to understand the cultural context which made it an important Indian ritual.[18]

The second item to note in Lyman's account is the fact that the assembly officially sanctioned exploits like his; moreover, it knew that offering financial incentives for evidence of dead enemies was money which "prompted some, and animated others, to a noble emulation."[19] Faced with an enemy who neither recognized nor accepted quarter, the assembly was concerned to turn people's minds from passive acceptance of the impossibility of doing anything to stop French and Indian raiders to an aggressive effort to do something, however limited, to destroy the menace where it lived. The net effect of offering scalp bounties was to ensure that the war on the frontier remained brutal and difficult.

The decision to offer financial incentives to induce some men to participate actively in the defense of the larger community was both part of and contributed to an important shift in the way people viewed the nature of military service. Scalp bounties, and later the bounties offered to able-bodied men for enlisting into active military service and for bringing with them the accoutrements of a soldier (gun, blanket, cartridge box, and bayonet), accelerated the tendency to turn defense into an economic activity which relied for its cutting edge on the community's ability to induce its poorer men, generally the young and unmarried, to undertake a task which, at least in theory, had previously been performed by a cross section of the local manpower, men who had been called into service because each of them had an obligation to help defend his community in time of danger. The nature of military service throughout most of British America was changing because the danger had moved away from the long and thickly settled towns near the coast to the sparsely inhabited regions of the interior. Only a small minority of the population faced the threat of French and Indian raiders on a daily basis. When men from more secure areas were called on for help, or to join major Anglo-American expeditions to extirpate the menace at its source by conquering Canada, they expected to be paid well for their services.[20]

The character of the war on the frontier between Native Americans and English colonists was set early and endured long; no-holds-barred conflict was the common element in relations until the eclipse of the frontier in 1890. Nearly all colonists were willing to accept the fact that nearly all Indians were savages and that the best—indeed the only possible—course of action was to exterminate the menace with whatever means were at hand. The principal restraints on conduct on both sides were lack of power to do more damage to the other side. The Indian tribes that resisted English encroachment lacked the resources, even with French help, to do more than slow the progress of the colonies' slowly expanding frontier. While the colonists, in truth, lacked the skill and knowledge to pursue and defeat Indian raiders, they chose to believe that only French support for the hostile tribes stood between them and a peaceful, ever-expanding occupation of the land. The French use of allied Indians was the most potent grievance the English had against their opponents. The colonists could just about comprehend that French Canadians, corrupted and debased by long association with the devilish tribes, would allow cruelty to dominate their military activity, but they could not understand how true Frenchmen, sent to defend Canada in large numbers during the final round of the imperial conflict after 1754, could descend to the point where they condoned, or at least did nothing to restrain, the behavior of their Indian allies.

What the colonists found especially repugnant in Indian behavior was the fact that they seemed to employ their special brand of cruelty on the defenseless, on women and children in frontier towns who generally had no means of resistance in the first place, and on men whom they had stripped of their ability to offer further resistance. The ill-treatment, even the murder, of men the colonists thought should have been viewed, in a European context, as prisoners of war was particularly shocking. They could not comprehend that Indians could butcher prisoners because they held the overwhelmed and surrendered in contempt, not as fit objects of compassion and assistance. But one of the marks of civilization they expected from Frenchmen was a willingness to apply European criteria to conflict in the wilderness, and they were outraged when Frenchmen seemed repeatedly unable or unwilling to enforce European standards of behavior on their allies.

The most notorious episode which proved French perfidy to colonial British Americans was the massacre of noncombatants in the aftermath of the fall of Fort William Henry to a French siege on August 9, 1757.[21] The fort, at the head of Lake George, had been built by a colonial expedition sent in 1755 to reduce the French post at Crown Point on Lake Champlain. The expedition had not achieved its intended goal but had managed to create Fort William Henry both to support a buffer zone protecting the frontier and to serve as a base for further advances toward Canada; that made it a post the French had to reduce. On August 1 the French commander, the marquis de Montcalm, began moving his force of nearly eleven thousand men south up Lake George from Fort Carillon at the Ticonderoga headland on Lake Champlain; his army included eighteen hundred Indians from many tribes, some from as far away as the shores of Lake Superior. By August 3 he had invested Fort William Henry, which the British commander at Albany did not have the resources to relieve because the main British effort that year was at sea on the way to attack Louisbourg on Cape Breton Island northeast of Nova Scotia.

According to the journal of Louis de Bougainville, one of Montcalm's senior officers, the marquis was counting on the psychological impact of his Indian allies to quicken the fall of the fort. "At three in the afternoon" on the first day of siege, Montcalm "notified the commander of the fort that humanity obliged him to warn him that once our batteries were in place and the cannon fired, perhaps there would not be time, nor would it be in our power to restrain the cruelties of a mob of Indians of so many different nations." It is difficult to say how far Montcalm actually believed the threat he made, but in the event it turned out that he spoke nothing but the truth. After the fort surrendered, the marquis appears to have done as much as he could to prevent the Indians from assaulting the surviving soldiers and noncombatants in the British camp, and to that end he had gotten what he thought was the chiefs' agreement "to restrain their young men." Montcalm seems to have understood that he was playing with fire, and Bougainville thought that "the guard we placed in the entrenched camp of the English did everything it could to prevent disorder." His comment on Montcalm's efforts affords some insight into the dilemma the French faced: "one sees by . . . [the precautions taken by the marquis] to what point one is a slave to Indians in this country. They are a necessary evil." To which a British colonist undoubtedly would have replied that any Frenchman with pretensions to humanity, knowing the explosiveness of his Indian allies, should not have relied so heavily on their support in the first place.[22]

The French precautions proved insufficient. What happened next is best told in Bougainville's own words:

At daybreak the English, who were inconceivably frightened by the sight of the Indians, wished to leave before our escort was all assembled and in place. They abandoned their trunks and other heavy baggage . . . and started to march. The Indians had already butchered a few sick in the tents which served as a hospital. The Abenakis of Panaomeska [now Old Town, Maine], who pretended to have recently suffered from some bad behavior on the part of the English, commenced the riot. They shouted the death cry and hurled themselves on the tail of the column which started to march out. The English, instead of showing resolution, were seized with fear and fled in confusion, throwing away their arms, baggage, and even their coats. Their fear emboldened the Indians of all the nations who started pillaging, killed some dozen soldiers, and took away five or six hundred. Our escort did what it could. A few grenadiers were wounded. The Marquis de Montcalm rushed up at the noise; M. de Bourlamaque and several French officers risked their lives in tearing the English from the hands of the Indians. For in a case like this the Indians respect nothing. . . . Finally the disorder quieted down and the Marquis de Montcalm at once took away from the Indians four hundred of these unfortunate men and had them clothed. The French officers divided with the English officers the few spare clothes they had, and the Indians, loaded with booty, disappeared the same day.

Bougainville knew that "all Europe will oblige us to justify ourselves" about events he abhorred; "my soul has several times shuddered at spectacles my eyes have witnessed":

Will they in Europe believe that the Indians alone have been guilty of this horrible violation of the capitulation, that desire for the Negroes and other spoils of the English has not caused the . . . [Canadians] who are at the head of these nations to loose the curb, perhaps to go even further? The more so since one today may see one of these leaders, unworthy of the name of officer and Frenchman, leading in his train a Negro kidnapped from the English commander under the pretext of appeasing the shades of a dead Indian, giving the family flesh for flesh. That is enough of the horror, the memory of which I would hope could be effaced from the minds of men.[23]

For the colonists, the Fort William Henry massacre was just the latest and largest in the series of atrocities for which they held the French responsible. Colonial newspapers reached new heights of indignation and outrage. The *New York Gazette* asked its readers to wreak an appropriate vengeance for this "horrible crime." "Will it not be strictly just and absolutely necessary from henceforward that we . . . make some severe examples of our inhuman enemies when they fall into our hands?" The *Pennsylvania Gazette* laid blame for the atrocities squarely on the "French nation," whose "perfidy and cruelty" were astonishing: "Is it the *Most Christian [French] King* that could give such orders? or could the most savage nations ever exceed such French barbarities?" Even the British commander in chief in North America held the French king ultimately responsible for the massacre because he had done nothing to condemn earlier, smaller atrocities committed by officers who held his commission. In truth, as Bougainville made clear, the French were in a bind. As a practical matter, the defense of Canada, difficult at best, would have been utterly impossible without the services of allied Indians. Since the start of the imperial frontier war in 1690, the French had invariably shown themselves willing to employ the means of defense they had at hand and, while not entirely comfortable with the results, had stuck by their decision. Having sown the wind, they were about to reap the whirlwind.[24]

The British colonists did not respond with the more extreme methods urged by some of their newspapers, principally because the character of the war was changing. Skirmishing in the no-man's-land between armies after August 1757 remained as cruel and brutal as it had always been; there were a few significant reprisals, most spectacularly the extirpation in October 1759 of the Saint Francis Indian village in the Saint Lawrence River valley by colonial rangers under the command of the renowned and redoubtable Robert Rogers. But most of the rangers' attention was devoted to scouting for, and protecting the advance of, the main British army, which, beginning with the campaign of 1758, was a juggernaut intended to roll up the appendages of French power and finally to crush the French viper in its nest in the Saint Lawrence valley. William Pitt's decision to spend British money and manpower unsparingly in North America turned the long sputtering frontier war between French and British colonial irregulars into a conventional war of conquest. The French were forced to pour resources into trying to defeat a European-style campaign of territorial conquest which they knew was more dangerous to them than a century more of border war. Hit-and-run raids, even of the scale of that which took Fort William Henry, could not deflect the British advance. The new British strategy of abundance also had implications for the way war was waged in North America. The flood of British troops brought British discipline to Anglo-colonial armies, and the resulting logistical demands absorbed all colonial attention and energy. The presence of so many British troops and resources allowed British commanders, in the arena where the decisive contest took place although not on its periphery, to impose for the first time European norms of military conduct on North American warfare.[25]

The final phase of the last French and Indian War was a departure from previous colonial military experience. Before 1758 conflict in North America was conducted on a very small scale compared with contemporary European wars, and with all the frustration and fear attendant on waging war with limited resources of manpower and money against an intractable and merciless foe over terrain and distances far more difficult than anything encountered in western Europe. The presence of people of another culture, one for which few Europeans had any affinity, first as opponents who threatened the survival of the settlements and then as difficult-to-manage pawns in imperial contests, made war in North America something of a throwback. By themselves, the colonies did not have the money or manpower to create large disciplined standing armies, led by professional officers with sufficient experience, to campaign effectively in the wilderness. The colonists were amateurs at war: there were never many men who possessed the requisite experience, prestige, and skill to serve as officers and lead to war their neighbors, who were themselves not merely undisciplined and untrained, but also unpromising material from which to mold effective forces. If there is a lesson here it is that when amateurs go to war against an opponent they simultaneously loathe and fear, they are apt to descend to the tactics of their opponents because they think they have no choice. Not that war waged in Europe by professionals was necessarily milder or more civilized by comparison; for example, the methods Britain used to suppress the rebel Highlanders who had supported Bonnie Prince Charlie in the Jacobite rising of 1745—what we would today call a campaign of counterinsurgency or pacification—generated as much brutality and suffering as anything in North America.[26] But the difference was that the pacification of the Highlands, while harsh, was orderly, purposeful, and decisive. The object was to create order, even though Highland society had to be broken and disrupted before the new model could be built on its remains. Such a comprehensive answer to the Indian menace was beyond the ability of the British colonists alone to achieve. So they muddled along in the years between 1690 and 1757, being terrorized by Frenchmen who had access to the services of many more, and more ferocious, Indian allies. Only when Britain changed the rules of the game in 1758 by investing unprecedented resources in the conquest of Canada did the colonists triumph.

When next the need arose for the colonists to create military forces—in 1775 to defend their political rights against encroachment by British imperial officials—

many members of the Revolutionary generation seem to have understood intuitively that relying on undisciplined and untrained short-service amateurs might create a situation where control might escape the hands of recognized political authorities. George Washington had many reasons for advocating the creation of a long-service Continental army that would be led and disciplined by virtuous and professional officers chosen for their probity and ability. First among them was the need to ensure that duly chosen political leaders kept control over the application of purposeful violence. Proper conduct in fighting the British would demonstrate to all nations the justice and truth of the American cause; the Americans, after all, were not savages fighting from behind rail fences and tree stumps, waiting to scalp dead and wounded British soldiers, but inheritors of a civilized European tradition who were asserting their rights by the measured application of force. Washington and like-minded leaders in every colony proved to be remarkably successful in preventing their conservative revolution from descending into the kind of violent disorder France would experience in its own revolution fifteen years later, but it was not an easy task.

The British, for their part, already possessed a disciplined and capable army, but they faced a tricky situation in determining how to use it. Their object was to promote in the American colonies a desire to return to a due submission to the empire, or, as they put it, to effect a reconciliation between the colonies and the mother country. By applying the right amount of force in conjunction with a program of what they thought were appropriate political compromises, the cleverest among them hoped to demonstrate clearly to all Americans that rebellion was militarily a hopeless cause and to induce all but a tiny minority of irreconcilables to accept reincorporation into the empire more or less willingly. To achieve their goal they had to strike the right balance between the carrot and the stick, and, to prevent the rebels from consolidating their position, do it as rapidly as possible with the minimum amount of destruction and residual ill feeling. As a practical matter, regardless of the soundness of their legal position, they could not go around hanging everyone they thought was a rebel to the crown. Such behavior was antithetical to their long-term interests and, given the size of the American population and the extent of the territory involved, was also something which required more manpower and money than they possessed.

The task of using force to achieve political objectives is never easy, and British field commanders were neither the first nor the last military officers to have trouble identifying what to do when and how to do it. The difficulty of accomplishing the mission was increased when imperial officials gave the commander of the first major campaign in 1776, Sir William Howe, a role as a peace commissioner and political negotiator in addition to his primary responsibility as chief field officer. Because he was required delicately to blend raw power and subtle diplomacy, Howe was not in a position to model his conduct on the Elizabethan conquest of Ireland or the Hanoverian suppression of the Jacobites in 1745. The British had to go on the offensive to recover something they had lost—political control over a significant number of their American colonists—and they thus carried the major share of responsibility for establishing the terms under which they would conduct that offensive. Howe's soldiers had to prove their unquestioned military superiority in a manner that kept both their own casualties and those of their opponents to a minimum, and thus created the shortest and quickest path to reconciliation.

Both Washington and Howe would have preferred to have waged war according to the rules of eighteenth-century European-style combat, using forces that were, at least in theory, equivalently organized, trained, equipped, and disciplined to fight each other within the formal linear tactical standards of the period.[27] The opportunity to force Washington to fight a battle which would significantly diminish the rebels' will to continue in rebellion, sooner rather than later, was Howe's best chance of accomplishing his objectives, but, while he was secure in the knowledge that the superior military ability of his British and German forces would give him the advantage in any stand-up, face-to-face combat, he understood, too, the need to conserve his forces. Washington was equally eager to fight in ways which proved the rectitude of his cause and diminished the risk that a war begun for the assertion of rights would degenerate into a social revolution, but he realized that it would take time to create an American army that would have a chance of beating his opponents.

So both leaders had to adopt compromise strategies. The rebel general had to stand on the defensive against the tactically superior British army, and the imperial commander, combining diplomacy and war, had to attempt to outmaneuver his opponent, inflicting pain and humiliation on the rebels while conserving his army for the day when they would have to acknowledge he was unbeatable and thus give up their quixotic rebellion. Both realized that brutality and terrorization on, and especially away from, the battlefield would erode support for their causes at home and abroad. Both generals did espouse, and tried to procure adherence to, standards of conduct that embraced notions of honor and the dispassionate, rule-driven conduct of war, but the character of the struggle made enforcement of such standards very difficult.

Combat on an eighteenth-century battlefield was, of course, nasty, debilitating, and deadly, even according to the most elevated standards of the age. Hard fighting was to be expected and was accepted as a normal part of war; on innumerable battlefields surviving participants reported, in these or similar words, that "no quarter was given on either side."[28] Several circumstances peculiar to this war, however, seem to have enhanced the willingness of soldiers on each side occasionally to fight more ferociously than European standards might call for. The fact that every American soldier could legally be hanged as a traitor to his king surely induced some Americans to fight harder and longer. The fact that the Americans could be hard to trap and unwilling to fight to a decision undoubtedly prompted some British soldiers to make the best of the chances they got. The fact that Britain had hired German mercenaries (commonly called Hessians), professional soldiers who maintained a reputation for ferocity, certainly gave both Germans and Americans ample reasons to increase the intensity of combat. The fact that the British tried to mobilize their Indian allies against settlements along the frontier without question drew savage responses from American frontiersmen. And, finally, the fact that the war for independence was nearly everywhere also a civil war provided incentive and opportunity for both rebels and loyalists to settle old grudges. What is of interest in the context of this chapter, however, is how and why these facts may have prompted men on both sides to act in ways which exceeded what a strict adherence to a standard of "civilized" European war might have allowed.

On some occasions officers made themselves appear to be more ruthless and brutal than they actually were, all in the service of what they considered to be such legitimate goals as gathering needed operational intelligence and protecting their men who had been captured by the enemy. Scouting ahead of and patrolling around the main British army created many situations where threats of noncombat violence seem to have been a constant and casual element in war making. In November 1776, for example, a force of Hessian jaegers led by Captain Johann Ewald was gathering intelligence ahead of the main British army as it made its way across northern New Jersey in pursuit of Washington's bedraggled force. Ewald thought nothing of forcing a local civilian to serve as his guide and, when American troops fired on his men from the far side of a bridge over an apparently substantial stream, "threatened the man with death unless he told [him] whether or not the water could be crossed above or below the bridge." The man complied, and disappears from the narrative: presumably Ewald, a cultured, disciplined, and professional soldier to the tips of his toes, did not kill him.[29]

In another instance a threat of violence in cold blood was made as a way of securing the safety of a man who, as a deserter from a rebel unit who had then enlisted in a loyalist regiment, would have been subject to hanging according to European standards. In July 1778 a sergeant and two men of the Queen's Rangers, a loyalist unit much feared by the rebels for its activity and intrepidity, were captured in an ambush in the south Bronx. The British commander of the rangers, John Graves Simcoe, later recalled that "the sergeant, having been in the rebel service, forced thereto by all want of work, was thrown into prison and threatened with death. Lieutenant-Colonel Simcoe offered a sergeant whom he had lately taken, in exchange for him, and threatening to leave to the mercy of his soldiers the first six rebels who should fall into his hands, in case of [Sergeant] Kelly's execution, soon obtained his release."[30]

There is no doubt that officers and men on both sides sometimes skirted the edge of approved conduct, especially in the matter of what could or could not be done to enemy soldiers who no longer possessed the power to resist. American propagandists who accepted the idea that the British army was at least capable of a higher standard of discipline than its American counterpart accumulated many examples of British atrocities, in part because Americans were more often in the position of trying to surrender than were the British. The great master of patriot iconography on canvas, John Trumbull, included in his series of battle scenes two paintings that showed perfidious British soldiers about to bayonet wounded American leaders who were trying to fend off death long enough to surrender to their tormentors. Artistic license aside, Trumbull was merely giving visual expression to stories current at the time: the death of Joseph Warren at Breed's Hill in June 1775 and the mortal wounding of Hugh Mercer at Princeton in January 1777 clearly proved to many Americans the brutality and immorality of the British aggressors.[31]

Washington was not squeamish about the bloody work sometimes entailed in face-to-face combat, but he was incensed by several episodes in January 1777 which proved to him that the British had not acted with honor and compassion toward wounded Americans trying to surrender. When Washington received the "dying affidavit" of Lieutenant Bartholomew Yates, who, having been wounded in action at Princeton, claimed that he had then been bayoneted and clubbed by a British soldier, the general "remonstrated sharply" with Howe, to whom he also forwarded the document. Howe responded quickly, claiming to "aver my abhorrence of the barbarity . . . set forth [in the affidavit], and am satisfied that the officers under my command are equally inclined to discourage such behavior, and to prevent it in every possible degree." He then appended an escape clause that did not satisfy Washington: "but the heat of action will sometimes produce instances that are only to be lamented." In early February Washington reported to Congress that while he acknowledged that Howe claimed to "disavow and detest" what happened to Yates, "I fear that too much encouragement is given to such barbarous behavior by the British officers," and offered as proof the recent case of another American officer who had been "slightly wounded in the thigh, but before he could get off the field, he was overtaken and murthered [sic] in a most cruel manner." Washington therefore fully approved the request of his subordinate, Adam Stephen, who wanted to inform the British commander "that unless such practices were put a stop to, our soldiers would not be restrained from making retaliation."[32]

If Howe chose to argue that the reins of command could sometimes regrettably go slack in the heat of battle, Washington could counter that cruelty seemed to be both a deliberate and pervasive element in much British military policy. The threat of massacre could come from the highest echelon, as, for instance, on November 15, 1776, when Howe coupled his demand for the surrender of rebel-held Fort Washington on the heights above the Hudson on the north end of Manhattan Island with the threat that, if the post did not immediately capitulate, it would be captured anyway and its defenders "put to the sword." Such threats, Howe could reasonably claim, were a common psychological weapon in European positional warfare, especially when a troublesome enemy post had to be reduced quickly, and it must be offered in Howe's defense that despite fierce American resistance—and one British officer's exhortation to "kill them, kill every man of them!"—the garrison was allowed to surrender on terms.[33] Washington remained suspicious, however, especially since evidence that the British were engaged in a "savage manner of carrying on war" was piling up by early 1777. He claimed to have "heard that orders were given at Trenton to make no prisoners, but [to] kill all that fell into their [British] hands, but of this," he did admit, "there is no proof."[34]

The depth of Washington's anger did not corrupt his honesty in reporting the facts as he knew them or, more importantly, lead him to rash behavior. Washington repeatedly condemned the pillaging and marauding of both the British and their German mercenaries in northern New Jersey in the wake of the American army's withdrawal; the conduct of those he called "infamous mercenary ravagers" had been so bad that, while he was willing to guarantee that the troops under his direct command would not molest a convoy of medical supplies sent to succor British and German wounded at Trenton and Princeton, he could not predict the behavior of militiamen who were "exceedingly exasperated at the treatment they have met with, from both Hessian and British troops." But in the matter of mistreating wounded American soldiers, Washington was willing to draw distinctions. "One thing I must remark in favor of the Hessians, and that is, that our people who have been prisoners generally agree that they received much kinder treatment from them, than from the British officers and soldiers. The barbarities at Princeton were all committed by the British, there being no Hessians there."[35]

Many Americans agreed with Washington's view of British behavior toward prisoners and held British officers especially liable: even if soldiers did commit atrocities in battle or in cold blood, their officers, like Montcalm at Fort William Henry in 1757, could and should be held responsible for any and all cases of misbehavior. Implicit in this view is the assertion that Americans should be accorded all the rights in combat the British would grant to a European antagonist and not be treated as rebels who could be dealt with summarily whenever they fell into British hands. For those who believed the British were already trampling on their political rights, the failure of British officers to enforce the acknowledged rules of war was only another part of the same conspiracy against America. In April 1777, for example, a committee of Congress lodged a stinging bill of particulars against the British forces whose "whole track" across New Jersey, it said, "is marked with desolation and a wanton destruction of property . . . the inhumane treatment of . . . prisoners . . . the savage butchery of those who had submitted and were incapable of resistance," and "the lust and brutality . . . of the soldiers in abusing women." Like Washington, the legislators did acknowledge that there were degrees of guilt. "The committee . . . learned that sometimes the common soldiers expressed sympathy with the prisoners, and the foreigners [Germans] more than the English. But this was seldom or never the case with the officers."[36]

The poor opinion of British officers was reflected by many Americans who came into a closer than desired contact with them. Take the case of Jabez Fitch, a Connecticut lieutenant who surrendered to the 57th Regiment at Long Island on August 27, 1776. Although Hessian soldiers hurled imprecations at the prisoners as they passed by, the soldiers of the 57th treated him fairly, taking his arms and ammunition but not robbing him of his clothing. Fitch clearly felt more threatened by some British officers who "were very liberal of their favourite term (rebel) and now and then did not forget to remind me of a halter." It is worth noting that Fitch had walked up to a group of British soldiers and offered himself as a prisoner; his reception might have been different had he tried to lay down his arms in the midst of a tough firefight.[37]

Perhaps the most notorious British officer in American eyes was Lieutenant Colonel Banastre Tarleton, the commander of the loyalist British Legion in the South after May 1780. Because he permitted his men to commit atrocities during a skirmish with some Virginia troops at the Waxhaws in South Carolina on May 29, Americans thereafter applied to him the epithet Bloody Tarleton, and considered him a man so brutal that the motto "Tarleton's quarter" became a synonym for no quarter. Tarleton's men were clearly, in the words of his biographer, "victorious and out of control." Coming upon a severely wounded American officer, Captain John Stokes, an excited and overzealous loyalist infantryman hurled a demand: "Do you ask for quarter?" When the officer replied, intemperately, "I do not; finish me as soon as possible," the soldier twice thrust his bayonet through the defenseless American:

> Another infantryman repeated the question and received the same answer. Twice he transfixed Stokes with his bayonet. Finally a humane British sergeant offered his protection. . . . The infantrymen continued to sweep over the ground, plunging their bayonets into any living American [after, the Americans claimed, they had sued for surrender and mercy]. Where several had fallen together, they used their bayonets to untangle them, in order to finish off those on the bottom.[38]

The willingness of British leaders to employ German mercenaries and, increasingly as the war went on, loyalist soldiers and Indian allies placed them in the same situation Montcalm had faced at Fort William Henry. No British commander could have been unaware that the Hessians had a reputation for rapacity and marauding, that many loyalists had an intense desire to revenge themselves on their rebel neighbors, or that the Indians would bring to war along the frontier all of the attitudes and techniques that had made them anathema to American colonists from the earliest days of settlement. By choosing to augment their forces in this way, the British implicitly accepted a large measure of responsibility for the actions of their allies. When, moreover, senior British officers in direct charge of main force units allowed there to exist among their subordinate commanders an ambivalence about how rebels were to be treated in and after battle, they showed that they had fully embraced the tar baby of simultaneously trying to break the hearts and minds of the rebellious colonists without losing their moral compass.

Washington himself chose to lend a tone and substance to military operations under his direct command that accorded with his strict, thoroughly eighteenth-century conception of how a virtuous and honorable officer should act. Like his British and German opponents he could not always control all of his own men, let alone the militia forces operating with or in support of his army, but he clearly understood that retaliating in cold blood to enemy provocation was not politic. "Tho' my indignation at such ungenerous conduct of the enemy [the British had burned the house and laid waste the farm of a New Jersey captain] might at first prompt me to retaliation, yet humanity and policy forbid the measure. Experience proves, that their wanton cruelty injures rather than benefits their cause; that, with our forbearance, justly secured to us the attachment of all good men."[39]

Washington's shrewd but lofty and detached reasoning was appropriate for the commander in chief of the American army. But one of the distinguishing features of the War of American Independence was the fact that the Americans fielded all manner and size of units in support of the main, European-style army, many of which were outside the control of the senior American military leaders. Washington could do little to control or stop the brutal give-and-take of the irregular war waged across the no-man's-lands that grew up around New York City after the British took that strategically important position in September 1776. Don Higginbotham's definition of irregular war is useful here: "A conflict of small flexible units which were local in their concerns and objectives, which were dedicated to partisan activity and to making the countryside uninhabitable to the enemy, and which resorted to fear and intimidation to hold the civilian population in line." One can distinguish further between a partisan war waged along the boundary between, and within the sphere of operations of, roughly equivalent, and therefore stalemated, main force units and a guerrilla war fought by small units, or even individuals, in the absence of significant main force units or where one side dominates the conventional battlefield but cannot entirely eliminate the other side, as at points in the campaign in the South in 1780–81.

Events in the Hackensack River valley in northeastern New Jersey in the relatively quiet year of 1778[40] remind us again that the War for American Independence was in many ways and in many places a civil war, that the imperial contest overlay preexisting levels of local social, religious, and political tensions of varying intensity and complexity.[41] The reality that a civil war was intertwined with British efforts to suppress a rebellion had a powerful, corrosive effect on the ability and willingness of men on both sides to moderate their actions and avoid involving civilians in military operations. While there were some standards by which both sides could model the conduct of armies that were, or aspired to be, professional forces, there were fewer conventions that could be used to restrain the mix of forces in the partisan war. In the Hackensack valley the adherents of the contending sides nibbled, bit, kicked, and scratched at each other across a countryside populated by prosperous and outwardly phlegmatic Jersey Dutchmen, whose own history of internecine religious controversy was exacerbated by the British occupation of Manhattan.

The first point here is that activity in the Hackensack valley looked very much like operations on the periphery of stationary armies in Europe. Each side jostled for position and advantage, trying to exploit the resources of the zone between the armies and to control the flow of information across that zone. Operations were directed mainly against civilian property and tried to avoid anything that smacked of indiscriminate killing. The object was to manipulate and utilize, not to terrorize. The British were interested in ensuring that the harvest of the hardworking farmers made its way, via purchase or confiscation, into their larders, an outcome which simultaneously reduced the amount of logistical support that had to come to them from Ireland and made Washington's supply problems just a little bit harder. Since the British had the greater need, superior local forces, and choice of time and place to move, their raids seem to have been largely successful. They moved through the countryside against little opposition and retired at their own pace after securing the harvest. The British had to balance their desire to seize food and break the back of rebel resistance with the competing need not to ravage the area so completely that farmers abandoned their fields and became hardened opponents of a restoration of British civil government.[42]

The British also tried to run intelligence networks across the valley in an effort to gain enough knowledge of enemy intentions that Washington would never be able to do anything they had not anticipated. These efforts led to friction of a kind that illuminates what each side thought was reasonable conduct in what Europeans would call a war of posts. One such episode began in late January 1778, when an overambitious local rebel militia commander sent two men deep into loyalist territory in an effort to disrupt some portion of the trade carrying Jersey foodstuffs to the British garrison at Manhattan. They stopped a wagon and in the ensuing struggle one of the militiamen shot and killed the driver, a prominent loyalist. Loyalists in Manhattan offered a bounty for the killer, and within a week four men had captured both of the militiamen and collected the reward. Loyalists wanted the men hanged immediately, but Sir Henry Clinton, the British commander, confined them to prison in chains and on a diet of bread and water. New Jersey authorities waited six months before attempting retaliation, probably because they did not want to roil the waters unnecessarily over an incident begun by an imprudent local commander. In early November 1778 they ordered a prominent loyalist prisoner to be subjected to the same treatment as the captive Americans, because, as the commissary of prisoners said, "Nothing short of retaliation will teach Britons to act like men of humanity." The ploy worked: nine days later the patriot prisoners were released from their irons. In late December 1778 Washington proposed an exchange of prisoners, probably in an attempt to end the episode before the loyalists could convince Clinton to change his mind. Clinton agreed, although he did assert that European military custom would have justified him in inflicting "any severities" on "infantry patrolling without a non-commissioned officer" who had killed a civilian. One can appreciate Clinton's humanity, while at the same time realizing that he knew a game of tit-for-tat would surely cripple his intelligence-gathering networks.[43]

The story shows that expediency and humanity could coexist in the no-man's-land between foes who could afford to subscribe to similar codes of conduct. But, as was the case in the conflicts between European colonists and Native Americans, an inability to force a decisive encounter could engender such frustration that brutality might explode when the enemy was caught at a disadvantage. British forces would occasionally sweep through the Hackensack valley, establish their presence, hearten the loyalists temporarily, forage for food, gather information, and attempt to catch some enemy force unawares. On the morning of September 28, 1778, a British force commanded by Major General Charles Grey surprised 150 Continental dragoons bivouacked at Old Tappan, at the upper end of the valley.[44]

Charles Grey had something of a talent for surprising Continental soldiers: he had inflicted heavy casualties on a regiment of Anthony Wayne's Pennsylvania brigade at Paoli, outside Philadelphia, a year before.[45] On both occasions his forces, led by the 2d Battalion of the Light Infantry, advanced during the night, attacked after midnight, and overwhelmed a sleeping foe with the bayonet. On both occasions there were claims from the American survivors that the British troops had massacred both wounded and surrendered Continental soldiers. At Old Tappan, the 2d Battalion burst in on the dragoons with shouts of "No quarters to rebels." Survivors claimed that their captors "sent to one of their officers . . . to know what was to be done with the prisoners. . . . In a few minutes thereafter, word was brought that the officers ordered all the prisoners to be killed."[46] Fifty dragoons were killed at some point during the attack, fifty more remained as prisoners, and twenty escaped. The British deputy adjutant-general later admitted in his journal that the light infantrymen were "thought to be active and bloody on this service, and it's acknowledged on all hands they might have spared some who made no resistance, the whole being completely surprised and all their officers in bed."[47] Another officer reported to his father in England that any credit due the light infantrymen "was entirely buried in the barbarity of their behavior."[48]

Embarrassment on this occasion seems to have been the result of a realization that some soldiers and perhaps a few officers had gotten carried away with the mission.

Grey himself bears some of the responsibility, for like Montcalm at Fort William Henry, he seems to have set the tone for his command. He is reported to have informed his superiors that in following orders he would not go out of his way to spare rebels, and in particular would grant no quarter to rebels if called upon to mount a night attack.[49] An argument can be made that any commander audacious enough to undertake an attack that increased the risk of injury to his own men in order to maximize the damage he might do to the enemy might also be inclined to allow his men to deal ruthlessly with prisoners who might impede defense against a counterattack that might come at any moment out of the darkness.

Senior commanders could be expected to understand the risks of allowing such latitude on the battlefield: during the battle at Germantown, fought on October 4, 1777, outside Philadelphia, Wayne's Pennsylvanians had surged forward against British light infantry skirmishers with shouts of "Have at the bloodhounds, revenge Wayne's affair" at Paoli. Smashing into the main British force, they had "pushed on with their bayonets and took ample vengeance" for the atrocities they believed the light infantry had committed against their comrades two weeks earlier. Their officers had "exerted themselves to save many of the poor [British] wretches who were crying for mercy," but "the rage and fury of the soldiers were not to be restrained for some time, at least not until great numbers of the enemy fell by our bayonets."[50] Probably no one wanted the game of tit-for-tat to get out of hand. British commanders had to balance their need to damage rebel military forces with the knowledge that a policy of deliberate brutality would impede the political process of returning rebels to allegiance to the crown. As a practical matter, moreover, British officers knew that the rebels were strong enough so that a policy of no quarter might someday redound to their own personal discomfiture.

On the other hand, many British leaders, prodded by the loyalists, were not averse to encouraging groups of shady characters to plunder rebels in the arc around Manhattan. They, again like Montcalm at Fort William Henry, wanted to extract whatever military advantage they could from the services of people they considered inferior or disreputable. While they may have tried to withhold official sanction for episodes like the Tappan attack, their ambivalent attitude undoubtedly contributed to the general deterioration of control over violence by both sides in areas neither one could control effectively.

What, then, are we to conclude from this look at constraints on war in colonial America? In the first place, contact with and hostilities against Native Americans who possessed customs and rituals that horrified the newcomers formed the principal element shaping English colonial attitudes about constraints on war in North America. Two points are vital here. The first is that the ruthlessness and cruelty displayed in abundance in these conflicts were not the fault of the Native Americans; the English conquerors of Ireland did not have to be taught how to be ruthless and cruel. The second point is that what the English settlers found so unsettling and anxiety inducing was the commingling of their fear and loathing of Native Americans with their frustration and despair at not being able to end more quickly the menace to their families and communities. Horrified at being unable to prevent the butchering of their people, they exploded in spasms of uncontrolled violence when they finally did manage to get their devilish tormentors into their power.

The second conclusion is in the form of a general principle: that control over the use of violence slips away on the margins, be it along the frontier between French Canada and British North America or in the contested area around Manhattan after 1776. Relying on irregular forces—that is, the untrained and undisciplined amateur colonial citizen soldiers mythologized by many contemporaries as the source of the republic's military strength—increased the inability to enforce some sort of common understanding of what was fair and what was not, especially in the matter of what people may be construed as noncombatants or no-longer-combatants. The greater the distance away from centralized monitoring, and probably also the smaller the numbers involved, the greater the opportunity for men to use violence to settle some personal score which may or may not have anything to do with the goals of the society that has authorized them to use purposeful violence in the first place.

Finally, it should be emphasized that the men whose behavior has been examined here were men of action who were forced to make hard decisions under difficult conditions. The fact that they thought they chose correctly—pragmatically as well as morally and ethically—is partly a function of the situations in which they found themselves. Their actions can and should be evaluated and judged, but we should also ask ourselves what we might have done in their places.

Gunther
Rothenberg

6

The Age of Napoleon

During the twenty-three years from 1792 to 1815, war passed through one of its great transitions. The limited dynastic wars of the kings ended, the wars of the nations began. But did this mean the end of international law and restraints on the conduct of war as they had evolved since the days of Hugo Grotius?

Some would answer yes. Though the century before the revolution, often called the Enlightenment, had not been peaceful—discounting revolts and colonial clashes, some sixteen wars were waged between various combinations of European powers—they argue that these wars of kings had evolved into formal affairs, pursued with limited means for limited objectives, fought by small disciplined professional armies commanded by an aristocratic class which felt itself joined by common bonds transcending national and political boundaries. With national hatreds absent or muted, and conduct governed by strict rules of war, hostilities had become well-regulated affairs into which, to quote Winston S. Churchill, "bad temper was not often permitted to intrude." One contemporary observer wrote that war now was waged so humanely "that farmers were able to till between the opposing sentries and loaded wagons passed through the picket lines without being bothered." Another contemporary, the Swiss international jurist Emerich de Vattel, boasted that "at the present war is conducted by regular armies. The ordinary people take no part and as a rule have nothing to fear from the enemy." And in the aftermath of the First World War, the historian Guglielmo Ferrero described these limited conflicts as "one of the loftiest achievements of the eighteenth century," the product of "an aristocratic and qualitative society" destroyed by the French Revolution.[1]

Clausewitz would have agreed with the latter contention. The conduct of war, he asserted, was determined by the nature of societies, "by their times and prevailing conditions." These, he wrote, referring to the aristocratic societies of the ancien régime, had changed fundamentally during the Age of Napoleon because the "people became a participant in war" and "the whole weight of the nation was thrown into balance." As a result military activity became more intense, escalating toward unrestrained violence, with international law and custom reduced to mere "self-imposed limitations, known as international law and custom" hardly worth mentioning.[2]

But closer investigation reveals that the idyllic picture of the moderate and humane nature of eighteenth-century war as well as the notion that after 1792 popular participation in war contributed toward ever more unrestrained violence and the total disregard of international law both are exaggerated. While jurists and philosophes wrote much about restraints in war, and though by the late Enlightenment their views constituted an intellectual consensus, in practice commanders of the ancien régime had been as ruthless as their successors and abandoned restraints when military necessity required it. The supposed limited wars saw bloody battles where quarter was denied, civilians were not spared, and when military necessity was invoked, vast areas, for instance the Palatinate in 1675 and again in 1689, and Bavaria in 1704, were deliberately laid waste. To be sure, at least in western Europe—in eastern Europe war always remained unrestrained—combatants adopted certain restraints. While no international treaties existed, a customary law of war, *jus in bello,* was widely recognized. To maintain discipline all armies adopted rules and regulations limiting certain practices, especially plundering and looting, and evolved codes of conduct, "the customs and conventions of the vocational/professional soldiers." During campaigns commanders concluded specific cartels and conventions stipulating proper treatment and exchange of prisoners and wounded, and generally acted according to accepted rules during sieges, capitulations, and surrenders. In practice, captured officers were treated well, though common soldiers often were abused to induce them to enlist in the captor's army. Moreover, the limited nature of war was primarily the result of objective factors, limited manpower, economic, and agricultural resources. When these limitations disappeared toward the end of the eighteenth century, more intense and prolonged wars became possible.[3]

Even so, professional soldiers knew the value of the laws and customs of war and observed them as best they could; military self-interest in fact was the paramount reason for the continuation of these practices during the Revolutionary and Napoleonic Wars. And all sides conducted themselves more or less according to this customary law. As during the earlier period, restraints were ignored when military necessity seemed to require it; and when there were radical political, ethnic, religious, or cultural differences between combatants fighting degenerated into murderous cruelty. At the outset of the Revolutionary Wars an enlightened French government stated its intent to wage war in a lawful, civilized manner. The National Assembly declared war in defense of the principles of justice and humanity and undertook to conduct hostilities with restraint toward civilians and promises of humane treatment for prisoners. Indeed, during the first year of war, 1792–93, armies observed most of the customs of limited war. The French army still contained a substantial proportion of regular units and fought the campaigns of 1792–93 primarily with regular commanders, men like Custine and Dumouriez, who, though often with little success, tried to enforce professional norms of conduct on their ill-disciplined troops. On the allied side, despite the Duke of Brunswick's threat that Frenchmen captured in battle would be treated as rebels, and except for their manner of attacking fortresses by bombarding houses and not fortifications to terrify noncombatants and induce the garrison to surrender, a practice contrary to eighteenth-century usage, Prussian and Austrian forces generally adhered to established procedures.[4]

A major shift occurred following the crisis of the Revolution in the summer of 1793. Controlled by Jacobin ideologues, the Convention introduced the concept of general mobilization and decreed the creation of a revolutionary army in which, as Robespierre put it, "military honor, the sign of the mercenary, would be replaced by the honor of the revolutionary."[5] The radical revolutionary regime had no use for restraint in war. "One should wage war à l'outrance or go home," Carnot wrote and he instructed commanders to "exterminate to the bitter end." This new radical attitude manifested itself in the treatment of prisoners of war. In September 1793 and May 1794 the Convention prohibited ransoming of prisoners and ordered that all émigré prisoners, and later British, Hanoverian, and Spanish captives as well, be shot as an "example of the vengeance of an outraged nation." Most commanders and troops, having considerable affinity for fellow soldiers and little liking for the revolutionary ideologues, and also fearing reprisals, evaded the orders, but some three thousand royalists and eight thousand Spaniards were massacred before the odious decree was repealed at the end of 1794.[6] And if the dogmatic revolutionary leaders declined to observe the customs and usages of war toward foreign soldiers, they were even less inclined to show restraint at home and suppressed domestic rebellions with unequaled ferocity. At the end of 1793 and during the first few months of the following year, republican troops under orders to "transfer the region into a desert," burned villages and indiscriminately slaughtered just under a quarter of a million armed as well as unarmed civilians in the Vendée. Carried out on the direct orders of a government, this possibly was the worst atrocity committed during the entire series of wars.[7]

Massacring poorly armed rebels, women, and children was one thing; waging war against the professional armies of foreign adversaries with ill-disciplined troops, animated by revolutionary principles but lacking training, soon proved impossible. War, Clausewitz wrote, has its own logic. Combat demanded proficient, well-trained, and professionally led troops, and two years of trial by fire had convinced Carnot, for all his rhetoric a former regular officer, the majority of senior commanders, regulars, and volunteers, as well as most junior officers and soldiers, that fighting ability and competence were more important than revolutionary dogma. This realization marked the beginning of the end of political indoctrination and of the powers of the Jacobin Deputies in Mission, political commissars in present-day terms, and a return to professional norms.[8]

This reversion came easier because professionalism had never entirely disappeared in the French army. There always had remained, Bertaud writes, "officers and sergeants who accepted the new order with little enthusiasm and continued to indoctrinate their men with the love of glory and the honor of the regiment." By the end of 1794 the experience of combat had eradicated the differences between professional and citizen soldiers and instead created a distinction between the troops who had been under fire and the politicians who had not. By 1795 professional leaders, regulars, and citizen soldiers turned neoprofessional regained control and soon returned to the traditional customs and usages between soldiers.[9]

Setting the tone, senior officers began to observe the civilities of the ancien régime. In 1796, for example, when General Marceau of the Army of the Sambre et Meuse had to be left behind fatally wounded to the Austrians, Archduke Charles sent his own surgeon to attend him and Marceau's funeral became an occasion for both armies, French and Austrian cannons joining in a final salute. The next year, when Mantua surrendered after a six-month siege, Napoleon refused to accept Marshal Wurmser's sword and openly praised his courage. In fact, Napoleon made it a practice to observe the rules of honor of the previous era and his generals followed suit; Marshal Soult, for example, raised a monument to Sir John Moore at La Coruña in 1809. Such gestures were returned and, on the whole, as Vagts wrote, "the balance in observing the rules of honor favors his [Napoleon's] enemies." Perhaps the most blatant example was the obsequious letter Archduke Charles sent to the emperor during the retreat from Ratisbon.[10]

Lower-ranking officers also observed the traditions of mutual respect between fellow professionals. In the Peninsula, British and French officers tried to take care of each other, while similar actions occurred elsewhere. Before the 1809 campaign French and Austrian officers exchanged addresses and made arrangements for mutual help in case they were taken prisoner, and even in Russia there were occasions where officers of the opposing armies exchanged courtesies and tried to negotiate better treatment for prisoners. Soldiers also tried to avoid inflicting unnecessary casualties on each other. During the Peninsular campaign and into southern France, for instance, Anglo-Portuguese and French forward pickets generally gave each other notice before an attack and avoided killing small enemy parties they encountered. Wellington approved of such accommodations. "I always encouraged this," he remarked, "the killing of a poor fellow of a vedette or carrying off a post could not influence the battle."[11]

Such amenities, however, were rarely extended when the opponent's blood was up during combat. Then, as an officer of the 53rd Light noted, "Soldiers of a defeated army can never feel quite sure that their lives will be spared by the enemy." At Austerlitz, for instance, up to the last hour the French refused to give quarter, while both at the Katzbach and at Waterloo the Prussians clubbed and bayoneted wounded French they came across. Keegan has suggested that, in addition to the tempers roused by the heat of battle, "extra-specific factors" influenced behavior toward wounded and surrendering enemies. Infantry tended to be compassionate toward defenseless fellow foot soldiers, while cavalry—always feeling superior to the footsloggers—felt little compunction in killing them out of hand.[12] There certainly is something to Keegan's notion, though, especially in close combat—Borodino comes to mind— infantry also was not inclined to show much mercy. Moreover, such incidents had not been uncommon in the heat of battle during the limited wars, and perhaps the treatment of those who were captured gives a better indication of actual restraint in war.

From a modern perspective, and even when compared with the period of limited war, the treatment of captives and wounded was less than satisfactory. Much depended on circumstances. Even Vattel had agreed that there were situations which permitted deviations from the established usages of war and during the Revolutionary and Napoleonic Wars it was widely accepted that military necessity permitted breaking normal rules and customs.[13] Military necessity was invoked when supplies were low, when prisoners became a burden, or when commanders considered them a threat to their own troops. In 1796, with some two thousand Austrian prisoners on hand and unable to feed them, Napoleon paroled the officers and released the soldiers, but after storming Jaffa in March 1799, claiming military necessity, Napoleon had several thousand Turkish prisoners shot—an action Chandler called "one of the grimmest and least excusable incidents" in his career. Perhaps realizing this, Napoleon later claimed that many of the prisoners had violated parole and that the enemy had shown no mercy to wounded or captured French soldiers and often had tortured them to death. During the bitter siege of Genoa in 1800, Masséna, with his own men on quarter rations, left some three thousand Austrian prisoners to starve on hulks in the harbor, though, in all fairness, he had offered to let the Austrian and British feed them, an offer they refused.[14]

Leaving aside such deviations, treatment of prisoners often conformed to established, admittedly unsatisfactory, standards. The Treaty of Amiens in 1802 expressly prohibited the practice of demanding ransom for the release of prisoners and called for their speedy repatriation once hostilities ceased. Conventions and capitulations were normally honored. After capitulating in 1801, Menou's army was transported from Egypt back to France with its weapons and baggage, while the Convention of Cintra in 1808, calling for the return of Junot's troops to France, was punctiliously observed by the British. One major violation occurred in Spain when Dupont's corps capitulated at Bailén in 1808 under terms stipulating safe-conduct to the nearest port and transportation to France. Here the Spanish junta broke its word. Only Dupont and a few senior officers were allowed to return home, the remaining captives were robbed and mobbed, and many of them casually murdered, by Spanish soldiers and civilians after their surrender. Survivors, initially held in prisons on the mainland were later kept on hulks in Cádiz harbor, where, deprived of food and medical care, and aided only by the occasional humanitarian intervention of British naval officers, many perished.[15]

If British military and naval officers tried to alleviate the lot of the French prisoners, their political superiors were not inclined to help. After the prisoners were transferred to their final destination, the small Balearic island of Cabrera, and left there with little provisions, in 1812 Marshal Suchet offered to exchange some two thousand healthy Spanish regulars for the sickest French prisoners. But Lord Wellesley, the British ambassador to Spain, vetoed the transaction, and in the end out of almost eighteen thousand men surrendered at Bailén only one in ten survived, in Napier's words "a disgrace to Spain and England."[16]

The invasion of Russia in 1812 brought new outrages against prisoners committed as usual by both sides. After Borodino, exhausted Russian prisoners unable to keep up with the column were shot by their escorts; others were killed when they became a burden during the retreat from Moscow. On the Russian side, according to General Robert Thomas Wilson, the British military representative to the czar, French prisoners were brutally abused, often made "the sport and victims of the peasantry."[17] In western Europe treatment of prisoners conformed more to established norms with officers always faring best, while the rank and file often were detained in unsanitary fortresses and deprived of food. Conditions in Austria were bad, but the situation in Prussia was described as the worst.[18]

Much depended on circumstances and personalities. Once the professionals regained control in France matters improved. Generally the French authorities did well. Russian prisoners taken at Zurich were well received in Paris and reportedly well fed. And under Napoleon conditions got even better. As a professional of the late Enlightenment, the emperor held that any harm done to the enemy should be limited to what was absolutely necessary. Napoleon, of course, was not a humanitarian and had ulterior motives. Whenever possible he intended either to incorporate prisoners into his own forces or have them return as friends to their own countries. After Jena he released the Saxon prisoners to their homes, and after Tilsit he returned Russian prisoners, freshly equipped and uniformed, to Czar Alexander. Austrian prisoners were promptly repatriated after 1806 and again after 1809, while despite the violation of the Bailén capitulation there were no reprisals against Spanish prisoners in French hands. Prussian prisoners also had little cause for complaint. Both Austrian and Prussian officers usually were paroled to live outside confinement; men were employed as farm help or in labor companies under retired French officers and received regular pay.[19]

On the other hand, Napoleon remained most suspicious of English prisoners and ordered them strictly guarded and confined to the "strongest and most distant fortresses." Perhaps in reaction, conditions for French prisoners in England deteriorated as the wars continued. During the early years soldiers commonly were employed as farm labor, while officers were paroled and frequently exchanged. In later years prisoners were treated decently in the zone of operations, but in England French prisoners, some fifty-five thousand in 1811 (including Danes, Dutch, and other allies), were confined to prisons and prison hulks where well over half died of malnutrition and various diseases.[20] Both "Britain and France," Best concluded, "had a good deal to be ashamed about." By contrast, in the field the British continued to treat their captives correctly and in the Peninsula did not hesitate to use force "to preserve our French prisoners from being butchered" by Spanish or Portuguese irregulars.[21]

Among the most troubling occurrences during this period were siege operations where the crucial distinction between combatants and noncombatants frequently disappeared completely and civilian sufferings—rape, pillage, torture, and killings—often exceeded that of the garrisons. Military customs made a clear distinction between towns that capitulated and those taken by assault. Many cities surrendered with little or no resistance—Vienna, for example, in 1805 and again in 1809, and here at least the population and the conquerors got along very well. But if an investment or siege was prolonged, civilians most likely would be left to starve before the garrison. Some seven thousand perished in Mantua, fifteen thousand in Genoa. Another issue was bombardments, often calculated to set civilian housing on fire, panic the population, and pressure the governor to surrender. Even when there were instructions to limit civilian damage, for example at Copenhagen in 1807, such collateral damage could not be avoided, especially when notoriously inaccurate Congreve rockets were used. After three days of bombardment much of Copenhagen was in flames with several thousand civilian casualties.[22]

If a fortress surrendered when summoned, it remained customary to spare the civilians, and even if there was a formal siege, capitulation on terms could be made. In 1807, for instance, after a long and bloody siege, Lefebvre allowed the Prussian garrison of Danzig to depart with the honors of war and took care to protect civilian life and property. Still, during the brutal and confused fighting in the confined space of fortifications and streets, atrocities occurred frequently. For instance, during the siege of Glatz in June 1807, a Saxon-Württemberg division under General Dominique Joseph Vandamme indiscriminately killed women and children. A Württemberg private, not a particularly bloodthirsty individual, remembered that "a breastwork facing us was mounted and . . . the Prussians along with their women and children were stabbed and shot to death and some were hurled over the walls."[23]

But if a town had to be stormed, usually a bloody affair for the assailants, troops frequently got out of hand. In such cases the customary codes provided no quarter for the garrison and permitted the town to be sacked, a practice rationalized both as an inducement and as a reward for the assault forces. However, even when a town was abandoned to pillage, this was limited to twenty-four hours and the "lives and honor of the citizens were to be protected," a restriction which often did not hold. Few Turks survived the Russian storming of Orchakov and Ismail in 1788 and 1790, and twelve thousand Polish civilians were massacred after Praga was stormed in 1794, while at Jaffa, Napoleon's men "neither spared the lives of men, or the honor of women," and most of the fifteen thousand Spaniards killed at Tarragona in 1811 were civilians. There were, however, honorable exceptions even in Spain. After a one-day bombardment of Valencia in 1812, Marshal Suchet told the governor, Captain General Blake, that "the laws of war do not permit the suffering of the people to go on, time has come to end them." Blake refused, but, even so, after a two-month siege, he and his troops were allowed to march out with the honors of war while Suchet, a general who believed that humane treatment paid dividends, spared the population.[24]

Even when a fortress was stormed, the garrisons often fared better than the civilians. Despite threats of no quarter, the soldiers usually were taken prisoner, while the enraged victors took out their frustrations on the population. When Zaragoza, a special case to be sure, fell in February 1809, after twenty-three days of bitter house-to-house fighting in which civilians participated, eight thousand Spanish soldiers were taken prisoner, but thirty-four thousand civilians, over two-thirds of the inhabitants, perished.[25]

Normally strictly disciplined professionals, Wellington's soldiers in the Peninsula were not immune to murderous outbursts after storming fortified towns, outbursts intensified by dislike of the Spanish population. General Sir William Francis Napier, both participant and historian of the Peninsular War, charged that "no wild horde of Tartars ever fell with more license upon neighbors than did English troops upon Spanish towns taken by storm."[26] It is only fair to note that other armies were no better and that much of the controversy about the behavior of British soldiers may well reflect later Victorian sensibilities.

The worst incidents occurred at Ciudad Rodrigo, Bajadoz, and San Sebastián. At Bajadoz in 1812, after the assault force suffered over thirty-five hundred casualties, the soldiers vented their anger on the population in three days of looting, murder, and rape. The following year, when San Sebastián fell after a sixty-nine day siege, the French garrison was accorded all the honors of war, while British troops killed half of the population and turned the town into ruins. Whether Wellington at Ciudad Rodrigo and Bajadoz or Lieutenant General Sir Graham at San Sebastián could have kept their men under better control has been debated. Some authors, including Sir Charles Oman, blamed Wellington for condoning the excesses, and Lady Longford concedes that officers made very little attempt to prevent it, seeing little wrong with the pillage and plunder. Historians also have tried to postulate that the killing of noncombatants was the result of the so-called siege mentality which caused enraged troops who had suffered extremely heavy casualties to lose all control. Napier, however, concluded that "this excuse will, however, scarcely suffice." The commanders, he claimed, should have done more to prevent these excesses.[27] Finally, the Spanish Cortés accused Wellington of ordering Graham to destroy San Sebastián to remove a threat to British commerce, an allegation angrily denied by Wellington, who wrote, "I do not know whether the conduct of the soldiers in plundering San Sebastian or the libels . . . have made me most angry."[28]

The impositions of a revolutionary regime, invasions, and occupations frequently aroused some degree of popular resistance, escalating into a full-fledged insurrection in the Vendée and a guerrilla, or people's, war in Spain. While most professional soldiers knew, and by and large observed the customs of war, the people in arms knew nothing of civilized warfare and waged war by means contrary to the military ethic. Wherever and for whatever cause civilians took up arms, military commanders responded with maximum violence to repress resistance, though none would rival the fanatic ferocity of the revolutionary generals in the Vendée. And invariably resistance and reprisals created a vicious circle with atrocities committed on all sides.[29]

When considering civilian resistance it is necessary to distinguish between militias, levies, and other regulated civilian bodies, and guerrillas. Contemporary international law and the customs of war recognized armed civilians serving in properly constituted bodies as entitled to protection, but offered no protection to self-constituted partisan and guerrilla bands.[30] But professional soldiers generally had little confidence in militias, and conservative governments as well as the Jacobin Convention, fearing the sociopolitical consequences, were reluctant to arm the population to fight invaders. The famous *levée en masse* of 1793 was, as Paret has demonstrated, not a military necessity but primarily designed to outflank the demands of the extreme left for a people's war. At the same time, the conservative Austrian government repeatedly canceled plans to arm the peasants along the Upper Rhine against French intrusions. Even when Vienna was threatened in 1797, the Archduke Charles vetoed calling out the levies of Tyrol and Styria. Then and later, the archduke opposed all schemes for wider popular participation in war "lest they might rouse the sleeping beast."[31]

In 1809 he reluctantly agreed with the formation of the *Landwehr,* not a militia but a uniformed second line, while the Tyrolean insurrection of 1809 was sanctioned by the emperor as long as it was controlled by regular officers, but abandoned quickly after the main army was defeated and the regulars withdrawn. Prussia organized a popular levy, the *Landsturm,* in 1813 to wage war against the French on the Spanish model, but a prudent government distrusted the concept and never implemented it. In Russia, of course, ad hoc peasant militias and partisan bands mercilessly harried the retreating French in 1812. Finally, when the Allies invaded France in 1814, Napoleon called for guerrilla war and in some cases the population did take up arms. In the south, Wellington recognized the distinction between legitimate resistance, authorized and controlled by the government, and unauthorized bands. He ordered the armed citizens either to openly join the forces of Marshal Soult or face reprisals—"villages will be burned and the inhabitants killed." In northern France, however, the Allies recognized no such distinctions and executed all civilians found carrying arms against them.[32]

While invaders were commonly disliked, active resistance was most frequently provoked by excesses of requisitioning. To be sure, all armies levied contributions, requisitioned, and on occasion let troops fend for themselves. But as commanders such as Custine, Carnot, Davout, Wellington, Archduke Charles, Napoleon, and many others realized, having an army living off the land could easily become counterproductive. All too often it led to looting and indiscriminate violence which eroded discipline, while taking supplies, especially in impoverished areas, threatened the population with starvation and provoked popular resistance. Therefore commanders tried to eliminate, or at least control, requisitioning and foraging. But it was difficult. The Austrians, perhaps the most conservative and professional army, often avoided requisitioning even when it placed them at an operational disadvantage, while in 1806 starving Prussian troops would not lift potatoes from fields. But such restraint had disappeared by 1814, when the Prussians, now less well disciplined and fired by national hatreds, turned into merciless marauders.[33]

In Spain, where Wellington paid considerable attention to supply, his commissariat often broke down and hungry men would steal what they needed to survive. While such self-help was tolerated, acts of violence were not.[34] Though clearly there were many times when restraints failed, and leaving sieges aside, Wellington authorized stern action to halt abuses. When during the campaign in southern France in 1814, looting by Spanish troops threatened to raise the peasants in arms, an enraged duke ordered them out of the country. He had not, he said, lost thousands of men "to enable the Spaniards to ill-treat and pillage the French peasantry." At the same time, when some British and Portuguese soldiers committed similar outrages, General Sir Edward Pakenham, Wellington's chief of military police, had them executed on the spot.[35]

Few armies, however, were as rapacious as the French. The French army always had relied heavily on requisitioning and, fighting primarily on foreign soil, had fewer scruples. Even if Carnot and some commanders initially tried to limit pillaging, the revolution elevated living off the land and war feeding war to the level of state policy and operational doctrine, a practice continued by the empire.[36] This behavior became explicit and continued throughout the wars. It was not that the French generals liked it. Requisitioning, a lawful practice, usually degenerated into marauding and pillaging, practices they knew wasted resources and destroyed discipline. But without it the French armies could not have sustained their operations. Moreover, French senior officers, including Napoleon and his marshals, as well as generals, officers, and soldiers, regarded looting as one of the compensations of war.[37]

Once it had started, civilian resistance was difficult to repress; countermeasures often escalated it. Despite the massacres and devastation in the Vendée, the region remained restive. In southern Italy popular resistance, shading into banditry, also remained endemic from 1798 on, tying down up to forty thousand French and satellite troops, though in Switzerland the French massacre of some twelve hundred men, women, and children at Stans in 1798 brought the population to heel.[38]

Spain, where resistance to requisitioning combined with xenophobia and religious zeal, became the classic example of a popular guerrilla war. While the French had little trouble dealing with the regular army when they invaded in 1808, provincial governments, the juntas, as well as individuals continued the fight. Both the terrain and the structure of Spanish society favored small, guerrilla war. Soon in much of the country there was a people's war against the invaders—attacks on minor posts, convoys, parties detached from the main body. Some of the guerrilla bands operated under government authority, others were self-constituted, but few of the Spanish, or later the Portuguese, irregulars spared wounded or prisoners, women or children.[39] Murder and torture were common, the French retaliating in kind. Of Napoleon's generals in Spain only Suchet, commanding in Aragon, succeeded, for a time at least, in meeting the insurgent challenge. He combined effective military action with political reform and sternly suppressed all looting. "The presence of a disciplined army and the organization of a competent system of internal administration," he wrote, "considerably improved conditions." Only in Aragon could French soldiers move about single and unarmed, while villages took up arms against the guerrillas.[40] But at best it was coexistence and as the insurgency consolidated and under mounting pressure from British and Spanish forces, Suchet, too, failed.

Although enjoying wide popular support, the Spanish revolt would undoubtedly have been crushed except for the presence of the small, but efficient British army, while without the guerrillas engaging up to three-fifths of the French strength, the Anglo-Portuguese forces might have been pushed into the sea. Despite their mutual dependence, relations between the British and the Spanish guerrillas were strained, even hostile. From the duke down, British soldiers detested the undisciplined and usually cruel resistance fighters, "almost useless in any serious operation," and the Spaniards reciprocated the feeling. It was neither the first nor the last time that regular soldiers would have trouble cooperating with irregular forces in liberating a country.[41]

Excluding the special circumstances of people's war, there is adequate evidence to support the contention that, despite the expanded scale of warfare during the Age of the French Revolution and Napoleon, longer in duration, with fighting more frequent and intense than before, and with the war effort much more broadly based and with national animosities rising, there remained substantial continuities with the traditional patterns restraining war. Professional soldiers were well aware of the laws and customs of warfare between civilized states, and by and large observed them. That this trend was motivated by the self-interest of the combatants does not detract from its beneficial humanitarian impact. There were, of course, exceptions and these conflicts witnessed numerous atrocities and violations of the customary law restraining conduct in war, but the basic existence and validity of these laws, the customs and usages of war, were never challenged.

John B.
Hattendorf

7
Maritime Conflict

"Mare quod natura omnibus patet," wrote the Roman
jurist Ulpian in the third century.[1] In the late nineteenth
century Captain Alfred Thayer Mahan expressed a complementary thought when he
declared: "The first and most obvious light in which the sea presents itself from the
political and social point of view is that of a great highway; or better, perhaps, of a
wide common in which men pass in all directions."[2] Both of these phrases echo the
first principle of modern international maritime law that has prevailed from the
seventeenth century to the present: the open sea is free to the ships of all nations.

Freedom of the seas is no romantic notion but something that reflects centuries of
man's experience and struggle at sea. The sea is an alien environment yet it is a place
of much human activity. For centuries man has valued the open sea as a medium for
communications across the globe. Thus, while the sea is not part of any state, it is an
area that falls under the law of nations to prevent it from becoming a place of anarchy,
while many share its use.

The notion of freedom of the seas recognizes a fundamental difference between
man's activities on land and those at sea. Such writers as Hugo Grotius in the
seventeenth century could base their ideas of freedom of the seas on the physical
inability of navies to control it and on the natural law postulate that all share everything that is in inexhaustible supply and can inoffensively be used by everyone.[3]
Today, when navies are more capable and few recognize natural law, these arguments
are difficult, if not impossible, to sustain. The fundamental basis for freedom of the
seas, however, does not lie in such legalistic notions. It is an appreciation of the fact
that maritime trade was, and is, an essential economic factor for many nations.
Unlike territory ashore that people own, cultivate, improve, and defend, the sea is
essentially a shared avenue of communication and commerce.[4]

Freedom of the seas means that the only permissible restraint on the navigation of any vessel, despite its nationality, its character as a merchant ship or warship, its cargo or destination, is that of proceeding with due regard for the rights of others to exercise like freedoms. Recognizing this as a basic principle, nations have developed over the past three centuries a set of common practices that flow from it and that have come to define and to restrain wartime activities at sea. Among these practices are recognition of the idea that, while no one owned the open ocean, nations could maintain sovereignty over their territorial waters and over their ships at sea. No nation has the right to require the ships of another nation to salute its vessels in the open sea. Thus, flying a national flag on board a ship is not just a quaint maritime tradition, but a means of identification and a recognition of the national laws under which the vessel sails.

Today, influenced by theorists, we think of freedom of the seas as the first principle of international maritime law. We recognize that the law of naval warfare is affected by it, even though many see the two subjects as separate bodies of law, existing side by side. The doctrines of belligerent and neutral rights, as well as humanitarian principles, further modify the conduct of war at sea. The practical development of common law and common usages to govern fighting at sea was slow and uneven. It grew originally neither from high flung idealism nor from a supranational power, but from pragmatic agreements among nations and from the practice of individual nations to control their subjects at sea. In short, law at sea grew from treaty agreements, and practice, with their acceptance as custom.

In the beginning the issues were entirely practical ones. Kings and princes had a particular interest in sharing the spoils of enemy property captured at sea and preventing maritime conduct that was at cross-purposes with their plans. Over many centuries these practices were modified by a range of other factors. In the historical development of legal restraints on the conduct of war at sea three categories of restraint can be delineated:

First, there are the inherent limitations of navies as weapons. This is a question of the technological capabilities that have varied over time and an issue of geographical position and constraint. As a category this is the fundamental basis upon which other restraints rest.

Second, there is the growth of administrative structures and of the methods to command and to control naval operations, all founded in the legal order of a particular nation. Only within the last century have these become international in character.

And third, there are the rules and principles of international law created through court decisions, treaties, scholarly analysis, and the customary practice of nations.

Our focus here on *jus in bello,* the constraints on warfare, suggests that our main interest is only in the third category. While it is common for modern specialists on the subject to limit themselves to that theme, I suggest that a broad historical understanding involves intertwining all three.

Early Development

In the Middle Ages a body of maritime law developed from decisions in maritime cases in local courts that became precedents for later practice. Among the most famous of these were the Rhodian laws compiled in the seventh to ninth centuries, the *Tabula amalfitana* developed in the tenth century by the city of Amalfi and the eleventh-century *Ordinamenta of Trani* in Italy, the *Rolls of Oléron* developed in the twelfth century on the west coast of France, the fourteenth-century *Leges wisbuensis* on the Baltic island of Gotland, and the *Consulato del mare* in Barcelona.[5] Among other things, some of these precedents provided for ways in which the king could share with the captor in his prizes.

As a way of following the main line of development in the law of naval warfare, it is useful to examine the experience of England as it grew to become a major naval power. As far back as records exist, the crown appears to have held all rights to the profits from the capture of enemy ships in wartime, whether made by armed merchantmen or by warships. The seamen who made the captures could only share by a grant from the king. As early as 1203 we find King John granting to the crews of galleys one half "the gains that they may make in captures from our enemies."[6] In 1276 and 1341 there are examples of the king suing in the common courts to obtain his share of the proceeds of the sale of prizes.[7] In these early times we can find evidence of other controls placed on the conduct of war at sea. In 1293 Edward I issued several similar orders. In one he issued a stay of the letters of marque that he had issued to allow private men-of-war to attack and capture Castilian ships.[8] In another he warned the seamen of the Cinque Ports, about to sail on a trading voyage to Gascony and Poitou, not to attack Normans or anyone from the realm of France.[9] And in a third he ordered the arrest of eleven German and Frisian ships that had entered English ports, seeking safety from storms, but which were carrying provisions and war materials to the enemies of England in Flanders.[10] The traces of legal jurisdiction over the conduct of sea operations in this period are scanty, but we know that some fundamental administrative and legal structures that later came to form English admiralty law began to appear at this time. Over time the courts of common law proved to be insufficient to handle the specialized problems of the sea. There is evidence that admirals began to conduct juridical proceedings as early as 1357, judging the appropriateness of captures at sea.[11] One finds such courts dispersed around the coast of England—the local courts of the admirals of the north, south, and west.[12] Their decisions were inconsistent and often irregular. To correct these problems in the beginning of the fifteenth century the king established a High Court of Admiralty. Shortly thereafter jurists compiled *The Black Book of the Admiralty* as a guide for the practices of the newly established court.[13] It would be another century before the

High Court of Admiralty began to reach its potential as a tribunal in prize cases, serving as a legal constraint on what should and should not be captured at sea.[14]

At the same time one can find another example. During a truce in the war with France about 1408 or 1410, France and England drew up an agreement against pirates and sea robbers, specifying among other things that no armed ship was to sail from either country without a license from the king.[15] Thus, from these few examples among many, one can see that the earliest forms of English law touching the conduct of war at sea concerned commerce and trade.

At the heart of it the issue was how to protect one's own trade and that of one's neutral trading partners at sea, while also doing maximum damage to one's enemy.[16] There were several aspects to the problem. It involved not only protection from an enemy during war but also protection from pirates during war and peace. When not engaged in a war, it involved ensuring the safety of one's trade from the depredations of other states which might be fighting one another.

The solutions to these problems were neither easy nor clear-cut. In wartime there were very heavy demands on navies, particularly when naval vessels had other duties, such as attacking enemy battle fleets or accompanying transports carrying land forces. Often the tasks were simply too much for navies alone to bear, and governments had to get assistance to carry them out.

Sovereignty of the Sea

In trying to solve the practical problem they faced, some governments declared ownership of the sea. They used this as a means to protect their trade. Going further, they used these claims as the basis for claims to a monopoly of commerce or for the exclusive use of the fisheries in particular waters.

England laid claim to the sovereignty of the British seas, demanding that foreign ships render a salute by lowering topsails and striking their flags when they met English warships sailing in a vaguely defined area which included the Channel, the North Sea, the Bay of Biscay and the seas surrounding Ireland and Scotland. Beginning in the thirteenth century this custom took form in the attempt of the king's ships to control piracy by inspecting foreign vessels. Later, during the reigns of James I and Charles I in the early seventeenth century, it began to be a serious issue in international relations. In 1652, when Admiral Martin Tromp failed to lower his flag to Robert Blake in the Straits of Dover, the English government used the incident as the pretext for beginning the First Dutch War.

England's claim to sovereignty over the adjacent sea was different from the claims which other countries had made in other waters. Most countries founded their claims on international treaties and other agreements. For example, through such arrangements Venice laid very strong claim to the Adriatic, which many other rulers recognized. In the Baltic, after the fall of the Hanseatic League, Denmark and Sweden vied for dominion within that enclosed sea, but for centuries most rulers accepted the king of Denmark's claim to full possession of the Baltic straits, and they paid to Denmark the sound dues on all ships that passed.

On a larger scale, Pope Alexander VI's two *Inter cætera* bulls of 1492 and the Treaty of Tordesillas in 1494 became the basis for Spain and Portugal each claiming exclusive rights to navigation. Although the original purpose of these documents was to prevent conflict by allocating land areas for colonies, Spain used them to lay exclusive claim to the western portion of the Atlantic, the Gulf of Mexico, and the Pacific, while Portugal claimed the Atlantic south of Morocco and the Indian Ocean.

With the establishment of the Dutch East India Company the Dutch were among the first to object to Portugal's claims. Hugo Grotius wrote one of the first major arguments against Portugal's claims favoring freedom of the seas. In the early 1600s Englishmen attacked his views and interpreted his ideas in the quite different context of British claims to sovereignty of the sea. Through the writings of Grotius and his critic, John Selden, this became the *mare liberum* and *mare clausum* controversy, which eventually formed the intellectual basis for many current ideas of international maritime law.[17] One should note, in this regard, that the scholarly debate between Grotius and Selden was less a determining factor than the voyages of Drake, Hawkins, Cavendish, and van Heemskerk in forcefully asserting the freedom of the seas while, simultaneously, trade patterns became firmly established.[18] These voyages clearly showed that it was not physically possible to exclude other nations from using broad expanses of the ocean for either commercial or military purposes.

By the eighteenth century claims to sovereignty over vast areas of the seas died out. In a broad general sense, however, remnants of them still form the basis for some claims to territorial waters. Although the legal basis for Britain's claim to territorial waters derives from more modern developments in law, other nations can trace their claims to different sources. For example, Denmark allocated parts of its claims to the Norwegian Sea and to the North Atlantic among Greenland, Iceland, Spitzbergen, and the Faeroe Islands. Consequently, the territorial waters in those areas can be seen as residual parts of the ancient claim. Some scholars have suggested that some claims to coastal limits extending for more than three miles also derive from such ancient claims. Thus in a historical sense the claims to sovereignty of the sea have played a role in the maritime law that restricts foreign warships in their activities in territorial waters.[19] Recently, for example, Libya has used its claim to the waters of the Gulf of Sidra to try to restrict U.S. naval activity off its coast.

Privateering

In trying to protect trade and to combat lawlessness at sea, the major problem was to find the ships and the manpower to combat piracy. Facing pirates in the broad expanses of the sea with ships of limited capacity and armed with short-range weapons, governments found it very difficult to acquire the resources to deal with the situation. Simultaneously, the work of pirates in destroying or capturing enemy trade was a significant contribution to any war effort. Continental powers found one solution to the problem in privateering. Through this method the government obtained ships and men to fight at sea, attracting seamen by the lure of adventure and the riches they might find in captured ships. By authorizing privately armed ships and privately paid seamen to go out at their own risk to attack enemy merchant ships, governments could divert at least some potential pirates from putting to sea, and they could fight some aspects of the sea war at little cost to the crown.

In addition to saving the crown naval expense, privateering took advantage of two other maritime practices. One of these was the licensing of privately owned ships to make reprisals against foreign trade for private losses at sea in both peace and war. After formal diplomatic protests had failed to bring satisfaction, the crown issued letters of reprisal authorizing a merchant to outfit a private warship to recover property from the responsible country up to the value of the lost property plus costs.[20] The other was the custom of arming merchant vessels for self-protection. In all cases, however, it was a general legal principle that seamen who made captures at sea had no legal title to their captures, unless they held a commission from the crown for this purpose.

It was very difficult to control the activities of privateers in the manner one could control a naval expedition in accomplishing precise objectives. The result of privateering warfare tended to be a haphazard plundering of enemy ships. In theory a government could also benefit from the licensing, control, and taxation of privateering. In Elizabethan England, however, this control was both feeble and corrupt. English officials lacked both the efficiency and the honesty to deal with privateering. All sorts of corruption and abuses occurred.[21] As one historian has observed, "Instead of controlling and taxing its subjects, the Crown entered with them into a race for private profit."[22] Yet English privateering did make a contribution in the late sixteenth century. Through its profits it was a positive influence in English commercial development and acted as a lever for further trade. It made a substantial contribution to the development of the shipping industry and greatly expanded the pool of maritime experience. In the war against Spain of 1585–1603, privateering was the most enticing aspect of a popular war.[23] In the distinctive circumstances of that time, privateering became a special vehicle for national feeling, and however crudely, laid both direction and constraint on war at sea. The regulations of the crown for issuing letters of marque and reprisal, at least, focused the privateers' attention on the enemy as the object of attack and provided for a basic method of dealing with captured goods through the admiralty courts.[24]

The accession of James I and England's peace with Spain brought on a new development in regulating warfare at sea. Although England was at peace, Spain continued to fight the Dutch in the Channel, the North Sea, and along the coasts of England. Not wanting to be involved, James I issued a proclamation in 1605, declaring what he believed were the rights and duties of neutrals. Among other things, he declared that belligerents could neither attack one another in English ports and harbors "nor hover and hang about the skirts of our Ports" to attack enemy merchantmen. When a belligerent ship of war should enter a port in neutral England where there was a merchant of the other side, the merchant was required to leave two or three tides before the man-of-war to prevent pursuit.[25]

The legal constraints on conduct of war at sea up to the early seventeenth century are important but fragmentary developments. They remind us that the origin of maritime warfare lies in the days when almost every major commercial vessel could defend itself and when naval weapons were relatively light and inexpensive. Historians have agreed that modern international law began only in the seventeenth century, but for the law of maritime warfare the main issue was already clear. The regulation of maritime warfare centered on the flow of commerce and balanced on the strategic and economic interests of the states concerned. In the modern era codification, refinement, and general acceptance of earlier pragmatic solutions followed.

The Beginning of the Modern Period

In the early and middle seventeenth century there was a shift in maritime warfare from that dominated by armed merchant shipping to that of a regular naval force. Up to this point the crown often hired vessels or depended upon merchants and cities to provide most vessels needed, relying heavily upon privateering for attacking the enemy. The development from private warfare to that conducted by the naval forces of the state was a gradual one in which privateering did not disappear for more than two centuries. Technological change undoubtedly brought with it specialization in design, armament, and other equipment which gradually made it more difficult to convert back and forth between the roles of merchant and warship. Nevertheless, even today, certain types of boats designed for pleasure have been equipped for war.[26] During this transition overseas commercial trading companies, such as the East India Company, took on responsibility for arming ships and protecting commerce. This was part of a larger development in which evolving sovereign states were assuming the responsibilities of private groups within the state. During this period the state began to pay more attention to the interests of its citizens, protecting them from foreign depredations. The effects of this development for sea warfare were increased restrictions on private warfare, the extension of admiralty jurisdiction, and the stabilization and more rigorous enforcement of the law in relation to captures made at sea.[27]

The Anglo-Dutch wars mark the first period in which the laws of naval warfare became more clearly defined through the decision of admiralty courts. While much that happened in this period was merely an extension of earlier precedent, the increasing number of legal decisions and the nature of the wars between competing maritime powers mark it as a key period in the development of maritime law. One of England's main objectives in the war was to destroy as much Dutch commerce as possible. "What matters this or that object?" Admiral George Monck asked. "What we want is more of the trade the Dutch now have."[28] To do this the English attacked all the Dutch ships they could find. To preserve their trade in the face of attacks, Dutch merchants resorted to all sorts of ruses to make their ships and cargoes appear to be neutral property, immune from capture.

The key issues in this period came from prize law cases involving the capture of ships at sea. In England the main figure in this early period was Sir Leoline Jenkins, who presided over the High Court of Admiralty from 1665 to 1685. A major theme of his tenure was the relationship between a neutral and a belligerent and many of his decisions became key cases for modern law. This question involved particular emphasis on three topics: determining what were enemy goods; what was contraband; and what constituted a blockade.

Enemy goods. To avoid the suspicion of carrying enemy goods in its ships, Sweden had agreed in a 1661 treaty to furnish its ships with passports that would exempt them from search, except in "just and urgent cause of suspicion."[29] The Dutch Republic strongly supported this method. However, many Englishmen felt that the system did not give assurance that the passport was an adequate description of the goods the ships carried. They preferred to rely on the right of visit and search, or certification of the nature of a cargo by an English minister at a neutral port.

Certification that a ship was carrying goods from one neutral port to another, from a neutral shipper to a neutral consignee was not enough. The real question was whether the cargo was ultimately destined for an enemy. The English raised the question, in two cases, of whether the law constrains a naval vessel from attacking: when enemy goods are in neutral ships and when neutral goods are in enemy ships. The Dutch, still wanting to preserve their trade, argued that free ships make free goods. The English argued the negative, enemy ships, enemy goods. By 1668 rules of law were established for both cases through a series of treaties between and among the principal maritime powers of Europe.[30] Practice at this time was not rigid, but it became clear that without a passport only a neutral ship carrying neutral goods was immune from capture. The establishment of the combined doctrine "Free ships, free goods; unfree ships, unfree goods" was a clear restraint on naval warfare in a period when nations wanted to expand their attacks on enemy trade. This doctrine meant that neutral goods in enemy ships could be captured, but neutral ships could protect enemy cargoes from capture. To understand this anomaly, however, one must appreciate that this compromise took place when nations were trying to develop their merchant marine fleets, at least for carrying their own goods. Thus, the major maritime powers were willing to give up the right of having their goods carried in the ships of other nations if they could continue to trade with their friends' enemies.[31]

Contraband. Another issue was the nature of cargoes. Here one encounters the idea of contraband or a prohibition on trade in particular commodities with an enemy. Munitions head any list of contraband with naval supplies and victuals following closely behind. By the end of the sixteenth century the idea was already current that if neutral trade prevented a warring nation from cutting off supplies to an enemy by banning all trade, one could at least ban selected articles that were most useful to an enemy in prosecuting a war. A century later in 1700 there was no consensus on the details of the law of contraband. While a belligerent had the right to intercept and confiscate munitions going to an enemy, he did not have the right to cut off all neutral trade to an enemy. The debate between belligerents and neutrals on the matter was unresolved, and it remained an issue of give-and-take in concessions, but without any fundamental compromise. Belligerents understandably wished to destroy all the vital supplies of their enemy, while neutrals always wanted to continue all their trade.[32]

Blockade. In the same period the issue of blockade became clear. Like other aspects of maritime law there was much precedent and there was much discussion of the issues under negotiation. From the 1640s onward nearly every commercial treaty had a more or less standard provision on blockade, listing free and noncontraband goods permitted for trade to enemy ports, except to those cities and places under siege or blockade. Thus, nations recognized blockade as a special circumstance. Only in 1742, in a treaty between France and Denmark, does one find the first reference to the idea that a blockade must be an effective one if it is to be regarded as a blockade at all.[33] The most peculiar aspect of the early law regarding blockade is that it was recognized in treaties for more than 150 years before it first became the basis for a legal decision in a prize court in 1798.

The European wars of the seventeenth and eighteenth centuries brought out the various issues and added to the range of admiralty court cases. At the same time the strategic situations in each naval war developed differing aspects of the larger problem. For example, France's shift of strategy from naval fleet combat to *guerre de course* in 1694 during the Nine Years' War showed the potential efficacy of a commerce raiding strategy in combating an opposing strategy based on naval fleets.[34] It illustrates the reasons why a nation that was not the predominant naval power would be reluctant to agree to constraints on warfare that mixed naval and privateering attacks on trade. During the first decades of the eighteenth century diplomats tried to keep their trade policies separate in two nearly simultaneous wars: the War of the Spanish Succession (1701–14) and the Great Northern War (1700–21). This raised a practical problem of neutral rights in circumstances where one nation was a belligerent in one war but a neutral in the other. In these years belligerent powers found themselves in the unusual situation of having to consider their neutral rights at the same time they planned attacks on enemy trade.[35] This, and the years that followed leading up to the Seven Years' War, gave rise to a legal principle that came to be called The Rule of the War of 1756. Illustrating the uncertain nature of maritime law, it in fact did not begin as a rule of law but as a British government policy to relieve some earlier restrictions on captures. This rule stated that neutrals lost their immunity to capture when they carried on trade with an enemy not normally permitted in peacetime.[36] Thus, wartime trade had to conform to the international treaties and national laws and policies of peacetime trade.

Military historians often point out that the French Revolution and the Napoleonic Wars mark the beginning of warfare in the modern age. Like other wars, however, they illustrate that those with the power to enforce restraints determine them. While France posed as the champion of neutral rights and freedom of the sea, it more often than not had to give way to Britain's belligerent rights while the Royal Navy controlled the sea. Napoleon's Berlin Decree and Britain's countering orders in council had a tremendous effect in temporarily shifting the flow of trade during the war. From 1793 to 1812 neutrals reaped dramatic profits from this shift, while the belligerents were reluctant to attack neutral trade for fear of making a neutral into an enemy. Yet as the war spread and the coalitions formed, neutrality itself was largely snuffed out. By 1812, when the United States went to war with Britain, the last important maritime neutral joined the conflict.[37] The principal and established issues of restraint in maritime warfare vanished for the moment.

By the beginning of the nineteenth century nations had clearly chosen sides in the arguments on international law, few were consistent in their views, and they resolved few major issues. In general, England opposed the principle of free ships, free goods supported by the Dutch, the Hanseatic towns, and sometimes France. On the other hand, the Dutch, the Danes, and the Swedes, and sometimes France and Spain objected to the English view of contraband that included naval stores such as pitch, tar, wood, rope, and sails as well as wheat and other food supplies. Britain and the young American republic fought over these issues in 1812, but had not resolved them. Britain continued to argue that a superior sea power had the right to close the seas to its enemies, and that its use of blockade and the impressment of seamen, together with the rules of contraband, continuous voyage, and enemy property, were justifiable rights for a belligerent in preventing neutrals from helping an enemy. Opposing this, the United States continued to maintain that the British position was a violation of freedom of the seas and the sovereignty of neutrals. Despite the fundamental disagreement, the issues did not lead to another war, as many predicted it would.[38] Conflicting national interests and strategies as well as changing technologies were firmly intertwined in the legal questions. Belligerents and neutrals were forced to balance contradictory interests at sea against pragmatic policies and strategies.

New Aspects

Slave trade. In the nineteenth century the abolition of slavery created a body of human rights law that provided for the peacetime use of naval force on the high seas. In this instance the law justified and guided an entirely new area of naval operations—searching and seizing vessels engaged in the slave trade. The English colony of Rhode Island and Providence Plantations had banned the importation of slaves as early as 1774, but it was not until after Denmark had abolished the importation of slaves in 1802, followed by Britain and the United States in 1807, that it began to have international effects. Both the Treaty of Paris of 1814 and the Congress of Vienna condemned the slave trade. In the 1820s the United States and Britain enacted laws declaring that the slave trade was a form of piracy punishable by death.[39] Yet for many years each nation had to send out its own warships for the purpose, being unwilling to allow warships from another nation to search merchant ships under its own flag. Although several attempts were made to form an international naval force to suppress the trade, Britain, with occasional assistance from France, Portugal, and the United States, took up the main effort in maintaining naval patrols off the West African coast. In the Webster-Ashburton Treaty of 1842, the United States and Britain agreed to maintain two squadrons for the suppression of piracy, operating separately but cooperatively. Later during the American Civil War, Britain and America finally agreed on a mutually acceptable approach to search and boarding, while also establishing three Anglo-American mixed courts of justice to adjudicate slave trading cases at Freetown in Sierra Leone, at Cape Town, and at New York. These courts lasted for less than a decade. While the antislavery patrols themselves were never fully effective and became ancillary to other strategic and political objectives,[40] they nevertheless provided a valuable precedent in the use of law to channel naval force.

A new structure of international relations. The first general European conflict after 1815 came with the Crimean War in 1854. The settlement of that war in 1856 resulted in major steps being taken toward resolving some of the knottier issues in maritime law. As part of the peace settlement in the Declaration of Paris the European powers agreed to outlaw privateering, France abandoned the doctrine of enemy ships, enemy goods, and Britain recognized the doctrine of free ships, free goods, thus abandoning the rule of 1756. Thus, noncontraband goods could not be seized on neutral ships. Britain formally agreed to accept in practice the principle that blockades had to be real and effective to be legally binding. This agreement was a major British concession that severely reduced the advantages of its naval supremacy. One can trace the reasons for this sudden change—on issues that had lain unresolved for so long—to the changed conditions of the time. The dramatic increase in technology and the specialized knowledge needed to man naval vessels were leading factors that made privateering and the impressment of merchant seamen far less attractive enterprises. The attitude prevailing at the time favoring economic liberalism and free trade played a role in securing the doctrine of free ships, free goods. Moreover, the diplomatic situation made it profitable for each side to make concessions to the other in order to preserve other diplomatic alignments.[41] A belligerent's natural desire to halt neutral trade with its enemy was balanced by the practical desire to avoid provoking a powerful neutral.

The United States did not sign the Declaration of Paris in 1856, because it could not agree to the article outlawing privateering.[42] Nevertheless, its actions in the following years showed that it clearly accepted the British policy. The American Civil War revealed no new principles of maritime law but reinforced the impression that in naval conflicts the more powerful state tends to use law for its own advantage, while the weaker state tends to argue from principle. Having the dominant naval power in the Civil War, President Lincoln did not authorize privateers and declared a blockade of southern ports in 1861. Asserting the North's belligerent right to blockade an enemy, the Union government argued that to be legal in international law a blockade needed only to present a high risk for an enemy, not an impervious wall. Moreover, the Lincoln government took up the doctrine of continuous voyage, a concept that Americans had found unjust half a century earlier. With a changed position they now sought to stop neutrals carrying contraband between two neutral ports if those goods were clearly bound to a blockaded Confederate harbor.[43] Similarly, in capturing the British merchant ship *Trent* in 1861, the United States attempted to stop Confederate representatives from reaching Britain and opposed Britain's claim that it had the right, in order to protect its own subjects, to receive unrecognized government special agents not possessing diplomatic character.[44]

Following the Crimean and the American Civil wars, a new structure of international politics began to appear in the latter half of the nineteenth century. For the moment it seemed that Britain had moved away from the issues of European balance of power politics and redefined its interests in broad imperial terms. Thus, it seemed that it lacked interest in defending the types of broad belligerent rights that it had earlier demanded. The development of technology continued to reduce the importance of the dispute between belligerent and neutral rights. The railroad, for example, provided an alternative means of transportation that seemed to make navies a less effective tool in halting enemy commerce on the Continent. Finally, many believed that the nature of war itself had changed. Prussia's wars in the 1860s and 1870s suggested that wars would be determined by short, decisive conflicts on land following national mobilization. These new conditions seemed to undermine the importance of such old issues as blockade, neutral rights, and contraband. The Spanish-American War only reinforced these perceptions. Immediately following that war President William McKinley went as far as to propose to the Hague Conference in 1899 that all private property should be immune from capture at sea.[45]

Code of naval warfare. In the same year U.S. Secretary of the Navy John D. Long ordered Captain Charles H. Stockton at the Naval War College in Newport, Rhode Island, to draft a code of naval warfare. Starting from the Hague Conference of 1899, Stockton went further and based his naval code on the 1863 rules for land warfare written by Francis Lieber, the German-born Columbia Law School professor. In general, Stockton sought to extend to the maritime sphere virtually everything that regulated land warfare. Among other things, he sought to narrow the limits for bombarding unfortified and undefended towns, to forbid reprisals in excess of an offense, to exempt coastal fishing vessels from capture, to provide definitely that free ships make free goods, to exempt mail steamers from capture, to except neutral convoys from search, and to classify contraband goods in a way that general international principles could be agreed upon. This first attempt to codify naval warfare was based upon a century of prize court decisions and American diplomacy promoting the freedom of the seas as well as the academic work of men such as Professor George Grafton Wilson of Brown University. It severely limited belligerent rights. The U.S. Navy adopted the code in June 1900 and it remained in effect for nearly four years. Secretary of the Navy William H. Moody withdrew it in February 1904,[46] so as not to put the United States at a disadvantage in case of war with a less principled state, and leaving American negotiators a free hand at The Hague Conference in 1907.

One of the key opponents of the Naval War Code was the naval theorist and historian Alfred Thayer Mahan. He argued that the United States should no longer view itself as a neutral but step into the shoes of a great naval power. It had to shift from the attitude of a neutral small country to that of a great maritime power. "Our weakness of a century ago is not expedient to our strength today," Mahan wrote to President Theodore Roosevelt. "Rather, we should seek to withdraw from our position of the flag covering the goods. We need to fasten our grip on the sea."[47] While Mahan did not convince Roosevelt on this particular issue, others in the navy and the

State Department agreed that the United States should reverse its traditional stance on the limitation of belligerent rights to adjust to the new conditions in international politics and America's changing role in them. As they observed the rise of German naval power, Mahan, Admiral George Dewey, and others argued that only in a common Anglo-American effort with a reversal of the traditional American stand could Britain and the United States successfully oppose Germany at sea, should it be necessary. But Theodore Roosevelt and his successors, William Howard Taft and Woodrow Wilson, as well as British prime ministers Arthur Balfour and Sir Edward Grey, continued to follow policies designed to further restrict belligerent rights. Both countries approved the German proposal for an international prize court and agreed at the London Conference in 1909 to reach compromise on other issues. At the time many observers heralded these events as substantial steps toward world peace through international law.[48]

Most importantly, the Declaration of London preserved what had been established at Paris in 1856, and it extended neutral rights and immunity by specifying a list that restricted contraband to a short list of munitions and war supplies, while at the same time establishing a much longer list of free goods, including raw materials for industry. The reform of maritime law along these lines ran directly counter to the contingency plans that naval officers were making at the same time for the possibility of an economic blockade of Germany.[49] In the event, neither the 1907 Hague Convention agreement for an international prize court nor the 1909 Declaration of London went into effect, although many accept the provisions of the declaration as customary law today.

The world wars. The events of the two world wars in 1914–18 and 1939–45 cast asunder the prevailing British and American assumptions and expectations about the nature of world politics and the role of international law that had developed in the waning years of the preceding century.

At the opening of World War I the British government began a maritime blockade that was as harsh as anything imagined in the Napoleonic Wars. This involved several new aspects, among them the British declaration in November 1914 that the whole North Sea was a military area and that "merchant shipping of all kinds, traders of all countries, fishing craft and all other vessels, will be exposed to the greatest dangers from mines that it has been necessary to lay and from warships searching vigilantly by night and day for suspicious craft."[50] In this dramatic change from previous practice the British government justified its action as retaliation for the indiscriminate mining of the main trade routes north of Ireland between Liverpool and North America by merchant vessels flying neutral flags.

Similarly, in February 1915 the German government announced that it would destroy every enemy merchant ship found within the war zone surrounding the British

Isles. Since British and Allied shipping often flew neutral flags to protect themselves, the Germans could give no recognition to neutral rights within the war zone. The German ambassador in Washington told the U.S. secretary of state, "the new German method of naval warfare is imposed and justified by the murderous character of the English method of naval warfare, which seeks to condemn the German people to death by starvation through the destruction of legitimate trade with foreign neutral countries."[51] At the end of January 1917 Germany went further and announced unrestricted submarine warfare, declaring its intention to prevent forcibly all navigation, including that of neutrals, to and from England or France. "All ships met within that zone will be sunk."[52]

At the end of the war in 1919 the Allies threatened to renew their blockade of Germany as a means of forcing Germany to accept the Versailles peace settlement. In reply to this demand the German delegate, Count von Brockdorff-Rantzau, reminded the Allies and his fellow countrymen of the wider moral issue involved in blockading an entire nation: "Crimes in war may not be excusable, but they are committed in the struggle for victory, when we think only of maintaining our national existence, and are in such passion as makes the conscience of peoples blunt. The hundreds of thousands of non-combatants who have perished since November 11, because of the blockade, were destroyed coolly and deliberately after our opponents had won a certain and assured victory. Remember that when you speak of guilt and atonement."[53]

In continuing the blockade after the armistice the Allies forfeited the legitimacy of what many accepted as a just war against the kaiser and turned it into an unjust war against the German people. With this it planted the seeds for renewed conflict.[54]

In conducting the blockade during the war there was another issue. The submarine was a new weapon and this in itself presented a problem. There was no established law for its use in wartime; few had even imagined that it could be put to use as either a commerce raider or as a tool to maintain a blockade. The opposing nations circumvented the traditional law and custom on the attack of trade that had grown up in the previous centuries. Rather than allowing the rules on enemy property, contraband, and neutral rights to constrain them, they sought to legitimize their conduct of war by a right of reprisal and retaliation for the enemy's extraordinary actions. This was a little used idea in the past. Governments had given privateers letters of reprisal in response to specific attacks on private property, but they had rarely justified attacks on neutral trade on the basis of reprisal. It should be remembered that in one of those rare instances the United States was so strongly opposed to the practice that it declared war in 1812.

Following the First World War diplomats made several attempts to deal with the broad issues of naval warfare through the naval disarmament negotiations held in Washington in 1921–22 and in London in 1930 and 1936. In an attempt to prohibit unrestricted submarine warfare against merchant ships, the delegates to the Second London Naval Conference issued a special protocol on the subject. By the time war broke out in 1939, more than forty countries had ratified or acceded to it, including all the major maritime powers. Given the experience that followed, Captain Stephen Roskill remarked, "The value of those signatures may be regarded as justification for cynicism about attempts to 'humanise' war."[55]

The belligerents employed the same policies in the Second World War as they did in the First World War. Although not fully accepted as a principle of international law, the idea of a war zone in which unrestricted warfare could take place was employed by both sides. In 1940 Germany declared an unrestricted war zone in the North Atlantic and the United States followed suit in the Pacific with its declaration of unrestricted submarine warfare against Japan.[56]

Naval war crimes. In pursuing war at sea the opposing sides raised broad issues of international law in terms of national policy and war crimes, yet the issue of individual responsibility in isolated circumstances should not be forgotten. For the little public attention they receive, war crimes committed at sea remain a fact. Among them are the torpedoing of the hospital ship *Llandovery Castle* by *U-86* in June 1918, and the murder of eleven survivors of *U-27* by the British Q-ship *Baralong,* whose crew seized them after their rescue from the sea by the steamer *Nicosian* in August 1915. In the Second World War the British submarine *Torbay* machine-gunned German survivors in the Mediterranean near Crete in June 1941, and in March 1944 the German submarine *U-852* methodically searched for and killed the survivors of the Greek ship *Peleus* in the South Atlantic. In these four examples only the Germans were tried and convicted for their atrocities, while the others escaped punishment and were even rewarded.[57]

The Postwar World

In the postwar world we are no longer surprised to see a nation use international law as a means to legitimize, rather than be deflected from its intention to use force. Nevertheless, even in such circumstances law can exert some constraint on the use of force. Like domestic crimes, a violation of international law may vary in its seriousness. "If recognition of this leads a state with a choice of means to select a less serious rather than a more serious violation, then the existence of law has exercised a beneficial influence."[58]

Since 1945 there has been a concerted effort among nations to rehabilitate and apply relevant portions of the traditional laws of naval warfare that had developed before 1914. A major force in this, undoubtedly, has been the war crimes trials and the work of the United Nations.

The International Military Tribunal at Nuremberg convicted Admirals Doenitz and Raeder of violating the 1936 London Protocol by ordering submarine attacks, without warning, on both neutral and enemy merchant vessels. On the other hand, the tribunal acquitted them of criminal charges in directing the attack against armed merchant ships. But it is still an unsettled point whether unrestricted submarine warfare against an enemy's merchant marine, as practiced by Allies and Axis alike in World War II, violates international law.[59] By traditional law a submarine must follow the rules of warfare applicable to surface ships.

In the years since the Second World War the U.S. Navy has emphasized the role of international law not only in war but in peace. Today the current *United States Naval Regulations* directs that "at all times, commanders shall observe, and require their commands to observe, the principles of international law. Where necessary to fulfill this responsibility, a departure from other provisions of Navy Regulations is authorized."[60]

American naval officers have ready access to this information. It is easily available in the *Commander's Handbook on the Law of Naval Operations,*[61] which cites the relevant provisions of recent treaties and national obligations as well as the Hague Conventions and the London Protocol of 1936. Issued by the U.S. Navy in July 1987, this manual presents the position of the United States and takes a major step in defining customary law on the subject. However, as Professor W. Michael Reisman has noted, "Manuals are not an end in themselves. They are an instrument for achieving an end: the prescription and application of a law of armed conflict which tempers the harshness and cruelty of combat and confines human and material destruction to targets of military necessity and utility."[62]

In the postwar era international law has had a clear effect on the conduct of naval operations at sea. While some may debate the legality of U.S. naval operations off Cuba in 1962, American leaders described it as a quarantine rather than as a blockade and this approach had the effect of reducing some belligerent activity normally associated with wartime blockades in the past. During other peacetime crises, both public opinion and international law played a role in constraining violence at sea, for example, in the 1973 Icelandic-British cod war.

In addition, the creation of general, humanitarian laws has become a further restraint on war at sea. Through the 1949 Geneva Conventions, the 1982 United Nations Conference on the Law of the Sea, and a range of other agreements, humanitarian law protects hospital ships, coastal fisheries and trade, as well as vessels on scientific, relief, and philanthropic missions. The laws surrounding the concepts of humanitarian treatment of peoples and the protection of the environment are also coming to constrain the conduct of war at sea.

While a variety of laws have begun to constrain maritime conflict in recent times, the fundamental problem remains today as it did in the seventeenth and eighteenth centuries. The effectiveness of legal restraint on naval activity continues to be a balance between strategic and economic interests—how one uses the sea and the practical policies that can be made at any given time.

Whether it be in the eighteenth or in the twentieth century, the major maritime power of the day is concerned when it finds itself confronted by suggestions that could constrain its naval power in a way that gives too great an advantage to a possible opponent. Whether the issue be neutral rights, an extension to territorial waters, seabed ownership, a code of naval warfare or naval disarmament, the fundamental issue is the same. As the U.S. chief of naval operations asked in 1989, "Are we willing to accept altering the traditional tenets of freedom on the high seas, tenets each of us hold so dearly, and is the risk of limiting the naval forces that have served us so well in maintaining the peace for more than 40 years outweighed by what I consider the uncertain possibility of improved international stability?"[63]

It is a difficult, slow, and uneven process to make new constraints for warfare. There are both rapid advances and dramatic reversions in its course. Once nations accept something as a rule or as customary behavior in war at sea there is no guarantee that it will always be a constraint. But if past practice is any guide, there is generally a price to be paid when a belligerent ignores the rules. While navies continue to assert the right of freedom of the seas as the first principle of maritime law, they are also becoming aware that they, too, are restrained by the legal regime of which they are a part.

Adam Roberts   8

Land Warfare: From Hague to Nuremberg

This is an account of a failure—of how some important and apparently successful diplomatic efforts to limit the cruelty and ferocity of war were followed by two world wars. These wars were not only conducted on a vast geographical scale, but there were also hideous excesses in the manner of their conduct, including on land the carnage of trench warfare, the use of gas, the breakdown of the distinction between soldiers and civilians, and extremes of cruelty in occupied territories. Why?

This story of failure begins with the two Hague Peace Conferences, of 1899 and 1907, at each of which a greater number of conventions and declarations on the proper conduct of war were concluded than at any other international conference either before or since. The story ends with the international military tribunals at Nuremberg in 1945–46 and at Tokyo in 1946–48: at these trials, whose legitimacy was hotly contested then as well as later, German and Japanese defendants were charged with a wide range of war crimes, conducted on a huge scale, and the great majority were found guilty.

The central questions addressed here are simple. Why did the laws of war apparently fail so comprehensively? What can be learned about the particular circumstances in which the laws of war can be useful or about the particular aspects of war which they can effectively tackle?

Failures are often more interesting to study than successes. They can show how even the best minds can get things terribly wrong; they can force us to refine our own thinking; and they can help us to get over the weaknesses of past approaches. This has been a century of false hopes, false Messiahs, and false Gods. It has also been a century of total war. Are we to view the laws of war as just one more twentieth-century failure?

Consideration of this question involves a peculiar difficulty which may as well be put bluntly at the outset. The laws of war are strange not only in their subject matter, which to many people seems a contradiction in terms, but also in their methodology. There is little tradition of disciplined and reasoned assessment of how the laws of war have operated in practice. Lawyers, academics, and diplomats have often been better at interpreting the precise legal meaning of existing accords, or at devising new law, than they have been at assessing the performance of existing accords or at generalizing about the circumstances in which they can or cannot work. In short, the study of law needs to be integrated with the study of history: if not, it is inadequate.

One Condemnatory View of the Entire Period

A clear thesis about the events between The Hague and Nuremberg can be found in a curious and in many ways eccentric book entitled *Advance to Barbarism,* published in London in 1948. Its author, F. J. P. Veale, hiding behind the pompous pseudonym of "A Jurist," put forward an argument of seductive simplicity:

> Through the ages, down to 1914, with certain temporary fluctuations, manners generally had become steadily milder and in warfare, in particular, primitive savagery had become gradually modified by an increasing collection of restrictions and restraints. Compliance with these restrictions and restraints is commonly held to mark the distinction between savage and civilized warfare. In savage warfare there are no rules and the enemy may be injured in any way physically possible. In civilized warfare certain restraints have long been recognized with relation to wounded and prisoners while hostilities are directed only against the enemy combatant forces. In this way a code of conduct was gradually established which became formally recognized by all civilized countries.
>
> A history of warfare, written in 1913, would be a simple record of this slow and fluctuating, but on the whole steady, progress.[1]

He went on to ask the obvious question about how such progress had been followed by the terrible calamities of the Second World War, which in turn had been followed by the execution of many of the German military leaders as war criminals. His judgment was particularly bitter, as he was a critic both of the Allied methods of combat in the Second World War and of the Nuremberg tribunal's decision that many of the German military leaders should be executed:

> How has it come about that within three decades it has become an accepted commonplace that the readiest way of winning a war is to ignore altogether the enemy's armed forces and to paralyse the enemy civilian population by devastating and systematic attacks from the air? The fate of Field Marshal von Keitel establishes a precedent which no one can doubt will be faithfully followed in the

case of all future professional soldiers of high rank who find themselves on the losing side.[2]

At this point Veale went so far as to attack the Nuremberg tribunal as itself violating the laws and customs of war:

It has always been considered a great step forward when the custom grew up of not killing prisoners of war but of merely detaining them until the end of hostilities. The killing of Field Marshal von Keitel was not, therefore, an innovation but was in effect a reversion to the original practice.[3]

There is much in Veale's view of the character of the two world wars that verges on the eccentric and should make us cautious of accepting his judgments without questioning them. Thus, he seems in some passages to be claiming that the Europeans had actually managed things in a civilized way in the first year of the war, in 1939–40. The rot, apparently, only really set in with the bombings of 1940, and then with the expansion of the war in 1941 from a European to a world war:

The war of 1940–45 was not conducted in accordance with the code of warfare subject to which for the preceding two centuries Europeans had been accustomed to wage war upon each other. Neither the Americans nor the Eurasians of the Soviet Union had any regard for what Europeans of past generations had been pleased to consider permissible in warfare. Throughout they fought in accord with their own views on this subject.[4]

The year 1940 was indeed the year when intercity bombing really began in earnest. It did so between Britain and Germany in late August.[5] It was on August 24, 1940 that the Luftwaffe dropped some bombs on London apparently by accident. On subsequent nights the Royal Air Force was sent to Berlin to bomb "military" targets. Strategic bombing (often a euphemism for city bombing) gathered momentum in the subsequent months. Veale, in choosing 1940 as his year for descent into barbarism, is saying, as many have said, that it was the use of air war in the Second World War which was the decisive departure from traditional limitations in war; and it was their manner of conducting war from the air which exposed the Allies as no better than the Axis. His nasty reference to the Americans and Eurasians further implies that the entry of the Soviet Union and the United States into the war in 1941 actually made matters worse.

Veale is surely right that air power played a significant part in the decline of the idea of restraint in war in this century. This view is widely shared. However, the particular version of it which Veale put forward, that air power constituted the core and essence of that decline, is far too simple. It is misleading to blame air power exclusively for what was a much larger and more instructive failure than Veale allows; just as it is erroneous to date the decline into barbarism as late as 1940.

The story of the decline of the laws of war begins very much earlier and has much more to do with land war than Veale's book says. Indeed, the idea that there was in the nineteenth century anything remotely like a golden age of the laws of war is historically untenable, and comes particularly ill from a Briton: British forces had deliberately bombarded or destructively raided towns in the United States in 1812–15, and in the Crimea in 1854–55. In the Far East, in Japan and China, the Royal Navy was involved in similar episodes. The laws of war had their value in the nineteenth century as they did later. However, if there was any progress at all in their application, it was halting and unsteady; and their codification, including at The Hague in 1899 and 1907, left many problems unsolved.

The Laws of War: Beginnings of Codification

Where did the laws of war stand on the eve of the First World War? They are an ancient and enduring part of the states system. Two paradoxes, one from the seventeenth century, one from our own times, show just how central their place in international relations is. At the time of the creation of the modern European states system in the seventeenth century, the law of war was actually the first part of international law to be developed in any depth. And now, in the last years of the twentieth century, the treaties which have more states parties to them than any other are the four Geneva Conventions of 1949.[6] Whatever criticism can be leveled at them, the laws of war cannot be dismissed as unimportant.

Up to the mid-nineteenth century the laws of war did exist, but in a form very different from today: in custom, in broad principles, in national laws and military manuals, and in religious teaching. The second half of the nineteenth century was not only an era of great belief in human progress in general, but also, though with less certainty, an era of belief in progress in controlling war. Indeed, that characteristic modern encapsulation of the laws of war—the multilateral treaty setting out principles in this field for states to follow—was only invented in the second half of the nineteenth century.

The passion for codification, which began with the 1856 Paris Declaration on Maritime Law, led to the 1868 Saint Petersburg Declaration, which contains the famous statement of principle, "that the only legitimate object which States should endeavour to accomplish during war is to weaken the military forces of the enemy." On the surface, this phrase appears simple and unexceptionable. Yet it has proved terribly problematical in the twentieth century.

The Hague Conventions of 1899 and 1907

On August 24, 1898, in the famous Imperial Rescript, Czar Nicholas II and the Russian government called for a peace conference. It does not appear that at that time they had in mind the laws of war as a principal subject of the proposed conference. Instead, the Russians—fearful, as so often since, of Western technological advances—wanted to see a general reduction of armaments and the complete avoidance of war. The czar had been influenced by discussions with Jan Bloch, author of *The Future of War,* which viewed recent technical developments with justified pessimism.[7] A key phrase in the Imperial Rescript conveys the sense of the time that there might be a war, that it might get utterly out of hand, and that disarmament was therefore imperative:

> The economic crises, due in great part to the system of armaments *à l'ou-trance,* and the continual danger which lies in this massing of war material, are transforming the armed peace of our days into a crushing burden, which the peoples have more and more difficulty in bearing. It appears evident, then, that if this state of things were prolonged, it would inevitably lead to the very cataclysm which it is desired to avert, and the horrors of which make every thinking man shudder in advance.[8]

Thus the Hague conferences were the result, not so much of blithe optimism, as of a real fear of new weaponry and of total war. That fear was also evident, in a different way, in the belated British response to the 1898 Rescript. Britain was the last of all the invited states to send in its acceptance. The foreign secretary, Lord Salisbury, wrote in terms which show that the British government's preoccupation with deterrence goes back at least to the last years of the nineteenth century. Indeed, his letter contains an interesting early use of the word *deterrent* in its modern meaning:

> There has been a constant tendency on the part of almost every nation to increase its armed force, and to add to an already vast expenditure on the appliances of war. The perfection of the instruments thus brought into use, their extreme costliness, and the horrible carnage and destruction which would ensue from their employment on a large scale, have acted no doubt as a serious deterrent from war. But the burdens imposed by this process on the populations affected must, if prolonged, produce a feeling of unrest and discontent menacing to both internal and external tranquility.[9]

The British, the Americans, and others, themselves sharing at least some of the Russian worry about the shape of a possible future war, pressed the Russian foreign minister to clarify the agenda of the proposed conference. Count Mouravieff replied on January 11, 1899, with a remarkable eight-point list, which showed just how deep was Russia's fear of new military-technological developments. The first item was a freeze on the size of "armed military and naval forces" and on their budgets with a view to subsequent reductions. The next three items were all attempts to stop new technical developments in land, sea, and air war by establishing certain prohibitions on deployment or use. For example, the second item on his list was:

2. To prohibit the use in the armies and fleets of any new kind of fire-arms whatever, and of new explosives, or any powders more powerful than those now in use, either for rifles or cannon. [10]

The more general codification and revision of the laws of war was the subject of items five to seven on his list. At that stage, in the mind of the Russian government, such codification seems to have been less important than the specific limits on armaments proposed in the first four items. Logically, general codification of the laws of war had a place: any prohibitions of the introduction or use in war of certain new weapons would be part of the laws of war, and might tally well with a more general effort at codification. Any such tidy theory, however, falls foul of the fact that at the 1899 Hague Conference, and on a Russian proposal, the question of limiting the use of certain armaments was considered by one body (the First Committee), and the revision of the laws of war by a quite separate one (the Second Committee). This artificial separation led the army member of the U.S. delegation to complain that "it would have appeared more logical" to consider many of the items dealt with by the First Committee as matters relating to the laws and customs of war: but this was not done. [11]

What happened as a result of these uncertain initiatives? In the eyes of the press and public, the 1899 conference was a failure. The 1898 Rescript naturally had been interpreted to mean that the conference thus summoned was a disarmament conference; and it was persistently so called. When it met at The Hague in 1899, the peace conference achieved nothing in the field of disarmament and was thus dismissed as a complete failure by most of the journalists covering it—an early example of the perennially poor coverage of the laws of war in the press. The Russian efforts to stop the manufacture and/or use of new weapons and materials failed almost completely: the Americans, with their love of technology, being particularly happy that they did.

Yet the 1899 Hague Conference did achieve a great deal in a field which had not been mentioned at all in the Rescript, namely, the laws of war. One American member of the conference subsequently went so far as to say that the peace conference accomplished a great and glorious result in "the humanizing of warfare and the codification of the laws of war" as well as in "the establishment of a permanent International Court of Arbitration." [12]

The 1899 conference did produce a Convention on the Law and Customs of War on Land. Although closely modeled on earlier texts, this was the first general codification of laws of land war in the form of a multilateral treaty ever to have been concluded. The conference also produced another Convention on Maritime War, and three prohibitory declarations: on the discharge of explosives from balloons (wonderfully archaic in view of subsequent technical developments), on projectiles diffusing asphyxiating gases, and on expanding dumdum bullets.

There was one inevitable but fateful failure at the 1899 Hague Conference. The legitimacy or otherwise of resistance in occupied territory has always been a very difficult problem in the laws of war. The negotiators at The Hague in 1899, and again in 1907, considered it at great length. Some argued that armed resistance was the inalienable right of the inhabitants of small countries brutally invaded; others that resistance merely prolonged war and confused otherwise clear distinctions between soldiers and civilians. It was disagreement about whether resisters in occupied territory should or should not be viewed as legitimate fighters, entitled to prisoner-of-war status, that led to the adoption of the famous Martens clause in 1899, whose magisterial words concealed the incurably incompatible interests of states:

> Until a more complete code of the laws of war is issued, the high contracting Parties think it right to declare that in cases not included in the Regulations adopted by them, populations and belligerents remain under the protection and empire of the principles of international law, as they result from the usages established between civilized nations, from the laws of humanity, and the requirements of the public conscience. [13]

These inspiring fudge words did not begin to solve the problem of the status of resisters—as subsequent developments, especially in the Second World War, were to comprehensively confirm.

The second Hague Peace Conference, held in 1907, built on the pattern of the first. Once again no general agreement on arms limitation was reached, but the conference, with an enlarged membership, did adopt no less than thirteen conventions, ten of them in the field of the laws of war. Eight of them dealt with one aspect or another of naval war. As to land war, the 1907 Hague Convention IV on the Laws and Customs of War on Land was just a slight revision of its 1899 predecessor; and the 1907 Hague Convention V on the Rights and Duties of Neutral Powers in Case of War on Land, also built, but rather more substantially, on the few provisions on this subject which had been contained in the 1899 Hague land war convention. The 1907 Hague Conference also replaced one declaration which had expired—the 1899 one on balloons.

A third peace conference was due to be held within eight years of the second. It never happened. The First World War had broken out.

Were the Hague peace conferences just an excessively optimistic attempt to make provision for that ultimate oxymoron, a humane war? It is easy to be cynical. However, the ways in which subsequent political and military events overtook them need to be examined before an answer can be attempted.

The results of the Hague conferences as they affected land war were incorporated in many writings, [14] and in military manuals—those crucial documents which provide a link between commitments entered into in international conferences and the actual training and practices of armed forces. [15] The Hague Conventions were to have a significant impact on events, but neither as complete nor as simple as some had hoped.

The First World War

The Great War—the name by which it used to be unwisely known—called into question many, though not all, of the assumptions of the Hague negotiators.

First, the question of neutrality. On August 3, 1914, as the first act of the war in the West, Germany invaded neutral Belgium—this being the easiest way of achieving the strategically important objective of knocking out France so that the German army could devote its attentions to its eastern neighbor. Just a few short years before, Germany had been one of the powers which bound themselves, in the 1907 Hague Convention V on Neutrality in Land War, to the proposition stated simply in its Article 1: "The territory of neutral Powers is inviolable." Here in the very opening phase of the war was a clash between legal principle and realpolitik: the latter won.[16]

The laws of war are problematical here not just for the obvious reason that there were violations, but also because of the belligerent reactions to those violations. In the First World War, perhaps more than in any other, violations of the laws of war were highly publicized in a war of propaganda. In Britain there was a vast literature on German attitudes to the laws of war and on German atrocities in Belgium—an issue which was clearly made to serve the cause of the Entente powers.[17] Thus, it was quickly shown that however much the lawyers may protest that *jus ad bellum* and *jus in bello* are separate subjects, there are in fact numerous and often uncomfortable connections between them: in particular, violations of *jus in bello* by one belligerent can be used by others as a justification for the use of force. Such violations were also used as a justification for expanded war aims—to such an extent that Liddell Hart was to call propaganda about the enemy's misdeeds "an artificial manure for the war effort."[18]

Within not much more than six months of the outbreak of the First World War there was another failure of the laws of war, again one which became a huge anti-German issue: the use in battle of the essentially new weapon of gas. Over 100,000 tons of poison gas were used in battle in the war. It was on April 22, 1915, that the first major gas attack of the war took place, when Germany released gas from several thousand cylinders on a front of six kilometers, quickly opening a gap in the Allied lines. The shock this caused was all the greater because Germany had, since 1900, been party to the 1899 Hague Declaration on Asphyxiating Gases, which had said: "The contracting Powers agree to abstain from the use of projectiles the sole object of which is the diffusion of asphyxiating or deleterious gases." Smart German lawyers could no doubt have argued that the declaration did not cover gas from cylinders, only from shells. Lord Kitchener, among others, attacked the German action as "contrary to the rules and usages of war." Some questioned the terms of this condemnation.[19] The British launched a propaganda campaign against the German use of gas, hoping among other things to influence neutral opinion in the United States. Gas went on to be used by Germany in Poland in May 1915, and then by the Allies at the battle of Loos in September 1915, at which a chemical projectile was used—by the British, and to some effect. Overall, gas was effective locally, but was not a war-winning weapon in the First World War.[20]

There were numerous other failures of the laws of war. At sea, German submarine warfare against merchant ships, and the Allied effort at what amounted to a starvation blockade of Germany and Austria, showed scant regard for traditional distinctions between soldiers and civilians.[21] In the air, bombing from airships and aircraft made its inaccurate and controversial debut in a series of minor operations. Many with direct experience of the war bemoaned what they saw as an almost complete failure of all notions of restraint. Thus, Basil Liddell Hart was later to write:

> The decline of civilized behaviour became steeper during the world-wide war of 1914–18. There was an appalling growth of brutality towards wounded and prisoners; inflated "atrocity" stories in turn produced a tendency to give no quarter; looting became rampant; historic buildings and other treasures of civilization were subject to destruction on the lightest plea of military necessity; and the rules of war designed to protect the civil population were callously violated in many directions. "Hate" propaganda multiplied all these evils.[22]

Liddell Hart's parade of accusations may not be right in every particular. For example, in the First World War the treatment of wounded and sick, and of prisoners, was not uniformly disgraceful. Stanley Spencer's paintings of scenes in the First World War, which are in the Sandham Memorial Chapel at Burghclere near Newbury in England, show the Red Cross emblem made in pebbles on a beach to protect a hospital area from air attack. Such efforts were common in many theaters of war and were judged worth making.

On some issues, a problem in the First World War was not that the law was flouted but that it contained gaps, and there was a lack of precision in certain texts. This was bound to be the case. War always throws up problems which had not been accurately foreseen by governments and their advisers. In respect of the treatment of prisoners of war, some such defects in existing texts were tackled in special agreements made between belligerents in Bern in 1917 and 1918, and after the war were to be put right in a new convention.

Overall, it is hard to resist the conclusion of one of the most detailed studies of the subject, Garner's *International Law and the World War,* that in respect of a wide range of matters "the existing conventions are either silent, inadequate, or out of harmony with present-day conditions. There is hardly one of the Hague conventions that cannot be greatly improved in the light of the experience of the recent war."[23] Yet in the interwar years little was to be done to revise the laws of war. Why was this so?

The First World War's greatest and most difficult challenge to the laws of war was nothing to do with violations, nor to do with reactions to those violations, nor with a lack of precision in existing texts. It lay in the terrible military slaughter caused by great armies engaging in machine-gun, shell, and trench warfare. The biblical text inscribed on the memorial at Hyde Park Corner in London to the men of the Machine Gun Corps who died in 1914–18 is only too apt: "Saul hath slain his thousands, but David his tens of thousands." The bloodstained battlefields of 1914 were very much as anticipated in the dire prophecies of Bloch and others at the time of the Hague conferences—as David Lloyd George said in a memorandum at the end of 1914, mentioning "Bloch's remarkable predictions on this subject."[24]

Ghastly as all this carnage of the land battles was, for the most part it was not contrary to the laws of war. The many legal analyses of the conduct of the belligerents said almost nothing about the horrors of trench warfare: law got separated from some of the real causes of moral concern. The respective armies, shooting at each other with unprecedented efficiency, were not conspicuously violating the central principle of the 1868 Saint Petersburg Declaration—"that the only legitimate object which States should endeavour to accomplish during war is to weaken the military forces of the enemy." On the main fronts at least, the belligerents conducted much of their action in accord with what Veale, in *Advance to Barbarism,* had seen as the heart of Europe's code of restraint right up to 1939:

The fundamental principle of this code was that hostilities between civilized peoples must be limited to the armed forces actually engaged.[25]

The distorted reflection of this principle in the First World War had been that societies had been massively mobilized for war, industry had produced the means of waging war in vast quantity, and the poor conscript soldiers in the front line had been overwhelmingly the targets and victims. This state of affairs did not commend itself to soldiers, lawyers, politicians, or public.

It is little wonder that, after the terrible experience of the First World War, few wanted to hear about existing or new rules to civilize warfare, and millions wanted to see war abolished altogether. Little wonder, too, that those whose job it was to think about future wars were less concerned about violating a body of law which had been consigned to a penumbra than about finding new means to secure decisive results without mutual suicide of armies. Little wonder, too, that some heretics, including Liddell Hart, were unenthusiastic about the prohibition of gas warfare, when it could at least sometimes be less lethal than a war of projectiles and explosives.[26]

There were many other respects in which the First World War called into question the fundamental assumptions of the laws of war. After that cataclysm only a very few exceptionally blinkered inhabitants of Europe could talk with real confidence of the distinction between "civilized" and "barbarian" warfare—a distinction which had been taken for granted in much previous discussion, including at the Hague peace conferences. The Great War had simply been more terrible than any savage or primitive war. The frequent use of the word *barbarian* to describe aspects of the hostilities had a special implication, that Europe was not superior (as it had previously thought) to most of the rest of the world.[27]

After the First World War

After the war, what was done—what could be done—to salvage the idea of limitations in war? Neither the shell-shocked surviving soldiers of the war, nor publics concerned to prevent any recurrence of war whatsoever, were at all anxious to address the task. There were, indeed, few ideas about how it might be achieved.

The ending of the war raised an issue which has been perennially difficult in the laws of war: the punishment of violations. The Hague Conventions had been notably vague on this subject. It is easy to criticize this vagueness as the result of a belief, as touching as it is remarkable, that somehow even in the thick of war international law could be self-operating in much the way that Jeremy Bentham had envisaged. A scrutiny of all the Hague Conventions yields a few scattered references to a state's responsibility for its armed forces, and the payment of compensation for violations. The main provision is in Article 3 of the 1907 Hague Convention IV on land war. (Remarkably, there had been nothing equivalent even to this modest provision in the 1899 convention.) Article 3 says:

A belligerent party which violates the provisions of the said Regulations shall, if the case demands, be liable to pay compensation. It shall be responsible for all acts committed by persons forming part of its armed forces.

The language is of course astonishingly vague. The words "if the case demands" give no hint as to what state or body can request, let alone enforce, the payment of compensation.

After the war, in the Treaty of Versailles of 1919, an attempt was made to solve this problem. Articles 227 to 230 of the Treaty of Versailles required Germany to surrender for trial members of its armed forces charged with violations of the laws of war. Subsequently, by arrangement with the Allied governments, Germany itself tried German offenders on charges formulated by the Allies, but very few were convicted.[28] It is easy with the wisdom of hindsight to scorn this halting and ineffectual procedure against offenders in a state which was defeated in war but not wholly conquered: but if we look at Iraq today and the conspicuous silence of the coalition powers on the question of Iraqi war crimes, have we made much progress on this issue?

In the interwar years there was no serious push to get nonparties to adhere to the existing pre-1914 conventions on the laws of war, and very few did so.[29] Nor was there any serious effort to get a new codification of the laws of war along the lines of what had been done at The Hague in 1899 and 1907. Efforts in this field were dispersed and spasmodic. However, a few formally binding treaties were concluded.

First, there was the 1925 Geneva Protocol on gas and bacteriological warfare. Like the Hague accords, it was the dubious and disappointing offspring of a conference which was intended to make much more dramatic inroads into the armaments problem than a mere prohibition on use. The conference from which it came had the ambitious title International Conference on the Control of the International Trade in Arms, Munitions, and Implements of War. The Geneva Protocol which eventually emerged is a classic laws of war accord in that it deals with prohibitions on use of certain types of weapon but not with prohibitions on possession. This has led to much criticism. However, the notorious difficulty of securing and monitoring chemical disarmament—a difficulty which is only too evident at the present time—meant that there was value, perhaps even wisdom, in having a freestanding prohibition on use.

The 1925 Geneva Protocol is often seen as a useless product of a reluctance to think seriously about the role of force in international relations—a reluctance which was indeed marked in the League of Nations period. Yet there is one interesting respect in which this prohibition of gas warfare, in the form in which it eventually came into force, was hardheaded. France, which was the depositary power for the Protocol, on ratifying it in 1926 made a reservation as follows:

> 1. The said Protocol is only binding on the Government of the French Republic as regards States which have signed or ratified it or which may accede to it.
>
> 2. The said Protocol shall *ipso facto* cease to be binding on the Government of the French Republic in regard to any enemy State whose armed forces or whose Allies fail to respect the prohibitions laid down in the Protocol.[30]

In ratifying the Geneva Gas Protocol in subsequent years, many other states—including the Soviet Union, Great Britain, the Netherlands, and Czechoslovakia—made virtually identical reservations. This meant that for many states the Protocol had the explicit character of being a limited no-first-use agreement, which could be (and later was) backed up by threats of retaliation if its terms were violated. In short, there was an element of intrawar deterrence in the Protocol.

The years between the two world wars saw few other accords. Much the most important were two Red Cross conventions concluded in 1929: the first on wounded and sick in land war; the second on prisoners of war. These enlarged on the provisions of earlier agreements: the 1906 Geneva Convention on Wounded and Sick, and that part of the 1907 Hague Regulations which dealt with treatment of prisoners of war. In both cases the new agreements were drawn up in order to overcome what were seen as defects in the law as it had applied in the First World War. For example, the 1929 Geneva Prisoners Convention introduced a prohibition of reprisals and collective penalties against prisoners, and spelled out in some detail the role of Protecting Powers in helping protect prisoners' interests.

Two major states never became parties to the 1929 Prisoners of War Convention: Japan and the Soviet Union. This was to have fateful consequences in the Second World War. In both countries there is an ancient tradition of viewing it as a matter of deep disgrace that a soldier should be taken prisoner. This is almost the opposite of a strand in American thinking, which sees the prisoner of war as hero. Such cultural attitudes are often more powerful than the texts of international agreements.

Other agreements in the interwar years were of less relevance to land war and in any case proved to be more fragile. Both in the 1920s and the 1930s unsuccessful efforts were made to get agreements restricting bombing from the air. In the 1930s agreements were reached trying to prohibit or limit attacks by submarines upon merchant ships, but they proved ineffectual in practice.

Throughout the interwar years in most European countries the intellectual climate was shaped by the fear that any future war would inevitably be worse than the First World War. The conclusion of an Inter-Parliamentary Union Enquiry in 1931 was typical of the times: "The real policy of peace should tend to prevent war, not to humanise it."[31] Fewer argued that war was inevitable but could be limited.[32] The prevailing view, emphasizing the complete prevention of war, is easily dismissed as idealism shown to have been absurd by the Second World War; note, however, that the theorists of nuclear deterrence in the post-1945 period have taken the same line, that war should be prevented not humanized.

The Second World War

The Second World War began in 1939 against a background of distinctly limited interest in the laws of war. At The Hague forty years earlier the focus had been on universal accords on the humanizing of war: in 1938–39 there were merely some limited attempts at deals between the future belligerents to avoid the worst excesses of mutual destruction, mainly as regards the use of gas and the bombing of cities.

The nonuse of gas in land war in the Second World War can be seen as one worthwhile success for the laws of war. True, Japan (which had never ratified the Geneva Protocol) used gas in China between 1937 and 1945; and in trials after the war, including some in the Soviet Union, Japanese officers were held responsible for this. At the outbreak of the war, several states, including Germany, declared that they would observe the prohibitions embodied in the 1925 Geneva Protocol, subject to reciprocity. Britain and France did so in proper legal form. Hitler said in a speech to the Reichstag: "Whoever fights with poison gas will be fought with poison gas. Whoever departs from the rules of humane warfare can only expect that we shall do the same."[33] This can be interpreted, more charitably than perhaps it deserves, as a grudging no-first-use statement. Although at the outbreak of the war in 1939 none of the powers was well equipped for offensive gas operations, the situation was far from static. New capabilities, and new and much more lethal gases, were developed. Moreover, situations arose or threatened to arise where the temptation to use gas was very strong. On June 15, 1940, in the wake of the evacuation of British forces from Dunkirk, Sir John Dill, the Chief of the Imperial General Staff, wrote as follows:

> At a time when our National existence is at stake when we are threatened by an implacable enemy who himself recognises no rules save those of expediency, we should not hesitate to adopt whatever means appear to offer the best chance of success.[34]

Preparations for possible use of gas against invasion went ahead, but no final decision was ever reached to use gas if Britain were invaded. On June 30, 1940, Churchill indicated that any such decision would have to be made by the cabinet.[35] However, it is abundantly clear from the military and cabinet memoranda on this issue that the illegality of first use of gas or chemical weapons was only one consideration; and that strategic arguments of various kinds as well as more general notions of honor loomed large. One could even conclude that Britain was deterred from making a conditional decision to use chemical weapons by the knowledge that Germany had large stocks and could retaliate in kind. As the war went on, the Allies increasingly used deterrent statements, and inspired leaks about new and more lethal gases, to discourage German, Italian, and Japanese use of gas in international military operations. To buttress this deterrent policy, production of chemical weapons was increased, especially in the United States.

By 1944 the problem had changed again. Churchill was actively considering the use of gas against Germany. He said to the Chiefs of Staff:

> I may certainly have to ask you to support me in using poison gas. We could drench the cities of the Ruhr and many other cities in Germany in such a way that most of the population would be requiring constant medical attention. We could stop all work at the flying bomb starting points. I do not see why we should always have all the disadvantages of being the gentleman while they have all the advantages of being the cad.[36]

Spiers's conclusion on the reasons for nonuse of gas in the Second World War is clear, and sobering:

For all belligerents, save the United States, the threat of counter-city retaliation was the most powerful deterrent to gas warfare. It reflected a peculiar combination of fears and assumptions—misperceptions about enemy gas potential,
inferences about possible enemy intentions derived from capabilities, and a conviction that any enemy, if attacked with gas, would retaliate in kind on a massive
scale.[37]

One other factor may have contributed something to the nonuse of gas in hostilities in the Second World War: the fact that it was not seen as a normal weapon, which
troops on either side had at hand and would expect to use in the ordinary course of
combat. There was a sense on both sides that its use in war required a political
decision at the highest level.

Thus the nonuse of gas in hostilities was certainly not due to the laws of war alone.
Intrawar deterrence was more important than legal commitments. If the laws of war
and in particular the 1925 Geneva Protocol had any part at all in the outcome, it was
by helping to keep gas in a special mental and operational category, and away from
the line of battle—and in providing one basis for declarations about reprisals in the
event that the adversary used gas. Here, then, is one respect in which the laws of war
and deterrence should not be seen as opposites.

For soldiers fighting on land, especially on the western fronts, the Second World
War was far less destructive than the first. The lists of names on war memorials in
England, the United States, and many other countries are far shorter for 1939–45 than
they were for 1914–18. This fact was not due to the laws of war, but rather to
developments in military technology (especially the tank) and strategy (the blitzkrieg
and its variants) which tended to favor decisive action rather than a war of attrition; it
was also due to the caution of the British and American governments, which were
reluctant to open up a front in France until it had a reasonable prospect of success.

As to soldiers, sailors, and airmen who were taken prisoner in the Second World
War, the rules were still widely observed but with two huge exceptions. The first
exception was Japan, which had not ratified the 1929 Convention and which treated
its prisoners appallingly, as the evidence at many postwar trials was to confirm.[38] The
second major exception was Germany in its treatment of Soviet prisoners. Hitler,
with his racist contempt for Slavs, used the Soviet Union's nonadherence to the 1929
Geneva Prisoners of War Convention as his thin excuse to ignore its provisions.
During the war the Soviet Union, while professing adherence to the Hague Regulations, never completely abandoned its view that soldiers who fell into enemy hands
were traitors who deserved no protection from their government, and it refused to
cooperate with the International Red Cross about prisoners.[39] Several millions of
Soviet prisoners died in German hands.[40]

One more issue about prisoners arose in, or rather at the end of, the Second World

War—and one which illustrates the difficulties of legislating for something as un-predictable as war. Hitherto, it had been assumed that at the end of a war all prisoners were simply repatriated. In the words of the 1907 Hague Regulations, Article 20: "After the conclusion of peace, the repatriation of prisoners shall be carried out as quickly as possible." There were similar provisions for repatriation in the 1929 Geneva Convention on Prisoners of War, Article 75. Yet in 1945 in Europe a problem arose which was to recur in subsequent wars from Korea to Kuwait: there were large numbers of prisoners who had excellent reason to fear that if they were repatriated to their own country, they would be persecuted or executed. Huge numbers were repatri-ated against their will to the Soviet Union and to Yugoslavia. Only in a few cases did humane Allied officers turn a blind eye and let them escape. The episode is a terrible blot on the Allied war record, and also reflects badly on the laws of war, which had been too rigid on this point. Only slowly, by changes in custom rather than in treaty law, has it begun to be accepted internationally that repatriation should not be forc-ible.[41]

Apart from these terrible disasters over prisoners, the worst outrages of the Second World War arose, not in relation to regular soldiers, but in relation to civilians: civilians in cities that were bombed, in cities that were besieged, and in occupied territories.

It is easy to condemn this involvement of civilians. Yet those fighting the Second World War on all sides were driven to this by an understandable desire to avoid the disasters of 1914–18. The Allied leaders, for example, did not wish to risk their troops in land war in Europe till they were certain they could prevail. Hence, Chur-chill and others placed great reliance on three methods of grinding the enemy down before any land assault: bombing, blockade, and resistance movements in occupied countries. All three methods put civilians in the front line; all three involved breaking down the distinction between soldiers and civilians which is at the heart of the laws of war. Yet such approaches originated from a serious moral as well as strategic purpose.

A good deal of the city bombing in the Second World War on both sides was plainly violative of existing standards; and in many cases it was not only of doubtful legality but also doubtful effectiveness. These aspects were perhaps most evident in the V-2 rocket raids on London which began on September 8, 1944. Being a grossly inaccurate weapon, the V-2 could only be used against cities—like its descendant, the extended-range Scud missile used by Iraq in 1991. In one of those grim ironies which seem to plague the history of international relations, Germany established the launching sites for the V-2s near The Hague:[42] the very city associated with the 1899 and 1907 agreements seeking to humanize war, and where the abortive 1923 Hague Air Rules had been negotiated.

If much of the city bombing was actually less effective than that aimed more precisely at military targets, the bombing of Hiroshima probably did hasten the end of the war. The justification that is constantly made for it, that it saved lives that would have been lost in any sea-land campaign to invade Japan, is a sad commentary on how strong remained the fear of an utterly destructive land war.

One of the most destructive aspects of hostilities, whether ancient or modern, is siege warfare. It is a part of war which largely escaped attempts to create specific written laws of war limitations until 1977.[43] The most terrible siege of the Second World War was that of Leningrad, whose heroism in the face of disaster engraves its name permanently in the history of war, even if that city's inhabitants have now, very understandably, elected to rename it Saint Petersburg. Here again was a grim irony. In the very city where in 1868 a declaration had been concluded "that the only legitimate object which States should endeavour to accomplish during war is to weaken the military forces of the enemy," over one million people died from the effects of the siege.[44] This was more than in all the modern infernos put together: more than the combined total of deaths in Coventry, Dresden, Hamburg, Tokyo, Hiroshima, and Nagasaki.

It was in occupied territories, especially German-held lands in the East, that some of the worst crimes against humanity occurred. When Hitler invaded Poland in September 1939 he gave the ominous instruction: "*Polen soll wie eine Kolonie behandelt werden.*"[45] The following month he and von Keitel, the Wehrmacht Chief of Staff, developed a plan for the administration of Poland which included the words:

> The administration has to work on its own responsibility and must not be dependent on Berlin. We do not want to do there what we do in the Reich. The responsibility does not rest with the Berlin ministries, since there is no German administration unit concerned.
>
> The accomplishment of this task will involve a hard racial struggle which will not allow any legal restrictions. The methods will be incompatible with the principles otherwise adhered to by us.[46]

This meant that the inhabitants of Poland (and the same would be true later of Russia) were not to be treated by the normal standards prevailing between civilized states. So it proved in practice. Some German acts, especially in the East, were unconscionable by any legal or human standard: the mass slaughter of Jews and gypsies, and of Soviet prisoners, being the most extreme examples. Much of this development had little to do with new technologies or methods of war: railways, barbed wire, and new gases played their part, but extermination was driven more by ideology and by an extreme revival of ancient hatreds than by any technological imperative.

In some occupied territories, from France in the West to the Soviet Union in the East, hideous cruelties were in part the German response to the acts of resistance movements. From the start, the Axis occupying authorities played up the threat posed by clandestine acts of armed resistance. They not only treated as outlaws those suspected of involvement, but also cruelly punished the inhabitants of any area where "outrages" had occurred. In the Warsaw uprising of August 1 to October 2, 1944, over 200,000 inhabitants were killed, of whom probably less than 20,000 were armed insurgents.[47] Such extremes of repression went well beyond anything that was permissible in the laws of war, and were later to be condemned in various trials at Nuremberg: but it could not be claimed that there was a clear, precise, and effective body of law relating to the problem of resistance in occupied territories. The position in international law of guerrilla forces opposing foreign occupations was uncertain.[48] There were no clear legal distinctions between different forms of resistance, violent and nonviolent. Indeed, to the extent (which was always debatable) that the laws of war had been considered as imposing on the inhabitants of occupied territories a duty of obedience to the occupier, they may have done positive harm to the inhabitants' position.[49]

Much that happened in Germany and its occupied territories raised an awkward question about the laws of war: on a strict legal interpretation, it could be asked whether these laws were applicable at all to some of the most serious atrocities. Some crimes, such as the treatment of Jews in Germany, were not covered by the laws of war because they involved the relations of a government with its own citizens, not those of the adversary. Some crimes occurred before September 1939, in what might be viewed as peacetime. Some countries, like Czechoslovakia, were occupied without any actual war. And finally, when there was an undoubted war, it was one in which some of the participants were not formal parties to the Hague Conventions, whose "general participation clause," read literally, said that the rules "do not apply except between contracting Powers, and then only if all the belligerents are parties to the Convention."[50] In short, along with vast human tragedies there was a muddle concerning the applicability of the law—a muddle of the kind which the conjunction between tidy legal categories and messy human realities often throws up. This raised further questions: were the laws of war broad enough, both in their provisions and in their scope of application, to encompass the range of problems produced by human conflict? Did they need to be supplemented by some new body of law?

The International Military Tribunals

Against the background of general muddle and failure, how can one justify the huge trial of major German war criminals at Nuremberg in 1945–46, at which nineteen of the twenty-two defendants were found guilty? And indeed the other trials of Axis defendants which took place in Nuremberg and elsewhere? These trials are sometimes accused of applying a body of law which had not up to that point been clear or fully applicable to the events under scrutiny; and they are often criticized as constituting nothing more than victor's justice. Are these complaints fair?

The charter of the Nuremberg tribunal, concluded by the Allies on August 8, 1945, got over part of the problem of the applicability of the law by inventing a new category of offense, crimes against humanity, which could take place before or during the war, and could apply to a government's offenses against its own citizens. This, like the simultaneous development of human rights law in the Charter of the United Nations, can be seen as creative law making. It is true that existing international law, developed at The Hague and elsewhere, contained gaps which, unless plugged in this convenient way, would have meant that important aspects of Axis atrocities could not be considered at Nuremberg. Yet the 1899 and 1907 Hague Conventions had foreshadowed such a solution to this problem by the inclusion of the Martens clause, cited above, which had clearly said that in cases not included in the regulations, the laws of humanity remain a source of law of key importance.

The judgment of the trial, delivered on September 30 and October 1, 1946, added to the Nuremberg Charter in asserting, in one further and important way, the universality of existing law. It said that the 1907 Hague Convention IV applied anyway to all countries because it was customary law. The exact words of the judgment on this point were:

> The rules of land warfare expressed in the convention undoubtedly represented an advance over existing international law at the time of their adoption. But the convention expressly stated that it was an attempt "to revise the general laws and customs of war," which it thus recognized to be then existing, but by 1939 these rules laid down in the convention were recognized by all civilized nations, and were regarded as being declaratory of the laws and customs of war which are referred to in Article 6(b) of the Charter.[51]

In one sense, this is like the passage in the script of a speech which Winston Churchill is said to have annotated with the marginal comment: "Argument weak here: shout." The claim that the Hague Regulations had achieved universal recognition by 1939 from that doubtful category of countries, all civilized nations, was questionable. Yet the passage is significant and even justifiable. With this statement, as with some other parts of the judgment, the judges from the victor powers were saying that irrespective of the adherence or otherwise of states to particular accords, irrespective of the legal niceties and the small print, there had to be some minimal universal standards.

In this and other ways, Nuremberg provides a curious counterpoint to The Hague. When they met in 1899, governments were confident that they represented civilized values and could be trusted to uphold them through voluntarily entering into legal accords. Now, less than half a century later, governments were being told (admittedly by other governments) that there are certain universal human standards that apply irrespective of whether they have acceded to a particular treaty. Further, the central role of governments was significantly tempered by the idea of personal responsibility: that superior orders are not a defense against a charge of war criminality. In short, the old society of states was having to yield, however slowly, to a society where governments were subject to certain overarching principles and could not order their citizens, even their officers, around just as they wished. Modern ideas of legal positivism, based on treaty law alone, were subtly yielding to older ideas of natural law.

On the basis of asserting the universality of standards which had not been quite universally accepted, were the Nuremberg and Tokyo tribunals justified in finding the great majority of their defendants guilty? It is easy—and it was well done by the defense lawyers at the trials—to point out that there had been terrible deeds on both sides in the war, and that in some areas, such as submarine warfare and city bombing, the Allies, just as much as the Axis powers, had ignored existing treaties and legal principles. However, there was one major category of crime in respect of which there was little comparison between the Allies and the Axis powers, and it was this category which, in the end, formed the basis for the conviction of most of the major war criminals. It concerned not combat, but treatment of those more or less *hors de combat*. The Axis atrocities against many of those who were directly under their control—whether Jews, prisoners of war, or inhabitants of occupied territories— formed the one really strong ground for conviction. It cannot have been wrong to punish these clear violations of the most elementary principles of decency, which in most cases were also contrary to the Geneva prisoners of war convention and the Hague land war convention. Thus, the convictions in the Nuremberg and Tokyo trials were in the end not so much about the initiation or conduct of military hostilities as about the treatment of largely defenseless people in the hands of the adversary. This crucial point was missed by Veale in *Advance to Barbarism,* just as it has been missed by many later critics of the Nuremberg trials.

The Laws of War in Two World Wars

How, then, is one to evaluate the performance of the laws of war in the half century from The Hague to Nuremberg? Clearly, the record of this first effort at internationally codified laws of war has to be viewed critically, and probably in the end judged harshly.

The laws of war should not be dismissed out of hand just because so many aspects of the two world wars were so terrible. Geoffrey Best has said of the period encompassing both world wars:

the circumstances most advantageous to observance of the law were when armies of not dissimilar race, religion and general ethical notions (i.e. armies able to recognize in their foes 'people of their own kind'), their minds unclouded by the grosser sorts of propaganda, and under the command ultimately of officers trained in the classic European or Europe-originated tradition, faced and fought each other in ways old-established enough to have accumulated a solid wrapping of law and custom. Much of the fighting on the European western front(s) in both world wars and much of the fighting at sea was of this kind. Deeds of chivalry and simple humanity continued to be met with, even when they might seem inconsistent with the political or other principles of the men evincing them. The Red Cross sign was generally respected in the ways due to it; quarter was usually given to soldiers who sought it in circumstances that did not make it impossible; prisoner of war camps varied in quality . . . but on the whole did not disgrace the governments responsible for them; . . .[52]

This is a justified conclusion. Yet it is possible to exaggerate the significance of the point about similar race, religion, and ethical notions. We know from civil wars—often the bloodiest and bitterest kind of war—that similarity of race or other factors do not necessarily lead to the acceptance of rules of restraint.

A second conclusion is suggested by the experience of twentieth-century warfare: the importance of the distinction between rules limiting actual combat and rules concerned with control of those within one's power—whether prisoners or civilians in occupied territory. In general, these latter rules are easier to implement. However, they were massively violated in the Second World War—and in such a way as to suggest that some belligerents had a dismissive view of the law as such.

A third conclusion is that the distinction between soldier and civilian, though crucial, is also tenuous. The crimes committed against civilians, especially in the Second World War, led Geoffrey Best to conclude a survey of restraints on war by land before 1945 with the question: "Has the civilian, as liberal Europe used to know him, become extinct?"[53]

Is more law the answer? Often when barbarism occurs in war there is a tendency to blame it on the insufficiency of detailed rules. Certainly in the two world wars the existing rules regarding the protection of civilians against the effects of hostilities were inadequate. However, it may be doubted whether the weakness of the formal rules was a principal cause of barbarism: deeper factors were involved, as is suggested by the dismal fact that certain clear and well-established rules were broken or circumvented.

Yet the idea that certain classes of people are entitled to a degree of protection and that this should be codified has refused to die. This was confirmed by the adoption of four new Geneva Conventions in 1949. These focused entirely on the protection of victims of war and not to any significant extent with limitations on weaponry or fighting. One may view all this as diplomats legislating for the last war, just as soldiers fight the last war: but it was necessary nonetheless. It was also a deeply ironic end to the process begun with the Imperial Rescript fifty-one years earlier, in which the control or elimination of certain weapons, or at least prohibitions on their use, had been the central question. Now it was largely abandoned, and the focus of the laws of war had become the protection of certain categories of people.

Where many at The Hague had been right was in the fear, expressed most clearly in Bloch's book, that war might happen; that it might be total; and that technology had put into the hands of man previously unimagined powers of destruction. Where they were too optimistic was in thinking that a formalized system of rules could either describe or circumscribe the actions of states each of which saw its interests differently and acted differently; or could cover the extraordinary range of situations which was to be thrown up by twentieth-century warfare.

The experience of land war in two world wars must raise a question as to whether formal legal codification is necessarily superior to the notions of custom, honor, professional standards, and natural law which preceded it. Codification in treaty form has such compelling virtues—verbal clarity, equal standards, the securing of formal acceptance by states—that it is bound to remain a central aspect of the laws of war. On the other hand, it risks being too rigid in face of changing situations and technologies; and it can make rules seem like artificial external impositions, rather than a natural outgrowth of the interests and experiences of a state and its armed forces.

Although the codification of the laws of war preceded the two world wars, it did not cause them; nor, on the whole, did it make them worse. There were, however, respects in which the laws of war may have contributed to tragedy. It is often said that one of the law's underlying purposes is facilitating future reconciliation between belligerents: if the conduct of a war is tempered by at least some codes of conduct, then there is less bitterness, and it may be easier to secure and maintain a peace between former enemies. To the extent that real or supposed violations led to bitterness and the desire for recrimination, as they did in the First World War, the laws of war failed in this purpose. At the end of the Second World War, reconciliation with Germany and Japan was achieved—but this owed more to fortunate circumstances, to prudent policy making, and to a general spirit of moderation after victory than to any specific legacy of the laws of war.

It is sometimes said that it is the losing side that resorts to violations of the laws of war. Such a view, though it has a grain of truth, is too simple. In two world wars violations occurred very early in hostilities and sometimes at least against a background of confidence in the final outcome. It may be nearer the mark to say that states which massively violate the laws of war risk seriously alienating international opinion and thus, as coalitions against them gain strength, become losers. However, that is hardly a universal truth, and the eventual victors in two world wars were not themselves innocent of violations.[54]

The real causes of the revival of barbarism in the two world wars went much deeper than the laws of war and usually proved more powerful. They lay in a combination of factors:

1. The opposition to liberal ideas of several early twentieth-century autocracies, and their positive belief in force.
2. The general body of ideas known as Social Darwinism, especially in its peculiar and virulent forms which saw races, nations, and/or classes as species; believed in the inevitability of violent struggle for supremacy between them; and saw that struggle as of cosmic historical importance.
3. Theories of war, derived from a shallow reading of Clausewitz, which saw battle and total war as being the essence of strategy.
4. The development of conscription and of machinery for moving conscripts, which created a new momentum toward total war.
5. The development through the industrial revolution of a complex division of labor within and between countries, which made it hard to maintain a clear distinction between soldier and civilian, or between a neutral and a belligerent power.
6. The growth of a popular press in many countries which was virulently nationalistic.
7. The emergence of new weapons—machine gun, long-range artillery, aircraft, submarine—which took war to new environments, which increased man's capacity for destruction, and which in some cases facilitated the posing of threats, not just to the adversary's front line, but to its society as a whole, including its cities and civilians.

New weaponry is listed last because it has perhaps been overrated as a cause of barbarism in two world wars. Land war in the Second World War, more technically advanced than in the first, was actually less catastrophic; and its worst excesses, whether in the siege of Leningrad or in occupied Yugoslavia, owed little to technology. In most cases the factors leading to extremes of violence and cruelty lay deeper: but they are not necessarily permanent. In particular, intolerant ideological worldviews, so prevalent for much of this century, are not necessarily a permanent feature of the human condition.

Following the Hague Conventions of 1899 and 1907, there was indeed an advance to barbarism in two world wars in this century. This is a sad conclusion for any who believe that treaty law alone can civilize or limit warfare. It suggests that much else is involved in the limitation of war. The advance to barbarism was not as technically driven as some of the simpler theories suggest, and had far more aspects.

Moreover, the customs and laws of war—though failing, in an all too instructive manner, to achieve what had been hoped for at The Hague—did not emerge entirely discredited. For all their limitations, they were strong enough to provide the basis for charges at Nuremberg and Tokyo; for the emergence of the four 1949 Geneva Conventions, which have secured the formal adherence of more states than any other treaties; and for the improbable and imperfect survival of laws of war ideas even in the post-1945 era of deterrence.

Tami Davis
Biddle

9
Air Power

The term *air power* refers to a type of military capability, but it also refers to an idea. The most dramatic manifestation of that idea, and the one with the greatest consequences for the law of war, is aerial bombing. The history of aerial bombing is an intricate and fascinating one, as it taps into something deep in the human psyche. For centuries men dreamed of mastering the skies. When that goal finally came to fruition it brought with it a sense of profound revolution which resonated strongly in the realm of military affairs. The sense of excitement generated by air power was accompanied by a sense of awe and foreboding. Technology had created the means for taking warfare to homelands in a more direct and frightening way than ever before. The revolution promised by bomber aircraft raised special problems for those who wished to confine the ravages of war through legal means. In particular it would create a host of thorny dilemmas for the general principle of discrimination, that is, the attempt to distinguish between combatants and noncombatants.

Some of these problems already were on the horizon by the time of the first Hague Conference of 1899, and they continue to plague us today. They reached a tangled and tragic crisis point during World War II when the means for massive bombing campaigns existed, but the means for making those campaigns discriminate did not.[1] Prior to the war, attempts to provide for discrimination through legal codification were not successful. Both the terms and the authority of those efforts were the subject of much debate and confusion. International legal efforts to clarify phrases such as "military objective" and "military necessity" were not successful, as individual states ultimately preferred to define them by themselves. This collective rejection arose out of a combination of fear, political mistrust, pessimism about the law of war in general, and the allure of the bomber airplane.

The experience of World War II showed that more discriminate forms of air warfare were the most militarily efficient. Since World War II a customary standard has gradually emerged which reflects, in a general way, world opinion on the issue of aerial bombardment and the law of war. Though this standard is not without its own problems, it represents an improvement over the chaos of the pre–World War II period. Moreover, it may be that in future warfare, ethics and efficiency will converge in the form of more accurate bombing technology—certainly the experience of Desert Storm suggests this. This serendipitous coincidence may help to bolster the prospects for adherence to international norms.

The Hague Conference of 1899

In the final year of the nineteenth century the Russians proposed the convening of an international conference to address issues relating to disarmament, the regulation of modern methods of war, and the arbitration of international disputes. Two things about the resulting 1899 Hague Conference are important with respect to air power. First, Commission I of the conference placed a five-year moratorium on the launching of projectiles and/or explosives from the air. Given the technology of the time, that meant from balloons. Projectiles dropped in this manner had not proven very effective, which is a key reason why the prohibition was enacted. The time limit of five years was suggested by an American delegate, Captain William Crozier, who argued that since balloon bombing was both indiscriminate and ineffective, it ought to be prohibited. He argued as well, however, that since such bombing might one day become an effective battlefield tool—capable of making war more decisive and shorter—the prohibition should not be permanent.[2]

Second, Commission II of the conference—which was assigned responsibility for codifying the law of war—produced Convention II with Respect to the Laws and Customs of War on Land. Several articles in the Convention II Annex had relevance for air power, including:

Article 25: The attack or bombardment of towns, villages, habitations or buildings which are not defended is prohibited.

Article 26: The commander of an attacking force, before commencing a bombardment, except in the case of an assault, should do all he can to warn the authorities.

Article 27: In sieges and bombardments, all necessary steps should be taken to spare as far as possible edifices devoted to religion, art, science and charity, hospitals, and places where the sick and wounded are collected, provided they are not used at the same time for military purposes. The besieged should indicate these buildings or places by some particular and visible signs, which should previously be notified to the assailants.[3]

The three articles offer general guidance requiring interpretation by those trying to implement it. The term *defended* (with respect to towns, villages, and habitations and buildings) was not defined, and the failure to come to grips with it would lead to subsequent confusion and misunderstanding. Delegates to the conference were cautious, and careful not to give away any advantages for themselves or to enable potential adversaries to gain an advantage. Even though the conference represented progress, it was a disappointment to the international public which held high hopes for genuine movement toward disarmament.

The Hague Conference of 1907

The second Hague Peace Conference was held in the summer of 1907. Delayed by the Russo-Japanese War, it was begun in a climate of more modest expectation. Germany was not in the mood for disarmament talks, and neither was Russia, concerned as it was to rebuild its status and military might after the embarrassing war it had just concluded. Britain's Liberal government was in favor of disarmament talks, but was not able to impose this attitude on the assembled states as a whole. The limiting of arms, which had been formally declared as the chief motive for the first conference, was not even included in the program for the second.[4]

It was in this inauspicious atmosphere that the balloon declaration was brought up for renewal. Further complicating this issue was the development of the zeppelin and the airplane. Air strength at home determined the stand taken by national delegates to aerial issues raised at the conference. States such as Germany, France, and Italy, which had ongoing aerial programs, were largely opposed to any continuing limitation on aerial bombardment. Britain, which lagged behind and saw air power as a threat to its shores and its naval supremacy, was in favor of the idea. The United States, with its geographic isolation, took a less than whole-hearted interest in the topic.[5] All of this meant that commitment to a meaningful continuation of the 1899 prohibition was lacking, and therefore nothing of legal significance came out of the conference on this point.

What did emerge, however, was a slight modification of the law of war on land, and the codification of a set of laws pertaining to naval forces. In recognition of new and potential aerial technologies, article 25 of the 1899 Land Warfare Convention was amended to read: "The attack or bombardment, *by whatever means,* of towns, villages, dwellings or buildings which are undefended is prohibited." Minor changes of language in the 26th and 27th articles did not alter their substance, and none of these changes brought greater clarity or force to the law.

Interestingly, however, the conference's Ninth Convention, Concerning Bombardment by Naval Forces in Time of War, was more precise than the Land Warfare Convention on the issue of bombardment. While the two conventions were not intended to conflict, in certain cases the material contained in them was not consistent. Article 2 of the Naval Convention identified particular military objects that were to be considered lawful targets for bombardment, including "military works, military or naval establishments, depots of arms or war materiel, workshops or plants which could be utilized for the needs of the hostile fleet or army, and the ships of war in the harbor."[6] Implied in this list is the notion that lawful targets can include industrial installations of value to the enemy war effort. The Naval Convention acknowledged that bombing was related to the military significance of the target rather than whether the city or town in which the target was located was defended, and it conferred permission to attack legitimate military targets wherever located.

Article 2 also made clear that commanders could not be responsible for "any unavoidable damage which may be caused by a bombardment." In this the framers of the article codified what had long been customary practice in warfare. Civilian casualties during a siege, for instance, were regarded as a burden upon the besieged commander—an inducement to end the siege. Collateral damage and resulting noncombatant casualties were considered part of the cost of warfare. The Lieber instructions, written to guide soldiers of the Union Army during the American Civil War, stated: "Military necessity admits of all direct destruction of life or limb of armed enemies, and of other persons whose destruction is incidentally unavoidable in the armed contests of the war."[7]

Regardless of what may have caused the difference between the Land and Naval Conventions, the existence of two sets of rules caused confusion and occasionally led to the assumption that naval forces had greater latitude in the execution of attacks than ground forces. As mentioned above, the focus of much misunderstanding was the troublesome term *undefended town*. It stemmed from a tradition in the law of war that sought to prohibit the attack of those places which could be easily occupied by an army or navy without the necessity of a resort to overwhelming military force. But specifying what places might now qualify proved confusing, especially as the criteria for legitimate targets were changing as the nature of warfare changed in the face of large-scale industrialization and mobilization. The Naval Convention accommodated this explicitly in Article 2, but the Land Warfare Convention did not. It is important to note, however, that in 1899 a German delegate to the conference, Colonel Gross von Schwarzhoff, stated that the prohibition in article 25 ought not to be interpreted so as to prohibit the destruction of any buildings whatever, and by no means when military operations rendered it necessary. His clarification, which met with no opposition from the subcommission and was noted in the subcommission's report of July 5, 1899, revealed the intentions of the drafters. As such, it offers a way of reconciling the two conventions. Writing just after the 1907 conference, legal scholar Percy Bordwell concluded: "Only where there are no fortifications, no troops, and no open resistance by the population, does this article apply."[8]

Despite this, confusion persisted. At the outset of World War I the British debated whether placing antiaircraft guns in London would make it a defended city. In the end the guns were emplaced.[9] This episode shows that a too-literal interpretation leads to an absurd situation. If a nation provides its towns with an air defense, does it open them to attack? If it provides no defense, are military targets within the towns immune from attack? In June of 1917 Lord Montagu of Beaulieu stated forthrightly that "it was absolutely humbug to talk of London being an undefended city. The Germans had a perfect right to raid London." This opinion was held as well by mathematician and military analyst Frederick Lanchester, who argued that London was a legitimate object of attack because it contained the administrative offices concerned with the direction of the war.[10]

The nonspecific nature of the Land Warfare Convention and the apparent contradiction between it and the Naval Convention would continue to cause problems for some time to come. Nonetheless, Conventions IV and IX of 1907, when read as their drafters intended, did allow for the attack of military targets in towns, and relieved an attacker of legal responsibility for collateral damage or collateral injury short of indiscriminate bombing. The conventions did not prohibit or even severely restrict the potential use of aircraft as a tool of war. That the conventions did not do more was a function of the unwillingness of states to depend for their national security on the law-abiding tendencies of others. It was, as well, a reflection of the lure of intriguing new technologies which tempted states away from categorical prohibitions that might eliminate a potential advantage in future warfare.

World War I

Arrangements for a third Hague conference were overtaken by the outbreak of World War I. In the Great War much of the aerial bombing that took place was directed at battlefield targets in support of troops in the field. But the war also saw emergent forms of strategic bombing—bombing done well behind the lines of battle in order to undermine an enemy's war economy and will to fight. The Germans began a rudimentary form of strategic bombing using zeppelins to raid the English coast and London. The French undertook some aerial raids against German military targets beyond the lines of battle, but both the number of planes and the physical damage done was limited. The air arm of Britain's Royal Navy bombed zeppelin sheds and other targets of special interest to that service.

In 1917 the Germans chose to open a new air offensive, this time with several types of bomber aircraft. The German "Giant" bomber, remarkable for its time, had a wingspan just short of a World War II B-29. The first two German raids directed against London were particularly important. In both cases a handful of aircraft were able to fly virtually unimpeded over the city in daylight and cause significant casualties.[11] The public outrage that resulted prompted the creation of an independent Royal Air Force (RAF) designed to defend the British homeland, and to launch reprisal raids against the Germans. The British got their reprisal offensive under way in the spring of 1918. It was headed by Major General Hugh Trenchard, former head of the army's Royal Flying Corps (RFC). Trenchard was an ironic choice for the position as he had initially opposed the formation of an independent air force, believing that air assets ought to be devoted exclusively to supporting armies in the field. But he took the job, believing that he could at least maintain good relations with the army, and thereby prevent too much harm being done.[12]

The German ground offensives of March 1918 meant that Trenchard never had anything like the resources he needed to carry out sustained strategic bombing. True to his RFC loyalties, much of what he did was actually battlefield related in nature, but he did devote a portion of his force to the attack of industrial centers in Germany. In a postwar dispatch explaining his strategy, he argued that he spread his attacks out over as many targets as possible in an effort to have the maximum impact on German morale. He defended himself on this point by arguing that "the moral effect of bombing stands undoubtedly to the material effect in a proportion of 20 to 1."[13] It is hard to know where this figure came from; it seems to have sprung, conveniently, from Trenchard's head. Historian Malcolm Smith has called Trenchard a master of the "wholly unfounded statistic."[14]

It is worth mentioning a few things about these World War I strategic raids. The technology of bombing in this period was so crude that it was often impossible for those on the ground to tell whether raids were aimed at military targets or not. Early in the war the French concluded that the Germans were bombing indiscriminately, and vice versa. In December 1914 French bombers, aiming at a German aircraft factory, bombed the town of Freiburg. German perceptions of the attack set in motion a cycle of reprisals and counterreprisals that continued through the war. In the confusion each side saw its own raids as legitimate and those of its enemy as indiscriminate.[15] The German raid on London of June 13, 1917, officially had as its targets docks, wharves, railways, government stores, and warehouses, but the chief damage was done to an East End council school, causing the deaths of many students.[16]

The frequent incidence of civilian death in World War I was not a direct indication that pilots were not trying to hit legitimate targets and spare innocent lives. Nonetheless, the circumstances led to a situation in which law of war considerations received almost no attention, except as a tool for blaming the enemy and justifying reprisal raids. As defenses improved, accuracy of attacks became even worse owing to the necessity of carrying them out at night—a cycle that would be repeated again in World War II.

For many Allied airmen the armistice of November 1918 was an interruption to their campaign, which had started to pick up momentum as large bombers were finally produced in numbers great enough to have an impact. The British had plans to bomb Berlin in 1919, and the Americans had plans to join in on the aerial offensives. But these were left frozen in place.[17] Men had gotten a rudimentary taste of the potential of bombers and were left to use their imaginations to fill in the rest.

The Interwar Years

During the interwar years a complex web of ideas and technologies emerged which affected not only the way the law of war was perceived, but also the development of military doctrine and efforts at disarmament. It is worth trying to explain each thread, and to show how they became woven together in some ironic and complicated ways.

Even before the development of aircraft, visionaries and a fair number of science fiction writers had speculated on the potential of flying machines as weapons. They spun elaborate and often frightening tales of aerial combat. In his 1908 book *The War in the Air,* H. G. Wells articulated a thesis, stating, "with the flying machine war alters its character; it ceases to be an affair of 'fronts' and becomes an affair of 'areas'; neither side, victor or loser, remains immune from the gravest injuries, and while there is a vast increase in the destructiveness of war, there is also an increased indecisiveness."[18]

After World War I speculation about the role of aircraft in future wars expanded greatly. Books and articles began appearing simultaneously and independently in many countries. The ideas they contained can be understood almost as primal or archetypal. People have a deeply ingrained fear of total vulnerability, and this is what the bomber threatened. No place would be safe; there would be no place to shelter or to hide, especially if poison gas bombs were used. And it was largely taken for granted that gas bombs would be used. Titles of popular fiction from the interwar years included *The Gas War of 1940, The Poison War, Invasion from the Air, Air Reprisal, Empty Victory,* and *The Shape of Things to Come.*[19]

The issue of civilian and homefront morale came to take on specific importance. As mentioned above, this was a theme given particular credence by Trenchard in the years after the war. Trenchard was not an intellectual or original thinker, but as chief of the air staff in the 1920s he had some influence on the development of ideas in his service. He converted to the religion of strategic bombing for reasons of organizational expediency, and became an outspoken defender of the faith. He justified his small World War I bomber force, and protected the postwar independence of the RAF by invoking the 20 to 1 rule. This emphasis on morale emerged on many levels after World War I, and was exacerbated by a general interwar climate of civil-military tension. Many in the military were concerned about the trend that took warfare away from armies and directly to homelands. They feared that civilians might not be able to bear up under the deprivations caused by direct attacks on them.[20]

This tapped into some broader psychosocial concerns about the alienation of the working classes and their dissatisfaction with impersonal, crowded urban life. Cities were viewed as nerve centers subject to easy disruption and chaos. Morale problems in Britain and France in the later stages of World War I, the Russian Revolution, and the German collapse the following year had made such concerns visceral to many, and events such as the British general strike of 1926 and the Paris riots of 1934 kept them real and raw. Even the financial collapse of 1929 seemed indicative of this trend.[21]

Italian Brigadier General Guilio Douhet's 1921 book *Command of the Air* provided many graphic passages about the possible face of future air warfare. Douhet, writing in reaction to the events of the Great War, argued that in the wars of the future, ground offensives would be futile, but aerial offensives would be vital to victory.[22] In his direct and often graphic prose, Douhet echoed a well-established attitude which assumed that the object of war is victory, and all methods essential to victory must be employed. Indeed, the struggle must be carried on beyond the mere armed forces of the enemy directly to the state itself.[23] To its proponents this position had its own kind of humane logic. Marshal von Moltke was noted for saying that the greatest kindness in war is to bring it to a speedy conclusion. Article 29 of the Lieber code argued that "the more vigorously wars are pursued, the better it is for humanity. Sharp wars are brief." About air war Douhet wrote: "Mercifully, the decision will be quick in this kind of war, since the decisive blows will be directed at civilians, that element of the countries at war least able to sustain them. These future wars may yet prove to be more humane than wars in the past in spite of all, because they may in the long run shed less blood."[24] Thus, Douhet sought to find virtue in unbounded escalation. Technology and industrialization seemed to give these ideas a new kind of determinism, making them appear the unforgiving reality of the future.

This view, however, worked at cross-purposes with another trend which manifested itself in the struggling efforts made by organizations like the League of Nations, and in events like the Washington Naval Conference. The intense desire for the resumption of law and order in a world gone mad for four years caused national publics to support international organizations, and international efforts for arms control and the maintenance of peace. The idea of prohibiting new weapons, including aircraft, was raised briefly at the Washington Naval Conference, but after some discussion the conferees concluded that it was impractical to limit the numbers or characteristics of either commercial or military aircraft. Instead, they chose to schedule a subsequent conference to devise rules for regulating aircraft in war.

The Hague Aerial Bombardment Rules

This follow-on conference opened at The Hague on December 11, 1922. Delegates working on the aerial bombing rules struggled with the term *military objective* and debated whether it was best to include that term in the regulations in the hopes that it would have a confining effect on aerial targeting. Ultimately they agreed on rules which included:

> Article 22: Aerial bombardment for the purpose of terrorizing the civilian population, of destroying or damaging private property not of a military character, or of injuring non-combatants is prohibited.

> Article 24: Aerial bombardment is legitimate only when directed at a military objective, that is to say, an object of which the destruction or injury would constitute a distinct military advantage to the belligerent.

Additional clauses of article 24 listed legitimate military targets, and attempted to prohibit indiscriminate bombing of residential areas. Listed as military targets were factories which produce military supplies, and lines of communication or transportation used for military purposes. Article 25 specified targets to be avoided to the greatest extent possible, including historic monuments and buildings dedicated to public worship, art, science, and care of the sick.[25] The 1923 Hague Rules of Air Warfare represented the best efforts of the delegates present. They struggled to articulate a code that would approximate fairness and humane behavior. But as no state was yet fully prepared to commit itself to such general constraints on a largely untested weapons system, the air rules were never adopted by any nation and thus must be viewed as a legal and political failure.[26]

Theories and Capabilities

The remainder of the decade saw a continuing spiral of concern about air war, but predictions ran well ahead of actual technologies. For all the dramatic rhetoric of the 1920s, aircraft and aircraft bombing did not evolve very quickly. Postwar financial problems had made it difficult for European powers to invest heavily in aeronautics. Through the decade the RAF spent much of its time flying wooden biplanes in aerial policing duties against tribes in such far-flung colonial territories as Somaliland and Mesopotamia (present-day Somalia and Iraq).[27]

Things began to change in the 1930s, however, as technical advances transformed wooden biplanes into metal monoplanes with retractable landing gear. In a last gasp effort at international cooperation, diplomats made an attempt to ban bomber aircraft at the Geneva Disarmament Conference of 1932. But an unpredictable political environment and technological momentum conspired against them. The problem of civilian aircraft which could be converted to military uses was a thorny one indeed, but the final blow to fragile hopes came when the Germans walked out of the conference in 1933. When Hitler announced the regeneration of the Luftwaffe, British fears of a knock-out blow from the air increased as the nation recognized its vulnerability, and that of London in particular.[28] Fear of air war existed alongside the desperate hope that bombers might deter war. Facing what now appeared to be an intractable Germany, the British began to ease constraints on defense spending and to establish a program of rearmament. But the latter, after the long locust years, was a challenging undertaking. Air staff members, in the tradition of Trenchard, emphasized the construction of bombers and an offensive doctrine. Chancellor of the Exchequer Neville Chamberlain saw the deterrent value of a bomber fleet, and considered such a force the most cost-effective option for rearmament.[29] But very little work had been done on the actual tactics and methods needed to prosecute strategic bombing successfully in the event deterrence failed.

The lack of attention to operational detail took a serious toll. When the new head of Bomber Command, Edgar Ludlow-Hewitt, set out on an inspection tour to assess the state of the organization, he was taken aback. His report in November 1937 was brutally frank; he found the command unprepared and vulnerable. Despite his own efforts to improve the state of navigation and crew training, he was still forced to admit as late as August of 1939 that "over 40 percent of a force of his bombers were unable to find a target in a friendly city in broad daylight." In the last two years before the outbreak of war, there were some 478 forced landings in Britain by pilots who had lost their way.[30]

Developments in the United States

The development of air doctrine in the United States took a slightly different course. Entering the First World War late, the United States had not had time to create the means for undertaking a strategic bombing campaign. With no aerial threat to American shores, there was no public clamor for a separate air force. Thus, remaining under the thumb of the army, the Air Service (and later Air Corps) had to stay in line with its parent service's infantry orientation. Army Chief of Staff John J. Pershing and Secretary of War Newton Baker were both opposed to independence for the air arm. Baker felt that the kind of long-range reprisal raids Britain had engaged in at the end of World War I were morally wrong and should not be considered by those making U.S. defense policy.[31]

The establishment of the Air Corps in 1926 gave American airmen a little more latitude, and in the 1930s they became more bold—articulating a vision of aircraft being used in independent, strategic missions. At the Air Corps Tactical School (ACTS), a small group of energetic instructors worked out a theory which presumed that precision bombing against key elements of an enemy's industrial infrastructure would make it impossible for that state to continue to prosecute a war successfully. Thinking in economic terms, they considered complex industrial states to be like interwoven webs, subject to unraveling by pulling on a central thread. They believed that massed bomber formations flying in daylight and using the latest technology for high-altitude precision bomb-aiming would be able to defend themselves and strike at their targets with high levels of accuracy and effectiveness. Events would later prove some of their assessments rather too optimistic.[32]

The Law on the Eve of War

In the years leading up to the outbreak of World War II, the guidance offered to air forces regarding targeting and the law of war was vague at best. The British *Manual of Military Law,* which was the reference of record prior to the war, contained the following sentence: "No legal duty exists for the attacking force to limit bombardment to the fortifications or defended border only. On the contrary, destruction of private and public buildings by bombardment has always been, and still is, considered lawful, as it is one of the means to impress upon the local authorities the advisability of surrender."[33]

Official legal guidance for U.S. air forces was not very helpful. U.S. Army Field Manual 27-10, *The Law of Land Warfare,* provided only what was contained in the 1907 Hague Conventions. At the Air Corps Tactical School in the early 1930s, students generally received only one lecture on international aerial regulations.[34] Naval guidance of 1941 pointed out that bombing strictly to terrorize civilians should not be carried out, and that due care should be employed in any bombardment. The guidance specified that the bombing of communications centers, lines of communication, workshops, plants, or factories was not prohibited.[35] The Luftwaffe's 1935 basic doctrinal statement *The Conduct of the Air War* suggested that the job of the service encompassed the capability to "carry the war from the beginning against the enemy's homeland [and to] attack his military power and the morale of the enemy population at the root."[36] Most air forces of the day made their personnel aware of the 1923 Hague Rules of Air Warfare, but lists of relevant articles were generally qualified with the statement that they were not legally binding. At the Air Corps Tactical School, for instance, the possibility of attacking capitals and centers of population was left open; students were informed that such targeting would be governed by political considerations during the course of a future war. International law, as a restraining force in and of itself, tended to be downplayed.[37]

The two most comprehensive interwar works on air power and international law, M. W. Royse's *Aerial Bombardment and International Regulation of Warfare,* and J. M. Spaight's *Air Power and War Rights,* took a largely pragmatic approach to questions of aerial bombing.[38] Royse's 1928 volume argued: "The history of bombardment regulation shows a distinct utilitarian development, in which the idea of military effectiveness dominates, and in which the doctrines of permissible violence and social sanction are of secondary importance as checks or influences."[39] In the late 1930s the Spanish Civil War and the Japanese bombing of Manchuria suggested that future air war might not be bound by any constraints at all. In response to the latter, Spaight wrote, in January 1938, an article tellingly titled "The Chaotic State of the International Law Governing Bombardment." Pointing to the inexplicit nature of the land and naval Hague rules of 1907, and their liability to be interpreted in different ways by different individuals or states, he complained, "It [the law of bombardment] is indeed in a state of baffling chaos and confusion which makes it almost impossible to say what in any given situation the rule really is."[40]

World War II

Responding in 1939 to a plea by President Roosevelt, Germany, England, and France agreed to limit bombing to strictly military objectives at the outset of the war. But all three powers reserved the right to take appropriate action in the event that their enemies reneged. In the spring of 1940 when many felt that the Germans had bombed Warsaw and Rotterdam indiscriminately, RAF aircraft still refrained from dropping their bombs if they could not find their assigned military targets. But during the Battle of Britain things began to change. On August 24, 1940, some German bombers went slightly off course and dropped bombs on London. RAF Bomber Command attacked Berlin the following night, as Prime Minister Winston Churchill argued that German cities increasingly ought to be the subject of British attacks. Thus began a gradual spiral toward all-out, gloves-off warfare that would lead to the infamous attacks on London, Coventry, Hamburg, and Dresden.[41]

This early stage of war did not see a single-minded clamoring for city targets, per se, however. The British sought to find and attack key German military targets in an effort to undermine the German war machine. This was difficult to do, however, as it was quickly discovered that bombers could not be counted on to always get through as Stanley Baldwin had predicted they would. In the early years of the war Bomber Command was a very weak offensive weapon with serious shortcomings, but in the dark days when Britain stood alone, Churchill considered it good for national morale to be able to wage an offensive of some sort. In an effort to cut losses, the British began flying mainly at night, and in the summer of 1941 they did a photo-reconnaissance study to determine their accuracy. The results, known as the Butt Report, were depressing indeed: "Of those aircraft recorded as attacking their target, only one in three got within five miles."[42]

Since cities were the one target that could be found and hit with some success at night, new plans were made and a directive was issued in early 1942 stating that Bomber Command operations henceforth would focus on "the morale of the enemy civilian population and in particular, of the industrial workers." The directive was followed up with an explicit instruction that the aiming points were to be the "built-up areas" of cities.[43] Soon after the decision for "de-housing" was made, Sir Arthur Harris was appointed as the new head of Bomber Command. As a disciple of Tren-chard, Harris had been reared on the morale aspect of bombing, so that, under Harris, the new focus was really the resurrection of a not-so-old idea. Harris undertook the new task with determination and tenacity.

For the next three years Bomber Command waged a dramatically brutal campaign —not only for those in Germany, but also for those who flew the long missions repeatedly through the cold and seemingly endless European nights. On occasion the right atmospheric conditions would facilitate vast firestorms in the cities below. Such raids were precisely what Harris was seeking, as he hoped and believed that they were an efficient and effective means of fighting Hitler's Germany.[44] As the man in charge of the most direct effort to strike down the abhorrent Nazi Reich, Harris was popular with the press and the British people.

The Americans began their bombing campaign in 1942, determined to implement their theories of attack against key node industries. In January 1943 Churchill and Roosevelt met at Casablanca and agreed on a round-the-clock combined bomber offensive that would allow Britain to continue to attack cities at night, while the United States would attack military-industrial targets by day.[45] Ultimately, unaccept-able bomber losses in 1943 finally convinced U.S. commanders that unescorted long-range daylight missions into Germany were not profitable.[46] The solution was an idea that had been discounted during the interwar years as unnecessary and even impossible—the long-range escort fighter.

Even after long-range escorts facilitated daylight raids into Germany, American planners still faced the considerable problem of achieving anything even approximat-ing true precision bombing. Large formations of bombers covered large areas which came under attack when the lead plane released its bombs, cuing all the others. In addition, the highly touted Norden bombsight, which worked well in trials in the clear air of the American Southwest, had significant difficulties in cloud-shrouded north-ern Europe. In November 1943 the commanding general of the United States Army

Air Forces, General H. H. Arnold, issued an order which declared that on bad days, U.S. forces should bomb through cloud by radar. This meant that in many cases their accuracy was no better than that of Bomber Command, and often it was worse.[47] Even when discrimination was the intent, the technical means available and the operating conditions of war did not fully permit it. Civilians died, and cultural property was destroyed; the ineluctable forces of total war operated ever more feverishly as time went on.

In the spring of 1944 control of the Allied strategic air forces was given over to General Dwight Eisenhower, who would direct them against a variety of targets—including transport and communications lines—in preparation for the Normandy landing. When control of the bomber forces went back to their respective commanders (General Carl Spaatz for the Americans, and Harris for the British), General Spaatz wanted to direct his forces against oil targets while Harris wanted to continue city bombing. By this time Bomber Command had honed its techniques to a point where, using radar guidance, it could strike specific locations with success. But Harris downplayed this and stuck to his countercity campaign, believing that he was perhaps just a few major raids away from forcing a collapse of German morale that would end the war.

Intelligence derived from Ultra intercepts indicated that Germany was growing critically low on synthetic oil, and that an intensified campaign against this commodity would be profitable. While Spaatz paid close attention, it is not clear that Harris took account of the information at all. Isolating himself at his headquarters at High Wycombe, he ignored intelligence indicating that German morale was indeed not suffering dramatically from the area bombing campaigns, while oil shortages were proving to be an increasing problem. Sir Charles Portal, who had been chief of the air staff since 1940, wished to bring Bomber Command in on the oil campaign, and he came to a standoff with Harris over targeting in the winter of 1944–45. Harris threatened to resign, and Portal backed down.[48] But cities and oil refineries were not the only targets attacked by Allied bombers at that point. Transportation and communication targets continued to receive attention since they were critical to impeding the German ground war. This campaign was successful as it dramatically curtailed German ability to move men and resources in the theater of combat operations. It meant collateral civilian deaths, however, among French and Germans alike.

The Culmination

The denouement of the World War II strategic bombing campaigns came in 1945 when Allied heavy bombers were available in large numbers and could fly with near impunity over German and finally Japanese air space. The raid most strongly associated with this period is that flown against the city of Dresden, one of Europe's great cultural centers, on the night of February 13–14, 1945. That night the city was packed with refugees fleeing the ground war. Through a harsh twist of fate the atmospheric conditions proved perfect for the creation of a firestorm. Under such circumstances air-raid shelters became suffocating incinerators which cooked those inside until their bodies were charred hulks and their body fats formed a thick layer on the floor. Kurt Vonnegut, who was in Dresden as a prisoner of war and managed to survive the raid, has claimed that the firebombing, "which had no military significance, was a work of art. It was a tower of smoke and flame to commemorate the rage and heartbreak of so many who had had their lives warped or ruined by the indescribable greed and vanity and cruelty of Germany."[49]

Was Dresden theater? In a sense, yes. The Allies hoped that a few dramatic raids late in the war might push Germany over the edge to surrender. And the idea of striking cities just behind German lines, in an effort to cause chaos and aid the Soviet ground advance, was one that had come to Churchill while he was preparing for Yalta; the notion of impressing Stalin with the strength of strategic air power was not lost on the prime minister.[50] In another sense though, Dresden was not theater at all. The most tragic thing about Dresden is that it was all too mundane. Dresden was a target on a list of targets. The weather in the region on the night of February 13–14 was favorable. Bombers were sent out all too routinely. The machine was up and running and had developed a momentum and logic all its own. American bombers, which came in after the British bombers had done their work, aimed at the city's railroad marshaling yards. But the city was already an inferno.[51]

Dresden foreshadowed what was to come in the Far Eastern theater. General Haywood Hansell, commanding U.S. strategic bombers in the Marianas, had, beginning in the autumn of 1944, tried to implement military-industrial targeting. But success had proved elusive due to Japan's constant cloud cover, and the jet stream made it nearly impossible for bombers to hold formation at 30,000 feet, much less bomb accurately. Impatient with the lack of progress and anxious to bring the war with Japan to a close, General Arnold replaced Hansell with General Curtis LeMay, who was charged with the task of making strategic bombing work—somehow—against Japan.[52] Ultimately, LeMay stripped the B-29s of their armament and had them fly low-level, nighttime incendiary raids against Japanese cities. After a couple of trial operations, LeMay launched his first big fire raid against Tokyo on the night of March 9–10, 1945. Over eighty thousand people died. Sixty-six Japanese cities would be burned before a new and unforgettable fire would be unleashed at Hiroshima and Nagasaki. The stated aim of these attacks was to destroy Japan's ability to sustain its war effort; but their unavoidable consequence was to kill large numbers of Japanese civilians.

Nuremberg

The International Military Tribunal at Nuremberg did not deal directly with the issue of aerial bombing. In defense of Luftwaffe chief Hermann Göring, Field Marshal Albert Kesselring testified that at Warsaw only military targets had been attacked, and that the bombing of Rotterdam had been undertaken because the army could not notify the air force to call off the attack once it was known that the city was going to capitulate. With respect to Coventry the Germans argued that the target had been an armaments factory, and that the indiscriminate bombing had been due to navigational inaccuracies.[53] Whatever one makes of this testimony it is nonetheless the case that the Allies, having experienced some navigational problems of their own, were not inclined to press the point. Evidence in other realms was viewed as sufficient to convict the defendants.[54] Addressing the topic frankly, Telford Taylor, chief counsel for war crimes at the war crimes trials of Nuremberg, noted in his final report that:

> Many of the provisions of the 1907 Hague Conventions regarding unlawful means of combat . . . were antiquarian. Others had been observed only partially during the First World War and almost completely disregarded during the Second World War. . . . If the first badly bombed cities—Warsaw, Rotterdam, Belgrade, and London—suffered at the hands of the Germans and not the allies, nonetheless the ruins of German and Japanese cities were the results not of reprisal but of deliberate policy, and bore witness that aerial bombardment of cities and factories has become a recognized part of modern warfare as carried on by all nations.[55]

The tribunal itself put no brake on this "recognized part of modern warfare."

Reflections and Conclusions

The aerial bombardment of World War II, and the questions of legality and morality it raises, still arouse passion and emotion. The problem must be approached on two levels. First, we must look back in an effort to understand the mentality of the time: why did leaders and policy makers act as they did, and what motivated their decisions? Second, we must ask ourselves, with the benefit of fifty years' perspective: what did we learn from this experience, and how should we think about air power and the law of war in the future?

When air forces failed to deter war in 1939, Allied statesmen faced a series of very difficult decisions. With the fall of France in 1940, Britain was certainly not well prepared to wage a successful bombing campaign against Hitler's Germany, but was even less well prepared to wage a successful ground campaign. Responsibility for an offensive fell to the bomber pilots, who, it was soon discovered, had a chance of carrying out repeated missions over Germany only under cover of darkness. And under such circumstances cities were the only viable targets. Those who implemented the campaign felt that it might have an impact on the German war effort, although the extent to which it would was hotly debated within planning circles. Nonetheless, the expectation of such a military effect gave it some legitimacy. In his book *Just and Unjust Wars*, Michael Walzer argues that in an extreme emergency—which is what the British faced in the early years of the war—and in view of the fact that they were confronting an evil as heinous as Nazi Germany, area bombing arguably could be defended as a last resort offensive. But he adds that Bomber Command should have shifted its aim points back to military targets as soon as possible, which was, as Walzer defines it, in 1944.[56]

Large organizations do not change quickly, however. And Portal's dilemma was not an insignificant one. Sacking Arthur Harris in the winter of 1944–45 would have amounted to a vote of no confidence in what Bomber Command had done up until then, and, with so many men lost in the campaign to date, would have been traumatic for the British public.[57] Nonetheless, it is hard not to question, in hindsight, why more British bomb tonnage could not have been dedicated to targets—like synthetic oil—which were having a discernible impact on the outcome of the war and were costing fewer civilian casualties.

American planners fixed their sights firmly on daylight targets, but they too faced a series of difficulties that often caused their operations to fall short of desires and expectations. American planners were dedicated to military targeting, some of them at least in part for moral reasons. With respect to the law of war, intent is important. But if you happened to be living in a German town during World War II, it would have seemed irrelevant. The reality was that American bombing was often grossly indiscriminate. Many have questioned, especially in recent years, the foundations of an American policy that led to participation in heavy raids on European cities, and to the firebombing of Tokyo and other cities in Japan. The spectrum of opinion on the issue is very wide, and the gulf will narrow only gradually, if at all, as the events themselves fade into the distance. Where some see hypocrisy or indifference, others see the fog of war, the burdensome pressures of command, and the vortex of total warfare. The Allies certainly believed the bombing campaigns would save the lives of many soldiers. The landing at Normandy would have been much harder, maybe impossible, with robust Luftwaffe opposition. The key question really is: how does one weigh the lives of one's own soldiers against the lives of enemy civilians?

Generals Arnold and LeMay thought they were using B-29s to help preclude the necessity for a ground invasion of the Japanese home islands. The firebombing of Japan took place while the battles of Iwo Jima and Okinawa were being fought to the last defender. Several years ago Paul Fussell wrote an essay called "Thank God for the Atom Bomb," which argued that those who are in foxholes have a different morality than those who are not. Fussell argued that those who were about to be told to charge the beaches of Kyushu with bayonets did not question the ethics of the atomic bomb.[58] The essay received an enthusiastic response—not least of all from veterans who found themselves in just the position Fussell described. But to pose the choice as either Hiroshima or invasion may be too stark, or even artificial. Some historians have argued that the choice was not simply between using the bomb and not using the bomb.[59]

There was great pressure on President Truman to end the war as quickly as possible. He believed, at least at the time of Hiroshima, that the bombing was a necessary military act. But one wonders if he believed that for the rest of his life. In hindsight we are obliged to ask the question: was there really no other way? And in doing so we must struggle over questions of diplomacy and negotiation—over the question of the emperor.[60] Michael Walzer has argued that Hiroshima was not a case of supreme emergency, but rather an act of political terror.[61] Different generations will ask different questions about the past. We have questioned Hamburg and Dresden and Tokyo and Hiroshima, and this kind of informed questioning may be an important first step toward the development of a consensus on standards for the future.

The murky laws on aerial bombardment that existed prior to World War II were much too weak a reed to constrain states. It is far from clear that a restrictive set of laws would have been adhered to during World War II, had they existed. Strategic bombing was a largely untested idea which seemed to many to hold the promise of making wars shorter, if more violent. Indeed, as we have seen, it was in part this lure, and the concern that other states might gain an advantage, that prevented adequate interwar restraints. The speculation about civilian morale and the nature of industrial society further blurred the already problematic concept of military target. In the United States the notion that one could attack the will of the enemy population was never entirely absent from discussions of aerial bombing, even if by the late 1930s attention was focused on military-industrial targeting. Indeed, the relationship between capacity to fight and will to fight—the oft-cited dyad of strategic bombing theory—has never been entirely clear in American air doctrine, and has been understood differently by different authors. In any event, all sides gave the phrase "military target" a wide interpretation during the war, and the intensity and duration of the conflict only added to the problem.

Setting aside such questions, and the emotion engendered by them, however, we can draw from the experience of World War II some clear conclusions that have important ramifications for the future of the law of war as it applies to air power. First and most important, city bombing—as attacks on the will of the enemy state— proved to be neither efficient nor effective. The United States Strategic Bombing Survey (USSBS) revealed that while bombing did affect the morale of civilian populations, heavy bombing was not proportionally more effective than moderate bombing, and sustained heavy bombing soon led to diminishing returns in morale effects. Lowered morale did not necessarily lead to active opposition to the war, and only in the very last stages of the war did it lead to diminished productivity at the workplace. The members of the British Bombing Survey Unit (BBSU) reached similar conclusions. In their final report they stated outright: "In so far as the offensive against German towns was designed to break the morale of the German civilian population, it clearly failed. Far from lowering essential war production, it also failed to stem a remarkable increase in the output of armaments." This was later supported by the British official history which stated that "after the German air defenses had ceased to be effective, [the general area offensive] had been revealed as an uneconomic and even irrelevant policy."[62]

World War II showed us convincingly that targets such as synthetic oil plants and key transport facilities—in other words, military targets more narrowly defined—contributed the most toward bringing the war to an end. The utility of oil and transport targets is documented clearly in the United States Strategic Bombing Survey, both in the European Summary Report and in individual reports on these specific target sets. The report of the British Bombing Survey Unit emphasized in particular the efficacy of transport targets. Recent scholarship has supported these conclusions. As historian Alfred Mierzejewski recently concluded, "Only when Germany was overrun and when Hitler died did the will to resist finally flicker out."[63]

Moreover, recent military experience in the form of Operation Desert Storm suggests some very similar conclusions. The most effective aerial bombing campaign in history was also the most discriminate. The coalition's focus on specific military targets, together with technology permitting unprecedented accuracy of weapon delivery, effectively precluded the kind of large-scale civilian fatalities that characterized the bombing campaigns of World War II.[64] And, in an age of instant television reporting, public reaction powerfully reinforced the coalition's policy to limit collateral damage.

These examples suggest at least the possibility of a broader trend with important ramifications for the law of aerial warfare. It may be that in future warfare, technology could produce a convergence between ethics and efficiency by permitting precise engagement of narrowly defined military targets. And this change in military technology may be paralleled by changes in civil technology: the effects of television on public opinion and thus, public influence on targeting, should not be underestimated. From the time of the Hague Conventions, popular opinion has been a driver in the development of the law of war. In an age of television it may become more important than ever before. If this is so, then any tension between effectiveness and discrimination would ease, and a key obstacle to broader adherence to the spirit of the Hague Conventions would be removed. Royse and Spaight were right to argue that utilitarian considerations always will take precedence in the heat of conflict. But if the most useful targets are also the most discriminate targets, and if technology makes discrimination possible, then the future may see behavior different than that which has characterized aerial warfare through the early part of this century.

This trend is thus a potential watershed in the history of the law of aerial warfare. By the same token, however, questions remain as to how this trend will develop in the future. It may well be, for example, that the military behavior of authoritarian states could differ importantly from that of industrialized democracies—it is far from clear that Saddam Hussein's attitudes on the desirability of discriminate targeting are identical to those of the coalition that opposed him in Desert Storm. His experience in the Battle of the Cities during the war with Iran may have inclined him to believe that there was utility to be gained from the deliberate targeting of civilians.[65] And, finally, trends should not be taken too far: civilians died in Operation Desert Storm, and some will certainly die in all future wars. But there is reason to hope that collateral casualty rates gradually will decline as technology continues to improve. And this trend will be further aided if all combatants—defenders as well as attackers—take responsibility for protecting civilian populations.

All in all then there may be grounds for optimism. In 1926 air theorist William C. Sherman wrote, "There has always been a sentiment among mankind to mitigate the horrors of war, as far as the nature of the thing permits."[66] In recent years the law of war has continued to develop with respect to aerial bombing. Protocol I of 1977, which was the result of an extended conference, sought, among other things, to limit the vulnerability of civilians to aerial bombardment. Even though it is a controversial document, the United States recognizes portions of it as being reflective of customary international law, and several United Nations General Assembly Resolutions have nudged the international community in this direction as well.[67] In an environment with no enforcement mechanisms, compliance always depends on the cooperation of the parties involved. The laws of war have been swept aside before, and there is always a risk that this may happen again. But the lessons of World War II, the improvements in target-finding capabilities, and the increasing impact of public opinion due to modern communications technologies all may point to a more hopeful trend for the future.

David Alan
Rosenberg

10

Nuclear War Planning

It is a specter that has terrified a generation. An international crisis escalates into full-scale conventional war. At some point in the conflict, tactical nuclear weapons are used at the battlefronts, followed inexorably by a theaterwide nuclear exchange. One of the superpowers, fearing defeat, uses a small number of nuclear weapons against targets in the other's homeland. Designed to show resolve and encourage de-escalation of the conflict, this strike instead causes the other superpower to react with a massive attack against the opponent's nuclear forces and perhaps its cities. The land- and sea-launched ballistic missiles of both sides pass each other in the thin atmosphere over the North Pole, and when they land, Western civilization comes to an end. The war unleashes a long-term environmental calamity of such proportions that most human, animal, and vegetable life in the Northern Hemisphere, if not the planet, is catastrophically altered, perhaps destroyed.[1]

These anticipated horrors were made possible by the invention of the atomic bomb in 1945. The A-bomb had an explosive yield equivalent to from tens of tons to five hundred thousand tons of TNT. The 1950s saw the perfection of the hydrogen bomb, a fission bomb coupled to a secondary device containing elements capable of harnessing the principles of nuclear fusion. The sequential detonations of the fission trigger and the secondary device could produce yields equivalent to tens of millions of tons of TNT. Both types of nuclear weapon caused their tremendous damage not just through prompt effects of blast, atmospheric overpressure, heat, and radiation, but also by their delayed effects of associated fires, radiation fallout, and, depending on the·number and yields of weapons used and their targets, climatic change as well.[2]

The power of nuclear weapons was enhanced by great advances in the speed of their delivery to their targets, starting with the intercontinental piston engine and then jet bombers, and climaxing in the development of multiple independently targeted reentry vehicles (MIRVs) on sea-based and intercontinental ballistic missiles. These missiles could rain unimaginable destruction in little more than half an hour. By the 1960s nuclear weapons of all kinds were ubiquitous in the military forces of the United States and the Soviet Union, and despite various innovations in doctrine, tactics, and conventional weaponry, their potential use lay at the base of the military strategies of East and West.[3]

Nuclear weapons appeared to have created the conditions necessary to achieve the heretofore hypothetical condition described by the nineteenth-century Prussian military philosopher Carl von Clausewitz as "absolute war." Real war, Clausewitz argued, was a case of "tension between two elements, separate for the time being, which discharge energy in discontinuous minor shocks." Absolute war could be considered "a case in which two mutually destructive elements collide," a state of "total discharge," in contrast to the partial and intermittent discharge of real war. Clausewitz held that absolute war was a "theoretical concept" that had not been realized because of the existence of a "non-conducting medium, [a] barrier that prevents a full discharge" between warring powers. This barrier was composed of a "vast array of factors, forces and conditions in national affairs that are affected by war," through which "no logical sequence could progress" as a result of its "innumerable twists and turns."[4] The power and speed of nuclear weapons, however, could sweep that barrier aside.

What constraints, old and new, judicial, procedural, or technological, have existed to constrain nuclear conflict and serve as Clausewitz's barrier to forestall total discharge? Further, have the constraints been adequate to their tremendous task?

Historians attempting to evaluate constraints on nuclear war are themselves constrained by certain factors that limit the extent of their analysis and the validity of their conclusions. First and most obvious, no nuclear weapon has been used in combat since 1945. Any judgments about the efficacy of constraints are speculative, based on assessments of what might have been.

Second, the evidentiary base for those assessments is incomplete, made up primarily of declassified strategic plans and concepts and programming analyses. No operational plans have ever been released, nor have any planning directives beyond 1960. While much progress has been made in gaining the release of cold war documents, the details of nuclear war plans remain closely guarded secrets.

Third, nuclear plans and concepts, like most war plans, were based on certain assumptions about when, where, and how military force would be employed. Those assumptions did not necessarily cover all or even the most likely circumstances by which nuclear war would begin. Further, even if the circumstances of a nuclear confrontation were predictable, the thoughts and choices of the civilian and military officials with power over nuclear decisions at the time of crisis were not. While clues are available in memoirs, oral histories, and government records, any assessment of how leaders' attitudes and actions might have modified prior constraints would be only a highly imaginative counterfactual scenario.

Finally, the evidentiary base is largely one-sided, composed primarily of American and British materials. While new disclosures from the former Soviet Union have shed light on some areas of cold war crisis and conflict, modern Soviet general staff archives remain closed. Historians thus must depend on memoirs, journalistic disclosures, and partially declassified Western intelligence analyses in attempting to divine the nature of Soviet nuclear war constraints.

Nevertheless, scholars now have access to a sufficient body of new data to begin to describe nuclear thought and potential actions. In particular, documents from the 1960s provide much new information about American and NATO plans which raise questions about whether certain long-heralded American concepts (such as the "no cities" counterforce strategy) were truly feasible at the time they were adopted. This information provides a useful case study of the problems of nuclear war constraints during the period when a full-scale nuclear confrontation was most likely.

Despite many international agreements and significant domestic legislation relating to nuclear arms, the overall legal framework for nuclear constraints is fragmentary and subject to conflicting interpretations. Existing legal restrictions were and are hardly specific enough to promise much efficacy in constraining actual operations. Most of them are found in the various international treaties and arms control agreements dealing with weapons testing, proliferation, deployment, and reduction. In addition, while the applicability of international law and the traditional laws of war to nuclear weapons is not clear-cut, some edicts proscribe particular targeting choices and first use of nuclear weapons under certain conditions. There are also American legal and constitutional provisions detailing governmental responsibility for nuclear weapons as well as legislation relative to efforts to outlaw American achievement of a first-strike counterforce capability.

The international agreements on nuclear weapons include the 1963 Limited Test Ban Treaty, the 1968 Nuclear Nonproliferation Treaty, and Soviet-American arms control agreements, particularly the 1972 treaties banning antiballistic missiles (the ABM Treaty) and limiting strategic arms (SALT I), the unratified 1979 strategic arms limitation treaty (SALT II), the 1987 agreement eliminating certain classes of land-based intermediate-range nuclear forces (INF Treaty), and the 1991 and 1993 strategic arms reduction treaties (START I and II).[5]

The test ban treaty served to bound the environmental impact of peacetime nuclear explosions, and it has also prevented the analysis of certain nuclear weapons principles. These include the "fratricidal" effects of ballistic missile warhead explosions on warheads following behind in an attack. The lack of conclusive data on these effects, which could only be confirmed through atmospheric tests, has limited confidence in the capability of nuclear forces to carry out an effective disarming first strike on enemy silo-based missile forces.[6]

The nonproliferation treaty, while not completely effective in preventing the spread of nuclear weapons, retarded development of large stockpiles by nations other than the five—the United States, the Soviet Union, the United Kingdom, France, and the People's Republic of China—that had them at the time of ratification. States with small numbers of weapons might not refrain from using them in the worst possible way—attacks on each other's population centers—but such attacks, while appalling, would not be likely to trigger a full-scale nuclear exchange. The future of nuclear proliferation has become much more perilous in the wake of the cold war, and it will cause dilemmas for policy makers concerned with constraints on nuclear war planning.[7]

The U.S.–Soviet arms control treaties restrain quantitative and qualitative aspects of the American and former-Soviet nuclear forces. The agreements reduce the destabilizing impact of certain nuclear offensive missiles, limit or reduce the numbers of offensive and defensive launchers and warheads, limit the number of warheads per launcher and the throw-weight of launchers, and bound or prohibit antimissile defenses. The treaties thus affect some of the capabilities of potential combatants but leave unregulated certain others, such as the yield or accuracy of warheads.

This is not to say that arms control treaties have not affected the prospects for nuclear war. They have contributed not only to an atmosphere of increasing trust between the United States and the former Soviet Union, but also to confidence that neither side will be the subject of the other's surprise first strike. This is because these treaties provide for extensive verification of the nuclear forces on either side. That verification, first by the SALT treaties' "national technical means" of reconnaissance satellites, and since the late 1980s by on-site inspections, has significantly increased each side's knowledge of the other's force structure, alert rates, launch procedures, and other military capabilities. While such knowledge permits greater precision in targeting enemy forces, it has also replaced inflated perceptions of enemy threats with hard data, and helped to mitigate arms race tensions.[8]

The most far-reaching steps to reduce the "use it or lose it" temptation that has dominated superpower nuclear strategy since the 1960s were the elimination of fast flying, highly accurate intermediate-range ballistic missiles by the INF Treaty and the agreement under START II to eliminate multiple independently targetable warheads on land-based intercontinental ballistic missiles (ICBMs).[9] These two agreements, however, were negotiated well after the period of the greatest Soviet-American tensions. Their successful conclusion was largely due to the unprecedented and unexpected Soviet-American political rapprochement at the end of the cold war, rather than to efforts to use arms control explicitly to restrain the potential use of nuclear weapons in a crisis or conflict. Should military tensions beset the new Russian-American relationship, leaders will find that the limits established for U.S. and Russian strategic arsenals (some 3,000 to 3,500 warheads by the year 2003) by the START II treaty have left residual strategic offensive forces equivalent to the American levels in the mid-1950s and Soviet levels in the early 1960s. Though the yields of most strategic warheads have been significantly reduced in the past three decades, stockpiles permitted under START II, if used against co-located urban and military targets, would still wreak immense devastation.[10]

Arms control has been limited in its ability to constrain nuclear planning for a number of reasons. First, nuclear war planning involves closely held secrets. It combines information on prospective targets derived from sensitive national intelligence with the actual capabilities of available nuclear weapons systems. It also reveals what each side considers necessary to deter enemy action in a nuclear crisis or to deny enemy objectives in a nuclear conflict. Nations are naturally reluctant to reveal such secrets to potential enemies.

Second, arms control did not become a major factor in international nuclear politics until the late 1960s. By 1967 Americans had what has been publicly estimated as a stockpile of more than 32,000 nuclear weapons, while the Soviets had some 6,000 to 15,000 weapons and had built the infrastructure to produce an additional 20,000 to 25,000 by the late 1980s.[11] Moreover, both sides had programs in place to produce the most destabilizing weapons—ICBMs with MIRV warheads— which they continued to implement into the late 1980s. While deployment of some weapons programs, particularly nationwide systems of nuclear-tipped antiballistic missiles, were curtailed by treaty, high-level decisions by both sides on what would or would not be subject to negotiation prevented restraints on other systems until the talks on real reductions in the late 1980s.

Finally, the arms control process is inherently limited by its focus on only selected aspects of the problem. There are, in essence, four components of nuclear strategy. The first is the weapons themselves. Nuclear weapons, for all their technological complexity and horrendous effects, are essentially no more than explosives to be employed against enemy targets. The second component is the delivery systems used to carry these weapons to their targets; the third is the bases for those delivery systems; and the fourth is the targets themselves. Unfortunately, only the bases and delivery systems are subject to verifiable arms control agreements. The number of warheads has been subject to negotiation since the late 1970s, but not their most threatening characteristics, such as yield and accuracy. This is because the warheads' internal workings contain many technical secrets about their design, manufacture, assembly, and efficacy. Similarly, targets have not been subject to agreement because their disclosure would expose the heart of war planning, and because targeting prohibitions could not readily be verified, much less enforced.

The constraints imposed by arms control agreements and other treaties, although selective in impact, are at least clear and specific. The limitations prescribed by international law are neither. There are three major criteria in international law by which to evaluate the appropriate use of any weapons in war: "the necessity to use them; the proportionality of their use; and the obligation not to cause unnecessary suffering." It has been argued that nuclear weapons cannot under any circumstances meet these tests, because of the indiscriminate and disproportional damage and suffering they inflict, and that they must, therefore, be illegal under international law. This assertion, however, has not been universally accepted. The Western nuclear powers—the United States, the United Kingdom, and France—in particular have resisted this interpretation.[12]

The United Nations Security Council has primary responsibility for maintaining international peace and security under the U.N. Charter, but it has passed no resolutions concerning constraints on nuclear use. The General Assembly, which is authorized to make recommendations to the Security Council on questions of peace and security, has passed a number of nonbinding resolutions. In November 1961 it adopted a Declaration on the Prohibition on the Use of Nuclear and Thermonuclear Weapons, proclaiming that "any state using nuclear and thermonuclear weapons is to be considered as violating the charter of the United Nations, as acting contrary to the laws of humanity and as committing a crime against mankind and civilization."[13]

The resolution was introduced by a consortium of Asian and African nations during debate on general disarmament, and was supported by the Soviet Union. It was opposed by the United States, which wanted it modified to preclude the threat or use of any armed force and reworded to prohibit not all use of nuclear weapons, but rather their use "in any manner contrary to the United Nations charter," thereby keeping the resolution consonant with the charter provision that explicitly preserved "the inherent right of individual or collective self defense" against an armed attack on a U.N. member.[14] The U.S.-backed amendment was defeated 50 to 28 with 20 abstentions, and the resolution itself passed with a vote of 55 to 20 (the United States, the United Kingdom, France, and seven other NATO members opposing) with 26 abstentions.

Additional General Assembly resolutions reaffirming this basic prohibition were passed in 1965, 1972, 1978, and 1980. Again the NATO nuclear powers voted no.[15] Lacking the weight of international law, these resolutions did not affect NATO war plans or strategic concepts. Although the Soviet Union voted for them, it is highly doubtful that its war planning reflected or was affected by this show of support.

The only clear restriction in international law on the use of nuclear weapons appears to be a general prohibition against attacks on civilian populations per se. This is a fundamental principle of the accepted laws of war first codified in the Hague Conventions of 1899 and 1907 and later by the Fourth Geneva Convention of 1949.[16] The huge blast radii of nuclear weapons, however, made it impossible to discriminate in planning between military and civilian targets. As the U.S. delegation to the United Nations stated in 1968, "civilian populations may not be attacked as such, but we recognize that the co-location of military targets and civilians may make unavoidable, certain injury to civilians."[17]

In 1974 two conferences on conventional arms convened to develop the concepts contained in the 1949 Geneva Conventions. Their work resulted in Protocols I and II of 1977, which reaffirm and extend the basic laws of war. Protocol I strongly endorsed the basic principle prohibiting weapons "which are of a nature to cause superfluous injury or unnecessary suffering." It also prohibited weapons that would cause "widespread, long-term and severe damage to the natural environment." Protocol II further prohibited attacks on "dangerous forces" like dams, dikes, and nuclear power plants.[18] Both protocols would seem, logically, to outlaw the use of nuclear weapons, or at least to place strict limits on targets. If "reasonably construed," they would prohibit nuclear targeting of any civilian population, cultural objects and places of worship, objects indispensable to the survival of the civilian population, the natural environment, and installations containing dangerous forces.

Nevertheless, NATO nuclear powers rejected this interpretation, arguing that the protocols did not apply to nuclear weapons. Their position was supported by the introduction to the preliminary draft protocol of 1973, which stated that nuclear weapons could not be governed by U.N. protocol, since they were currently the subject of "international agreements and negotiations." Although the final draft was more ambiguous, the United States, the United Kingdom, and France have consistently held that the agreement applies only to conventional weapons, and that "special agreements [are] needed on nuclear weapons."[19] The United States signed Protocol I only with the understanding that "the rules established by this Protocol were not intended to have any effect on and do not regulate or prohibit the use of nuclear weapons."[20] As long as NATO nuclear powers insist that nuclear weapons can only be regulated through bilateral or multilateral disarmament negotiations, nuclear weapons will occupy the anomalous position of appearing logically inconsistent with the laws of war, but not legally proscribed.

An equal ambivalence surrounds the first use of nuclear weapons. Some authorities hold that first use is manifestly illegal, based on widespread general international agreement and the prohibition of first use of armed force under the U.N. charter, except when authorized by the United Nations. Yet the charter does permit use of force in individual or collective self-defense. One major authority has therefore argued that the U.N. charter legally bars a nation from "starting a war with nuclear weapons" but "does not prohibit another kind of first use—using nuclear weapons to repel a conventional attack."[21]

In summary, there does not appear to be any international law accepted by the nuclear powers that significantly restricts or restrains the use (either first or second) of nuclear weapons, except when blatantly used to initiate hostilities. Even such aggressive use may not contravene the laws of war if it is a preemptive strike in self-defense at the nuclear forces of an enemy that has provided unambiguous warning of its intention to attack. In short, nuclear weapons are largely outside the sphere of international legal controls.

Thus international law gives great latitude to governments which have nuclear weapons, and claim the right to use them in self-defense, in determining if, when, and how such weapons will be used, and how nuclear confrontations will be contained or curbed. The answers to such questions are found in the systems of laws, executive regulations, national and alliance policy statements, strategic and operational plans, and the actual weapons, delivery, communications, and warning systems of the nuclear nations.[22] These serve as the most important constraints on planning for the use of nuclear weapons. The American case is arguably the most complex and will be used to illustrate the problems involved in imposing nuclear planning constraints at the national level.

The U.S. Constitution of 1789 and the Atomic Energy Act of 1946 provide the legal basis of American nuclear command and control. Article II, Section II of the Constitution declares that "the President shall be commander-in-chief of the army and navy of the United States." The Atomic Energy Act empowers the president to consent to and direct "production of atomic bombs, atomic bomb parts, or other military weapons utilizing fissionable material," to have delivered "such quantities of fissionable materials or weapons to the armed forces for such use as he deems necessary in the interest of national defense," and "to authorize the armed forces to manufacture, produce, or acquire any equipment or device utilizing fissionable material or atomic energy as a military weapon."[23]

This presidential authority is limited primarily by the authority given to Congress under the Constitution to budget funds for the armed services and to declare war. Through the end of the cold war, however, congressional budgetary control over nuclear weapons production was limited by the extraordinary secrecy surrounding the nation's nuclear stockpile. Only the Joint Committee on Atomic Energy, beginning somewhat belatedly in the early 1950s and continuing up to its dissolution in 1977, had access to stockpile information. For most of its existence the Joint Committee actively supported development of America's nuclear capability and served mainly as a conduit for Atomic Energy Commission funding requests for weapons. Likewise, the House and Senate armed services committees and defense appropriations subcommittees have traditionally been strong advocates rather than critics of administration budget requests.[24] It was not until 1969 that Congress began seriously to challenge defense spending and selected aspects of American nuclear strategy. During the Nixon administration the Senate effectively blocked funding for extensive deployment of the Safeguard antiballistic missile system. It also attempted, unsuccessfully, to impose curbs on deployment of MIRV warheads and on U.S. capability to achieve a kill against hard targets such as enemy missile silos. In 1983 the House passed a resolution in favor of a nuclear freeze, but the amendment was never approved by the Senate.[25]

The failed hardware restraint measures might, if adopted, have limited the performance of future U.S. forces, but they would not have affected existing forces and then-current war plans. Further, budgetary constraints would not necessarily constrain planning for nuclear war. Unless Congress limited presidential authority to command the armed services, an a priori act both unlikely and unconstitutional, presidential policy choices would still guide nuclear force employment. If those policies mandated certain targeting priorities, such as hard target kill counterforce, the military would be obliged to attempt to implement them even if the weapons funded by Congress could not perform the task.

Congressional authority to declare war may be no more effective than budgetary controls as a constraint on nuclear employment. Should nuclear war begin with a surprise enemy attack, or clear warning of an imminent attack, the president would not be able to consult Congress before launching a retaliatory or preemptive strike. Even in the 1950s, when the United States could have expected several days' or weeks' strategic warning, the realities of nuclear war appeared inconsistent with congressional war-making authority. In 1956 President Dwight Eisenhower confided to his diary that there was very little the nation could do during the month before an impending Soviet attack to reduce its expected losses, except to launch a surprise attack of its own. The obstacles to such a course of action appeared insurmountable. It "would be not only against our traditions," he wrote, "but it would appear to be impossible unless the Congress would meet in a highly secret session and vote a declaration of war which would be implemented before the session was terminated. It would appear to be impossible that any such thing would occur."[26]

By the late 1960s, with ballistic missile forces on both sides, warning time was measured in hours if not minutes. The 1973 War Powers Act authorized the president to deploy forces in hostile situations but required that he provide Congress a written report within forty-eight hours detailing why the forces were deployed, for how long, and for what type of conflict. The president would have to withdraw the forces in sixty days unless Congress had declared war or voted to extend the time limit, or if U.S. forces were under "armed attack."[27] The contrast between the time frame established by Congress and the anticipated tempo of a nuclear confrontation is striking. Virtually all the critical decisions in a nuclear exchange would have to be made long before congressional war-making authority came into play. The major exception might be a protracted conventional conflict which could escalate into nuclear war. Although Congress would have time to act, it could not rule out the use of nuclear weapons, before or after declaring war, without infringing on the president's authority as commander in chief.

It is thus the preparations made to exercise that authority—in other words, the policies, plans, procedures, and physical safeguards established within the U.S. executive branch—which are the most substantive nuclear controls. Successive administrations have wrestled with balancing concerns about deterring Soviet aggres-

sion against anxiety about the threat of unintended or uncontrolled nuclear operations.[28] The history of American attempts to establish constraints on nuclear planning
can be divided into two periods. Between 1945 and 1960 the West relied on nuclear
weapons almost without constraints. From 1961 on American and NATO leaders
moved to impose a variety of policy, planning, procurement, and physical checks on
existing and planned nuclear forces.

Through 1960 the two greatest external factors feeding nuclear proliferation were
the tremendous imbalance between Soviet and Western conventional forces in Europe
and, after 1949, the threat posed by Soviet nuclear weapons. As a counter, the United
States relied on rapid expansion of its nuclear weapons capability and planned nuclear
offensives. In 1948 an American month-long bomber campaign against 70 Soviet
cities with 133 atomic bombs was projected as reducing Soviet industrial capacity 30
to 40 percent and killing 2.7 million people. By 1955, when the U.S. stockpile
numbered 2,280, an American atomic campaign was expected to cause the "total loss
of 118 out of 134 major Soviet cities" and to kill 60 million people. Full execution of
the first Single Integrated Operational Plan (SIOP) in 1961 would have killed 285
million people in the Soviet Union and People's Republic of China.[29]

What planning constraints were established over the arsenal capable of wreaking
such awesome destruction? Far fewer than might be supposed. From 1945 through
1974 the United States had no detailed national nuclear weapons employment policy.
Indeed, National Security Council (NSC) policies relating to nuclear weapons were
so general as to place virtually no limitations on their use. The first of these was
approved in the fall of 1948, in the midst of the first Berlin crisis. It was intended to
resolve confusion over whether the military was authorized to plan for the use of
atomic weapons. President Truman had rejected the first Joint Chiefs of Staff (JCS)
atomic war plan the previous spring and ordered a conventional alternative, a directive which was subsequently reversed by Secretary of Defense James Forrestal. The
NSC originally intended to address the issue of when and how nuclear weapons might
be used, but instead chose to endorse an air force originated paper that forcefully
argued against limiting military options.

NSC 30, United States Policy on Atomic Warfare, concluded that "in event of
hostilities, the National Military Establishment must be ready to utilize promptly and
effectively all appropriate means available, including atomic weapons, in the interest
of national security and must plan accordingly." Nevertheless, "the decision as to the
employment of atomic weapons in the event of war is to be made by the Chief
Executive when he considers such decision to be required."[30] NSC 30 gave the
military freedom to plan for nuclear war according to their own best judgment. Such
judgment was embodied in a special annex to what became the annual Joint Strategic
Capabilities Plan (JSCP). Annex C to the JSCP was approved by the JCS and was

used by military planners overseas and in the newly established Strategic Air Command (SAC) to prepare operational plans for nuclear war.

Military planners initially identified the Soviet urban industrial base as the most lucrative attainable target set. In 1949 the JCS added "retardation" targets, fixed installations in the Eastern bloc which could be struck to slow the Red Army's invasion. In August 1950, responding to the need to defend the U.S. homeland, the JCS gave highest priority to blunting Soviet capability to deliver atomic bombs against the United States and its allies. This drove the United States toward a preemptive strategy, and provided a powerful dynamic to increase the numbers both of installations targeted and of nuclear weapons required. To get the most from then-limited resources, SAC planned a simultaneous strike on all target systems, overwhelming the Soviet air defense network, to get the bombers through with minimal losses. This operational approach permitted little discrimination between the civilian and military target categories established by the JCS.[31]

In 1951–52 the State Department developed a proposed set of procedures for making a decision on nuclear use. It recommended that the JCS should either initiate or immediately review any proposal that nuclear weapons be used, and that the president would then consult with the secretaries of defense and state and the chairman of the Atomic Energy Commission before making his decision. Time permitting, he would also consult with congressional leaders, the American people, allied governments ("especially those whose consent is required before their bases can be used by the United States for atomic strikes"), and the United Nations. Although Truman did not approve or even comment on this proposal, the incoming Eisenhower administration came to view it as "established procedure."[32]

The question of consulting allies is especially interesting. In 1943, while cooperating with Great Britain on atomic development, the United States had signed an agreement stating that neither the United States nor Great Britain would use atomic weapons without the other's prior consent. This restriction, however, was removed by a new modus vivendi adopted in January 1948, which nullified existing atomic energy agreements between the United States, Great Britain, and Canada.[33] By 1950 the United States had deployed nuclear modified bombers and atomic weapons minus their cores of fissionable material to air bases in the United Kingdom, and was negotiating to do the same in Canada. In January 1952 President Truman and Prime Minister Winston Churchill agreed that no nuclear strike would be launched from U.K. bases without the consent of the British government. No other requirements for consultation were agreed to, although Truman assured the British he intended to keep communications open. Under Eisenhower the NSC ultimately wrote into national policy that the president should consult with allies before using nuclear weapons, but only if time permitted.[34]

Except for the question of procedures for considering nuclear use and possible consultation with allies, the Eisenhower administration appears to have actively discouraged the development of constraints on nuclear war planning. During an October 1953 NSC discussion on the role of nuclear weapons in national policy, JCS chairman Admiral Arthur Radford sought to clarify exactly how the weapons might be used, as a basis for U.S. force planning in both general war and limited conflicts, and for use in upcoming talks with the British. He proposed that a policy for the graduated use of nuclear weapons be adopted, one which assigned first priority to attacking "military forces operating against us or our allies," followed by their supporting structure. "Unrestricted atomic operations" would be launched only "in retaliation for such attacks on the west."[35]

President Eisenhower, however, was satisfied with language which specified that "in the event of hostilities, the United States will consider nuclear weapons to be as available for use as other munitions." The only clarifying (yet nonbinding) guidance, issued in January 1954, declared that "in certain cases," such as an atomic attack on the United States or Western Europe, "the use of nuclear weapons by the United States would be automatic," while in others, such as limited hostilities, the advantages of immediate use would have to be weighed against the possibility that it "would increase the danger of their strategic use by the enemy, lose the support of allies, expose them to devastation, or widen the Hostilities."[36]

By the mid-1950s the question of whether the United States should plan for limited nuclear operations, in contrast to full-scale nuclear war, was practically moot. By the end of 1954, after the failure of France to ratify the European Defense Community agreement, the inability of member states to meet the 1952 Lisbon conventional-force goals, and an intensive evaluation of the implications of the new nuclear technology in 1954 by a multinational committee of military officers called the New Approach Group, NATO moved to adapt its future strategy so as to rely on the power inherent in both strategic and tactical American nuclear weapons. NATO strategic concepts approved between 1954 and 1957 mandated that in the event of a Soviet attack, theater nuclear forces would be employed "from the outset" in conjunction with an "instant and devastating nuclear counteroffensive by all means available," particularly SAC, against the Soviet Union itself. It was emphasized that "in no case is there a NATO concept of limited war with the Soviet Union." Between 1952 and 1958 the number of nuclear weapons allocated for war planning purposes to NATO's commanders grew from 80 to more than 3,500.[37]

In April 1956, NSC 30 was finally superseded as American policy on atomic warfare by a paragraph in NSC 5602/1, the current statement of Basic National Security Policy: "It is the policy of the United States to integrate nuclear weapons with other weapons in the arsenal of the United States. Nuclear weapons will be used in general war and in military operations short of general war as authorized by the President. Such authorization as may be given in advance will be determined by the

President."[38] Like NSC 30, this statement placed no particular constraints on nuclear war planning, and it was interpreted to mandate planning for primarily full-scale nuclear conflicts. In the spring of 1956, with the apparent concurrence of the president, Secretary of Defense Charles Wilson ruled that the JCS should plan that "in a general war, regardless of the manner of initiation, atomic weapons will be used from the outset."[39]

NSC 5602/1 also introduced the important new concept that presidential authority over nuclear weapons could be transferred in part through predelegation. In 1956, even before the relevant systems were deployed, President Eisenhower approved advance authorization for the use of nuclear weapons in air defense. In May 1957 he issued an "authorization for the expenditure of nuclear weapons," which apparently gave U.S. theater commanders advance permission for nuclear response under a variety of emergency conditions. The instructions involved required extensive review and were not finally approved until 1959. In late 1959 and early 1960 Eisenhower authorized the secretary of defense to send additional, still classified, instructions on nuclear weapons expenditure to theater commanders and the commander of SAC. These authorizations appear to have been continued through at least 1964.[40] One source indicates that the four-star commanders were permitted to predelegate their authority to their three-star subordinates in charge of corps, numbered fleets, and air forces, further weakening the constraint inherent in strict presidential control.[41]

Another possible avenue for constraining nuclear war planning was through national policy pronouncements on war objectives. Between 1945 and 1960 three such statements were approved. The first was appended to NSC 20/4, the November 1948 statement of general U.S. objectives "with Respect to the USSR to Counter Soviet Threats to U.S. Security." It mandated reducing "the power and influence of the USSR to limits which no longer constitute a threat to world peace, national independence and stability in the world family of nations," but it rejected "a predetermined requirement for unconditional surrender," occupation of the Soviet Union, or other specific expectations, except that any surviving "bolshevik" regime should not control enough military resources to threaten any other regime.[42] The Truman administration's war plans were prepared under this statement.

In 1954 the Eisenhower administration approved a specific declaration of objectives for general war, beginning with the goal of achieving "a victory which will insure the survival of the United States," while preserving allies to the extent possible and reducing the capabilities of the Soviet Union (and if necessary Communist China) to wage war. Among the other objectives was one to enlist the support of the people in the Soviet Union and its satellites in the allied war effort, a goal that appears inconsistent with a nuclear offensive. During NSC discussion of the paper, however, President Eisenhower noted that "in such a war the United States would be applying a force so terrible that one simply could not be meticulous as to the methods by which the force was brought to bear."[43] In March 1959 Eisenhower approved a new statement of war aims which eliminated this modifying objective, and indeed removed any semblance of constraint that war objectives might have placed on war planning. NSC 5904/1 reaffirmed that the United States should prevail and survive, and that it should bring the Soviet Union and Communist China "to the point where they have lost their will or ability to wage war against the United States and its allies." The only limitation proposed on the nuclear offensive was, if feasible without jeopardizing other war aims, "to avoid unnecessary destruction and casualties in all countries not involved in the war."[44] In 1960 Secretary of Defense Thomas Gates overruled a majority of the Joint Chiefs to reaffirm Wilson's earlier directive that JCS planning be guided by the principle that general war was any "war with the USSR." No possibility that such a conflict could be contained at the conventional level was to be considered.[45]

The decision not to impose policy constraints on nuclear war planning reflected the views of the commander in chief about the nature of nuclear war. Eisenhower desired to insure that the U.S. commitment to employ nuclear weapons in event of attack on the United States or Europe was not subject to misperception by the Soviet leadership. He believed that the more terrible the prospect of a nuclear war appeared, the more deterred the Soviet Union would be from ever starting one. Further, Eisenhower understood that the United States had become vulnerable to attack for the first time in its history. Explicitly limiting a U.S. nuclear response, either by encouraging a retaliatory as opposed to preemptive strategy or by imposing limits on the number or types of nuclear weapons procured, would have strengthened congressional Democrats who had declared a "bomber gap" in 1956 and a "missile gap" from 1957 to 1960.[46]

The president may still have entertained notions of controlling the execution of U.S. war plans in circumstances other than a surprise attack, but the plans themselves had become exceedingly complex, requiring careful adherence to timing of attacks and bomber routes to targets. Further, between 1959 and 1961, U.S. nuclear capability had nearly doubled, from 12,305 weapons to more than 23,000.[47] Army and navy planners were concerned that lopsided emphasis on nuclear capability was leaving the nation unprepared to fight the limited, conventional conflicts that they argued were the most likely future challenges under the emerging U.S.-USSR nuclear stalemate. While the arguments revolved around issues of forces and budgets, they offered opportunities to propose constraints on war planning.

The first set of proposals looked to reducing the size of the planned SAC offensive. In August 1956 the navy began to examine a possible "minimal target system, the threat of destruction of which would deter the USSR."[48] By the next summer army and navy planners jointly presented a critique of SAC's weapons requirements, demonstrating that more weapons than needed were being assigned to installations targeted for attack. In late 1957 an alternative undertaking target list was proposed. It sought to create an exclusively retaliatory target list of highest priority targets that would be struck if the United States had only 25 percent of its current nuclear strike force remaining after a Soviet first strike. The alternative list emphasized Soviet government control and population centers and targeted residual Soviet nuclear capability only to the extent profitable. Designed to supplement existing target lists, it also had the potential to replace them if the decision were made to shift funds from nuclear systems to preparing for limited conventional wars. Work on the alternative list continued into 1960.[49]

The alternative undertaking would not have altered the operational approach in existing plans for a comprehensive counterforce and urban-industrial attack. That issue was addressed by two other initiatives. The first was a navy argument in favor of "finite deterrence, controlled retaliation" that built both on the targeting concepts underlying the alternative undertaking and on the anticipated deployment of the Polaris ballistic missile submarine. Polaris missiles based on relatively invulnerable submarines could be withheld and used selectively against Soviet targets to "apply political coercion if we like to gain national objectives more advantageous than simple revenge."[50] Although the primary targets for such attacks were urban-industrial concentrations, overall casualties were expected to be considerably lower than in the combined attack on military and urban targets. Further, the invulnerability of the submarine-based missile force would enhance deterrence by alleviating pressures to use or lose targetable land-based forces.

The anticipated development of ballistic missiles also gave rise to a very different initiative for controlling nuclear war, the "no cities" counterforce strategy advocated primarily by analysts at the Rand Corporation, an air force contractor. Retaliation against Soviet population centers was perceived as a confession of weakness.[51] The appropriate response was to target unexpended Soviet nuclear capability, including mobile ICBMs, while withholding attacks on urban centers in expectation that the Soviets would do the same. This retaliatory damage-limiting concept would constrain SAC's total response by breaking it up into more discrete options.[52]

In the spring of 1958 President Eisenhower moved to investigate whether future requirements for strategic forces could be reduced without weakening U.S. defense posture. He directed the NSC to undertake an analysis of what would constitute a minimum adequate deterrent and retaliatory capability, and subsequently of whether counterforce or urban-industrial targets were best suited to deterrence. The so-called Hickey Committee of the NSC staff completed its report in February 1960. Consistent with the war aims of NSC 5904/1, the committee focused not on what targets would best deter but on what would allow the United States to prevail in war. It proposed an optimum mix of counterforce and urban-industrial targets, similar to, if smaller than the list already being targeted by SAC. When Secretary of Defense Gates created the Joint Strategic Target Planning Staff (JSTPS) in August 1960 to consolidate the services' nuclear planning, the Hickey report was provided to it as guidance in the preparation of the first SIOP.

The new JSTPS, directed by the commander of SAC, completed SIOP 62 in December 1960, to enter into force at the start of the 1962 fiscal year in July 1961. The plan governed the operations of all American strategic and many theater nuclear forces and was designed to be executed either in retaliation or as a preemptive measure. It contained assurance of delivery factors of from 75 to 97 percent against each target category (nuclear targets, other military targets, and the urban-industrial base), resulting in considerable redundancy in order to assure destruction of the specified targets. The target list included 3,729 individual installations, many of which were co-located so as to be included in a single designated ground zero (DGZ). The plan had fourteen to sixteen attack options, all based on alert time. Within 15 minutes' warning, 1,004 delivery systems, carrying 1,685 weapons yielding some 2,100 megatons, were to be launched against more than 650 DGZs in the Sino-Soviet bloc. With strategic warning of 14 hours or more, 2,244 bombers and missiles, carrying 3,267 weapons yielding more than 7,800 megatons, would attack a total of 1,060 DGZs, including those in more than 150 urban areas. Eight hundred of the DGZs were defined as military targets.[53]

SIOP 62 represented a technical triumph in the history of war planning. In less than fifteen years the United States had mastered a variety of complex technologies and acquired the ability to destroy most of an enemy's military capability and much of the human habitation of a continent in a single day. SIOP 62 incorporated operational choices that aimed to reduce the friction of war, coordinate and protect bomber forces, and integrate bomber and missile forces at the cusp of two eras in warfare. It was an American Schlieffen Plan, an ultimate strategy for war winning under all circumstances of war initiation, with an even less tenable basis in political and military realities than the German plan, infamous for its inflexibility, executed in 1914.

The JSTPS was not insensitive to the issue of constraints. SIOP 62, as the JCS briefing for President Kennedy emphasized, was not so inflexible as to preclude options. It was possible to withhold attacks against most targets in the satellite nations. (Only radar sites, surface-to-air missile batteries, and other defensive targets would have to be hit.) It was also possible to withhold attacks against cities. There were, however, strong arguments against making such a choice. The plan was designed to be executed as a whole, and there would be no way to adjust it rapidly to decisions to withhold. In particular, forces withheld might not survive for later use if needed: "Thus, withholding of a portion of the planned attack could degrade our plan and the forces committed to it to the point that the task essential to our national survival might not be fulfilled." Furthermore, "limiting attack to military targets" would have "little practical meaning as a humanitarian measure," since atomic weapons are "relatively non-discriminating, especially with respect to fall-out." With so many military targets located near population centers, it was impossible to reduce civilian casualties substantially through withholding, or to convince the Soviets that the United States was seeking to do so. It was far better to execute the plan in its entirety, if necessary, than to risk the nation's survival by seeking to impose constraints at the last minute.[54]

The incoming Kennedy administration could not simply reverse fifteen years of American war planning by high policy fiat. In addition to confronting the technical realities involved in changing the SIOP, there were political limitations. The Democrats had been elected in part on their promise to close the missile gap, and the best the new administration could hope for was to constrain nuclear war plans gradually, bringing them under control by incremental actions. Although Kennedy explicitly declared in March 1961 that the nation's arms would not be used to strike first, no such directives were sent to the Pentagon. Indeed, during the Kennedy and Johnson years no specific NSC statements on national security policy, war aims, or national nuclear employment policy were issued, despite the fact that a number of such statements were drafted, and the JCS made clear that they would have found such guidance valuable. Rather, pointed National Security Action Memoranda (NSAMs) were issued to prod the bureaucracy and improve responsiveness to presidential initiatives. Rarely did these memoranda become policy per se. Except in one significant instance relating to the Berlin crisis of 1961, no attempt was made to mandate nuclear employment policy from the White House.

Instead, Robert McNamara used the enhanced powers of his Office of Secretary of Defense (OSD) to regulate the procurement of both nuclear delivery systems and nuclear weapons, and he also mandated changes in JCS guidance for the SIOP. For example, whereas in the 1940s and 1950s the JCS had sent requirements for nuclear weapons through a military liaison committee directly to the Atomic Energy Commission, in the 1960s, McNamara's office provided a formal statement of nuclear requirements. This kept the 1961 stockpile of 23,000 weapons from doubling by the end of the decade, as 1961 JCS requirements dictated, and it leveled off at some 32,500 weapons in the mid-1960s.[55] In fact, McNamara came into office inclined toward a strategy of finite deterrence, and he had little faith in first-strike counterforce. The briefing he received on SIOP 62 in Omaha in February 1961, however, convinced him that it would be extremely difficult to revise American war plans or cut forces back to a finite deterrent level. Seeking alternatives, he was very impressed with a subsequent briefing on the Rand "no cities" counterforce concept, and he had consultants draft a military strategy section of a basic national security policy statement to mandate such an approach.[56]

The Kennedy administration's attempt to reformulate nuclear strategy was accelerated and focused by the second Berlin crisis, which began in 1958 and continued into the mid-1960s. The "Deadline Crisis" from November 1958 to March 1959 had led the Eisenhower administration to adopt a strategy based on the theory that a single large probe, perhaps as much as a division moving down the Autobahn, was all that was needed to force the Soviets to back down or accept general war.[57] By the fall of 1961 the intensive review of American military strategy in general and military options in Berlin led to directives to revamp American war planning. What was ultimately accomplished, however, was far less than the administration desired. The process illustrates the difficulty of imposing meaningful constraints on nuclear planning even when the stakes are high and time is available to design reforms.

In October 1961 two directives were approved as the basis for reshaping American nuclear strategy. The first was NSAM 109, U.S. Policy on Military Actions in a Berlin Crisis, which laid the groundwork both for a series of graduated conventional and nuclear responses in a Berlin crisis, and for American efforts to promote a flexible response strategy for NATO. The second was the National Strategic Targeting and Attack Policy prepared by the Joint Chiefs of Staff and approved by Secretary McNamara as guidance for redesigning the SIOP.

NSAM 109 built upon a variety of studies and proposals. These included an April 1961 policy statement, based on a study prepared by former Secretary of State Dean Acheson, which proposed reorienting NATO strategy for localized, conventional contingencies such as a clash over Berlin, because a massive Soviet attack on Europe was unlikely. It also built on JCS studies ordered by Secretary McNamara of how many divisions NATO would require to hold out over specified periods against a Soviet invasion of Europe without resort to nuclear weapons. The structure of NSAM 109 was furnished by an OSD study, initiated in the army staff toward the end of the Eisenhower administration, which examined the full range of possible Soviet actions and allied countermeasures that a Berlin crisis could precipitate, focusing on those considered most likely.[58]

NSAM 109 described a four-phase preferred sequence for military operations over Berlin, from dealing with localized harassment of Western access, to challenging significant blockage, to expanding conventional ground and air operations in Europe and maritime pressures worldwide in the face of continued obstruction of access, and finally to the employment of nuclear weapons. The fourth phase called for responding to continued Soviet intransigence in the face of "substantial non-nuclear" pressure with, first, "selective nuclear attacks" to demonstrate a willingness to use such weapons; second, "limited tactical employment" to gain tactical advantage and/or to increase pressure on the Soviets; and finally, if all else failed, general nuclear war. This planning directive was provided to the JCS and General Lauris Norstad, the Supreme Allied Commander, Europe (SACEUR), as well as to NATO allies (though some, like the French, were never shown phase four) for discussion and approval.[59]

One question that concerned the Kennedy White House and the McNamara Pentagon, for which NATO was not responsible, was how the United States might wage general nuclear war if such a contingency became unavoidable. Over the summer of 1961 key deputies in the NSC and OSD examined the implications of new intelligence that the Soviet Union's intercontinental nuclear forces were much smaller than had been thought. By mid-August they produced a critique of SIOP 62 and the outline of an alternative strategic concept. The ultimate distribution of this concept remains unclear, but a copy was apparently transmitted from the White House to the JCS in September.[60]

The only available documentary evidence of this effort indicates that it explored how to capitalize on gaps in Soviet air defenses to launch a limited surprise first strike aimed at neutralizing Soviet ICBM, IRBM, and bomber forces. Ten B-52 bombers, each carrying four H-bombs and two nuclear-tipped air-to-surface missiles, would infiltrate at night at an altitude of 500 feet to carry out a synchronized attack with U.S. ICBM and Polaris missiles against ICBM and bomber bases deep within the Soviet Union. This would be followed up by a relatively small number of strikes by airborne alert B-47 bombers and theater land- and carrier-based aircraft against Soviet theater nuclear forces. Damage estimates projected that the Soviets would have two or less of their ICBMs remaining, as well as thirty IRBMs, forty-five medium bombers, and five sea-launched ballistic missiles.[61] Possible Soviet responses were considered limited: if they attacked U.S. cities, a maximum of 9 million American fatalities were anticipated; if the Soviets responded against European cities, 36 million might perish. The United States would retain the bulk of its nuclear forces to deter such city attacks, however. Further analysis indicated that if Soviet nuclear forces were alerted at the time of a U.S. attack, many more of their forces would survive. Soviet countercity strikes against the United States and Western Europe would cause more than 100 million deaths.[62]

Despite the transmission of this study to the JCS, it appears to have played no role in revising SIOP 62. Some off-line contingency planning may have been undertaken in the Joint Staff, but its ultimate fate is shrouded in mystery. The new SIOP guidance, which had been debated by the JCS through the summer of 1961, was presented to Secretary McNamara on October 23 and approved two days later.[63] Recently declassified material provides new insights into the changes it mandated. SIOP 63, as completed in June 1962, broke SIOP 62 into five attack options, some designed for preemptive execution, others for retaliation. There were three tasks for destruction to specified levels of, respectively, Soviet nuclear capability, other military forces, and the urban-industrial base. The five attack options did not address each target category (much less any subsets) separately. Rather, the options were cumulative, each adding a target category to the previous one. All required expending thousands of nuclear weapons and were subsequently criticized as "five options for massive retaliation."[64] They permitted the president to order strikes "against nuclear threat targets only, against nuclear threat plus other military targets, or against nuclear threat plus other military plus urban-industrial targets." Provisions were included for withholding attacks, by task, against satellite countries and the People's Republic of China, or against military and government controls in the Moscow or Peking area, so as to permit a negotiated settlement. Finally, "selected forces of high survivability" were kept in reserve "to be employed as the last resort threat in any retaliation situation," apparently against the Soviet urban-industrial base.[65]

The new SIOP was prepared over the protests of SAC, which expressed "doubt that there were sufficient forces available to withhold a reserve for later use, doubt that forces held in reserve would survive, and doubt above all that the command and control system [which had been built with emphasis on surviving only long enough to get the Emergency War Order through to launch the forces] would operate long enough or effectively enough to launch and direct them."[66] As the Soviet Union deployed increasing numbers of strategic forces, such doubts would grow. Nevertheless, this basic design for the SIOP remained the foundation of U.S. nuclear employment strategy for more than a decade and a half.

The planning set in motion by NSAM 109 carried forward into 1962. In January President Kennedy and his advisers met with General Norstad, and reviewed and possibly amended the command and control procedures within his command for the selective and limited use of nuclear weapons.[67] On June 20 (*after* he had given his famous speeches at Athens, Greece, and Ann Arbor, Michigan, announcing the counterforce shift in U.S. nuclear targeting policy) Secretary McNamara was briefed on SIOP 63.[68] Then on August 18 President Kennedy and his advisers were briefed on the status of Berlin contingency planning. A wide array of options had been identified, for initiatives short of military force in Phases I and II, and for tripartite (U.S., U.K., and French) or quadripartite (plus German) military initiatives in Phase III, which would be turned over to NATO control if allied forces came under attack. Phase IV, which was defined by the United States as beginning with any use of nuclear weapons, whether in response to Soviet use, for demonstration purposes, or "to avoid defeat of major military operations," had been prepared for by nuclear annexes attached to the plans for each type of military operation to be used in Phase III, and a specific nuclear-only plan for the demonstrative use option.[69]

Kennedy seems to have been doubtful about the prospects for success of the options mandated by NSAM 109. He interrupted the briefer's explanation of the subtleties of and allied difficulties with nuclear use in Phase IV to remark: "I suppose if we get involved in a war in Europe we will have no choice but to use nuclear weapons."[70] This frustration may have fed the president's caution when faced two months later with the Cuban missile crisis, which appears to have had little impact on the efforts to change American nuclear planning. Guidance issued for SIOP 64 on November 14, 1962, "had very few substantive changes from previous guidance."[71]

Barely ten months later, however, on September 12, 1963, American nuclear planning reached a significant but until now unheralded milestone. The Net Evaluation Subcommittee (NESC) of the NSC reported its findings to President Kennedy and the full NSC on the results to be expected in a nuclear war from 1964 through 1968. After the briefing the president asked the head of the subcommittee, Air Force General Leon Johnson, "whether, even if we attack the USSR first, the loss to the U.S. would be unacceptable to political leaders." Johnson responded "that it would be, i.e., even if we preempt, surviving Soviet capability is sufficient to produce an unacceptable loss in the U.S." Secretary McNamara further emphasized that "there was no way of launching a no-alert attack against the USSR which would be acceptable," and "thus, preemption, today or in 1968 is not an acceptable course of action."[72]

Subsequent studies indicated that even with 1,950 Minuteman ICBMs (in contrast to the 1,100 to 1,300 then approved by McNamara for procurement through 1968), the least the United States could hope to suffer in retaliation for a preemptive attack on a smaller than expected future Soviet missile force was 28 million American and 60 million Western European dead. Against a "medium" Soviet force and with a nationwide civil defense program, the United States could expect 58 to 95 million dead and 75 to 100 million allied fatalities, depending on whether 950 or 1,950 Minutemen were deployed.[73] Further OSD analysis raised even more questions about whether the United States could use offensive or even existing air and planned missile defense weapons systems to limit damage and reduce casualties in the United States.[74]

As a result McNamara seized on the concept of "Assured Destruction," a secure second-strike capability that under any conditions could destroy half of Soviet industry and 20 to 25 percent of the population in large cities, as a basic measure for the size of the American programmed force. While the attack options in the SIOP did not change to reflect this priority, guidance issued through 1974 gave highest priority to assigning weapons to urban-industrial targets first, then to nuclear threat and other military forces. "The capability of destroying urban-industrial targets was to be assured even with inadequate warning of an attack" on U.S. strategic forces.[75]

The end of counterforce preemption as a serious option, however, did not represent an end to the counterforce mission for SIOP-assigned U.S. nuclear forces. First, it is not clear whether President Lyndon Johnson was made aware of the NESC's findings when he took office after Kennedy's death. Johnson was not at the September NSC meeting. McNamara declared in 1983 that he had warned both presidents against initiating nuclear use, but he has not provided dates or details of those discussions. The defense secretary did tell Johnson that "neither side can blunt an attack by the other" at a December 5, 1963, NSC meeting on Soviet military capabilities, and Johnson received a brief on executing the SIOP from JCS Chairman Maxwell Taylor on December 9, and a full JCS SIOP brief in August 1964, but there is no indication what the president understood or decided about executing the war plans available to him.[76]

Second, the United States did not abandon damage limitation as a task for strategic offensive forces. Rather, the emphasis was placed on second-strike counterforce, which involved targeting residual Soviet nuclear forces after a first strike on the West, or launching U.S. forces on less than perfect (i.e., early) warning of a Soviet preemptive strike in hopes of destroying as many enemy missiles and bombers on the ground as possible. This had become an extremely difficult challenge. Attacking Soviet follow-on forces was now less feasible than in the early to mid-1960s, when many of those forces had to undergo a laborious fueling and arming sequence prior to launch, including mating missiles to their nuclear warheads, which were stored separately.[77] In addition, new calculations involving heretofore unconsidered results of nuclear explosions—electromagnetic pulse, atmospheric ionization, and the dust created by near-surface explosions—suggested that the problem was far more complex than had been supposed. Taking into account the rapid growth of the Soviet ICBM force, such complexities appeared to have "pushed the counterforce problem beyond coherent calculation."[78] The only way to carry out the assigned task seemed to be to place even greater emphasis on redundant cross-targeting of available systems, thereby increasing the likelihood of unintended damage to nonmilitary targets.

In less than a decade from 1961 American nuclear force structure changed dramatically. The bomber force was significantly reduced. One thousand fifty-four hardened and dispersed land-based ICBMs were deployed, as were 41 submarines armed with 656 ballistic missiles. The SIOP, however, remained basically unchanged. SIOP 64 was replaced by SIOP 4 in 1966 (the annual designation of the plan having been dropped). It continued the patterns begun by the first flexible response plan, SIOP 63, designed in 1961. While withholding of attacks on cities was provided for, large-yield warheads, redundant cross-targeting of warheads to achieve high damage, and damage criteria based only on the primary effects of nuclear explosions (blast and overpressure) rather than such secondary effects as fire and radiation meant that even attacks on military targets would produce high civilian casualties. SIOP 4 remained the basic U.S. nuclear war plan through the mid-1970s.[79]

McNamara had wanted to introduce greater flexibility and discrimination into nuclear war planning. When he left office in 1968, he described the lack of more controlled and deliberate response options as "one of the main weaknesses in our posture today."[80] Nevertheless, his embracing of assured destruction meant that he put little effort into pressuring the JCS or the JSTPS to make the SIOP more discriminate, while the demands of the continuing counterforce requirement also tended to work against discrimination.

Two other factors complicated the push for greater flexibility and restraint. The first was the escalating requirement for MIRV warheads on SLBMs and ICBMs to counter the anticipated deployment of a Soviet antiballistic missile system. McNamara left office calling for nearly six thousand independently targeted missile warheads by 1976. With several warheads on each missile, a decision to use even one meant the destruction of multiple targets. The single warhead missiles retained were less accurate and had a greater yield per warhead than the multiple warhead missiles that were deployed.[81] The second problem was the enormous technical difficulty involved in perfecting and deploying systems that would permit greater flexibility and selectivity in nuclear force employment. In particular, limited and discriminate nuclear options required effective "tactical warning" sensors and "attack assessment" (TW/AA) networks to provide information on enemy nuclear operations, including the size and targeting of incoming attacks; the capability for rapid retargeting of ballistic missiles to accommodate changed circumstances; and secure and enduring command, control, and communications (C3) systems to allow the president (or his successor) to transmit orders for strikes over a protracted period with confidence that they would be received.

The capability to "classify the attack, as small or large, for example, accidental or deliberate, selective or indiscriminate, against cities or not, against high command or not" was critical in supporting "a decision as to an 'appropriate' retaliatory response."[82] It was not until 1971, with the launch of the first operational Defense Support Program (DSP) orbital infrared detection satellite designed to detect missiles in the powered-launch phase, that potential warning time could be extended from the 15 minutes afforded by the Ballistic Missile Early Warning System radar to "perhaps" 27 minutes. DSP-type systems improved "the capability to assess an attack and even evaluate the likely intentions of the attacker, and [did] so by a wide margin over other warning and surveillance systems." They "promised for the first time . . . to make flexible response options more than a remote possibility."[83]

Likewise, the capability to retarget missiles rapidly was not available until nearly a decade and a half after SIOP 63's guidance was approved. Through the mid-1970s it took as long as 90 days to retarget the Minuteman force. On an emergency basis the target tapes of a single missile might be changed in 9 hours. The command data buffer system, which became operational in 1975–76, enabled the retargeting of a Minuteman III missile with three MIRV warheads in 36 minutes. In addition, guidance software changes increased the number of execution plans prestored in missile launch control centers from 100 to 200. With respect to submarine-launched ballistic missiles, even if the submarines had had a rudimentary capability for rapid retargeting, the SLBMs' lack of accuracy and the fact that a single missile launch might give away the submarine's location diminished their potential in limited strikes.[84]

Creating a survivable command and control system was the most difficult problem. Such a system "would require a considerable capability to assemble, evaluate, and utilize information, almost certainly in an extremely fast-moving situation, probably with normal information systems, communications, and command operating under great stress, overload or other abnormal conditions, and perhaps with impaired or degraded capabilities."[85] From the 1960s on major improvements were made to the American strategic C3 system, including backup communications links to the bombers, ICBMs, and submarines; airborne and other mobile command posts for the president and major commanders, improved TW/AA systems, and improved intelligence gathering capabilities against the Soviet Union. One major study of the results of this vast and expensive modernization program concluded in the mid-1980s, however, that even in response to a limited attack against U.S. nuclear forces, the vulnerabilities of the command system would "encourage comprehensive retaliation." Further, "a limited Soviet counterforce attack would not be unambiguously limited, and it would trigger preplanned operations that, in conjunction with extensive collateral damage to the command system, would create strong pressures for organizing retaliation around a single plan that releases most of the SIOP retaliatory forces. Regardless of what calculations political leaders might make at the time, they would have to select the plan that would achieve everything they would expect to accomplish in retaliation for the duration of the conflict."[86]

Despite this dismal prognosis, efforts continued in the 1970s and 1980s to increase options available to the Western alliance in general, and the president of the United States in particular, in using nuclear weapons. The main thrust of these efforts was to create punctuation points or pauses in a nuclear confrontation to provide the opportunity for reevaluation before entering into a general nuclear exchange.

Soviet military capability grew tremendously during this period, not just strategic nuclear forces but theater nuclear forces and significantly modernized conventional ground and tactical air forces as well. Efforts begun in the 1960s to strengthen NATO's ability to fight conventionally continued, but there was great political reluctance among the European allies, and limited economic ability, to develop the capacity for fighting a protracted conventional war of up to thirty days before using nuclear weapons. Nevertheless, the 1960s initiatives left their mark on NATO planning: a new strategy of flexible response was formally approved in December 1967. Recently published discussions confirm that this concept was defined as "direct defense [of NATO territory] in event of attack," to be followed by "deliberate escalation of the level of military force in accordance with the level of an attack," and finally "general nuclear release."[87]

Implementing such a strategic concept meant first, that the alliance would have to increase controls on nuclear weapons to insure that their use was indeed deliberate, and not the result of actions by individual field commanders. Second, it required that NATO have a series of plans for using such weapons across a range of possible war-initiation contingencies. Third, it meant that NATO needed agreement among its members as to when and where nuclear use might be initiated and for what political and military objectives. Finally, the concept mandated modern theater and tactical nuclear forces, and their associated command systems, which would allow NATO to employ nuclear weapons in a controlled and discriminate manner.

The first two requirements were more readily met than the latter two. NSAM 160, promulgated by the Kennedy administration in June 1962, required that Permissive Action Links (PALs) be fitted to all nuclear weapons in Europe, beginning with those on Quick Reaction Alert aircraft. The first PALs were five-digit combination locks fitted on the warhead containers of nearly a dozen tactical and theater weapon types. These were later replaced by electronic locks with six- to twelve-digit codes and limited try features, which after too many attempts would cause electrical circuits to self-destruct, disabling the weapon.[88]

By 1973, to meet the second requirement, there were myriad nuclear-employment options available. According to General Andrew Goodpaster, SACEUR at the time, these included "the controlled battlefield use of nuclear weapons, possible air defense use of nuclear weapons, possible use at sea, going from there into the more extended battle area which might include use of close-in interdiction purposes, extending even to counter-nuclear, counter-air, always in a tactical role against military targets and beyond that we have plans, prepared plans and capabilities of conducting the full scale use against fixed targets of military significance and the threats against [NATO's European] command extending throughout the Warsaw Pact area."[89] Some of these options were fully preplanned while others were partially preplanned against mobile targets. The key concept in plans for tactical or battlefield use was a nuclear "package," defined as "a discrete group of nuclear weapons by specific yields for employment in a specified area during a limited time frame to support a corps tactical contingency. It should be treated as a single entity for the purposes of request, release and control." Any nuclear use would have to meet the dual criteria of military effectiveness and avoiding collateral damage.[90]

The requirement for agreement among NATO members on nuclear use resulted in the establishment in early 1967 of the Nuclear Planning Group (NPG), composed of NATO defense ministers who met twice a year to consider nuclear policy. The NPG adopted a set of "provisional political guidelines for the Initial Defensive Tactical Use of Nuclear Weapons by NATO" in November 1969, which stated that since "any initial use of nuclear weapons would result in a qualitative change in the nature of warfare, such use by NATO should have a fundamentally political purpose." This statement appeared to reject nuclear war-fighting strategies in favor of a deterrent posture, but it did not specifically constrain nuclear operational planning. Because NATO members could not agree to rule out or commit themselves in advance to any particular form of nuclear employment, a variety of options were planned, so as to be available as needed.[91]

Debates aimed at turning the guidelines from a provisional statement to a final one, covering not just initial use but follow-on use and general nuclear response, continued for sixteen years. Finally, in October 1986, a statement of General Political Guidelines for the Employment of Nuclear Weapons in the Defense of NATO was approved. While the political purpose of initial nuclear use was reaffirmed, selective early use of nuclear weapons against military targets (as opposed to less militarily effective demonstration use) was approved, particularly initial use "mainly on the territory of the aggressor including the U.S.S.R." aimed at "destroying targets in depth" in hopes of "reversing the attack and splitting the Warsaw Pact coalition."[92] The difficult process of crafting a NATO agreement on the circumstances of nuclear use illustrates the problems involved in determining ahead of time how, when, and where constraints would (or would not) be applied.

By the time NATO at last adopted its General Political Guidelines, its nuclear forces had undergone a long, difficult political struggle for piecemeal modernization. The force posture achieved served to define the political guidelines for use rather than the other way around.[93] One of the most bitter debates concerned the neutron bomb, which the Carter administration ultimately chose not to develop, and which, although revived by the Reagan administration, was never deployed overseas. The neutron bomb, or more accurately the Enhanced Radiation Warhead for tactical missiles and artillery shells, appeared to some to be a significant new limitation on nuclear forces, designed to reduce collateral damage in attacks on invading Soviet armored formations. To others, however, its reduced collateral effects appeared to make nuclear war more likely by blurring the distinction between nuclear and conventional weapons.[94] NATO's 1979 decision to deploy Pershing II IRBMs and ground-launched Cruise missiles to counter Soviet deployment of MIRVed SS-20 IRBMs led to even greater controversy in 1983–84. The ability of these U.S. single warhead weapons to reach the Soviet Union from bases in Western Europe made them a critical part of the strategy of deliberate escalation, but also made them tempting targets for a Soviet preemptive attack. In the end, however, the political resolve their 1983–84 deployment so forcefully demonstrated resulted in the signing of the INF Treaty in 1987. The subsequent destruction of an entire class of weapons represented the ultimate constraint on their use.[95]

In the 1970s and 1980s the American nuclear policy process finally reached maturity. In 1974, 1980, and 1981 the Nixon, Carter, and Reagan administrations respectively issued a presidentially approved statement on nuclear employment policy. These statements went beyond the calculated ambiguity of the Truman and

Eisenhower policies on atomic warfare, and spelled out target categories, the purposes their destruction would serve, and the general characteristics and constraints of employment plans. Each policy statement was then expanded upon by a more detailed Nuclear Weapons Employment Policy (NUWEP) issued by the OSD which spelled out, in increasing detail as the years went on, specific attack options. Together these documents provided the detailed, civilian-approved guidance for specific nuclear war planning by the JCS in Washington and the JSTPS in Omaha.[96]

The first of these presidential policy statements, National Security Decision Memorandum (NSDM) 242, did not change the general character of the SIOP target categories established thirteen years before. Rather, this so-called Schlesinger strategy, named for the initiatives begun by the then–Secretary of Defense James Schlesinger, resulted in hybrid nuclear planning which emphasized neither counterforce nor countervalue. The new policy mandated escalation control through the development of limited nuclear options against various subsets of these target categories, as well as regional nuclear options to deal with Soviet threats in various theaters, capitalizing on the technological advances in warning, attack assessment, retargeting, and command and control. These options were designed to permit the use of strategic nuclear forces while reducing the likelihood that a general nuclear exchange would result. Whether this could actually have been done became the subject of much public debate. U.S. presidents were at least provided with more choices than the limited number of SIOP options available in SIOP 63, SIOP 64, and SIOP 4.

NSDM 242 also emphasized "the existence of non-targets, i.e., places that it would be in the U.S. interest to preserve from destruction." Previously, constraints had been established "on the amount of fallout on allied and neutral territory, constraints by SACEUR on collateral damage in Eastern Europe and constraints on damage within allied territory; there was also the city withhold option. However, on the whole, it had been assumed that collateral damage to places of value to an adversary other than designated targets was a 'bonus.' [NSDM 242] explicitly recognized that it might be very much to the U.S. advantage to prevent damage to certain places or things of value in the Soviet Union, e.g. population centers."[97] The new guidance also established a requirement for a secure reserve force to influence intrawar and postwar bargaining. Finally, it established the objective of using nuclear weapons to impede Soviet postwar recovery, enabling the United States to reconstitute itself more rapidly than the Soviet Union. This objective ended the emphasis on assured destruction established by Secretary McNamara. NSDM 242 and its associated NUWEP became the guidance for SIOP 5 and its revisions from 1976 through 1981.

President Jimmy Carter came into office intending to further reduce U.S. requirements for nuclear weapons by emphasizing minimum deterrence. By this time, however, intelligence assessments of the unprecedented Soviet military buildup, including the now declassified Team B analysis of Soviet Strategic Objectives, an Alternative View, indicated that the Soviets had approached nuclear strategy from perspectives very different from those that had gained acceptance in the West in the 1960s.[98] As a result Carter initiated the Nuclear Targeting Policy Review, an in-depth study of Soviet military doctrine, in hopes of more tightly focusing U.S. strategy. This extensive survey of Soviet thought, plans, and programs concluded that Soviet decision makers considered victory in a nuclear war possible and preferred short, decisive conflicts, either conventional or nuclear. The Carter administration thus began to consider how to fight a protracted nuclear conflict with the Soviet Union to deny Soviet war aims.

Presidential Directive (PD) 59 of June 1980 mandated certain changes in nuclear weapons employment policy. In particular, economic recovery targeting was de-emphasized, in favor of targeting logistics and war-supporting industries. As a result "literally thousands of industrial targets" were dropped from the SIOP.[99] PD 59 also redefined the secure reserve force and sought to make it more survivable, in expectation of a protracted conflict. The two most important changes, however, were to emphasize targeting military and political leadership, including command posts and communications facilities, to the point that it was made a separate targeting category, and to increase emphasis on targeting Soviet general-purpose forces, including supply depots, marshaling points, airfields, and storage facilities, with strategic weapons. PD 59 was approved too late to serve as guidance for the Reagan administration's first SIOP, and a new National Security Decision Directive, NSDD 13, was approved in October 1981. This document, which appears to have reaffirmed most of PD 59's conclusions, served as guidance for SIOP 6 and its revisions, which governed American nuclear strategy through the end of the cold war.[100]

By the 1980s the U.S. government had gone as far as it could in developing and refining constraints on nuclear war planning, considering the persistent problem of command and control in a nuclear environment. While government officials had labored hard for more than twenty years to effect options and establish restraints, most realistic decision makers were aware that the circumstances leading to the outbreak of a superpower war could not be predicted, and that any use of nuclear weapons was likely to get out of hand rapidly. The major attack, selected attack, and limited nuclear and regional nuclear options that reportedly comprised the SIOP were admirable attempts by reasonable men to enhance deterrence and, if it failed, to control nuclear use and retard the slide toward Armageddon. Nevertheless, in view of the sheer numbers of weapons involved, the magnitude and diversity of their destructive power, and the unprecedented uncertainties of nuclear war, no constraint was assured, especially if human passions overwhelmed human rationality.[101]

These concerns were reinforced by the growth of Soviet nuclear forces under the umbrella of the SALT I and SALT II treaties, a political stalemate over procurement and deployment of additional strategic offensive forces, and a major public debate over the morality of continued nuclear deterrence. In response the Reagan administration turned to other, less direct approaches to restraining nuclear planning. The first was oriented toward the midterm future: the Strategic Defense Initiative (SDI) looked to using a variety of technologies for protection from ballistic missile attack. By the time he announced SDI in 1983 Reagan had already experienced at least one SIOP briefing, and clearly found existing options and constraints inadequate to his needs.[102] The second approach involved developing conventional military strategies for near-term implementation, to deny the Soviet Union a speedy victory in Europe without resort to nuclear weapons. In 1982, NSDD 32, the Reagan administration's statement of national security policy, required the U.S. military to be capable of fighting a protracted conventional war. Many of the military initiatives of the 1980s, including the U.S. Army's Air-Land Battle Doctrine, the U.S. Navy's Maritime Strategy, and NATO's strategy for Follow-on Forces Attack, must be understood not just as spurs to conventional procurement, but as manifestations of this policy.[103]

The end of the cold war relieved the pressure that had generated enormous stockpiles of nuclear weapons and planning for how to use and defend against them. Nevertheless, the question of how to control nuclear weapons will remain so long as the weapons themselves exist, although we can draw some useful insights into this problem from the historical record we have considered. First, the central issue in the control of nuclear weapons is time. By the 1970s the tempo of potential nuclear conflict had reached the point where time, or lack thereof, became the critical determinant of when and how nuclear forces might be used. Even with the advent of theater nuclear packages and limited strategic options in the 1970s, nuclear war plans were designed as worst-case scenarios, ready for immediate execution upon the alerting or generation of assigned forces. While these plans may have been tailored to deal with more discrete target sets than in the 1960s, they were still designed to treat military contingencies, neglecting the political circumstances surrounding the opening of hostilities. With adequate time for contemplation and decision, war plans might be updated and modified to fit the circumstances of war initiation and, perhaps, even to reflect the basic legal and moral mandates that the superpowers had deemed inapplicable. Without adequate time, leaders would have been left with preplanned and possibly unsuitable options.

Second, it may well be that nuclear weapons are simply not amenable to the kind of organizational and planning controls with which decision makers have tried to master them during the past forty-five years. The most effective constraint on nuclear weapons appears, in the end, to be an extraordinary reluctance to use them, out of fear of the consequences. The applicability of international law may be in dispute, and national policy may serve to illuminate the problem rather than to resolve it, but basic human instincts have built a barrier against Clausewitz's full discharge of total war. Even without access to the frightening statistics in official briefings on executing the SIOP, the public is aware of the horrendous possibilities of nuclear war. The military and civilian leaders who have been exposed to the details, and who bear ultimate responsibility, find the prospect even more sobering.

It seems possible that an opportunity now exists for a new beginning. The time available to decision makers has increased dramatically as the threat of a Soviet invasion of Western Europe has disappeared, and the prospects for global conflict have dissipated. Large numbers of targets have been dropped from existing war plans.[104] The incentive for early intercontinental use of nuclear weapons is virtually negligible, and incentives for theater use are likely to be almost equally low for the foreseeable future. Can strategies be devised to take advantage of this opportunity? Considerable flexibility is now possible in nuclear planning. Capitalizing on continuing improvements in retargeting technology and intelligence and warning capabilities, emphasis can be put on adaptive planning to fit the circumstances, rather than on rigid planning to meet, however inappropriately, all circumstances of war initiation and military operations. START II will eliminate many of the time pressures associated with "use it or lose it" systems built during the cold war, and the treaty (when ratified and implemented) will ensure that once the reduced force levels are attained, they will be legally constrained from rising again. It might even be possible for East and West to retain nuclear forces without having them aimed at particular targets.

This last eventuality was initially discussed by physicist Freeman Dyson in the 1980s.[105] Even if it occurs, however, it will not end the quest for nuclear constraints. While the superpowers will have moved back from the brink of Armageddon, special attention will have to be given to new dangers like the use of nuclear weapons in regional or even internal crises, and threats by outlaw states to use them to coerce their neighbors or perceived enemies. Neither problem can be resolved by better nuclear employment planning. Both must be addressed through diplomacy first, including stringent physical controls on remaining stockpiles and strong enforcement of counterproliferation measures. The fewer nations with nuclear weapons and the means to use them, the more manageable the problem. If these controls fail and nuclear attacks are threatened by renegade powers, a conventional military response for the purposes of prevention and preemption would clearly be preferable to a nuclear response.

The question becomes more difficult, however, if the renegade succeeds in launching a nuclear attack, resulting in enormous destruction and high casualties. Would such an attack, most likely by a nation with limited nuclear capability, justify preemptive or punitive nuclear strikes in response? Would it be possible to define the conditions necessary for nuclear retaliation, the military objectives to be served, and the appropriate targets for nuclear weapons under these conditions?

A framework might be provided by the 1977 protocols to the Geneva Convention. With the cold war over and START II limitations in place, the objections initially raised by the nuclear powers to applying these restrictions to nuclear weapons may no longer have legal validity or political utility. For the first time in forty-five years it appears possible that nuclear weapons can be used without initiating Armageddon. The question now is whether the international community, in cooperation with the nuclear powers, is ready once again to seek to impose constraints on even limited use.

George J.
Andreopoulos

I I
The Age of National
Liberation Movements

One of the most distinguishing features of the post-1945 era in international politics is the emergence of national liberation movements.[1] What this term immediately brings to mind is a whole set of movements that sought to integrate territorially oriented nationalism with social-reformist themes.[2] *Emancipation* in one form or another became a code word, as did *peoples;* the latter figured prominently in the 1977 Geneva Protocol I when the provisions of the 1949 Geneva Conventions were extended via article 1 §4 to "armed conflicts in which peoples are fighting against colonial domination and alien occupation and against racist régimes in the exercise of their right of self-determination."[3] The term *peoples* which in the postwar period had begun life as a rather nebulous concept in the aspirational provisions of the U.N. Charter (in particular, article 1 §2, "to develop friendly relations among nations based on respect for the principle of equal rights and self-determination of peoples") had ended as a term guaranteeing legal protection in the use of force of the type that traditional international law had reserved only for organized states.[4] To its supporters, such a development constituted a long-overdue corrective in the international community, reflective of the changes that the conduct of warfare had undergone in the previous thirty years; to its critics, the international personality bestowed upon peoples was a purely political construct imposed by Third World states in their perennial quest to legitimize struggles that sometimes may be indistinguishable from terrorism. Regardless of where one stands on this issue, one thing is certain. As Michael Howard has noted in this volume's introductory chapter, the emergence of national liberation movements reintroduced the older concept of *jus ad bellum,* "legitimizing the conflict not in terms of the authorities fighting it or the methods they use but of the cause for which it is fought."[5]

To assess the impact of the national liberation movements on the laws of war, I shall examine the following issues: (*a*) the prevailing tendencies in international politics in the aftermath of World War II; (*b*) the new dimensions in the conduct of warfare as exemplified in the practice of national liberation movements; (*c*) the challenges that the emergence of these movements posed for traditional international legal concepts and for the regulations on warfare; and (*d*) some of the key facets of the Algerian War, the event that contributed more than any other single event to the legitimation of national liberation movements in their quest for self-determination. As must be obvious by now, the subject necessitates as much a discussion of *jus ad bellum* as *jus in bello* issues.

The end of the Second World War brought to the forefront the underlying tensions between the United States and the Soviet Union.[6] The period 1946–53 was to witness the emergence of a series of potential/actual conflicts which raised the stakes in the superpower confrontation and led to the consolidation of the bipolar nature of the international system: the Iranian Crisis, the Greek Civil War, the 1948 events in Czechoslovakia, the Berlin Crisis, the Chinese revolution, and finally the Korean War. For American policy makers, this series of events necessitated the creation of a worldwide network of bases and the forward deployment of forces, as well as a series of regional alliances (NATO, SEATO, CENTO, ANZUS) whose main purpose was to deter any contemplated challenge by rendering its costs prohibitively high. For Soviet policy makers, these events led to the tightening of their control over the nations of Eastern Europe as a way of consolidating what they considered to be their legitimate sphere of influence: the *quest for security* became the code word for repressive policies articulated by unrepresentative regimes. The confrontation was quickly transcending the traditional great power rivalries of the past by acquiring a distinct zero sum game mentality. Until Khrushchev's enunciation of the doctrine of peaceful coexistence in the early 1960s, the feeling among both policy makers and large sections of the public was that accommodationist strategies were doomed; the way to survive was not by compromise but by the eventual demise of the opponent's system.

As the East-West conflict was entering its global phase, another powerful determinant of political developments appeared in the Third World—nationalism. Third World countries constituted, with few exceptions, a challenge to be met not so much in military terms, but primarily in terms of the type of development to which the indigenous people would aspire. Since each superpower had implicitly ceded to the other a sphere of unchallenged influence, the Third World was to become the *terra nullius* of geostrategic considerations: namely, the terrain where few, if any, legitimate interests were taken for granted. The rising tide of Third World nationalism intersected with the East-West conflict to produce explosive situations: situations in which the criteria employed to assess the legitimacy of a nationalist struggle had less to do with the merits of the case and more with its perceived impact on the East-West conflict. What the cold war framework did was to bring forward the social-reformist themes in the ideology of certain national liberation movements, themes which were most often drawn from Marxism. At the same time, it downplayed the nationalist themes, which were drawn from the European tradition of territorially oriented nationalism and the Wilsonian notions of self-determination that were equally incompatible with colonial rule, as the cases of the Front de Libération Nationale (FLN) in Algeria and of Ethnike Organosis Kypriakou Agonos (EOKA) in Cyprus were to demonstrate.

In such a context the inherent instability of colonial regimes led to a series of insurgent challenges that compounded the international community's traditional ambivalence (lack of consensus) in dealing with the sensitive issues associated with civil war situations. The overt politicization of the symbols of recognition, whether dealing with rebellion, insurgency, or belligerency, led to the disappearance of the concern for correlating status with facts; as Falk aptly noted at the time, "These symbols of legal status have themselves been virtually discarded, and governments determine their relations to competing political elites on the basis of their preferences, capabilities, and foreign policy goals, as well as on the basis of what their adversaries are doing or would tolerate."[7] However, the deep ideological cleavages in the international system were only part of the problem; what made the whole picture infinitely more complicated were the nature of these insurgent movements and their conduct of warfare.

Guerrilla (or irregular) warfare became particularly important in the post-1945 period, although as a mode of warfare it is as old as war itself.[8] It is the type of warfare which has traditionally empowered weaker forces to confront stronger ones, relying on the elements of constant mobility and surprise attack. Its main vehicle is the civilian soldier, a notion that encapsulates not only the inextricable link between the fighter and the population on whose behalf the struggle is waged, but the fighter's categorical refusal to be reduced to a single identity.[9]

Clausewitz was the first thinker to seriously undertake the effort to synthesize the characteristics of irregular warfare. Despite the fact that in his major work *On War* the section on irregular warfare remained in rough draft,[10] it nevertheless influenced all subsequent studies on the subject. He outlined five conditions for the effectiveness of irregular warfare and in the process captured some of its essential dimensions.[11] In particular, he noted the importance of avoiding major confrontations with the enemy; rather by nibbling "at the shell and around the edges" he would force the enemy to overstretch his resources, thus enhancing the overall effectiveness of the resistance.[12] Another critical dimension relates to the organizational characteristics of insurgent groups. Although the type of actions they engage in are characteristic of strategic defense, they must never allow their actions to turn into tactical defense; on the contrary, they must maintain a technically offensive posture by making skillful use of the element of surprise attack (i.e., raids and/or ambushes).[13] Thus, the necessity to opt for confrontations in which they can use sudden, overwhelming force, coupled with the ability to withdraw in unfavorable circumstances and prepare for a subsequent counterattack under more favorable ones, constitute key operational characteristics of guerrilla warfare.

While Clausewitz focused on the operational dimension, it was Mao Tse-Tung who articulated the political dimension of guerrilla warfare.[14] This need emerged as a result of the Chinese Communist party's near disastrous confrontation with the Kuomintang in 1927. This experience convinced Mao that a reorientation of the traditional Leninist strategy was long overdue. Shifting the focus to the peasantry as the main vehicle for the revolutionary struggle and following his axiomatic definition of revolution as revolutionary war, he addressed two major issues, (a) the building of a Communist army and (b) the development of tactics responsive to the needs of an objectively weaker military force.[15] The crux of the matter was to obtain the best intelligence possible on the enemy's strengths and weaknesses and in the meantime deny similar accessibility to the enemy's forces. If successful, such a strategy would enable one to concentrate superior forces at selected places, choose the time and place of fighting (something that was brilliantly adhered to by the Vietcong during the Vietnam War),[16] and avoid all potentially unfavorable engagements.[17]

To achieve this, Mao proposed the integration of intelligence tactics with popular mobilization. Such an undertaking could materialize via an ingenious use of Lenin's concept of the united front.[18] Contrary to Lenin's vision of the united front as a tactic used to position the party for the eventual seizure of power by a dedicated elite of professional revolutionaries, Mao focused his attention on the population at large and sought to forge a permanent rather than a temporary link. As Johnson has aptly noted:

> Mao conceived of a united front with the mass of the population so that the people could serve as the source of his army's manpower and as its intelligence-collecting network. In order to obtain this desired level of cooperation from the population . . . the revolutionary directorate had to discover some issue salient among the masses which the party could champion; the party thereby gains access to the people's sympathies and is able to organize the masses for guerrilla warfare.[19]

Such a link—which at the strategic level emerged as the "mass line" concept—could only function if based on a continuous interaction between the party and the population; hence, Mao's emphasis that the party should avoid at all costs espousing policies not grounded on popular aspirations, however inchoate these may be. In the meantime, the people should be educated on "the political goal of the struggle and the political organization to be used in attaining that goal."[20] Such an interactive relation is intended to produce both a party (and a fighting force) responsive to popular needs and a politically conscious and readily mobilized popular base.[21] Thus, Mao's prescriptions were anchored on the importance of politics in shaping and controlling warfare[22] (one of the most crucial elements in Clausewitz's theory of war) and on the need for a broadly based fighting force. The obsessive concern with maintaining "a unity of spirit" with the local inhabitants is well reflected in the famous "Eight Points for Attention": (1) Speak politely. (2) Pay fairly for what you buy. (3) Return everything you borrow. (4) Pay for anything you damage. (5) Do not hit or swear at people. (6) Do not damage crops. (7) Do not take liberties with women. (8) Do not ill-treat captives.[23] Of these eight maxims only one refers to the interaction with enemy forces (no. 8). The first and foremost criterion of military virtue is the way the guerrilla fighter behaves vis-à-vis his own people. It is the application of the mass line concept to the rules of warfare.

As a result of this continuous interaction between party and people the lines become blurred—the party is the people and vice versa; likewise in the case of war the distinction between combatant and noncombatant is rendered meaningless since it fails to capture the essence of the civilian soldier. During the Vietnam War the National Liberation Front (NLF) named its paramilitary forces Dan Quan, meaning civilian soldiers, indicating thus that the United States was not fighting against a guerrilla army but against the Vietnamese nation.[24]

It is not difficult to understand the enormous advantages that such a strategy, if properly adhered to, entails for the guerrilla forces. Most importantly, it places the onus of indiscriminate warfare on the enemy. The guerrilla's ability to melt into the population, or—to use Mao's famous formulation—to be the fish who inhabit the water (the people), makes one of the most fundamental principles of the laws of war untenable, namely, the distinction between combatants and noncombatants. Captured guerrillas have routinely failed to abide by the provision of article 4 of the 1949 Geneva Convention III on Prisoners of War that would qualify them for prisoner of war status.[25] A similar problem is posed with villages, homes, and shelters. Since the guerrilla fighters live primarily among the civilian population and use the villages as bases of operations and for intelligence-gathering networks, it is increasingly difficult for their opponents to distinguish, during the course of operations, the genuine homes from those that may function as guerrilla hideouts or fortifications. Once again, the opponent must shoulder the burden of indiscriminate conduct.[26]

The inability to discriminate between combatants and noncombatants (the product of the guerrillas' refusal to accept a single identity, that of either civilian or soldier) coupled with the inability to force a decisive encounter (the product of the guerrilla's strategy to choose the time and place of engagement) would often generate levels of frustration among their opponents that would result in questionable rules of engagement (like forced resettlements of village inhabitants) or outright brutalities (wholesale massacre of innocent civilians) as the following examples from the Algerian and Vietnam wars indicate.

During the Algerian War (1954–62), the French forces often resorted to reprisals against the inhabitants of villages believed to have harbored guerrillas and to have acted as operational bases for terrorist attacks against them.[27] In addition, they set up regroupment camps where huge numbers of villagers were relocated as a means of stripping FLN guerrillas from the much-needed civilian cover for their activities; the conditions in these camps were often deplorable. According to a report by Monsignor Rodhain, general secretary of Secours Catholique Français, by the late 1950s there were more than 1.5 million displaced persons.[28] The French government was charged by the Provisional Government of the Algerian Republic (GPRA) with setting up the equivalent of concentration camps in clear violation of article 3 of the 1949 Geneva Convention IV on the protection of civilian persons.[29]

During the Vietnam War the My Lai massacre came to symbolize one of the lowest points in an already deeply unpopular war. One of the principal figures in that massacre was Lieutenant William Calley, who was charged with four counts of murder. At his court-martial the defense counsel attempted to highlight, among other things, both Calley's inadequate training in the laws of war and the fact that upon arrival in Vietnam he had been instructed that all Vietnamese (men, women, and children) were potential enemies. This prompted the following exchange:

Q: I am talking to you about the training that you received—I don't know who would give it to you. It had to do with the enemy you would face and what you could expect, who they might be and information in that general area?
A: Well, there was never any word of exactly who the enemy was, *but to suspect everyone, that everyone was a potential enemy and that men and women were equally as dangerous and because of the unsuspectedness of children, they were even more dangerous* [author's emphasis].[30]

A similar argument was used when Calley sought to appeal his conviction to the Court of Military Appeals. Once again the appellate defense counsel argued, among other things, that Calley was acting in ignorance of the laws of war and that since his commanding officers had informed him that only "the enemy" would be there, he genuinely believed that there were no innocent civilians at My Lai; thus he bore no "criminal responsibility for their deaths." The Court of Military Appeals did not accept this and the other arguments presented by the defense and upheld Calley's conviction.[31]

Such attacks on civilians are expected to enhance the guerrilla fighters' standing with the population at large. In fact, in many cases their strategy is predicated on their opponents' indiscriminate counterattacks as a means of mobilization of the civilian population. Bearing in mind that in most cases the guerrillas begin with a small core of supporters, their enemy's superior forces and the often indiscriminate use of their firepower constitute an indispensable component in the strategy of massive mobilization. If successful, this strategy would contribute to the transformation of what began as a military struggle into a political one.

The emergence of national liberation movements raised a whole set of legal and political issues concerning the international community's attitude toward (*a*) the nature and (*b*) the rights and duties of these entities. The most fundamental issues were those concerning their legal status (i.e., whether they could be subjects of international law) and the conditions under which they could resort to the use of force.

Before the issue of the internationalization of the wars of national liberation came up on the agenda of the United Nations, the international community considered them as internal wars in which the insurgents could only receive the benefits and rights of international law (including the application of the relevant provisions of the Hague and the Geneva Conventions) "when they had developed characteristics sufficiently analogous to those of States to be granted belligerent rights or to be recognized as the new government in power."[32] How should the international community respond to a quest for belligerent status (which was the international community's way of saying that the said movement was a legitimate contender for power), when in most cases these movements did not control territory to an extent that would enable them to exercise government-type functions? Moreover, how could the international community sanction the use of force when, according to article 2 (4) of the U.N. Charter, it was expressly forbidden except in cases of individual or collective self-defense (article 51 of the Charter)? And even in that case "this inherent right" referred to U.N. members (i.e., states). Finally, on what basis did national liberation movements represent the people and how could the international community assess the representative character of these movements? These questions were to generate a series of arguments in which legal reasoning and political considerations were very often coextensive. To the supporters of these movements the bottom line was the need for the progressive development of international law; to the critics the bottom line was the attempt of these movements to acquire all the rights that international legal status could confer, while being unable and/or unwilling to live up to the concomitant responsibilities.

The first concern addresses the controversial issue of recognition. While there are indeed certain rules specifying the requirements for belligerent status and (eventually) recognition, a closer examination of state practice indicates that very often political considerations are as important a determinant as international legal norms in these situations. Two examples can be cited. During World War I the Paris-based Polish National Committee was recognized as cobelligerent by France and Britain, even before the formation of an independent Polish state. During World War II the British government de facto supported Tito's partisans in Yugoslavia, while in the meantime recognizing the London-based royalist government as the legitimate government of Yugoslavia.[33]

The variance of state practice with legal rules may have an adverse impact on the enforcement of certain fundamental norms. For example, the granting of belligerent status to a guerrilla movement will imply that their captured members will have to be treated in accordance with the provisions of the 1949 Geneva Convention III relating to prisoners of war. However, as noted above, guerrilla warfare is premised (at least during the initial stages) on continuous mobility and the absence of a permanent base. Their mode of operation prevents them from developing the type of infrastructure that will enable them to grant similar treatment to captured enemy soldiers.[34] Thus, the granting of belligerent status places the guerrillas at an advantage since it gives them a right (to be treated as prisoners of war) without the concomitant responsibilities (to treat likewise their opponents). Despite these problems, the historical record indicates that the correlation between material capacity to fulfill certain obligations and recognition is not as high as it is often claimed, and that the concern about certain requirements as preconditions for recognition has failed to translate into an applicable set of objective criteria.

The second concern addresses the issue of the use of force. In an effort to legitimize their use of force, national liberation movements have used the plea of self-defense, attempting thus to base their claim on article 51 of the U.N. Charter. At first the self-defense argument was rationalized as a delayed response to colonial aggression. Thus, in the initial stages of the Algerian revolution the FLN argued that their resort to armed struggle was a delayed response to the illegal invasion and occupation of Algeria by the French in 1830; an illegal act to which the Algerian people never acquiesced.[35] This, however, was not an argument confined to national liberation movements. India, for example, argued that its 1960 annexation of Goa was, among other things, a legitimate response to Portuguese colonial aggression which had occurred in 1510, that is, 450 years earlier.[36] But this argument had no legal basis because at the time most of the colonies were acquired, the use of force was a legitimate instrument for the acquisition of territories. In addition, as Quincy Wright argued in his criticism of the Indian position, the fact that a considerable amount of time had lapsed without challenging this "continuing aggression" ipso facto nullified all claims to a legitimate exercise of the right of self-defense.[37] Similar criticisms have been raised against the Organization of African Unity's (OAU's) use of the continuing aggression argument in support of African liberation movements.[38] To be sure, national liberation movements could point to minor sporadic acts of resistance as indicative of the reluctance to acquiesce to colonial conquest as the FLN did; but the nature of these acts was mostly of a symbolic rather than substantive nature. The international community's rejection of this argument was understandable, since if accepted, it would open a Pandora's box for all sorts of new territorial claims offered as delayed responses to illegal acquisitions of territory with unpredictable, if not outright explosive, consequences.

A second argument for the use of force has sought to link self-defense with the right of self-determination. This argument draws from the Declaration on Principles of International Law concerning Friendly Relations and Co-operation among States in Accordance with the Charter of the United Nations adopted by the General Assembly during its 25th session in 1970.[39] According to this view, the recognition of the principle of self-determination as an international legal principle implies in the words of the Declaration that "the territory of a colony or other Non-Self-Governing Territory has, under the Charter, a status separate and distinct from the territory of the State administering it." The separate and distinct status of the territory in question empowers the peoples to resist any "forcible action" which deprives them of their right to self-determination. "In their action against and resistance to such forcible action . . . such peoples are entitled to seek and receive support in accordance with the purposes and principles of the Charter." Thus self-determination internationalizes the conflict, which in turn empowers the peoples concerned to seek support from the U.N. Charter in cases of forcible action to deprive them of that right. As the record shows, U.N. resolutions, especially those approved unanimously (as was the case with the resolution approving this Declaration) are worded in a way that allows for wide-ranging interpretations.

Supporters of national liberation movements have argued that the 1970 Declaration legitimizes armed resistance to forcible denial of self-determination. For them, forcible denial is manifested by the imposition or maintenance by force of colonial or alien domination.[40] In fact, one scholar has argued that the Declaration asserts that liberation movements have a *jus ad bellum* under the Charter.[41]

This interpretation has been challenged on several grounds. First, that the resolution's provisions do not equate the maintenance of a colonial regime with forcible denial of self-determination; thus, the use of force is only legitimate when used in defense against armed attack rather than in the initiation of force to achieve self-determination. Second, that the resolution makes no mention of armed resistance, but simply of resistance. This ambiguity, critics argue, can be construed as referring to forms of resistance that do not involve the use of force. Finally, that the clause on the "purposes and principles of the Charter" can be interpreted in such a way as to legitimize only the type of assistance that is consistent with the overriding duty of U.N. members to "maintain international peace and security," as the United States representative argued, while voting for the resolution.[42]

Although this second argument was less problematic than the first one, namely, the use of the self-defense argument in favor of the right of self-determination rather than against the notion of continuing aggression, it did not settle the dispute. On the contrary, the rather broadly phrased General Assembly resolutions that both preceded and followed the 1970 Declaration simply confirmed the continuing controversies over the legitimate use of force. To be sure, the Declaration unquestionably established the right of peoples to self-determination as an international legal right; how-ever, the use of force in the exercise of that right was considered a questionable proposition, particularly in cases where the peoples were to initiate rather than respond to the use of force.[43]

The central importance of the right to self-determination in any discussion con-cerning the status and empowerment of national liberation movements reflects pri-marily two postwar developments in the international community. The first has to do with an increasing concern for the promotion and protection of human rights as evidenced in the relevant provisions of the U.N. Charter, the Universal Declaration of Human Rights, the International Covenant on Civil and Political Rights, and the International Covenant on Economic, Social, and Cultural Rights, among others.[44] To be sure, this concern had to confront well-entrenched rules, especially those associated with the domestic noninterference clause, as expressed in the Charter. The creative tensions between domestic jurisdiction and human rights concerns were to generate strong pressures for change. Article 73, for example, of the U.N. Charter commits U.N. members who administer non-self-governing territories to "develop self-government, to take due account of the political aspirations of the peoples, and to assist them in the progressive development of their free political institutions." Like-wise, article 21 of the Universal Declaration of Human Rights states, "Everyone has the right to take part in the government of his country, directly or through freely chosen representatives . . . [and] the will of the people shall be the basis of the authority of government." What these and similar provisions did—granted that most of them were of an aspirational nature—was to question the proposition that matters of domestic jurisdiction should be kept insulated from the international community. It was becoming increasingly difficult for U.N. members to sustain adherence to the high standards of the Charter's Declaration Regarding Non-Self-Governing Territo-ries, while at the same time remaining indifferent to the way colonial territories were treated by fellow member states. The second development had to do with the interna-tional community's slow and tortuous adjustment to the challenge posed by the Algerian War of Independence. This war contributed more than any other single event to the passage of Resolution 1514 (XV), the Declaration on the Granting of Indepen-dence to Colonial Countries and Peoples, on December 14, 1960,[45] and to the pre-mature recognition of movements fighting wars of national liberation. To understand the importance of this war, we will briefly examine some of its key aspects.

The Algerian War was to become the test case for the relevance of the traditional distinction between international and internal wars. The nature of the war remained in dispute between the French and the FLN until the very end. For the French, the war was nothing more than an internal rebellion to be suppressed by all means necessary in order to restore domestic order. For the FLN, it was a war of national liberation which entitled them to the protection offered by international legal norms. The conflict lasted for almost seven and a half years and was fought with uncommon ferocity.[46] Almost from the beginning it was termed a *sale guerre* (dirty war). It was a characterization that reflected both the predisposition of the participants and the issues at stake: for the Algerians it was the long-overdue overthrow of colonial rule; for the French, coming on the aftermath of the humiliating defeat in the Indochinese War, it represented the last opportunity to reverse the passing of national greatness and the concomitant demise of *la mission civilisatrice.*[47] What compounded the problem was the existence of a million and a half Algerians of French descent, the *pieds-noirs.* For them any change in the status of Algérie-Française was tantamount to a threat to the very existence of their community. Thus, both sides could lay claim, with varying degrees of success, to the alluring imagery of a popular struggle.

At the outbreak of the conflict, the FLN's initial proclamation stated that its goal was national independence to be achieved through (*a*) restoration of the Algerian State, within the framework of the principles of Islam, (*b*) the preservation of all fundamental freedoms without distinction of race or religion, and that one of its key external objectives was the internationalization of the Algerian problem.[48] The latter objective was a reflection of the FLN's realization that internationalization would both enhance its legitimacy and assist it in the efforts to obtain much needed foreign military and financial assistance. It was a brilliantly executed strategy which quickly became the blueprint for future liberation movements.

In order to bolster its credentials as the authentic representative of the Algerian people, the FLN presented itself as a "nation-party"; this formulation projected the image of an inclusive formation, open to the whole of society, rather than an exclusive one reflecting sectional interests.[49] Moreover, it sought to create nationwide institutions of a governmental character. In this context it summoned delegates to a congress in August 1956 which chose members for two bodies: the National Council of the Algerian Revolution (CNRA), a legislative body, and the Committee of Coordination and Execution (CCE), an executive body; the latter was replaced by the Provisional Government of the Algerian Republic in September 1958.[50] Finally, with the skillful use of mass demonstrations and strikes, such as the 1955 and 1956 strikes on the anniversary of the French invasion of Algeria, as well as the 1957 strike at the time of the U.N. General Assembly debate on the Algerian question, the FLN strengthened its claim concerning the emancipatory nature of the struggle.[51]

The war began on November 1, 1954, when the FLN launched a series of guerrilla attacks on French rural outposts. Initially, the FLN attempted to justify its actions on the basis of the aforementioned argument about a delayed reaction to the colonial aggression of 1830.[52] However, this did not take the FLN very far and it quickly switched to the argument relating to the right to self-determination. The Algerian rebels felt that if the international community were to endorse that right, then their use of force could be legitimized as an exercise of self-defense against French military efforts to suppress it. It was a small step "from declaring that a people are entitled to independence to declaring that they may use force if independence is denied."[53] Thus it could be argued that the Algerian FLN was the first national liberation movement to articulate the use of force as the only means of sustaining the legitimate quest for self-determination. To be sure, this was a convincing argument to the already converted group of Afro-Asian states who supported the FLN from the beginning; but it is instructive to remember that no state sought to obtain a formal U.N. condemnation for the use of force by the FLN.[54]

The French government's reaction was typical of most governments when faced with such a problem. It resolutely refused to consider the conflict as anything other than an internal one, in which domestic law and order provisions were applicable. In a speech to the National Assembly a few days following the initial attack, the prime minister Mendès-France declared that "one does not compromise when it comes to defending the internal peace of the nation, the unity and integrity of the Republic. The Algerian departments are part of the French republic. . . . Ici c'est la France!"[55]

Mendès-France's pronouncements were to be echoed by successive prime ministers and reflected a growing concern over France's diminishing imperial role, a role which was perceived as coextensive with national survival. Such a perspective rendered ipso facto colonial wars as "the measure of the nation."[56] What transformed, however, the Algerian War into a virtual last stand case was the intersection of two powerful factors: (*a*) the genuine belief held among sections of the French population and the pieds-noirs that Algeria was indeed part of France, and (*b*) the defeat in Indochina which had generated strong ill-feeling among army officers toward the politicians and the institutions of the Fourth Republic. A group of disillusioned young officers began articulating what came to be known as the doctrine of *guerre révolutionnaire,*[57] which was to be the French answer to the Maoist strategy of guerrilla warfare. Their near obsession with the notion of a ubiquitous Communist challenge, which in the case of Algeria was pure fiction,[58] coupled with their strong conviction that the politicians had abandoned the army in Indochina, militated against any compromise solutions in Algeria. The stage was thus set for the sale guerre in the villages, the Casbahs of the cities, and the "inhospitable crags and passes of the High Atlas."[59]

This was primarily a guerrilla war whether fought in urban or rural areas. With no set battles or fixed fronts, the French army was engaged in operations against an enemy who was everywhere and nowhere; against "a wily, slippery and often invisible enemy whose strongholds and solace lay in the souks and casbahs of the cities."[60] It was a conflict that exhibited the classic patterns of irregular warfare whereby a vastly inferior force can repeatedly frustrate its enemy due to the skillful use of the elements of concealment and surprise attack. Yet despite its modest successes, the Armée de Libération Nationale (ALN, the military arm of the FLN)[61] never posed to the French forces the type of challenge that the Viet Minh did during the Indochinese War. Although there was a noticeable growth in both numbers and skill, particularly after gaining sanctuaries in Morocco and Tunisia in March 1956, the ALN "in Maoist terms . . . was never able to move their war beyond the opening stage of guerrilla war and terrorism."[62]

On the other hand, this did not translate into major operational successes for the French forces. In fact, as the war progressed, both the nature of the French commitment and the anger of the officers grew. It was the Socialist-led government of Guy Mollet which in 1956 decided to commit the conscription army to the cause of Algérie-Française, resulting by the end of the year in the presence of 500,000 troops on Algerian soil, a tenfold increase since November 1954.[63] And it was the officer corps which read in this commitment a confirmation of their determination to achieve total victory; a victory in the pursuit of which considerations of controlled warfare were an irritant at best and a dangerous illusion at worst.

The most notorious example of total war during the Algerian conflict was undoubtedly the Battle of Algiers.[64] During 1956–57 the FLN carried on a series of terrorist activities in the city of Algiers; this constituted a major escalation of the conflict which up to that point had focused on the villages, the mountainous areas, and the rebel strongholds along the borders with Tunisia and Morocco. The French response was swift and decisive. Major cleansing operations were mounted by French forces; they cordoned off the Casbah and engaged in a systematic effort to dismantle the FLN cells and arrest their leaders. These search-and-destroy missions lasted for nine months and became known as the Battle of Algiers. They were conducted with extreme brutality and included the routine torture of FLN members and suspected sympathizers. In particular, the 10th Paratroop Division of the Foreign Legion, called in to restore order and commanded by General Jacques Massu, stood out for its consistent and widespread use of torture;[65] although the Battle of Algiers was finally won by the paratroopers, "the methods employed . . . to win the battle had probably done more than anything to discredit the cause of Algérie française in the eyes of both French and world opinion."[66] This battle has been vividly portrayed in a powerful and deeply disturbing film by Italian filmmaker Gillo Pontecorvo. In this film Ali La Pointe, an illiterate street dweller, personifies the anonymous civilian soldier in the service of revolutionary justice. Counterpoised to him is the cool, calculating Lieutenant Colonel Mathieu whose main task is to identify and destroy the FLN structure in the autonomous zone of Algiers.[67]

At the time of the Algerian conflict the principal instruments governing the conduct of warfare were the 1907 Hague Conventions, in particular Convention IV (relating to the Laws and Customs of War on Land) and the four 1949 Geneva Conventions concerning the protection of the victims of war.[68] The former "was so outdated as to be virtually forgotten."[69] Concerning the Geneva Conventions, the

French government had ratified them in 1951 without reservations, hence it was bound by their provisions. The question arose whether these provisions were applicable in the context of the Algerian conflict.

In cases where the conflict was of a noninternational character, article 3, which was common to all four conventions and provided a fundamental baseline for humanitarian conduct irrespective of the nature of the conflict, was to come into force. From the initial stages of the conflict, the FLN tried to reach an agreement with the French government concerning the applicability of article 3 of the conventions. In these efforts, the FLN sought to enlist the assistance of the International Committee of the Red Cross (ICRC). In 1958 the ICRC (on the basis of the provision in article 3 concerning the offer of its services to the parties to the conflict) presented a draft agreement by which both parties would pledge themselves to observe the provisions of article 3.[70] This and similar efforts by the FLN to reach a "special agreement" with the French government on the "whole body of humanitarian problems which had arisen in the course of the Algerian war"[71] failed primarily due to France's persistent refusal to admit the applicability of the said conventions to the conflict.[72] Finally, in a gesture of strong symbolic value, the GPRA declared its intention to accede to the Geneva Conventions by formally depositing the necessary instruments of ratification with the Swiss government, an action which it took on June 20, 1960. The accession was well-timed. Coming when the FLN's infrastructure had survived the most serious challenges of the war, and with the de facto and de jure recognition of the GPRA by a growing number of states, the FLN had made an important step toward international legitimacy.[73] To be sure, the French government would persist in its refusal to the very end; however, its position was becoming increasingly untenable. With the ICRC's assessment that the provisions of article 3 were indeed relevant to the conflict and with 500,000 French troops on Algerian soil, the claim that the whole thing did not even qualify as an "armed conflict not of an international character" was absurd. As one commentator aptly noted, "The refusal of France . . . to recognize that these conflicts fall within Art. 3 has, it is thought, been determined by political consideration and not by any objective assessment of the facts."[74]

The lack of formal agreements did not prevent both sides from adhering to certain provisions concerning the treatment of prisoners and internees, although it should be stressed that their conduct left a lot to be desired.[75] The FLN claimed that throughout the conflict captured French soldiers were given prisoner-of-war status. The ICRC was unable to visit FLN camps to assess the accuracy of these claims. This however had more to do with France's refusal "to authorize such missions rather than to the unwillingness of the FLN to receive them." The French on the other hand did acknowledge a certain informal responsibility regarding the treatment of prisoners and internees. Thus, they authorized repeated ICRC visits to Algeria to inspect French prisons and detention centers. From February 2, 1955, to the end of the war ten ICRC missions were allowed in Algeria. The green light for these missions was given on one condition: that the resulting ICRC reports would be communicated only to the French government, and that the ICRC delegation would focus exclusively on the conditions of detention,[76] thus avoiding unpleasant subjects like the grounds on which people were being imprisoned/detained (terrorists, guerrilla sympathizers). The potentially embarrassing nature of the information included in the ICRC reports was confirmed when, in January 1960, the report of the seventh ICRC mission was leaked to *Le Monde*. The revelations created enormous pressure on the government not only to improve the conditions in the prison camps but to seek a speedy conclusion to the whole conflict.[77]

Nothing however was to generate greater outrage in French public opinion than the stream of stories associating the French military and police forces with widespread use of torture and related practices. And it was the very use of torture that in the end convinced most French people that the cause of Algérie-Française was not worth the enormous strain that it was placing on the societal fabric.

The use of torture confronted France with a serious challenge to its self-image as the articulator of both the Declaration of the Rights of Man and Citizen and of the mission civilisatrice. The latter was supposed to project to the colonized people some of the values codified in the former, in particular, notions relating to constitutional government and the rule of law. The Algerian problem was to force upon the national agenda a critical question: to what extent could the goals of the mission civilisatrice be sustained in a context in which their enforceability was becoming coextensive with their violation? a context in which these continuing violations were undermining the normative underpinnings of the grand legacy of the French Revolution.

These concerns came to haunt the French government from the early stages of the Algerian conflict. In January 1955 Interior Minister François Mitterrand authorized Inspector-General Roger Wuillaume to conduct an investigation on the allegations of ill-treatment of individuals under arrest, the authority under which these methods were employed, and the extent to which these methods were, under certain conditions, producing the desired effect.[78] The resulting report, which was based on interviews with police officers and sixty-one detainees, concluded that although some statements concerning the use of certain forms of ill-treatment may have been exaggerated, they were on the whole, accurate.[79] Three things stood out in Wuillaume's Report. First, despite the admission that what amounted to torture was being practiced against detainees, the term *torture* was not used as a term of reference, save for the concluding part of the report in which Wuillaume stated in one sentence that "certain [forms of ill-treatment] are really very serious and have the character of true tortures."[80] Instead, the less offensive *sévices* (form of ill-treatment) and the even more clinical *procedures* were used throughout the report. Second, the attempt to distinguish on the advice of medical specialists, between those sévices which could be used, under certain conditions, in a risk-free way and those which could not (he cited the case of the water pipe as an example of the former and that of the use of electricity as an example of the latter).[81] Finally, the stunning conclusion that certain procedures, if used moderately, were not more inhumane than food, drink, or sleep deprivation; moreover, that these procedures must be recognized and officially sanctioned. Such a stance on this "delicate problem" would, according to Wuillaume, avoid two major pitfalls. On the one hand, the official attitude of ignorance concerning these excesses, and on the other hand, the official attitude of false indignation, forcing the police to comply with legal procedures. Both were untenable: the former because public opinion was alerted, the latter because "Algeria is in need, especially under existing circumstances, of a particularly efficient police."[82]

The Wuillaume Report marked a turning point in governmental perceptions of the use of torture. By sanctioning the discriminate use of torture and accepting the suggestion on the counterproductive nature of further investigations to identify responsible individuals, the report set the stage for what was to follow: namely, the decentralized nature of the decision-making process concerning the range of acceptable illegality. Having already placed the process outside the realm of the law, the government ipso facto guaranteed immunity coupled with a certain room for discretionary conduct on the part of officials in the field (whether the military or the police). What the criterion of efficiency implied was that the greater the challenge in the field, the greater the leeway for the responsible official to identify the precise contours of "acceptable illegality"—a task facilitated by the very arbitrary nature of the concept in question. It was this arbitrariness that allowed senior officers like Jacques Massu to justify the use of torture techniques in his personal account of the Battle of Algiers. Massu's defense was to minimize its extent and set it within the context of a response proportional to the challenges facing the French forces in Algeria.[83]

Acceptable illegality was to prove instrumental in the waging of *guerre révolutionnaire*. Torture was one of the main instruments that practitioners of counterinsurgency warfare employed to break up the support network enjoyed by the FLN. The argument was that given the guerrillas' ability to "melt into the population" so as to blur the combatant/noncombatant distinction, it was in the very same population that French forces had to focus to extract the necessary information concerning the extent and whereabouts of their enemies' activities. However, in their eagerness to break up the support network, French forces were antagonizing the very group whose assistance was necessary if they were to move from the phase of destruction of the enemy organization, to the phase of construction of a new order with the support of the indigenous populations. The situation on the battlefield awakened the French forces to the fact that these two steps were not sequential, as the doctrine would have it, but overlapping and contradictory.[84] What compounded the contradictory nature of that process was that the very notion of acceptable illegality was playing into the FLN strategy of popular war; the wider the search for FLN sympathizers, the greater the number of potential detainees subjected to special procedures, hence the greater the erosion of popular support for the pacification efforts of the French forces.

What rendered the use of torture such a devastating weapon in the hands of the FLN was that contrary to other emergency measures, its status was not relevant to the nature of the conflict. French practices clearly violated both domestic and international law provisions. In particular, the use of torture was in clear violation of article 186 of the French Penal Code, of article 5 of the Universal Declaration of Human Rights, and of common article 3 of the 1949 Geneva Conventions (since, as aforementioned, the ICRC had concluded in favor of its applicability to the Algerian conflict).[85] Thus, regardless of whether the confrontation was a war, or a conflict of a noninternational character, or even a rebellion, torture was an indefensible practice on all conceivable grounds. To be sure, French forces could point to the use of torture by their opponents and the horrible mutilations to which Muslim Algerians were subjected by FLN forces for refusing to abide by FLN directives. For example, in his book on the Battle of Algiers, Massu included pictures of mutilated faces with their noses and lips sliced off (the punishment was meted for disobeying the FLN directive banning smoking, an activity which was, according to the FLN, profiting the French).[86] However, such a perspective promoted the principles of proportionality and efficiency as the ultimate criteria for conduct within a clearly extralegal framework. It was not any more a question of lawful activities which violated the rules of proportionality; rather it was a question of clearly illegal behavior which was anchored on a dubious understanding of proportionality. When Paul Teitgen, Secretary-General of the Algiers Prefecture, resigned over his inability to prevent Massu's "war crimes,"[87] his frustration exemplified the lack of any credible argument in defense of the conduct of the French paratroopers in Algiers.

Finally, a few words on what was undoubtedly one of the most disturbing features of the Algerian conflict: the use of terror, or the indiscriminate use of violence as a means both of instilling fear in the enemy and of rallying potential supporters to the cause (most often it is a combination of both). The purpose of the former is to expose the inability of the guerrilla's opponent to protect the civilian population and hence increase the pressure for negotiated settlement and/or withdrawal; the purpose of the latter is by exposing the very inability of the opponent, to enhance the stature of the guerrillas and promote the justness of the cause. The use of terror, however, is most likely to produce counterterrorist measures of equal ferocity and of an equally indiscriminate nature, in a spiral of mindless violence leading to a new form of total war; a war waged not against the guerrillas but against the people as a whole. As mentioned earlier, guerrilla strategy is predicated on placing the onus of indiscriminate warfare on the enemy, although many of its practitioners (including Mao) insisted on the discriminate use of terror by guerrilla forces (at most targeting select groups of civilian or military officials, but not the population at large).[88]

The use of terror whether discriminate or indiscriminate is in clear violation of the laws of war since it presupposes the most extreme form of an indirect engagement with the enemy outside the framework of all rules and regulations governing the conduct of warfare.[89] During the Algerian conflict, the FLN used violence indiscriminately, particularly during the Battle of Algiers. In its most extreme form this manifested itself with the placing of bombs in areas where civilians would attend to their daily routines (bus stations, offices, cafés, restaurants); these bombings were followed by the assassination of several French officials.[90] The French response came quickly with the widespread use of counterterrorist tactics. In accordance with the doctrinal provisions of the guerre révolutionnaire, they launched sweeping cleansing operations to sever the bond between the "fish" and the "water" by denying the fish access to the water. The operations sustained a veil of suspicion that came to engulf ever larger numbers of people as potential guerrilla sympathizers. This resulted in the rounding up of whole neighborhoods for questioning and the routine use of torture to counteract the perceived tendency of sheltering and supplying the guerrillas.

In the countryside French forces routinely evacuated villages which were then declared "forbidden zones" to be subjected to either artillery fire or aerial bombardment (or both); the underlying assumption being that any human presence within the forbidden zone was tantamount to an enemy presence (an eerie precursor to the Vietnamese experience of "free-fire zones").[91] According to a report commissioned by Paul Delouvrier, French Delegate-General for Algeria, and published in April 1959, the number of people whose villages had been declared forbidden zones, or "who have been resettled in areas too far to allow access to the former village," was around 200,000.[92]

Moreover, as the war progressed, French forces made increasing use of the aforementioned regroupment centers. Here again, the purpose was to deny the guerrillas access to the population and to protect the latter from insurgent influences. However, this forced resettlement led to the denial for huge numbers of people of their means of livelihood, thus reducing them to a state of total dependence. According to the April 1959 report, the sanitary conditions and food and clothing distribution were so inadequate that they undermined the prospects for survival of large numbers of regrouped persons.[93] Probably the greatest indictment of these practices came from Raphael Lemkin, the moving force behind the Genocide Convention, who in a memorandum submitted to the Conference of Independent African States in 1959 argued that "there is a recent development which increases the violence of genocide in Algeria. This is the case of the resettlement of hundreds of thousands of civilians and their families who were forcibly transferred and assembled in places similar to concentration camps. . . . This type of resettlement constitutes genocide under Article II (c) of the Genocide Convention."[94]

What all of these counterterrorist measures indicated was that no matter how deplorable some of the FLN's methods were, the conflict was reaching a stage where it was becoming difficult to distinguish between friendly (or at least neutral) and hostile noncombatants. This is not a legal distinction but a political one and it is something which can not and should not be decided by the commanders in the field since it is a political call to be made by the responsible government at home. In his novel *Lieutenant in Algeria,* based on his experiences during the Algerian War, Jean-Jacques Servan-Schreiber offers a very revealing exchange between two French officers on the merits of the official policy toward suspected fellaghas. One of the officers, Captain Julienne, expresses his concern over the killing of Arabs who do not carry arms: "you can't rule out the possibility that the victims aren't fellagha but maybe honest fellows from the village—which wouldn't do much good to our relations with the population." To this, Lieutenant Martin replies ("with a condescending but friendly manner"):

You're right, a hundred per cent right—in theory. Unfortunately, in practice you'll find that you're faced with a choice. Either you consider *a priori* that every Arab, in the country, in the street, in a passing truck, is innocent until proven guilty—and allow me to tell you that if that's your attitude you'll get your men bumped off . . . *or you do your duty honourably, which is to say you put the fellagha out of commission and look after our men the best you can. In that case, there's only one way: treat every Arab as a suspect, a possible fellagha, a potential terrorist—because that, my dear sir, is the truth* [author's emphasis]. And don't come back at me with words like *justice* and *charity*. They have nothing to do with it. I don't say they don't exist: I say all that's not in the same boat. You can talk about that in Paris with the politicians who got us into this mess. But once you're here, raising problems of conscience—and presuming the innocence of possible murderers—is a luxury that costs dear, that costs men, my dear sir, young men, innocent too, *our* men.[95]

The FLN had succeeded in turning a military into a political conflict; as a result, the French had ended up fighting not against the FLN guerrillas but against the Algerian nation. Once this stage is reached the legitimacy of the guerrillas is not the key issue; the war has to stop because the only way that it can be fought is "by setting out systematically to kill civilians or to destroy their society and culture."[96]

In the meantime the Algerian question was gathering momentum in the General Assembly of the United Nations with the support of the organization's African-Asian group of states. In four years' time the African-Asian bloc had managed to move from inscribing the Algerian question in the agenda of the tenth session of the General Assembly (1955) to obtaining a draft resolution recognizing the right of the Algerian people to self-determination during the fourteenth session of the General Assembly (1959).[97] And although the 1959 draft resolution did not muster the necessary two-thirds majority for its adoption, it signaled that the passage of such a resolution was simply a question of time.

And so it was. On December 14, 1960, the General Assembly approved the draft resolution on the Declaration on the Granting of Independence to Colonial Countries and Peoples submitted by forty-three African and Asian countries. What became Resolution 1514 stipulated, among other things, that "all peoples have the right to self-determination; by virtue of that right they freely determine their political status and freely pursue their economic, social and cultural development."[98] During the discussion preceding the vote the Algerian question figured prominently in the statements made by delegates, especially those of the African-Asian group which had sponsored the draft resolution.[99]

A few days later the General Assembly approved resolution 1573 on the Question of Algeria; a resolution which recognized "the right of the Algerian people to self-determination and independence."[100] It would take a little over a year, after the passage of resolution 1573, for the French government and the National Liberation Front to reach the Evian settlement (March 1962), which paved the way for Algerian independence. In the end the FLN had achieved more than Algeria's independence; its prolonged struggle had contributed to a major reconsideration of the legitimacy of national liberation movements. The international community had taken the first and decisive step in a new direction.

National liberation movements appeared at a time when the East-West conflict was engulfing the Third World. As a result, their agendas very often acquired a reach which was wholly disproportionate to their actual aims. To be sure, many of these movements were heavily influenced by Marxist notions of class struggle and socio-economic emancipation, as was the case with the Viet Cong in Vietnam, SWAPO in Namibia, the MPLA in Angola, or Zanu in Zimbabwe. However, the one-dimensional emphasis on the socioeconomic aspects of their platform was reflective of a mentality that sought to place all conflicts along the continuum of an East-West confrontation. As a result, nationalist themes which were drawn as aforementioned from the European traditions of territorially oriented nationalism and the Wilsonian notion of self-determination and which were equally incompatible with colonial rule were totally subsumed under notions of a ubiquitous Communist challenge. The case of the Algerian War is typical of a colonial power's failure to understand the importance of the nationalist themes as a key source of popular mobilization. A similar argument has been made in the case of the U.S. involvement in Vietnam: namely, that the conflict should have been perceived not as a cold war struggle but as an anticolonial struggle, the unfinished business "of an interim settlement of a later colonial war between the Viet Minh and the French. . . . This erroneous categorization (i.e. as a Cold War conflict), made in 1945–46 and again in 1954 and continued through the early 1970's, at least, determined the nature of our response."[101]

The quest for self-determination most often entailed confrontations with financially and militarily superior opponents. With varying degrees of success national liberation movements adopted the strategy and tactics of the weak, namely, guerrilla warfare. Of particular relevance was the guerrilla's steadfast refusal to adopt a single identity, that of either civilian or combatant, thus placing the onus of indiscriminate warfare on the guerrilla fighter's opponents. Such a strategy was geared toward the transformation of a military conflict into a political one; a transformation that in the long run would place unsustainable burdens on the opponents' armed forces and society. What was the impact of this transformation on the rules and regulations governing the conduct of warfare?

To begin with, it reintroduced with certain qualifications the notion of *jus ad bellum*. The principle of self-determination ipso facto legitimized the struggle irrespective of the prospects for military success. In this context the Algerian conflict had a profound effect on the international community's perception of national liberation movements. The adoption of the Declaration on the Granting of Independence to Colonial Countries and Peoples by the U.N. General Assembly was indicative of a trend toward the acknowledgment of self-determination as a legal right. In addition, the fact that the GPRA was recognized by twenty countries at the time of the resolution's adoption pointed toward the legitimation of recognition on the basis of the quest for self-determination. This meant that a growing section of the international community was prepared to recognize governments which had failed to satisfy the traditional criterion of effectiveness, provided that these governments promoted the aforementioned principle. To be sure, there was nothing new in the violation of the criterion of effectiveness; what was new was that this criterion was *consistently overtaken* by the principle of self-determination, especially in the context of struggles against colonial rule.[102]

On the issue of the use of force the international community's attitude was more ambivalent. On the one hand, many member states were prepared to acknowledge the legitimacy of the resort to force if self-determination was denied; in fact, some went so far as to argue that the denial of self-determination constituted ipso facto aggression against the people concerned, thus entitling the latter to the use of force in self-defense. However, despite the repeated condemnations of colonialism, this view never acquired the legal status that its proponents sought; instead, the international community was prepared to tolerate (i.e., not condemn) rather than endorse the use of force, particularly in cases where national liberation movements were to initiate rather than respond to the use of force.

Despite these qualifications, the reintroduction of the *jus ad bellum* in the calculus of the conduct of warfare was to generate major controversies. To its supporters it constituted an acknowledgment of the failure of the traditional international law to address the needs of colonized peoples. To its critics it constituted an attempt to shift the focus from the reciprocal obligations of belligerents under *jus in bello* provisions to the one-sided rights of the belligerent in quest of self-determination. The fear expressed by the critics was that the so-called justness of the cause would allow national liberation movements to take shortcuts in their operational conduct, thus placing the two belligerents on unequal footing.[103]

What was the impact on *jus in bello* provisions of the progressive acknowledgment of self-determination as a legal right? On the one hand, it led to the premature recognition of governments whose limited exercise of governmental functions often prevented them from adhering to certain regulations of the Geneva Conventions (for example, those relating to the provisions of adequate services to prisoners of war). On the other hand, however, the prospect of internationalizing the conflict would act as an incentive for national liberation movements to apply the laws of war. Adherence to the Geneva Conventions would become the litmus test of their willingness to become legitimate members of the international community. The FLN's eagerness to point to the application of the Geneva Conventions to the French-Algerian conflict in their well-argued *White Paper,* as well as the GPRA's accession to these Conventions were indicative of the fundamental importance attached to this incentive.[104]

To be sure, accession to conventions does not imply adherence to their provisions in practice. Critics of national liberation movements would point to the illegality of the whole strategy of guerrilla warfare, the blurring of the combatant-noncombatant distinction, and the impossible burden placed on their opponents as a result. National liberation movements were vulnerable up to a point to this criticism. During the Algerian conflict the FLN made a special effort to indicate that its military arm, the ALN, satisfied all four requirements of article 4A §2 of Geneva Convention III, and as a result its captured combatants had to be treated as prisoners of war.[105] While this was true for one category of combatants, the moudjahidines, it was not true for either the moussabilines or the fidaiyines.[106]

The inability to draw the combatant-noncombatant distinction was to lead the guerrilla's opponents into questionable and often outright illegal practices. In their attempts to eliminate the access of the fish to the water they employed strategies and tactics that were marked by certain disturbing similarities across place and time. In the Algerian War the doctrine was called guerre révolutionnaire; in the Vietnam War it was counterinsurgency warfare; in both cases pacification constituted one of the central tenets. In the Algerian War villagers were relocated into regroupment centers and the evacuated villages declared "forbidden zones" to be subjected to artillery fire or aerial bombardment; in the Vietnam War villagers were taken to government-run camps and the evacuated villages declared "free-fire zones" to be likewise subjected to aerial bombardment or artillery fire. In both cases operational conduct was premised on treating everyone as a potential enemy. In Jean-Jacques Servan-Schreiber's semifictional account of the Algerian War, Lieutenant Martin warned Captain Julienne to "treat every Arab as a suspect, a possible fellagha, a potential terrorist"; in the Vietnam War, Lieutenant Calley was instructed "to suspect everyone, that everyone was a potential enemy."

The everybody is a potential enemy mentality exemplified an intriguing paradox. Initially, opponents of national liberation movements had accused them of violating the strict separation between *jus ad bellum* and *jus in bello* by subsuming the latter under the former. However, as the struggle unfolded, their opponents were to resort to a form of warfare that exhibited the very conflation of the two notions that they had sought to keep apart. Thus, in the Algerian War, the case of Algérie-Française and the containment of the ubiquitous Communist challenge were to become the *jus ad bellum* that ipso facto marginalized most *jus in bello* considerations. In the same vein, during the Vietnam War, the specter of falling dominoes was to witness the growing emasculation of constraints and the adoption of questionable rules of engagement. This conflation marks the transformation from a military into a political conflict and it signals, whether one likes it or not, the legitimization of the guerrilla's struggle. In the words of Walzer, "The struggle against them is an unjust struggle as well as one that can only be carried on unjustly. Fought by foreigners, it is a war of aggression; if by a local regime alone, it is an act of tyranny. The position of the anti-guerrilla forces has become doubly untenable."[107]

Paul Kennedy
and George J.
Andreopoulos

12
The Laws of War: Some
Concluding Reflections

This concluding chapter briefly synthesizes some of the key elements of the preceding chapters and offers reflections on the main challenges facing the enforcement of humanitarian norms in warfare on the eve of the twenty-first century.

Among the major themes in this volume is the critical issue, Who is included in, and who is excluded from the laws of war? In seeking to answer that apparently simple question, one gains insights into the social order, the political assumptions, and the economic structures of the group in question. The ritualistic, carefully constrained form of hoplite warfare seems unreal and bizarre to modern ears, until one comes to learn that it nicely reflected a society of roughly egalitarian, independent, and prosperous peasant farmers, able to afford hoplite armor and weapons, and thus be in the phalanx, keen to demonstrate their martial values but just as eager to minimize casualties and to have the fighting over before the harvesting began.

In much the same way the emergence of a separate class of feudal knights, each rich enough to have a horse, groom, armor, and other equipment, was soon reflected in ideas about chivalry, especially the *jus militare,* the laws of the knights. In some way, internal restraints on the conduct of war reach a height here, in the sense that feudal society provided an answer to the critical issue of the enforceability of the customary rules of warfare. In the special royal courts, where heralds and knights debated, and lawyers pleaded, one can see how a particular social class sought to police itself, at the same time demonstrating its distinction from and superiority over other classes. Unsurprisingly, when the age of chivalry was replaced by wars of the nation-states and their professional standing armies, the officer corps of each side usually preferred to treat each other with respect, even when conquered in battle, as Napoleon treated defeated generals with respect or, for that matter, as German fighter pilots treated the captured Douglas Bader with respect.

However admirable those mutual courtesies, the obverse side—who is not in the in-group—makes for far bleaker reading. Generally speaking, it looks as if two major distinctions were made, between fighting men and others within their own society—layfolk, clergy, women, children—and between one's own forces and those of another race, religion, or color. The first of these distinctions was commonplace and is, indeed, readily understandable: as armed forces were evolving their own internal rules of war, it was generally accepted that noncombatants' lives and property should be respected, provided that noncombatants would not take advantage of their immunity by assisting the other side, refusing to surrender towns, or joining in surprise or surreptitious attacks on military units. While the origins of this distinction can be traced to the efforts of medieval churchmen to achieve immunity for nonknightly social orders, its consequence over time was the evolution of the important distinction, so far as *jus in bello* is concerned, between the treatment of combatants and noncombatants which governs much of modern thinking and practice.

But in all periods noncombatants had obligations as well as rights; namely, that their immunity from damage and harm was predicated upon their obligation to abstain from hostile acts. If they took action against one party's armed forces, they automatically lost immunity. Similarly, a neutral country could not plead its neutrality if it helped one of the combatants. In sum, this was very much a two-sided understanding; just as professional armies of nation-states were willing to adhere to the rules of warfare among themselves, so also were they willing—in theory, if not always in practice—to respect those not involved in fighting provided the latter did not take advantage of their immunity. From an officer's viewpoint these distinctions helped to make military life more predictable, controllable, and enforceable. It was and is natural, therefore, that regular armed services intensely dislike counterinsurgency warfare, fighting opponents who can't be distinguished from local civilians and who may use indiscriminate acts of violence to achieve their political ends. It is one of the many darker ironies of twentieth-century history that, just as the codification of laws respecting noncombatants achieved further refinements, a whole surge of revolutionary struggles, civil wars, and insurgencies have made discriminate warfare more difficult than ever to implement.

The second group excluded from *jus in bello* considerations were alien peoples, whether that referred to Persians in the fifth century B.C., or Muslims and heathens during medieval Europe's crusades, or the North American Indians and other aboriginal peoples in the way of European expansion. Time and again there occur cases of people slaughtered indiscriminately on the grounds that they were not considered part of the international community. Englishmen, for example, who killed without restraint in Ireland, found it easy to use the same reasoning and brutal methods in exterminating Indians. Only those with similar cultural traditions were entitled to be treated with restraint in wartime, a judgment based on entirely subjective criteria.

Combatants resorted to this judgment frequently, as witnessed in the reciprocal and more tolerant practices of the British and French forces toward each other—as opposed to their treatment of the Indians—in the North American wars; in the British officers' preference to consort with captured Frenchmen as opposed to Spanish allies in the Peninsular War; in the German treatment of American and British prisoners in World War II as opposed to Russians and Ukrainians on the eastern front, or Serbs and Greeks on the Balkan front.

Given the extent of the atrocities against civilian victims during World War II, it was clear that the laws of war had to take a quantum leap, from applying the established rules for the conduct of armed forces in wartime to incorporating essential human rights norms—especially, the notion of humanitarian conduct regardless of distinctions between combatant and noncombatant, Christian and heathen, or black and white.

Another central concern in these essays is whether *jus in bello* practices worsened or improved the longer war lasted. During the Thirty Years' War and the Napoleonic Wars, as armies became more professional, they steadily lost their original religious or revolutionary fervor, began to see how much in common they had with soldiers on the other side (especially in the treatment of prisoners of war), and opted for restraints over a no-holds-barred conflict. Geoffrey Parker termed this the *democratization* of war, while Michael Howard preferred the word *professionalization;* both detected a widening acceptance of *jus in bello* prescriptions. By contrast, as the Peloponnesian War intensified, more and more of the commonly held rules were disregarded, with Athens conducting what was increasingly a total war waged by and against the whole populace, in and out of the regular campaign season, and regardless of the economic and even the social consequences. Similarly, our own century, which began with such earnest hopes at the two Hague conferences, saw an intensification of violence and the adoption of increasingly indiscriminate and total forms of warfare.

Technological and economic changes have clearly had much to do with the repeated breakdowns of the efforts to preserve *jus in bello* practices. These practices flourish best, the historical record suggests, among societies which are relatively static and socially hierarchic, when there exist common codes among the fighting forces of the combatants, and where membership in the armed forces is prestigious and chivalric, even glamorous. But when that static society begins to crumble, as occurred when the age of chivalry gave way to the age of the condottieri and then national mercenary armies, or when hoplite society was challenged by the newer methods, including the all-year-round fighting of Athens, restraints in war are imperiled.

In our own century technology has so often confounded efforts to preserve *jus in bello* practices. The technology of the white-hot battlefield, dominated by heavy artillery, mortars, and the machine gun, caused so many casualties that military and civilian leaders cast around for other, nonbattlefield measures to bring the enemy to its knees. They found them in the swift development of the submarine and, especially, the airplane. The former gave a further twist to the already traditional, and much disputed, policies of the maritime blockade, not only by applying pressure on the enemy's population, food supply, economy, and morale as an alternative to launching massive assaults on land, but also by doing it in a way—undeclared torpedo or gun attacks on merchant ships and their crews—that nineteenth-century combatants simply had not contemplated.

The airplane blurred still further any distinctions between combatant and noncombatant forces simply by reaching beyond the front lines. The more a government drew upon national resources and mobilized its entire society to gain total victory, the more its foes felt it necessary to destroy the sinews of war and people's morale by direct attacks upon places of work, railway lines, ports, and workers' homes. To be sure, there were sometimes technical reasons for this operational clumsiness, as in Royal Air Force Bomber Command's choice of area bombing during 1942–44, when the lack of a good bombsight and difficulties of navigation and targeting in the dark and clouds made specific bombing impossible. However, even when those difficulties had been overcome, there was little effort to revert to discriminate attacks because of the belief that destroying the enemy civilians' morale was an important part of winning the war.

While the U.S. Army Air Forces in Europe during World War II did subscribe to discriminate bombing, the same was not the case with the firebombing of Japan's cities. It is significant that the Pacific conflict, which saw so many *jus in bello* provisions disregarded, concluded with the explosion of two weapons which, because of their power, could not possibly discriminate between combatants and noncombatants.[1]

Yet, however novel the power and means of their delivery, the bombs dropped at Hiroshima and Nagasaki could be justified by two lines of argument as traditional as warfare itself: namely, *exemplary violence* and *military necessity.*

Exemplary violence is one of the more paradoxical elements in a field full of paradoxes. Knowing the passions aroused in the religious wars of early modern Europe, it comes as no surprise to learn of appalling incidents such as the sack of Drogheda in Ireland by Cromwell's troops. It is probably more disturbing that contemporaries justified such action on the grounds that the customary rules of siege warfare proclaimed no quarter if a city refused to open its door and was then taken; and, further, that a horrible but legitimate sack would have the effect of inducing other towns and cities to surrender swiftly, thus bringing the bloodshed to a halt. By much the same logic airpower advocates in the interwar years could argue that a massive air attack, by destroying an enemy's industries and causing its population to see the folly of continuing the war, would shorten the conflict and was therefore humane. Hiroshima itself can also be seen as an act of exemplary violence, hurting the foe so badly that surrender was induced out of a fear of further punishments, thus reducing overall casualties. However, the historical record does not offer a clear-cut lesson on this issue: in many instances, indiscriminate warfare has led not to the silencing of the opponent, but to an escalation of atrocities, and to counterterror as a response to terrorist strategy and tactics. The idea that a conflict must undergo a short phase of extreme brutality so as to ensure a humane conclusion is one of the most disturbing oxymorons in the elusive quest for humanitarian norms.

Perhaps the biggest challenge facing these norms is the argument of military necessity. This is, by its very nature, subjective; everything hangs upon a decision by generals and/or politicians as to what they judge to be needed. The sack of Drogheda, for example, was also justified by the need to keep up troop morale, in addition to the argument that the English army's position was precarious unless the Irish troops they had captured were wiped out. The colonists in North America, uneasy at what the Indians might do to them, pleaded military necessity as they strove to eliminate the real or perceived threat. Germany's disregard of Belgian neutrality in 1914 or, for that matter, its unrestricted U-boat campaign against neutral shipping in 1917 constituted violations of international legal norms, yet Berlin argued that these were the only ways of winning the war. In a similar vein, General Massu justified the widespread use of torture and related practices by his paras during the Battle of Algiers as the only credible response ("an eye for an eye, a tooth for a tooth") to the FLN challenge for the control of the city of Algiers. To commanders in the field, military necessity becomes a particularly attractive line of argument if an action of dubious legality holds out the prospect of saving their soldiers' lives. Whether the Hiroshima and Nagasaki bombs and the consequent Japanese surrender saved the lives of 500,000 or only 30,000 Allied troops from the bitter fighting which would have occurred during a later invasion of the home islands remains debated; however, one would have to look very hard for an American serviceman in 1945 who would contest the argument that dropping the bomb was militarily necessary to save lives, and thus justified. It is yet another irony of the laws of war that time and again one encounters instances where to reduce battlefield casualties increased pressure was put upon civilians.

Given the fact that the whole subject of constraints on warfare allows for such catchall excuses, where does this leave all the recent efforts to modify the relevant legal instruments? In particular, to what extent are some of these efforts contributing to the international community's successful handling of certain major challenges of the post–cold war era?

Undoubtedly the 1977 Geneva Protocols Additional to the Geneva Conventions are among the most controversial of these efforts, especially Protocol I which deals with international armed conflicts. Several Western countries have refused to ratify Protocol I, primarily on the grounds that in accordance with article 1 §4, it offers the legal protection of the Geneva Conventions to peoples who "are fighting against colonial domination and alien occupation and against racist regimes in the exercise of their right of self-determination." According to its critics, such language "would politicize humanitarian law and eliminate the distinction between international and non-international conflicts. It would give special status to 'wars of national libera-tion', an ill-defined concept expressed in vague, subjective, politicized terminol-ogy. . . . In fact, we must not, and need not, give recognition and protection to terrorist groups as a price for progress in humanitarian law."[2] In addition, it has been pointed out that national liberation movements, due to the nature of their struggle, could not fulfill all their obligations under the convention; that the loaded labels of "colonial," "alien," and "racist" make it unlikely that opponents of these movements would accept such a characterization necessary for the applicability of the relevant provisions of Protocol I; and that the legitimization of the international character of these conflicts would license foreign intervention in the domestic affairs of certain states.[3]

To be sure, the concern about a special status for national liberation movements was reflective of certain statements by delegates to the plenary sessions of the diplo-matic conference convened to develop these protocols, as for example the Chinese delegate's insistence that the new protocols should incorporate a distinction between just and unjust wars. However, this and similar views were not even supported by the delegates of the national liberation movements present at the conference and were quickly consigned to oblivion.[4]

It is beyond the scope of this chapter to offer an assessment of Protocol I. Suffice it to say, however, that some of these criticisms are exaggerated. Concerning the special status of national liberation movements, there are two solid safeguards in the proto-col: first, the preamble reaffirms that both the provisions of the Geneva Conventions and of the protocol "must be fully applied in all circumstances to all persons who are protected by those instruments, *without any adverse distinction based on the nature or origin of the armed conflict or on the causes espoused by or attributed to the Parties to the conflict*" [our emphasis]; second, according to article 96 §3 of the protocol, the authority representing the people must make a declaration to the depository [Swiss government] indicating its willingness to abide by the protocol's provisions. Such a declaration will have the effect that "the said authority *assumes the same rights and obligations as those which have been assumed by a High Contracting Party to the Conventions and this Protocol*" [our emphasis]. As the head of the U.S. delegation to the conference noted, "members of armed forces of liberation movements are not granted protection simply because they may be deemed to be fighting for a just cause; the Protocol and the Conventions must apply equally to both sides if they are to apply to the conflict at all."[5]

As far as the terms *colonial domination, alien occupation,* and *racist regimes* are concerned, these were used to refer to Portuguese rule, to the Israeli occupation of the

West Bank and Gaza, and to the South African regime of apartheid, respectively. They undoubtedly allow for all sorts of interpretations, but do they really undermine the credibility of the protocol? If one takes into consideration that the term colonial domination refers almost exclusively to the rule of Western powers in the Third World, which is dying anyway, and the fact that secessionist struggles do not sustain any noticeable sympathies among the supporters of the protocol, what one is left with are "racist regimes" and "alien occupation." Given the fact that apartheid is being phased out and that Israel is not a signatory of the protocol, its provisions hence not being applicable to the West Bank conflict, the range of application of this most controversial of provisions is exceedingly small (a controversial candidate for the "alien occupation" label may well be the Moroccan occupation of the Western Sahara, which has led the Moroccan government into a prolonged confrontation with Polisario). As one analyst has aptly noted, "If it [Article 1 §4] opens up a Pandora's box at all, it is an unexpectedly small one."[6]

However, all these discussions on specific provisions of the protocol leave out what is arguably the most important dimension: the general trend toward the *substantive intersection between human rights law and the laws of war*. Traditionally, these two bodies have pursued different trajectories: human rights law has focused on the relationship between states and their own nationals in peacetime, while the laws of war have concentrated on the treatment of both combatants and noncombatants by their opponents in wartime. And while the provisions of the 1949 Geneva Conventions applied almost exclusively to the conflicts between states, common article 3 came to be seen as "the short bill of rights for non-international armed conflicts."[7] In this context, common article 3 marked the beginning of a growing realization that the strict compartmentalization of international and noninternational conflicts was often unsustainable, especially when certain noninternational conflicts reached the level of manpower involvement and witnessed the kinds of force that one would normally associate with international conflicts. Since then, the international community has progressively acknowledged that certain basic humanitarian norms are applicable irrespective of the status of the individual (whether combatant or noncombatant) and that certain fundamental guarantees against arbitrary behavior on the part of the authorities (for example, on issues of penal procedure) should be respected whether in wartime or peacetime. This trend is well reflected in the two 1977 Geneva Protocols: for example, article 75 of Protocol I and articles 4 and 6 of Protocol II are based on the relevant provisions of the Universal Declaration of Human Rights (articles 5 and 11) and the International Covenant on Civil and Political Rights (articles 14 and 15).[8]

Nowhere is this trend toward the intersection between human rights law and the laws of war more apparent than in the current debate about a "new world order" and the concomitant discussions on the operationalization of the doctrine of humanitarian intervention. The concept of the new world order was thrust into the limelight as a result of the U.S. reaction to the Iraqi invasion of Kuwait. The end of the cold war, according to former President Bush, provided a unique opportunity to transcend the perspective of a regional conflict as a reflection of the ongoing superpower confrontation; rather, for the first time since its inception, the U.N. Security Council could undertake truly collective actions against aggression, and in the process confirm the status of *collective security* and the *rule of law* as key constitutive elements of this new world order.

However tempting these visions of a new world order are, the first case study of this new era (the Gulf War) has emerged with a mixed record at best. On the positive side the war witnessed the unprecedented cooperation of the great powers in pursuit of collective security. The series of Security Council resolutions issued with the concurring votes of the five permanent members between August 2 and November 29 (when resolution 678 authorized member states "to use all necessary means" to implement resolution 660, namely, Iraq's withdrawal from Kuwait) was indeed a first step toward a more effective use of the United Nations machinery.[9] In addition, the wide support among Third World countries for the aforementioned resolutions seemed to indicate that the traditional North/South cleavages may not stand in the way of the newly found consensus. Finally, the invocation of the Fourth Geneva Convention of 1949 in resolution 674 of October 29, 1990, and the reaffirmation in that resolution that Iraq "is liable under the Convention in respect of the grave breaches committed by it, *as are individuals who commit or order the commission of grave breaches* [our emphasis],"[10] raised the possibility that high ranking Iraqi officials may be subjected to prosecution for violations of the laws of war as a result of their occupation policies in Kuwait.

On the negative side the war witnessed the Security Council drawn into approving "the shift from sanctions to military measures without the sort of finding evidently contemplated by the language of Article 42"[11] of the U.N. Charter. Article 42 clearly states that action by air, sea, or land forces to maintain or restore international peace and security can take place only after the Security Council has concluded that non-military actions have failed. Such a Security Council finding was never issued; on the contrary, the Security Council was pressured into endorsing resolution 678, thus authorizing the coalition to go to war on its behalf. Concerning the conduct of the war, the Security Council exercised no control whatsoever over the nature and scope of the mission, or over the operational conduct of the coalition forces. The latter has become a key aspect of the debate on the lessons from the Gulf War. As the conduct of the coalition forces comes under closer scrutiny, troubling questions have been raised about the U.S. Air Force's targeting strategy, the quest for Iraq's center of gravity, and the extent to which despite all the publicity about precision-guided bombs (smart bombs), the overwhelming use of unguided weaponry (dumb bombs) may have been responsible for substantial civilian damage, especially when air attacks shifted to the supply lines and the electrical system.[12]

If the Gulf War experience raises intriguing questions about the role of the United Nations in a traditional interstate conflict, the follow-up Operation Provide Comfort raises similar questions about the U.N. role in an intrastate conflict. The United Nations' insistence (as reflected in Security Council resolution 688) that "Iraq allow immediate access by international humanitarian organizations to all those in need of assistance in all parts of Iraq and to make available all necessary facilities for their operation" placed the question of forcible humanitarian assistance in protection of persecuted groups (in this case, the Kurds) on the agenda irrespective of the Iraqi government's wishes. Did this signal the beginning of a substantive erosion of sovereignty in cases of gross violations of human rights, and the dawning of a right to humanitarian intervention? Are we witnessing the emergence of the protection and promotion of human rights as the new *jus ad bellum* for the post–cold war era? Former U.N. Secretary-General Javier Perez de Cuellar hinted strongly in this direction when in a speech at Bordeaux he claimed that "we are witnessing what is probably an irresistible shift in public attitudes towards the belief that the defence of the oppressed in the name of morality should prevail over frontiers and legal documents."[13] And in a recent book on famine relief in Sudan, the authors noted that "by overriding Iraqi sovereignty to provide humanitarian assistance and protection to the Kurds, the U.N. Security Council has paved the way for the current discussion of a *new humanitarian order in which governments are held—by force, if necessary—to higher standards of respect for human life* " [our emphasis][14].

Despite the welcoming signs of a new humanitarian concern that transcends borders, a closer look at Operation Provide Comfort indicates that there were unique features in that operation which render any talk of substantive change premature. In particular, there was the fact that the operation was anchored in the concern that the conflict in Iraq would pose a threat to international peace and security "due to refugee flows and crossborder incursions"; and the additional fact that allied action took place in the aftermath of the Gulf War when "coalition powers had considerable reason to feel responsible for the plight of refugees, not least because of their previous and unfortunate incitements to Iraqis to rebel."[15] Thus, the extent to which humanitarian intervention can be imposed against a government's will remains open. After all, a later intervention, Operation Restore Hope in Somalia, was rendered possible primarily because of the absence of any form of government in the country; but even under these most favorable circumstances, the enabling U.N. resolution had to refer to the Somali situation as posing a threat to international peace and security in accordance with the provisions of article 39 of the Charter.

The linkages between serious violations of international humanitarian law and threats to international peace and security have been reinforced as a result of the international community's belated response to the crisis in Bosnia-Herzegovina. After months of debates on the nature and extent of humanitarian assistance and the passage of unenforceable resolutions, the Security Council finally approved the establishment of an international tribunal to "prosecute persons responsible for serious violations of international humanitarian law committed in the territory of the former Yugoslavia since 1991."[16] In fact, the enabling resolution (827) adopted on May 25, 1993, characterized the situation in the territory of the former Yugoslavia as a continuing threat to international peace and security, a finding consistent with the Security Council's earlier resolution 808 of February 22, 1993.[17]

In his report to the Security Council on the establishment of the international tribunal, the secretary-general reaffirmed that the 1907 Hague Convention IV Respecting the Laws and Customs of War on Land and the Regulations annexed thereto together with the provisions of the 1949 Geneva Conventions for the Protection of War Victims are among the instruments of conventional international humanitarian law which have become part of international customary law and are relevant to the conflict in the territory of former Yugoslavia.[18] This reaffirmation coupled with the earlier endorsement of the Statement of Principles (August 26, 1992) by all states participating in the London conference on Yugoslavia left little doubt as to the body of international humanitarian law applicable in the Yugoslav conflict.[19]

It is too early to assess the impact of the decision to establish the international tribunal. Skeptics can describe it as a symbolic gesture, reflective of the international community's reluctance to deal decisively with the more pressing issue, namely, the reversal of advantages gained by the use of force. In addition, several questions have been raised concerning the effectiveness of the tribunal.[20] However, irrespective of the nature of the tribunal's eventual contribution, its establishment does create certain interesting precedents. What is of particular relevance here is an issue that relates to the legal basis for its establishment.

The tribunal was created by a decision of the Security Council on the basis of Chapter VII of the United Nations Charter. This procedure, as the secretary-general acknowledged in his report to the Security Council, was rather unusual. Under normal circumstances an international tribunal would be established upon the conclusion of a treaty, "drawn up and adopted by an appropriate international body (e.g., the General Assembly or a specially convened conference), following which it would be opened for signature and ratification."[21] However, the need "for an effective and expeditious implementation of the decision to establish an international tribunal"[22] necessitated the bypassing of the General Assembly.[23] This decision marked the first time in the history of the United Nations that the Security Council established, as an enforcement measure, *a subsidiary organ of a judicial nature* under article 29 of the Charter. And it was the first time that a judicial organ's life span was directly linked to the restoration and maintenance of international peace and security.[24]

While these developments are welcome because they strengthen the aforementioned linkages between grave breaches of international humanitarian law and threats to international peace and security, they do not address a critical facet of the relationship between *sovereignty* and *humanitarian assistance*. Given that the international community is not prepared to link all violations of humanitarian law to threats to international peace and security, what if anything can it do in cases where these linkages cannot be sustained? The answer is hardly encouraging.[25]

It is a sign of the times that some of these concerns regarding the problematic relationship between sovereignty and humanitarian assistance have found their way into the secretary-general's report to the General Assembly entitled *An Agenda for Peace*. In his report the secretary-general acknowledges the growing permeability of national boundaries:

National boundaries are blurred by advanced communications and global commerce, and by the decisions of States to yield some sovereign prerogatives to larger, common political associations. . . . [T]he time of absolute and exclusive sovereignty . . . has passed. . . . It is the task of leaders of States today to understand this and to find a balance between the needs of good internal governance and the requirements of an even more interdependent world.[26]

A few pages later though, this carefully worded balance is weakened by the exigencies of a ritualistic reaffirmation of sovereignty. Discussing the issue of preventive deployment in conditions of crisis within a country, the report emphasizes that

the United Nations will need to respect the sovereignty of the State; . . . humanitarian assistance must be provided in accordance with the principles of humanity, neutrality and impartiality; . . . humanitarian assistance should be provided *with the consent of the affected country and, in principle, on the basis of an appeal by that country* [our emphasis].[27]

What this document seems to indicate is that if a government engages in massive repression against its own people, only the very same perpetrator government can appeal for humanitarian assistance; hardly a visionary perspective for the new world order. Thus, while the United Nations is groping for a new humanitarian order, what we have witnessed so far are flashes of boldness, but with the primacy of sovereignty little diminished.

But the challenges will not go away. A growing number of states are facing a resurgence of ethnic, religious, racial, and socioeconomic cleavages with a diminishing capability of providing satisfactory solutions. Borders are becoming increasingly porous and a whole set of problems such as famine, disease, and overpopulation create huge numbers of displaced persons as well as "massive migrations of peoples within and beyond national borders."[28] These trends are blurring the traditional distinction between national and international security concerns and the pressures on the international community to act will increase. Particularly vulnerable are multi-ethnic units, as recent events have demonstrated (Yugoslavia, Czechoslovakia). In this context wars of secession may well replace the anticolonial wars of the 1950s, 1960s, and 1970s as the national liberation struggles of the 1990s. So far, the United Nations and the regional organizations (especially the OAU) have been extremely reluctant to apply the right to self-determination to secessionist struggles. Current events, however, may force upon us a serious rethinking of the types of groups that are entitled to self-determination. If that materializes, then the provisions of the 1977 Geneva Protocol I, in particular the reference to peoples fighting against alien occupation, may well open the dreaded Pandora's box. Some of the winners of the anticolonial struggles may well turn out to be the losers of the secessionist struggles.

In conclusion, as we move into the turbulent post–cold war era, the following considerations must be borne in mind:

1. The trend toward the substantive intersection between human rights law and the laws of war will continue.
2. The uneasy cohabitation between *sovereignty* and *humanitarian assistance* will be seriously tested especially as a result of the breakup of multiethnic units and of the new challenges which are blurring the traditional distinction between national and international security.
3. The calls for humanitarian assistance will not transform the concept into the new *jus ad bellum* of the post–cold war era; however, it will increasingly be used as a basis for legitimizing intervention in cases where there is a threat to international peace and security in accordance with the provisions of Article 39 of the U.N. Charter.
4. The growing intersections between human rights law and the laws of war may result in a serious rethinking of the right to self-determination. If the right to self-determination were to encompass secessionist struggles, then the provisions of Protocol I may come back to haunt those nation-states that have, in the past, been the protocol's greatest beneficiaries.

Notes

1. Constraints on Warfare

1. Carl von Clausewitz, *On War,* trans. Michael Howard and Peter Paret (Princeton: Princeton University Press, 1976), 75.

2. Ibid., 76.

3. See, e.g., Harry H. Turney-High, *Primitive War* (Columbia: University of South Carolina Press, 1949). For a full bibliography, see William T. Divale, *Warfare in Primitive Societies* (Santa Barbara, Calif.: Clio Press, 1973).

4. For the agonistic element in war, see Robert E. Osgood and Robert Tucker, *Force, Order and Justice* (Baltimore: Johns Hopkins University Press, 1967).

5. For a good survey of the development of medieval theory, see Frederick H. Russell, *The Just War in the Middle Ages* (Cambridge: Cambridge University Press, 1975).

6. See Hedley Bull and Adam Watson, eds., *The Expansion of International Society* (Oxford: Clarendon Press, 1984), esp. 75–85, 118–26.

7. See Ronald Inglehart, *The Culture Shift in Advanced Industrial Society* (Princeton: Princeton University Press, 1990).

8. On this see Geoffrey Best, *Humanity in Warfare: The Modern History of the International Law of Armed Conflict* (London: Weidenfeld & Nicolson, 1980).

9. For this and further documentation, see Adam Roberts and Richard Guellf, eds., *Laws of War* (Oxford: Clarendon Press, 1982), 30.

10. Ibid., 45.

11. Ibid., 390.

2. Classical Greek Times

1. Describing rules as informal does not, of course, mean that they were easily ignored, nor does legal enactment guarantee conformity in practice. General treatments of the problem include Pierre Ducrey, *Le traitement des prisonniers de guerre dans la Grèce antique* (Paris: Boccard, 1968), 288–301; Jean Pierre Vernant, "Introduction," in *Problèmes de la guerre en Grèce ancienne,* ed. Jean Pierre Vernant (The Hague: Mouton, 1968), 18–22; Jacqueline de Romilly, "Guerre et paix entre cités," ibid., 207–20; Yvon Garlan, *War in the Ancient World,* trans. Janet Lloyd (New York: W. W. Norton, 1975), 23–77; Peter Karavites, *Capitulations and Greek Interstate Relations,* Hypomnemata 71 (Göttingen: Vandenhoeck and Ruprecht, 1982); Pierre Ducrey, *Guerre et guerriers dans*

la Grèce antique (Paris: Payot, 1985), 280–82; W. Robert Connor, "Early Greek Land Warfare as Symbolic Expression," *Past and Present* 119 (1988): 3–27.

2. See Everett L. Wheeler, "Ephorus and the Prohibition of Missiles," *Transactions of the American Philological Association* 117 (1987): 157–82.

3. H. L. Hart, *The Concept of Law* (Oxford: Oxford University Press, 1961).

4. Rule 1: Frank E. Adcock and D. J. Moseley, *Diplomacy in Ancient Greece* (New York: St. Martin's, 1975). Rules 2–4: Garlan, *War*, 57–64; Ducrey, *Traitement*, 295–304; W. Kendrick Pritchett, *The Greek State at War*, 5 vols. to date (Berkeley: University of California Press, 1971–), vol. 2, 246–75; Raoul Lonis, *Guerre et religion en Grèce à l'époque classique: Recherches sur les rites, les dieux, l'idéologie de la victoire*, Annales littéraires de l'Université de Besançon 238 (Paris: Les Belles Lettres, 1979); Karavites, *Capitulations;* M. G. Goodman and A. J. Holladay, "Religious Scruples in Ancient Warfare," *Classical Quarterly* 36 (1986); 151–71; Ducrey, *Guerre*, 271–75. Rule 5: Garlan, *War*, 61. Rule 6: Pritchett, *War*, vol. 2, 147–55. Rules 7–8: Ducrey, *Traitement*, noting (334–36) that the Peloponnesian War was a watershed. Rules 9–12: Victor D. Hanson, *The Western Way of War* (New York: Alfred A. Knopf, 1989), esp. 15–18, 25–26, 177–84.

5. Greek versus non-Greek warfare: Raoul Lonis, *Les usages de la guerre entre Grecs et barbares,* Annales littéraires de l'Université de Besançon 104 (Paris: Les Belles Lettres, 1969), in a thorough review of the evidence, points out that the practice of war between Greeks and barbarians need not necessarily have been more brutal than between Greeks, but offers abundant evidence for breaches in the rules, especially during the Persian Wars of 490–479 B.C., and the wars between the western Greeks and the Carthaginians. Cf. Ducrey, *Guerre*, 271–83. Breakdown after 450 B.C.: Josiah Ober, *Fortress Attica: Defense of the Athenian Land Frontier, 404–322 B.C.*, Mnemosyne Supplement 84 (Leiden: E. J. Brill, 1985), 32–50.

6. Homeric warfare: Gordon S. Kirk, "War and the Warrior in the Homeric Poems," in *Problèmes*, 93–117; H. van Wees, "Kings in Combat: Battles and Heroes in the *Iliad*," *Classical Quarterly* 38 (1988): 1–24. Date of *Iliad:* P. E. Easterling and Bernard M. W. Knox, eds., *Cambridge History of Classical Literature* (Cambridge: Cambridge University Press, 1985), vol. 1, 42–51. Although some sort of mass fighting surely antedates the hoplite reform of the early seventh century B.C., it seems to me to go too far to claim (as does Pritchett, *War*, vol. 4, 44) that the equipment changes of the seventh century had no significant impact on the techniques of battle or on Greek society. Evolution of hoplite equipment and the phalanx: Victor D. Hanson, "Hoplite Technology in Phalanx Battle," in *Hoplites: The Classical Greek Battle Experience,* ed. Victor D. Hanson (London: Routledge, 1991), 63–84.

7. Solonian classes: David Whitehead, "The Archaic Athenian Zeugitai," *Classical Quarterly* 31 (1981): 282–86. Plot size and draught animals: Ober, *Fortress*, 19–23. The unit of measurement (*medimnos*) is equivalent to about 1.5 bushels. The actual yield of an average hoplite farm would not have been anywhere near 300 bushels of grain, but the figures were meant to refer to total wet and dry yield, including olive oil, wine, and perhaps other sorts of produce as well.

8. Cost of armor: A. H. Jackson, "Hoplites and the Gods: The Dedication of Captured Arms and Armour," in *Hoplites,* 229; at least 30 drachmas in the late sixth century B.C.

9. In 479 the Athenians fielded eight thousand hoplites at Plataea, at a time when a

good number of Athenian hoplites were serving as marines on the Athenian triremes (Herodotus 9.28.6, 8.131). Athenian demography in the period of the Persian Wars: Jules Labarbe, *La loi navale de Thémistocle* (Paris: Les Belles Lettres, 1957), 199–211; in general Mogens H. Hansen, *Demography and Democracy* (Herning, Denmark: Systime, 1985). It is important to remember that slaves were also part of the society, and in some poleis (e.g., Sparta) the nonfree population was a very significant part of the total population. The size of the Athenian slave population is unknown, but I doubt it was very large before or after the wealthy imperial period of the mid- to late-fifth century; see Ellen M. Wood, *Peasant-Citizen and Slave: The Foundations of Athenian Democracy* (London: Verso, 1988). Robert Sallares, *The Ecology of the Ancient Greek World* (London: Duckworth, 1991), 53–60, has recently argued that the slave population of Attica was only about twenty thousand, about one-sixth that of the citizen (native-born adult males and their families) population.

10. Athenian cavalry: Glenn R. Bugh, *The Horsemen of Athens* (Princeton: Princeton University Press, 1988).

11. Role of cavalry in battle: Bugh, *Horsemen,* 35–38. This issue will be treated in much more detail in a forthcoming book by Iain Spence. In the fifth century B.C. at Athens the state supported the rich cavalryman with a financial subsidy for his cavalry mount: Bugh, *Horsemen,* index s.v. *katastasis.* Link in Greek ideology between fighting for one's land and citizenship: Pierre Vidal-Naquet, *The Black Hunter,* trans. Andrew Szegedy-Maszak (Baltimore: Johns Hopkins University Press, 1986), 94–99.

12. Methods of fighting: Hanson, *Western War.* Sparta: Paul Cartledge, "Hoplites and Heroes: Sparta's Contribution to the Technique of Ancient Warfare," *Journal of Hellenic Studies* 97 (1977): 11–23.

13. Limited damage to cropland: Victor D. Hanson, *War and Agriculture in Classical Greece,* Biblioteca di studi antichi 40 (Pisa: Giardini, 1983). Casualty rates: Peter Krentz, "Casualties in Hoplite Battles," *Greek, Roman and Byzantine Studies* 26 (1985): 13–20. Krentz's figures may actually be too high since they necessarily derive from well-attested great battles in which casualties were probably atypically high.

14. War without strategy: Hanson, *Western War,* 19–26; Josiah Ober, "Hoplites and Obstacles," in *Hoplites,* 173–96. On Sparta's vulnerability to helot insurgency, see the recent exchange by Richard J. A. Talbert, "The Role of the Helots in the Class Struggle at Sparta," *Historia* 38 (1989): 22–40; Paul Cartledge, "Richard Talbert's Revision of the Spartan-Helot Struggle: A Reply," *Historia* 40 (1991): 379–85. Use of social disruption strategies in the Peloponnesian War: Ober, *Fortress,* 35–37.

15. Marathon: Herodotus 6.113–17; Pausanias 1.15.4, 1.32.6. Plataea: Herodotus 9.70.4–5.

16. War atrocities: Thucydides 2.67.4, 3.32.1, 2.5.7, 3.68, 5.116.4, 7.86–87. Sustained pursuit by Syracusans: 7.72–85. Pylos: Thucydides 4.3–41; Decelea: Thucydides 7.19–28.

17. Compare Geoffrey E. M. de Ste Croix, *The Origins of the Peloponnesian War* (Ithaca, N.Y.: Cornell University Press, 1972), who places the blame for the war squarely on Sparta. Whether or not one accepts this verdict, Ste Croix's book is a superb collection of the sources and modern scholarship.

18. Josiah Ober, *Mass and Elite in Democratic Athens: Rhetoric, Ideology, and the Power of the People* (Princeton: Princeton University Press, 1989), esp. 53–95.

19. The constitution of the Five Thousand: Edward M. Harris, "The Constitution of

the Five Thousand," *Harvard Studies in Classical Philology* 93 (1990): 243–80. Importance of the navy to democracy: Ober, *Mass and Elite,* 83–84.

20. Athenian empire: Russel Meiggs, *The Athenian Empire* (Oxford: Oxford University Press, 1972).

21. The focus of hoplite warfare on decisive battle is the central thesis of Hanson, *War.*

22. Thucydides 1.140–44, 2.60–65.

23. Pericles' strategy: Josiah Ober, "Thucydides, Pericles, and the Strategy of Defense," in *The Craft of the Ancient Historian: Essays in Honor of Chester G. Starr,* ed. John W. Eadie and Josiah Ober (Lanham, Md.: University Press of America, 1985), 171–88.

24. Raids into Peloponnese: H. D. Westlake, "Seaborne Raids in Periclean Strategy," *Classical Quarterly* 39 (1945): 75–84. The Megara strategy: T. E. Wick, "Megara, Athens, and the West in the Archidamian War: A Study in Thucydides," *Historia* 28 (1979): 1–14.

25. First year of the war and its events: Thucydides 2.1–33, with Donald Kagan, *The Archidamian War* (Ithaca, N.Y.: Cornell University Press, 1974), 43–69.

26. Spartan innovations in the Decelean War: Thucydides 1.19–28, 8.5–44; Xenophon, *Hellenica* 1.1.1–1.6.38, 2.1.1–2.2.23; Plutarch, *Lysander.* Cf. Donald Kagan, *The Fall of the Athenian Empire* (Ithaca, N.Y.: Cornell University Press, 1987).

27. New warfare of the fourth century: Ober, *Fortress,* 37–50.

28. Athenian stability: Ober, *Mass and Elite,* 17–20.

29. Athenian work on the city walls: Richard E. Wycherley, *The Stones of Athens* (Princeton: Princeton University Press, 1978), 7–25. Theban stockade: Mark Munn, "Agesilaos' Boiotian Campaigns and the Theban Stockade of 378–377 B.C.," *Classical Antiquity* 6 (1987): 106–38. Border defenses: Ober, *Fortress,* passim.

30. Development of siege artillery and its effect on military architecture: E. W. Marsden, *Greek and Roman Artillery,* 2 vols. (Oxford: Clarendon, 1969, 1971); Yvon Garlan, *Recherches de poliorcétique grecque,* Bibliothèque des écoles françaises d'Athènes et de Rome 223 (Paris: Boccard, 1974); Josiah Ober, "Early Artillery Towers: Messenia, Boiotia, Attica, Megarid," *American Journal of Archaeology* 91 (1987): 569–604.

31. Ober, *Fortress,* 220.

3. The Age of Chivalry

1. Maurice H. Keen, *Chivalry* (New Haven: Yale University Press, 1984), 5, 88, 107–13; Philippe Contamine, *War in the Middle Ages,* trans. Michael Jones (Oxford: Basil Blackwell, 1984), 210–12. On the dating of Vegetius, see Walter Goffart, "The Date and Purpose of Vegetius' *De re militari,*" *Traditio* 33 (1977): 65–100.

2. The quotation is from John Michael Wallace-Hadrill, "War and Peace in the Early Middle Ages," *Transactions of the Royal Historical Society,* 5th ser., 25 (1975), as reprinted in his collected *Essays in Early Medieval History* (Oxford: Basil Blackwell, 1975), 19–38, at 19. On Roman laws of war, see Frederick H. Russell, *The Just War in the Middle Ages* (Cambridge: Cambridge University Press, 1975), 7–8, and Maurice H. Keen, *The Laws of War in the Late Middle Ages* (London: Routledge & Kegan Paul, 1965), 104, 137. For the Ostrogoths and the Huns, see John Michael Wallace-Hadrill, *The Barbarian West,* 3d ed. (London: Hutchinson University Library, 1967), 33.

3. On *bellum Romanum*, see Keen, *Laws of War*, 104; Contamine, *War*, 283–84; Russell, *Just War*, 129; against non-Christians, James Muldoon, *Popes, Lawyers, and Infidels: The Church and the Non-Christian World, 1250–1550* (Philadelphia: University of Pennsylvania Press, 1979). The quotation is from Wallace-Hadrill, "War and Peace," 20.

4. "Christianae fidei atque religionis sacramenta susciperent et Francis adunati unus cum eis populus efficerentur." My translation, from *Éginhard: Vie de Charlemagne*, ed. Louis Halphen, Les classiques de l'histoire de France au moyen âge (Paris: Les Belles Lettres, 1947), 26.

5. Contamine, *War*, 266–68; Russell, *Just War*, 31–32.

6. Wallace-Hadrill, "War and Peace," 30–35.

7. Carl Erdmann, *The Origin of the Idea of Crusade*, trans. Marshall W. Baldwin and Walter Goffart (Princeton: Princeton University Press, 1977; orig. ed., 1935). Compare Keen, *Chivalry*, 44–63, esp. 45–50; Jonathan Riley-Smith, *The First Crusade and the Idea of Crusading* (London: Athlone Press, 1986); and the critique of Erdmann by John Gilchrist, "The Papacy and War against the 'Saracens'," *International History Review* 10 (1988): 174–97.

8. On early codes of knightly conduct, see Karl Leyser, "Early Medieval Canon Law and the Beginnings of Knighthood," in *Institutionen, Kulture und Gesellschaft im Mittelalter: Festschrift für Josef Fleckenstein zu seinem 65. Geburtstag*, ed. Lutz Fenske, Werner Rösener, and Thomas Zotz (Sigmaringen: Jan Thorbecke Verlag, 1984), 549–66; and Janet Nelson, "Ninth-Century Knighthood: The Evidence of Nithard," *Studies in Medieval History Presented to R. Allen Brown*, ed. Christopher Harper-Bill, Christopher J. Holdsworth, and Janet Nelson (Woodbridge, Suff.: Boydell & Brewer, 1989), 255–66. H. E. J. Cowdrey, "The Peace and the Truce of God in the Eleventh Century," *Past and Present* 46 (1970), 47–67, is the best short account of its subject. Georges Duby, *The Three Orders: Feudal Society Imagined*, trans. Arthur Goldhammer (Chicago: University of Chicago Press, 1980) has much of interest on these matters, as does the stimulating collection of essays by Thomas Head and Richard Landes, eds., *The Peace of God: Social Violence and Religious Response around the Year 1000* (Ithaca, N.Y.: Cornell University Press, 1992).

9. Leyser, "Canon Law and Knighthood," 564–65.

10. Leyser, "Canon Law and Knighthood," 564–65. As Leyser points out (ibid., 566), the distinction between the armed noble and the unarmed commoner was not new in the eleventh century. But it was increasingly sharply drawn from about 1100 on: see Keen, *Chivalry*, 23–30; Contamine, *War*, 31.

11. Leyser, "Canon Law and Knighthood," 562.

12. Keen, *Laws of War*, 19. It is worth noting that *pauper* in medieval Latin meant "powerless," not "poverty-stricken." In practice, of course, there was considerable overlap between the two conditions.

13. Keen, *Laws of War*, passim; Keen, *Chivalry*, 18–43.

14. On *jus ad bellum* versus *jus in bello*, see James T. Johnson, *Ideology, Reason, and the Limitation of War: Religious and Secular Concepts, 1200–1740* (Princeton: Princeton University Press, 1975), 3–80; and Russell, *Just War*, passim. On crossbows, see Contamine, *War*, 71–72, 274; and on contemporary reactions to gunnery, Contamine, *War*, 274; and Malcolm Vale, "New Techniques and Old Ideals: The Impact of Artillery on War and Chivalry at the End of the Hundred Years War," in *War, Literature, and Politics in the*

Late Middle Ages, ed. Christopher T. Allmand (New York: Barnes and Noble Books, 1976), 57–72.

15. In addition to Keen, *Laws of War,* passim, see Maurice H. Keen, "The Jurisdiction and Origins of the Constable's Court," in *War and Government in the Middle Ages: Essays in Honour of J. O. Prestwich,* ed. John Gillingham and James C. Holt (Woodbridge, Suff.: Boydell & Brewer, 1984), 159–69. The willingness of both French and English courts to hear cases brought even against their own supporters for breaches of military law probably reflects the fact that both kings claimed to be the legal king of France. Such cases helped to reinforce the legitimacy of both sides' claims to rule over all of France. In Germany the mechanisms for enforcing the law of arms were much less developed. Military custom in Spain, however, was highly regularized, even between Christian and Muslim combatants. See, for example, José Enrique López de Coca Castañer, "Institutions on the Castilian-Granadan Frontier, 1369–1482," in *Medieval Frontier Societies,* ed. Robert Bartlett and Angus MacKay (Oxford: Clarendon Press, 1989), 127–50.

16. N. A. R. Wright, "The Tree of Battles of Honoré Bouvet and the Laws of War," in *War, Literature, and Politics,* 12–31.

17. Unless otherwise noted, the information that follows is derived from Keen, *Laws of War,* passim.

18. The quotation is from Keen, *Laws of War,* 24. The reluctance of some of the greatest nobles of late thirteenth-century England to accept the king's wages in war had disappeared by the mid-fourteenth century. For discussion, see Michael Prestwich, *War, Politics and Finance under Edward I* (London: Faber and Faber, 1972), 67–91.

19. Keen, *Laws of War,* 63–81.

20. Keen, *Laws of War,* 85.

21. Contamine, following Hostiensis and John of Legnano, distinguishes seven different types of conflict, four licit and three illicit: *War,* 283–84; see also Russell, *Just War,* 129–30. I follow Keen, *Laws of War,* 104–18, in offering four, but in place of truce, which Keen regards as a type of war, I have substituted the laws of siege, which seem to me sufficiently distinct to warrant separate treatment. All such schemas are, of course, arbitrary.

22. The quotation is from Keen, *Laws of War,* 104. On *guerre mortelle* at Crécy, Poitiers, and Orléans, see Keen, *Laws of War,* 105; and Malcolm Vale, *War and Chivalry: Warfare and Aristocratic Culture in England, France and Burgundy at the End of the Middle Ages* (London: Duckworth, 1981), 157. On the red banner as its sign, see Keen, *Laws of War,* 104–6, and the discussion of the battles of Lewes and Evesham below.

23. Robert Bartlett, "'Mortal Enmities': The Legal Aspect of Hostility in the Middle Ages." I am grateful to Professor Bartlett for permission to cite his unpublished paper.

24. The best account of these battles is now David A. Carpenter, *The Battles of Lewes and Evesham, 1264/65,* British Battlefield Series (Keele: Mercia Publications, 1987). Full references to the sources can be traced there.

25. For discussion, see Robert C. Stacey, "Crusades, Crusaders, and the Baronial *Gravamina* of 1263–1264," in *Thirteenth Century England, III,* ed. Peter R. Coss and Simon D. Lloyd (Woodbridge, Suff.: Boydell and Brewer, 1991), 137–50.

26. Carpenter's translation, *Battles of Lewes and Evesham,* 27, of a passage in an unpublished chronicle from Battle Abbey.

27. Clive H. Knowles, "The Resettlement of England after the Barons' War, 1264–1267," *Transactions of the Royal Historical Society,* 5th ser., 32 (1982), 25–41.

28. Keen, *Laws of War,* 137–55; the quotation is on 106. For Spanish customs on the distribution of booty, see James F. Powers, *A Society Organized for War: The Iberian Municipal Militias in the Central Middle Ages, 1000–1284* (Berkeley: University of California Press, 1988).

29. Jean Froissart, *Chronicles,* trans. and ed. Geoffrey Brereton (London and New York: Penguin Books, 1978), 71–77, saw clearly the importance of the English fleet as a repository for plunder.

30. Christopher T. Allmand, "The War and the Non-Combatant," in *The Hundred Years War,* ed. Kenneth A. Fowler (London: Macmillan, 1971), 163–83; Keen, *Laws of War,* 189–97.

31. Keen, *Laws of War,* 137–38, 251–53; on neutrality, 208–9.

32. Quoted in John Gillingham, *The Wars of the Roses: Peace and Conflict in Fifteenth-Century England* (London: Weidenfeld and Nicolson, 1981), 1, 255, whose argument I am following.

33. Contamine, *War,* 256–57; Vale, *War and Chivalry,* 156–61.

34. Keen, *Laws of War,* 88.

35. Froissart, *Chronicles,* 143–44.

36. Keen, *Laws of War,* 156–85. The quotations are on 157–58 and 180.

37. Quotation from Keen, *Laws of War,* 173; see also Contamine, *War,* 289–90.

38. My treatment of sieges follows Keen, *Laws of War,* 119–33; the quotation is on 121–22. The rules of siege warfare appear to have been already well established by the mid-twelfth century: see, for example, the *Gesta Stephani,* ed. Kenneth R. Potter, rev. Ralph H. C. Davis, Oxford Medieval Texts (Oxford: Oxford University Press, 1976), 30, 34–42, 84, 128–36, 180–84, 186. The emphasis on treason, however, appears to have been a later development.

39. I am following Keen, *Laws of War,* 108–18. The term itself betrays the royalist bias of the theorists. From the point of view of the feudal lords who waged it or of the peasantry who suffered from it, there was nothing covert about such a war.

40. Keen, *Laws of War,* 237. On the triumph of this principle, see also Keen, *Chivalry,* 235, 239–43; and Vale, *War and Chivalry,* 147–74.

4. Early Modern Europe

My thanks for assistance and references in preparing this chapter go to John Beeler, Mitzy Carlough, Charles Carlton, Steven Collins, Robert Cowley, Barbara Donagan, Fernando González de León, Mark Grimsley, J. F. Guilmartin, Jr., Russell Hart, Sir Michael Howard, Jefferson McMahan, Allan Millett, Jane Ohlmeyer, Mark Shulman, Nancy van Deusen, Joanna Waley-Cohen, and, most of all, John Lynn.

1. Martin van Creveld, "The Gulf Crisis and the Rules of War," *Military History Quarterly,* vol. 3, no. 4 (Summer 1991): 23–27.

2. See the suggestive article of John A. Lynn, "How War Fed War: The Tax of Violence and Contributions during the *Grand Siècle,*" *Journal of Modern History* 65 (1993): 286–310; and Fritz Redlich, *De praeda militaris: Looting and Booty, 1500–1815,*

Vierteljahrschrift für Sozial- und Wirtschaftsgeschichte, Beiheft 39 (Wiesbaden: Steiner, 1956).

3. For details see, respectively, Alberico Gentili, *De jure belli, libri tres* (1588–89; complete ed., Hanau, 1598), 2.19 (English ed., Oxford: Oxford University Press, 1933); J. P. Myers, "'Murdering Heart . . . Murdering Hand': Captain Thomas Lee of Ireland, Elizabethan Assassin," in *Sixteenth Century Journal* 22 (1991): 47–60; Geoffrey Parker, *The Army of Flanders and the Spanish Road: The Logistics of Spanish Victory and Defeat in the Low Countries' Wars, 1567–1659* (Cambridge: Cambridge University Press, 1972), 66.

4. For example, in volume 7 of the *Tractatus universi juris* (Venice, 1584) are published five major treatises on the laws of war written in Italy between about 1360 and 1560: see G. Soldi-Rondinini, "Il diritto di guerra in Italia nel secolo XV," *Nuova rivista storica* 48 (1964): 275–306. See also Philippe Contamine, *War in the Middle Ages*, trans. Michael Jones (Oxford: Basil Blackwell, 1984), 260–302; Redlich, *De praeda militaris*, 1; and Frederick H. Russell, *The Just War in the Middle Ages* (Cambridge: Cambridge University Press, 1975).

5. H. E. J. Cowdrey, "The Peace and the Truce of God in the Eleventh Century," *Past and Present* 46 (1970): 42–67; and James T. Johnson, *The Just War Tradition and the Restraint of War: A Moral and Historical Inquiry* (Princeton: Princeton University Press, 1984), 124–28.

6. An early example of modern articles of war was the *Lex pacis castrensis* (1158) of Emperor Frederick Barbarossa; the first code enacted as permanent legislation by a state was issued by the States-General of the Dutch Republic in 1590. For a detailed discussion of the articles of one state, see Barbara Donagan, "Codes and Conduct in the English Civil War," *Past and Present* 118 (1988): 65–95.

7. Fairfax quoted, amid an important discussion of theory and practice of the laws of war in seventeenth-century England, in Donagan, "Codes and Conduct," 78.

8. See Henry J. Cohn, "Götz von Berlichingen and the Art of Military Autobiography," in *War, Literature and the Arts in Sixteenth-Century Europe*, ed. J. R. Mulryne and M. Shewring (London: Macmillan, 1989), chap. 2; Keith M. Brown, *Bloodfeud in Scotland, 1573–1625: Violence, Justice and Politics in an Early Modern Society* (Edinburgh: John Donald, 1986), 5; and Redlich, *De praeda militaris*, 2–3. Gentili, *De jure belli*, 3.8 (Eng. ed., 2:323–27), provides an interesting discussion of suitable punishments for defeated leaders.

9. Ian Gentles, "The Impact of the New Model Army," in *The Impact of the English Civil War*, ed. John S. Morrill (London: Collins & Brown, 1991), 99. See also David Underdown, *Pride's Purge: Politics in the Puritan Revolution* (Oxford: Oxford University Press, 1971), chaps. 4–5.

10. Balthasar Ayala, *De iure et officiis bellicis et disciplina militari, libri III* (Douai, 1582), 1.2 (quotations from the 2-vol. ed. of J. Westlake, Washington, D.C., 1912, 1:10–11). Francisco de Vitoria, *Relectio de iure belli* (1539; ed. L. Pereña Vicente, Madrid, 1981), 182, had advanced virtually identical arguments.

11. For the theories see James T. Johnson, *Ideology, Reason and the Limitation of War: Religious and Secular Concepts, 1200–1740* (Princeton: Princeton University Press, 1975), esp. 134–46; Johnson, *Just War Tradition*, esp. 94–103; and John R. Hale, "Incitement to Violence? English Divines on the Theme of War, 1578–1631," and John R. Hale,

"Gunpowder and the Renaissance: An Essay in the History of Ideas," in J. R. Hale, *Renaissance War Studies* (London: Hambledon Press, 1983), 487–517. For a later example of the lack of influence of theory on the practice of war, see Armstrong Starkey, "War and Culture, a Case Study: The Enlightenment and the Conduct of the British Army in America, 1755–1781," *War and Society* 8 (1990): 1–28.

12. "Lo que se responde a Su Santidad," October 1585, Archivo General de Simancas [hereafter AGS], *Estado*, 946/248; Philip II to the count of Olivares, his ambassador in Rome, July 22, 1586, AGS, *Estado*, 947/110. See also Lucio Serrano, *Correspondencia diplomática entre España y la Santa Sede durante el pontificado de S. Pio V*, 4 vols. (Madrid, 1914), 1:310, Philip II to Don Luis de Requeséns, August 12, 1566 (and many more).

13. See Simon L. Adams, "The Protestant Cause: Religious Alliance with the West European Calvinist Communities as a Political Issue in England, 1585–1630" (D. Phil. diss., Oxford University, 1973); G. Groenhuis, *De Predikanten. De Sociale Positie van de Gereformeerde Predikanten in de Republiek der Verenigde Nederlanden voor c. 1700* (Groningen: Wolters-Noordhoff, 1977), 77–107; Sverka A. Arnoldsson, *Krigspropagand i Sverige före Trettioåriga Kriget* (Gothenburg, 1941).

14. Ayala, *De iure*, 1.2.23 (16–17). The phrase "heinous offense" is significant since it was used by lawyers to denote capital crimes.

15. Ibid., 1.2.14–15 (11–12).

16. Gentili, *De jure belli*, 3.7 (Eng. ed., 2:320); Marquis of Santa Cruz to Philip II, August 8, 1588, in Avelino de Freitas de Meneses, *Os Açores e o Dominio Filipino (1580–1590)* (Angra do Heroísmo: Instituto Histórico da Ilha Terceira, 1987), 1:66; Starkey, "War and Culture," 14–15; and David Syrett, "The Failure of the British Effort in America, 1777," in *The British Navy and the Use of Naval Power in the Eighteenth Century*, ed. Jeremy Black and Philip Woodfine (Leicester: Leicester University Press, 1988), 174–75.

17. Francisco de Valdés, *Espeio y deceplina militar* (Brussels, 1589), fo. 40v. See also Sancho de Londoño, *Discurso sobre la forma de reduzir la disciplina militar* (Brussels, 1589), fo. 23v: "[the soldier] has more opportunities to misbehave than any other group of people."

18. Thomas Woodhouse to Geoffrey Fenton, September 23, 1586, after the battle of Ardnary, in H. C. Hamilton, ed., *Calendar of State Papers Ireland: Elizabeth, 1586–88* (London: Her Majesty's Stationery Office, 1877), 161; Charles H. Carlton, *Going to the Wars: The Experience of the British Civil Wars, 1638–1651* (London: Routledge, 1992), 174.

19. See the admirable discussion in Michael Walzer, *Just and Unjust Wars: A Moral Argument with Historical Illustrations*, 2d ed. (New York: Praeger, 1992).

20. Carlton, *Going to the Wars*, 174. The same response is documented in non-Western cultures; see, for example, the brutal treatment of Ming loyalist cities in China after their capture by Ch'ing forces in the 1640s, narrated in Frederic E. Wakeman, *The Great Enterprise: The Manchu Reconstruction of Imperial Order in Seventeenth-Century China*, 2 vols. (Berkeley: University of California Press, 1985), 1:558–65, 655–61, and 2:817–18.

21. Josh. 6:21, 24.

22. See Soldi-Rondinini, "Il diritto di guerra," 299; Volker Schmidtchen, *Kriegswesen im späten Mittelalter: Technik, Taktik, Theorie* (Weinheim: VCH, 1990), 65–71; Alfred

Vanderpol, *La doctrine scholastique du droit de guerre* (Paris: Pédone, 1919), 146–49; and Redlich, *De praeda militaris,* 17–19. For twentieth-century views, see William V. O'Brien, *The Conduct of Just and Limited War* (New York: Praeger, 1981).

23. The flooding of Walcheren—seemingly the first such example of the war—was reported by de Wacken and Beauvoir to the duke of Alba, Middelburg, June 27–28, 1572, Archives Générales du Royaume, Brussels [hereafter AGRB], *Audience,* 343/84f. The constant danger of inundation in Holland during the 1570s is well described in G. 't Hart, "Rijnlands Bestuur en Waterstaat rondom het Beleg en Ontzet van Leiden," *Leids Jaarboekje* 66 (1974): 13–33.

24. Francisco de Valdés to Don Luis de Requeséns, September 18, 1574, AGS, *Estado,* 560/91. Orange's letter (to Marnix) is discussed in Robert Fruin, *The Siege and Relief of Leiden in 1574,* trans. Elizabeth Trevelyan (The Hague: Nijhoff, 1927), 84–85.

25. See W. Hays Park, "Rolling Thunder and the Law of War," *Air University Review,* vol. 33, no. 2 (January–February 1982): 2–23; and Hays Park, "Linebacker and the Law of War," ibid., vol. 34, no. 2 (January–February 1983), 2–30.

26. Philip II to Requeséns, October 22, 1574, AGS, *Estado,* 561/122. See the remarkably similar logic used to rule out the strategic bombing of the Red River dikes in a memorandum of John T. McNaughton, assistant secretary of defense, January 18, 1966, in M. Gravel, ed., *The Pentagon Papers: The Defense Department History of United States Decision-Making on Vietnam* (Boston: Little Brown, 1971), 4:43–48. For another unusual modern example of restraint, the decision not to drop the first atomic bomb on Kyoto, see Otis Cary, *Mr. Stimson's Pet City: The Sparing of Kyoto, 1945,* Moonlight Series no. 3 (Kyoto: Amherst House, 1975).

27. François de La Noue, *Discours politiques et militaires* (1587; ed. Frank E. Sutcliffe, Geneva: Droz, 1967), 391–401, 638–42.

28. John H. Elliott, "Revolution and Continuity in Early Modern Europe," in John H. Elliott, *Spain and Its World, 1500–1700: Selected Essays* (New Haven: Yale University Press, 1989), 92–113; Peter Clark, ed., *European Crisis of the 1950s: Essays in Comparative History* (London: Allen & Unwin, 1985); Geoffrey Parker, *Europe in Crisis, 1598–1648* (London: Collins, 1979), 17–28.

29. William Beech, *More Sulphur for Basing: or, God Will Fearfully Annoy and Make Quick Riddance of His Implacable Enemies, Surely, Sorely, Suddenly* (London, 1645). See also the fire-eating tract written in the Netherlands in 1583 by Luis Valle de la Cerda, *Avisos en materia de estado y guerra para oprimir rebeliones* (Madrid, 1599), fos. 31–33v, 37v–39, justifying the execution of all rebels, with references from Deuteronomy, Cicero, the Justinian Code, Cyprian, Augustine, and Thomas Aquinas.

30. Donagan, "Codes and Conduct," 86; Geoffrey Parker, *Spain and the Netherlands, 1559–1659: Ten Studies* (London: Collins, 1979), 110.

31. Bulstrode Whitelocke, *Memorials of the English Affairs* (Oxford: Oxford University Press, 1853), 3:351.

32. *Henry V,* act 3, sc. 3, lines 7–18; Wellington to George Canning, February 3, 1820, in [Duke of Wellington], *Despatches, Correspondence and Memoranda of Field Marshall Arthur, Duke of Wellington* (Millwood, N.Y.: Kraus Reprint, 1973), 1:93. See also the excellent discussion in J. W. Wright, "Sieges and Customs of War at the Opening of the Eighteenth Century," *American Historical Review,* 29 (1934): 629–44; and Maurice H. Keen, *The Laws of War in the Late Middle Ages* (London: Routledge & Kegan Paul, 1965), 119–33.

33. Carlton, *Going to the Wars,* 173.

34. Quotations from Archief van het Aartsbisdom Mechelen (Belgium), *Fonds Kloosters: Cortenberg,* 2/345 ("Den capiteijn antwoerde nu de furie over was, niet en souden cunnen doet"); and E. Symmons, *A Military Sermon, Wherein by the Word of God, the Nature and Disposition of a Rebel Is Discovered* (Oxford, 1644), 35. My thanks to Craig Harline for the first reference and to Barbara Donagan for the second.

35. Francisco de Vitoria, *Relectio de iure belli,* in Francisco de Vitoria, *Political Writings,* ed. Anthony Pagden and J. Lawrance (Cambridge: Cambridge University Press, 1991), 293–327.

36. Requeséns to Philip II, December 30, 1573, AGS, *Estado,* 554/14. Explicit discussions of the customs of war by leading military practitioners are exceedingly rare. For a detailed account of the duke of Alba's policy toward rebellious towns, albeit based on secondary sources, see Léon van der Essen, "Kritisch onderzoek betreffende de oorlogvoering van het Spaans leger in de Nederlanden in de XVIe eeuw, namelijk de bestraffing van opstandige steden. I. Tijdens het bewind van Alva," *Mededelingen van de Koninklijke Vlaamse Academie van Wetenschappen, Letteren en Schone Kunsten van België: Klasse der Letteren* 12 (1950), no. 1.

37. Morillon to Granvelle, June 3, 1572, in Charles Piot, ed., *Correspondance du Cardinal de Granvelle, 1565–86* (Brussels: F. Hayez, 1884), 4:231–34, records Mechelen's refusal to accept a garrison. Alba's determination to make the town pay for this may be found in Alba to Philip II, August 21 and September 6, 1572, and to Cardinal Pacheco, September 1, 1572, in [duke of Alba], *Epistolario de Fernando Alvarez de Toledo III Duque de Alba,* 3 vols. (Madrid, 1952), 3:187, 193–94, and 197. His later justifications appear in Alba to Philip II, October 2 and 13, 1572, and Alba to Don Juan de Zúñiga, October [27], 1572, ibid., 3:219–21, 230–31, and 238–39.

38. Esteban Prats to Philip II, November 30, 1572, in *Colección de documentos inéditos para la historia de España,* vol. 75 (Madrid, 1880), 127; Jean Richardot quoted by Louis P. Gachard, *Rapport sur les différents séries de documents concernant l'histoire de la Belgique qui sont conservés . . . à Lille* (Brussels, 1841), 234. See other contemporary letters concerning the brutality of the sack in Piot, *Correspondance,* 4:455–68, 490–94, 504, and 547.

39. Mondoucet, the French agent who accompanied Alba on campaign, to Charles IX, September 25, 1572, in L. Didier, *Lettres et négociations de Claude de Mondoucet* (Paris: Leroux, 1891), 1:48; and Alba to Philip II, November 19, 1572, in Alba, *Epistolario,* 3:249.

40. Van der Essen, "Kritisch onderzoek," 23–26.

41. "I recall that the burning of the town of Duren [in 1543] by the emperor Charles V secured the submission of the whole province of Gelderland in a single day": Alba to Philip II, November 19, 1572, in Alba, *Epistolario,* 3:248.

42. Alba to Zúñiga, October [27], 1572, in Alba, *Epistolario,* 3:239. Even as the sack of Mechelen continued, Oudenaarde, Dendermonde, Leuven, Diest, and Tongeren all sent delegates to surrender and ask for mercy.

43. See Barbara Donagan, "The Thirty Years' War: The View from England" (paper given at the Sixteenth-Century Studies Conference, Philadelphia, 1991).

44. See the details in Gustav Droysen, "Studien über die Belagerung und Zerstörung Magdeburgs, 1631," in *Forschungen zur deutsche Geschichte* (Göttingen, 1863), 3:433–606; and Karl Wittich, *Dietrich von Falkenberg, Oberst und Hofmarschall Gustav Adolfs:*

Ein Beitrag zur Geschichte des dreissigjährigen Krieges (Magdeburg, 1892). On the propaganda surrounding this event, see W. Lahne, *Magdeburgs Zerstörung in der zeitgenössischen Publizistik* (Magdeburg, 1931); and Donagan, "The Thirty Years' War."

45. Details in Ian Gentles, *The New Model Army in England, Ireland and Scotland, 1643–1653* (Oxford: Oxford University Press, 1992), 357–63.

46. Ormonde to Charles II, September 1649, in John T. Gilbert, *A Contemporary History of Affairs in Ireland* (Dublin: Irish Archaeological and Celtic Society, 1880), 2:270. All other quotations come from James Burke, "The New Model Army and the Problems of Siege-Warfare, 1648–51," *Irish Historical Studies* 27 (1990): 1–29.

47. Gentili, *De jure belli*, 3.7 (Eng. ed., 2:315). For examples of executions following unconditional surrender, see van der Essen, "Kritisch onderzoek," 31–35; Haarlem in 1573: Joke W. Spaans, *Haarlem na de Reformatie: Stedelijke cultuur en kerkelijk leven, 1577–1620*, Hollandse historische reeks vol. 11 (The Hague: Nijhoff, 1989), 44–46; several towns in England and Ireland in 1648–51: Burke, "The New Model Army."

48. Two published fragments of seventeenth-century court-martial records give some idea of their work: J. Adair, "The Court Martial Papers of Sir William Waller's Army, 1644," *Journal of the Society for Army Historical Research* 44 (1966): 205–23; Godfrey Davis, ed., "Dundee Court-Martial Records, 1651," *Scottish Historical Society Miscellany, vol. 3*, Scottish History Society, 2d ser., vol. 19 (Edinburgh, 1919), 3–67. For the Spanish Army of Flanders see also Lucienne van Meerbeeck, *Inventaire des Archives des tribunaux militaires* (Gembloux, 1939).

49. See "Lo que a Su Magestad ha parecido advertir sobre la relación de los excessos que se dize se han hecho en los Estado de Flandes," Instituto de Valencia de Don Juan, 36/40; Mateo Vázquez to Philip II, April 11 and 15, 1574, ibid., 44/57–58; and the reports of the "Juntas grandes y particular," ibid., 45/329.

50. See Pierre Génard, "La furie espagnole: Documents pour servir à l'histoire du sac d'Anvers en 1576," *Annales de l'Académie royale d'archéologie de Belgique* 32 (1876); and Karl S. Bottigheimer, "The Restoration Land Settlement in Ireland: A Structural View," *Irish Historical Studies* 18 (1972): 9–12.

51. Keen, *Laws of War*, 133, 243–44, 254–57.

52. In AGRB, *Secrétairerie d'État et de Guerre* [hereafter *SEG*], 11/82v, Parma's instruction for Don Alonso de Lerma, December 29, 1588, sent to negotiate the ransom of captured soldiers from the Spanish Armada, is the first mention I have found of the formula "one month's wages plus 'entertainment'" as the standard ransom.

53. The *cuartel general* of October 25, 1599, was reissued on May 14, 1602, and October 18, 1622; see copies in Algemeen Rijksarchief, The Hague, *Staten van Holland*, 2604 nr. g; and Bibliothèque Royale, Brussels, MS 12622-31, fos. 273–75v. The English versions of the 1602 and 1622 arrangements were printed as an appendix to Henry Hexham, *The Principles of the Art Militarie Practiced in the Warres of the Vnited Netherlands* (London, 1637); see Maurice J. D. Cockle, *A Bibliography of Military Books up to 1642* (London, 1900), 108–9. An important collection of documents on the ransom and exchange of prisoners by and from the Spanish Army of Flanders may be found in AGRB, *SEG*, 175bis/46–72.

54. Lucienne van Meerbeeck, "Le service sanitaire de l'armée espagnole des Pays-Bas à la fin du XVIe siècle et au XVIIe siècle," *Revue internationale d'histoire militaire* 20 (1959): 493, notes that a French military hospital abandoned in the Spanish Netherlands in

1677 was immediately placed under special protection, guaranteed by the joint insignia of France and Spain.

55. Philip IV to Don Francisco de Melo, May 17, 1644, AGS, *Estado,* 2251, unfol.

56. Marquis Sfondrato to Don Miguel de Salamanca, June 4, 1640, Archivo Histórico Nacional, Madrid, *Estado libro* 972, unfol. See also a position paper prepared by the Spanish high command at this time, regretting the restraints imposed on their conduct of war by the ability of the peasants to contract out of hostilities by paying contributions: AGRB, *Conseil privé espagnol* 1573/259–62v (papers of Pieter Roose); and the examples from the Thirty Years' War cited by Redlich, *De praeda militaris,* 45. On the medieval *appatis,* see Keen, *Laws of War,* 251–53.

57. The marquis of Worcester (formerly Lord Glamorgan) to Charles II, ca. 1666, in *Historical Manuscript Commission: Twelfth Report, Appendix Part ix: Beaufort Manuscripts* (London: Her Majesty's Stationery Office, 1891), 60. For the military changes mentioned in this paragraph, see Geoffrey Parker, *The Military Revolution: Military Innovation and the Rise of the West, 1500–1800* (Cambridge: Cambridge University Press, 1988), chaps 1–2.

58. See Redlich, *De praeda militaris,* 58–77; and Lynn, "How War Fed War."

59. See Barbara Donagan, "Understanding Providence: The Difficulties of Sir William and Lady Waller," *Journal of Ecclesiastical History* 39 (1988): 433–44; and Blair Worden, "Oliver Cromwell and the Sin of Achan," in *History, Society and Churches: Essays in Honour of Owen Chadwick,* ed. Derek Beales and Geoffrey Best (Cambridge: Cambridge University Press, 1985), 125–45.

60. See G. Bacot, *La doctrine de la guerre juste* (Paris: Economica, 1987), chap. 3; Geoffrey Best, *Humanity in Warfare: The Modern History of the International Law of Armed Conflicts* (London: Weidenfeld & Nicolson, 1980), chap. 1; M. Howard, ed., *Restraints on War: Studies in the Limitation of Armed Conflict* (Oxford: Oxford University Press, 1979), 5–6; and Johnson, *Ideology, Reason and the Limitation of War,* chap. 4.

61. Gerhardt and Locke quoted in Theodore K. Rabb, *The Struggle for Stability in Early Modern Europe* (Oxford: Oxford University Press, 1975), 119–20; the peasant Bible in Geoffrey Parker, *The Thirty Years' War* (London: Routledge & Kegan Paul, 1984), 179.

62. Rabb, *The Struggle for Stability,* argues the case for the chaos of the mid-century wars giving rise to absolutism and also produces a dazzling array of "no more war" writings and pictures.

63. Requeséns to Philip II, December 30, 1573, AGS, *Estado,* 554/146.

64. Details in Alois Gerlo and Rudolf de Smet, eds., *Marnixi epistulae. De briefwisseling van Marnix van Sint-Aldegonde. Een kritische uitgave* (Brussels: University Press, 1990), 1:206–32.

65. Carlton, *Going to the Wars,* 249–52. But there were exceptions: some royalists continued to hang captured parliamentarians out of hand (see examples in ibid., 255–64); and the parliamentarians in the Second Civil War showed far more rigor toward their defeated enemies (see Burke, "The New Model Army").

66. For examples of early modern live and let live systems, see Henri Drouot, *Mayenne et la Bourgogne, 1587–1596: Contribution à l'histoire des provinces françaises pendant la Ligue* (Paris: Picard, 1937), 1:309–15; John S. Morrill, *The Revolt of the Provinces: Conservatives and Radicals in the English Civil War, 1630–1650* (London:

Longman, 1976), 36–42; and Hubert Salm, *Armeefinanzierung im dreissigjährigen Krieg: Der niederrheinisch-westfalische Reichskreise, 1635–59*, Schriftenreihe der Vereinigung zur Erforschung der neueren Geschichte, vol. 16 (Münster: Aschendorff, 1990), 164–76. For World War I, see Tony Ashworth, *Trench Warfare, 1914–1918: The Live and Let Live System* (New York: Holmes & Meier, 1980).

67. Robert A. Stradling, *The Armada of Flanders: Spanish Maritime Policy and European War, 1568–1668* (Cambridge: Cambridge University Press, 1992), 40–45.

68. Quotations from Christian Streit, *Keine Kameraden: Die Wehrmacht und die sowjetischen Kriegsgefangenen, 1941–45* (Stuttgart: Deutsche Verlags-Anstalt, 1978), 9; and Christopher Duffy, *Red Storm on the Reich: The Soviet March on Germany, 1945* (London: Routledge, 1991), 274. Both works document the meticulous execution of these policies. See also Horst Boog et al., *Das deutsche Reich und der zweite Weltkrieg* (Stuttgart: Deutsche Verlags-Anstalt, 1983), 4:413–40; and Omar Bartov, *Hitler's Army: Soldiers, Nazis and War in the Third Reich* (Oxford: Oxford University Press, 1991), 106–78.

69. Thomas Churchyard, *A Generall Rehearsall of Warres Wherein Is Five Hundred Severall Services of Land and Seas* (London, 1579), sig. Qii, Qiiiv.

70. See Patricia Seed, "Taking Possession and Reading Texts: Establishing the Authority of Overseas Empires," *William and Mary Quarterly* 49 (1992): 183–209; Philip W. Powell, *Soldiers, Indians and Silver: The Northwards Advance of New Spain, 1550–1600* (Berkeley: University of California Press, 1969), pt. 3; Anthony Pagden, *The Fall of Natural Man: The American Indian and the Origins of Comparative Ethnology* (Cambridge: Cambridge University Press, 1982), 80–90; and, more generally, Johnson, *The Just War Tradition*, 69–84.

71. Richard Meinertzhagen, *Kenya Diary (1902–1906)* (London: Eland, 1983), 178. By way of example, see the author's personal tally on 143–44, 146, 152 and 158, and the quotations in Robert F. Jones, "The Kipkororor Chronicles," *Military History Quarterly*, vol. 3, no. 3 (Spring 1991): 38–47. Thomas Churchyard advanced a remarkably similar justification for the brutality of the English in Elizabethan Ireland: there were so few troops and so few victuals, he asserted, that a policy of terror was unavoidable (Churchyard, *A Generall Rehearsall*, sig. Qiv).

72. Robert Axelrod, *The Evolution of Cooperation* (New York: Basic Books, 1984), 173–89.

73. *Henry V*, act 4, sc. 7, ll. 1–4.

5. Colonial America

I thank Professor Paul M. Kennedy, Sir Michael Howard, and Dr. George Andreopoulos for the opportunity to help plan the series on the laws of war and for their gracious invitation to contribute one of the chapters.

1. Nicholas P. Canny, "The Ideology of English Colonization: From Ireland to America," *William and Mary Quarterly*, 3d ser., vol. 30, no. 4 (October 1973), 583, 593.

2. Ibid., 582.

3. Edward Waterhouse, "A Declaration of the State of the Colonie and Affaires in Virginia, with a Relation of the Barbarous Massacre," in Warren M. Billings, ed., *The Old Dominion in the Seventeenth Century: A Documentary History of Virginia, 1606–1689* (Chapel Hill: University of North Carolina Press, 1975), 224.

4. J. Frederick Fausz and Jon Kukla, eds., "A Letter of Advice [from George Wyatt] to the Governor of Virginia, 1624," *William and Mary Quarterly*, 3d ser., vol. 34, no. 1 (January 1977), 126.

5. Two accounts by men who were familiar with contemporary English military tactics help us understand how the New England settlers fought Native Americans in the mid-1630s: Lion Gardener, "His Relation of the Pequot Warres," in *Collections of the Massachusetts Historical Society*, 3d ser., vol. 3 (1833), 136–60; and John Underhill, *News from America* (London, 1636), in *Collections of the Massachusetts Historical Society*, 3d ser., vol. 6 (1837), 2–28.

6. Gardener, "Relation," 144.

7. Fausz and Kukla, eds., "Letter of Advice," 126. See also Alden T. Vaughan, "'Expulsion of the Salvages': English Policy and the Virginia Massacre of 1622," *William and Mary Quarterly*, 3d ser., vol. 35, no. 1 (January 1978), 57–84.

8. See Harold E. Selesky, *War and Society in Colonial Connecticut* (New Haven: Yale University Press, 1990), 3–11, for an account of the settlers' confrontation with the Pequots. The number of casualties inflicted by the Pequot raid, as well as the population of the three towns, is reported by John Mason in *A Brief History of the Pequot War* (Boston, 1736), ix–x.

9. Underhill, *News from America*, 25–27.

10. For an excellent explanation of the rituals of torture and cannibalism with which some Iroquoian peoples surrounded their war making, see Bruce G. Trigger, *The Children of Aataentsic: A History of the Huron People to 1660* (Montreal: McGill-Queen's University Press, 1987). For an imaginative reconstruction of how the English colonists incorporated these experiences into their intellectual world, see Richard Slotkin, *Regeneration through Violence: The Mythology of the American Frontier, 1600–1860* (Middletown, Conn.: Wesleyan University Press, 1973).

11. Cotton Mather, *Decennium Luctuosum: An History of Remarkable Occurrences in the Long War, which New-England hath had with the Indian Salvages, from the year 1688, to the year 1698, faithfully Composed and Improved* (Boston, 1699).

12. Samuel Penhallow, *The History of the Wars of New-England with the Eastern Indians, or a Narrative of Their Continued Perfidy and Cruelty* (Boston, 1726). The pagination is from the 1726 edition. A second edition, "with a memoir, notes, and appendix," was published by the New Hampshire Historical Society in 1824.

13. Ibid., 6.

14. Ibid., 20–23.

15. Richard R. Johnson, "The Search for a Usable Indian: An Aspect of the Defense of Colonial New England," *Journal of American History*, vol. 64, no. 3 (December 1977), 623–51.

16. Penhallow, *History*, 21–22.

17. Ibid., 23.

18. James Axtell and William C. Sturtevant, "The Unkindest Cut, or Who Invented Scalping?" *William and Mary Quarterly*, 3d ser., vol. 37, no. 1 (July 1980), 451–72.

19. Penhallow, *History*, 10.

20. On the development in Connecticut of incentives as a way of organizing military activity, see Selesky, *War and Society*.

21. Louis Antoine de Bougainville, *Adventures in the Wilderness: The American Journals of Louis Antoine de Bougainville, 1756–1760*, ed. Edward P. Hamilton (Nor-

man: University of Oklahoma Press, 1964) contains an eyewitness account of the massacre, on which I draw below. Guy Fregault, *Canada: The War of the Conquest* (Toronto: Oxford University Press, 1969), 151–56, is a concise modern account. A longer recent treatment that seeks to provide a context for the event is Ian Steele, *Betrayals: Fort William Henry and the "Massacre"* (New York: Oxford University Press, 1990), 149–85.

22. Bougainville, *Adventures*, 159, 170.

23. Ibid., 172–73, 175.

24. Fregault, *Canada*, 153–54. On sowing the wind, see Hos. 8:7.

25. On the nature of the final French and Indian War, see, for example, Selesky, *War and Society*, pt. 2.

26. W. A. Speck, *The Butcher: The Duke of Cumberland and the Suppression of the '45* (Oxford: Basil Blackwell, 1981), chaps. 6 and 7. See also John Prebble, *Culloden* (London: Martin Secker & Warburg, 1961), chaps. 3 and 4.

27. Washington constantly asked Congress to create a long-service standing army that could be equipped and trained to match his opponents, most famously in his letter of September 24, 1776, to John Hancock, the president of Congress, in John C. Fitzpatrick, ed., *The Writings of George Washington*, vol. 6 (Washington, D.C.: U.S. Government Printing Office, 1932), 106–16.

28. Marion Balderston and David Syrett, eds., *The Lost War: Letters from British Officers during the American Revolution* (New York: Horizon Press, 1975), 124.

29. Johann Ewald, *Diary of the American War: A Hessian Journal*, trans. and ed. Joseph P. Tustin (New Haven: Yale University Press, 1979), 23.

30. John Graves Simcoe, *Simcoe's Military Journal: A History of the Operations of a Partisan Corps called the Queen's Rangers* (New York, 1844), 78–79.

31. Both paintings now hang in the Yale University Art Gallery. On Trumbull, see Theodore Sizer, *The Works of Colonel John Trumbull, Artist of the American Revolution* (New Haven: Yale University Press, 1950). Examples of this form of atrocity abound; see, for instance, the account of the massacre of Connecticut troops at Fort Griswold in Groton by British, Hessian, and loyalist forces under the turncoat Benedict Arnold. See William Heath, *Memoirs*, ed. William Abbatt (New York: William Abbatt, 1901), 282–84; and Christopher Ward, *The War of the Revolution* (New York: Macmillan, 1952), 627–28.

32. Fitzpatrick, *Writings of Washington*, 7:15–16, 103.

33. Henry P. Johnston, *The Campaign of 1776 Around New York and Brooklyn* (Brooklyn, N.Y.: Long Island Historical Society, 1878), 278; and Alexander Graydon, *Memoirs of His Own Time* (Philadelphia, 1846), quoted in Richard M. Ketchum, *The Winter Soldiers* (Garden City, N.Y.: Doubleday, 1973), 147.

34. Fitzpatrick, *Writings of Washington*, 7:109.

35. Ibid., 6:466, 480; 7:108. Howe did try to restrain his troops; see Ira D. Gruber, *The Howe Brothers and the American Revolution* (New York: Atheneum, 1972), 145–46, 242–43.

36. Frank Moore, ed., *Diary of the American Revolution from Newspapers and Original Documents* (New York, 1860), as quoted in Henry S. Commager and Richard B. Morris, eds., *The Spirit of 'Seventy-Six: The Story of the American Revolution As Told by Participants* (New York: Harper & Row, 1975), 525–27.

37. W. H. W. Sabine, ed., *The New-York Diary of Lieutenant Jabez Fitch* (Hollis, N.Y.: Colburn & Tegg, 1954), 31, 137–38.

38. Robert D. Bass, *The Green Dragoon: The Lives of Banastre Tarleton and Mary*

Robinson (New York: Henry Holt, 1957), 81. Well before May 1780 Tarleton had acquired among rebels a reputation for ruthlessness, but his activities had stayed within the bounds of what other Europeans would have deemed acceptable. In skirmishing against American dragoons in Westchester County, New York, in July 1779, for example, Tarleton found a most effective way of subduing the militiamen aiding the dragoons. "I proposed to the militia terms, that if they would not fire shots from buildings, I would not burn [those buildings]. They interpreted my mild proposal wrong, imputing it to fear. They persisted in firing till the torch stopped their progress, after which not a shot was fired." In Dorothy H. Hinitt and Frances R. Duncombe, *The Burning of Bedford, July 1779* (Bedford, N.Y.: Bedford Historical Society, 1974), 19. For more on the civil war in the South see, inter alia, Robert S. Lambert, *South Carolina Loyalists in the American Revolution* (Columbia: University of South Carolina Press, 1987). American soldiers in the South were guilty of actions similar to those of Tarleton's men at the Waxhaws; see, for example, Bass, *Green Dragoon*, 168.

39. Fitzpatrick, *Writings of Washington*, 7:443.

40. Don Higginbotham, "Reflections on the War of Independence, Modern Guerrilla Warfare, and the War in Vietnam," in *Arms and Independence: The Military Character of the American Revolution*, ed. Ronald Hoffman and Peter J. Albert (Charlottesville: University Press of Virginia, 1984), 12. The account of partisan war in northeastern New Jersey that follows draws heavily on Adrian C. Leiby, *The Revolutionary War in the Hackensack Valley: The Jersey Dutch and the Neutral Ground, 1775–1783*, 2d ed. (New Brunswick, N.J.: Rutgers University Press, 1980), chaps. 8–11. See also John Shy, "Armed Loyalism: The Case of the Lower Hudson Valley," in John Shy, *A People Numerous and Armed: Reflections on the Military Struggle for American Independence* (New York: Oxford University Press, 1976), 181–92. I have chosen not to consider what was appropriate conduct in guerrilla war, on the theory that the further a conflict slips away from some centralized control, the less it can be influenced by some centralized, specifically military norms, and becomes absorbed in and directed by what each individual thinks his society will tolerate, or by what he thinks he can get away with. Such activity becomes criminal, not military.

41. On the internecine aspects of the war of independence, see Paul H. Smith, *Loyalists and Redcoats: A Study in British Revolutionary Policy* (Chapel Hill: University of North Carolina Press, 1964); and Robert M. Calhoon, *The Loyalist Perception and Other Essays* (Columbia: University of South Carolina Press, 1989), esp. chap. 8, "Civil, Revolutionary, or Partisan: The Loyalists and the Nature of the War for Independence." On the war in the no-man's-land around New York City, see also Philip Ranlet, *The New York Loyalists* (Knoxville: University of Tennessee Press, 1986); Catherine S. Crary, "Guerrilla Activities of James DeLancey's Cowboys in Westchester County: Conventional Warfare or Self-Interested Freebooting?" in *The Loyalist Americans: A Focus on Greater New York*, ed. Robert A. East and Jacob Judd (Tarrytown, N.Y.: Sleepy Hollow Restorations, 1975); and Hinitt and Duncombe, *The Burning of Bedford*.

42. Leiby, *Revolutionary War*, 160, 153.

43. Ibid., 149–50. Similar situations continued to crop up until the British evacuated Manhattan in November 1783. In a notorious case, the hanging of rebel Capt. Joshua Huddy by loyalist Capt. Richard Lippincott in March 1782 created a dilemma for Washington that lingered until November. Washington, with a rashness born of frustration, threatened to hang a British captain, Charles Asgill, in retaliation if Lippincott were not

executed for the murder of Huddy. Although Clinton seems to have again been embarrassed by his inability to control the loyalists, he turned Lippincott over for trial by military court-martial, which court found that he had only been following the orders of his loyalist superior. Washington, who had no wish to hang Asgill, wriggled out of his promise of retaliation by accepting an appeal for clemency from the French ambassador based on the fact that because Asgill had been taken prisoner at Yorktown the French had an interest in his fate and would not allow him to be used as a pawn to satisfy the debased standard to which the conduct of war had fallen in America. See Douglas S. Freeman, *George Washington: A Biography*, vol. 5 (New York: Charles Scribner's Sons, 1952), 412–14, 419–20, 425; Frederick B. Wiener, *Civilians under Military Justice: The British Practice since 1689 Especially in North America* (Chicago: University of Chicago Press, 1967), 113–22; and Katherine Mayo, *General Washington's Dilemma* (New York: Harcourt, Brace, 1938).

44. The following account is drawn principally from Leiby, *Revolutionary War*, chap. 9; and D. Bennett Mazur and Wayne M. Daniels, *Baylor's Dragoons Massacre, September 28, 1778: Excavation of a Burial Site—A Report to the Board of Chosen Freeholders, Bergen County, New Jersey* (Bergen County, N.J.: Board of Chosen Freeholders, 1968).

45. Paul D. Nelson, *Anthony Wayne: Soldier of the Early Republic* (Bloomington: Indiana University Press, 1985), chap. 3.

46. Leiby, *Revolutionary War*, 170.

47. New-York Historical Society, *Collections . . . for . . . 1883, The [Stephen] Kemble Papers, Vol. I: 1773–1789*, ed. Edward F. DeLancy et al. (New York: New-York Historical Society, 1884), 163. The Second Battalion of the Light Infantry was created by combining the light infantry companies of nine regular regiments (ibid., 353).

48. Mazur and Daniels, *Baylor's Dragoons Massacre*, 9.

49. Ibid., 8.

50. Nelson, *Anthony Wayne*, 60.

6. The Age of Napoleon

1. Winston S. Churchill, *Marlborough: His Life and Times* (New York: Charles Scribner's Sons, 1934), 2:38; G. H. v. Behrenhorst, *Betrachtungen über die Kriegskunst* (Leipzig: G. Fleischer, 1798), 1:203; Emerich de Vattel, *The Law of Nations, or the Principles of Natural Law*, trans. Charles G. Fenwick (Washington: Carnegie Institution, 1916), 283; Guglielmo Ferrero, *Peace and War* (New York: Macmillan, 1933), 63–64.

2. Carl von Clausewitz, *On War*, ed. and trans. Peter Paret and Michael Howard (Princeton: Princeton University Press, 1976), 75, 609–10. See also Howard's essay "Temperamenta Belli: Can War Be Controlled?" in *Restraints on War*, ed. Michael Howard (Oxford: Oxford University Press, 1979), 1–8.

3. I have adopted the term vocational/professional from Geoffrey Best, *Humanity in Warfare* (New York: Columbia University Press, 1980), 60–61. On the changing material base for war, see William McNeill, *The Pursuit of Power* (Chicago: University of Chicago Press, 1982), 144–46.

4. Best, *Humanity*, 78–81; Jules Basdevant, *La révolution française et le droit de la guerre* (Paris: Latose, 1901), 50–53, paints a rather too favorable picture. For details on efforts to reduce pillaging in one of the armies, see John A. Lynn, *Bayonets of the Republic: Motivation and Tactics in the Army of Revolutionary France, 1791–94* (Urbana,

Ill.: University of Illinois Press, 1984), 97–115. For the Austrian ańd Prussian restraints, see Hoffman Nickerson, *The Armed Horde, 1793–1939* (New York: G. P. Putnam, 1942), 77–81.

5. Jean-Paul Bertaud, *The Army of the French Revolution: From Citizen Soldier to Instrument of Power,* trans. R. R. Palmer (Princeton: Princeton University Press, 1988), 191.

6. On execution of prisoners, see among others Alfred Vagts, *A History of Militarism* (New York: W. W. Norton, 1937), 119–20; Ramsey Weston Phipps, *The Armies of the First French Republic,* 5 vols. (London: Oxford University Press, 1926–39), 1:322–23; Best, *Humanity,* 81–82. The French need not have worried. The Duke of York had ruled out reprisals.

7. Simon Schama, *Citizens: A Chronicle of the French Revolution* (New York: Alfred A. Knopf, 1989), 791–92. Jacques Godechot, *The Counter-Revolution: Doctrine and Action, 1789–1804,* trans. S. Attanasio (New York: H. Fertig, 1971), 223–24. For an overall account of the Vendée rebellion, see Charles Tilly, *The Vendée,* 2d ed. (New York: Wiley, 1967).

8. Gunther E. Rothenberg, *The Art of Warfare in the Age of Napoleon* (London: Batsford, 1977), 111–13; Lynn, *Bayonets,* 89–91.

9. Bertaud, *Army of the Revolution,* 190–91. The growing tensions and differing attitudes between combat soldiers and the revolutionary leadership are emphasized by Rainer Wohlfeil, *Vom stehenden Heer des Absolutismus zur allgemeinen Wehrpflicht,* in *Handbuch zur deutschen Militärgeschichte* (Frankfurt: Bernard und Graefe Verlag, 1964), 2:35. Cf. Samuel F. Scott, "The French Revolution and the Professionalization of the French Officer Corps," in *On Military Ideology,* ed. Morris Janowitz and Jacques van Doorn (Rotterdam: Rotterdam University Press, 1971), 32–47.

10. Rothenberg, *Art of Warfare,* 90–91, 113–14; Bertaud, *Army of the Revolution,* 280–84, 296–300. Compare Geoffrey Best's observations in *War and Society in Revolutionary Europe, 1770–1870* (New York: Oxford University Press, 1986), 200–201. On Napoleon see Vagts, *Militarism,* 121; and on Charles see Gunther E. Rothenberg, *Napoleon's Great Adversaries: The Archduke Charles and the Austrian Army, 1792–1814* (Bloomington: Indiana University Press, 1982), 136.

11. Jennings L. W. Croker, *The Croker Papers* (London: J. Murray, 1884), 1:433; William F. P. Napier, *History of the War in the Peninsula* (1862; reprint ed., New York: AMS Press, 1970), 5:63.

12. John Keegan, *The Face of Battle* (New York: Random House, 1976), 194, 200–201.

13. Best, *Humanity,* 18–19, 49–50, 58, 101.

14. David G. Chandler, *The Campaigns of Napoleon* (New York: Macmillan, 1966), 236. On the siege of Genoa, see Rothenberg, *Art of Warfare,* 218–19; Marcellin de Marbot. *Mémoires du Général Baron du Marbot,* 3d ed. (Paris: E. Plon, 1891), 1:95–98, 110–11.

15. Georges Pariset, "Les captifs de Baylen: Les pontons de Cadix," *Revue des études napoléoniennes,* July–December (1931): 209–29.

16. Napier, *War in the Peninsula,* 3:177.

17. For French actions, see Marbot, *Mémoires,* 2:594. General Wilson quoted in A. Brett-James, *1812: Eyewitness Accounts of Napoleon's Defeat in Russia* (New York: St. Martin's Press, 1966), 224. By contrast, for efforts by Russian officers to protect

prisoners, see report by a German conscript, *Kanonier des Kaisers: Kriegstagebuch des Heinrich Wesemann,* ed. H. O. Wesemann (Cologne: Verlag für Wissenschaft und Politik, 1971), 68–69.

18. Bertaud, *Army of the Revolution,* 256–57; Paul Reyroles, "Les prisonniers de guerre étrangers pendant la période révolutionnaire et de l'Empire," *Mémoires de l'Académie de sciences, artes et belle lettres* 119 (1966–69): 113–70.

19. John R. Elting, *Swords around a Throne: Napoleon's Grande Armée* (New York: Free Press, 1988), 616–21.

20. J. M. Bulloch and E. E. Cope, "British Prisoners in France, 1803–1813," *Notes and Queries* 174 (1938): 92–96, 114–19; 175 (1938): 76–78, 202–3, 256–58; Rothenberg, *Art of Warfare,* 90.

21. Best, *Humanity,* 125; on Spain see Rothenberg, *Art of Warfare.*

22. For a discussion of traditional siege customs, see John W. Wright, "Sieges and Customs of War at the Opening of the Eighteenth Century," *American Historical Review* 39 (1934): 629–40. There is an excellent discussion of siege problems during the Wars of the Revolution and Napoleon in Best, *War and Society,* 99–102.

23. For Danzig see Gunther E. Rothenberg, "The Honest Soldier—Lefebvre," in *Napoleon's Marshals,* ed. David G. Chandler (New York: Macmillan, 1987), 227–31. For the incident at Glatz see Jakob Walter, *The Diary of a Napoleonic Footsoldier,* ed. and trans. Marc Raeff (New York: Doubleday, 1991), 15.

24. Phipps, *Armies,* 5:393; Best, *War and Society,* 101.

25. Raymond Rudorff, *War to the Death: The Sieges of Saragossa, 1808–1809* (New York: Macmillan, 1974) is the standard account.

26. Napier, *War in the, Peninsula,* 1:60.

27. Ibid.; Elizabeth Longford, *Wellington: The Years of the Sword* (New York: Harper & Row, 1969), 271–73, discusses the controversy. The latest on this debate is Jack A. Meyer's "Wellington and the Sack of Bajadoz: A 'Beastly Mutiny' or a Deliberate Policy?" *Proceedings, 1991,* Consortium on Revolutionary Europe, 251–57. Meyer concludes that "Wellington did indeed authorize the plundering of all three Spanish cities."

28. Charles J. Esdaile, *The Duke of Wellington and the Command of the Spanish Army, 1812–14* (New York: St. Martin's Press, 1990), 156.

29. The problem of how to distinguish between legitimate popular resistance forces and illegitimate guerrilla bands continued to plague generals during the American Civil War and the Franco-Prussian War. General Sheridan, an observer in Moltke's headquarters, is reported to have advised the Prussian that only severe measures, "the smoke of burning villages," would repress the *francs-tireurs.* Stig Förster, "Moltke und das Problem des industrialisierten Volkskriegs im 19.Jahrhundert," in *Generalfeldmarschall von Moltke: Bedeutung und Wirkung,* ed. Roland G. Foerster (Munich: Oldenbourg Verlag, 1991), 104–7.

30. Henry W. Halleck, *Halleck's International Law,* ed. S. Baker, 3d ed. (London: K. Paul, Trench, Trubner, 1893), 1:561–62.

31. Peter Paret, "Conscription and the End of the Old Regime in France and Prussia," in *Geschichte als Aufgabe,* ed. Wilhelm Treue (Berlin: Colloquium, 1988), 168. See also Bertaud, *Army of the Revolution,* 99–104. For the Austrian reluctance to use levies and militias, see Rothenberg, *Great Adversaries,* 46–48, 118–19; and Rothenberg, "The Archduke Charles and Popular Participation in War," *Proceedings, 1982,* Consortium on Revolutionary Europe, 214–24.

32. Halleck, *International Law,* 1:561–62; Napier, *War in the Peninsula,* 5:62.

33. Lynn, *Bayonets,* 113–15; Best, *Humanity,* 90 and n.18.

34. Edward J. Coss, "The British Soldier in the Peninsular War: The Acquisition of an Unjust Reputation," *Proceedings of the Annual Meeting of the Western Society for French History* 18 (1991): 248–49.

35. Napier, *War in the Peninsula,* 5:30–31, 61–63.

36. Best, *War and Society,* 92–93, 103–5.

37. Elting, *Swords,* 553–73; Best, *Humanity,* 91–96.

38. Rothenberg, *Art of Warfare,* 118–20.

39. Charles Esdaile, "Heroes or Villains? The Spanish Guerrillas in the Peninsular War," *History Today* 38 (1988): 29–35.

40. On French counterinsurgency in Aragon, see Don W. Alexander, *Rod of Iron: French Counterinsurgency in Aragon during the Peninsular Wars* (Wilmington: Scholarly Resources, 1976), 50–61, 92–94, 222–23.

41. Among the literature on the Spanish experience, the summary in Best, *War and Society,* 168–80, is perhaps the most perceptive. The war in Spain and Portugal emerges as a war of attrition in David Gates, *The Spanish Ulcer: A History of the Peninsular War* (New York: W. W. Norton, 1986). For Wellington's views on the guerrillas see Esdaile, *The Duke of Wellington,* 73–74, 78; for the views of some of his officers and soldiers, see Rothenberg, *Art of Warfare,* 186.

7. Maritime Conflict

1. Quoted in Lassa Oppenheim, *International Law: A Treatise,* ed. Hersch Lauterpacht, 8th ed. (London: Longmans, Green, 1955), vol. 1, 582, n.1. The Latin quotation may be translated as "The sea is open to everyone by nature."

2. Alfred T. Mahan, *The Influence of Sea Power upon History, 1660–1783* (1890; Boston: Little, Brown, 1949), 25.

3. Hugo Grotius, *The Law of War and Peace* [*De jure belli ac pacis,* 1625], trans. Louise R. Loomis (Roslyn, N.Y.: Walter J. Black, 1949), bk. 2, chap. 2, par. 3, 80–81.

4. Oppenheim, *International Law,* 593–94.

5. Ibid., 80.

6. Reginald G. Marsden, ed., *The Law and Custom of the Sea,* vol. 1, *1205–1640,* Publications of the Navy Records Society, vol. 49 (London, 1915), 1.

7. Ibid., 8, 69. Before 1630 commissions for outfitting private men-of-war were indiscriminately termed letters of marque, letters of reprisal, or letters of marque and reprisal.

8. Ibid., 19–20.

9. Ibid., 20–21.

10. Ibid., 21–31.

11. Ibid., 81–84. See also Frederic Rockwell Sanborn, *Origins of the Early English Maritime and Commercial Law* (New York: Century, 1930).

12. See Reginald Marsden, "The Vice-Admirals of the Coast," *English Historical Review* 22 (1907): 468–77; 23 (1908): 736–57.

13. Sir Travers Twiss, ed., *The Black Book of the Admiralty,* 4 vols. (London, 1871).

14. For the early history of the admiralty courts, see the introductions in Reginald Marsden, ed., *Select Pleas in the Court of Admiralty,* Publications of the Selden Society (London, 1894), vol. 1, *1527–1545* (London, 1897), vol. 2, *1545–1602.*

15. Ibid., 116.

16. See D. A. Gardiner, "History of Belligerent Rights on the High Seas in the Fourteenth Century," *Law Quarterly Review* 48 (1932): 521–46.

17. See William E. Butler, "Grotius and the Law of the Sea," and G. I. A. D. Draper, "Grotius's Place in the Development of Legal Ideas about War," in *Hugo Grotius and International Relations,* ed. Hedley Bull, Benedict Kingsbury, and Adam Roberts (New York: Oxford University Press, 1990), 177–207, 209–20.

18. Thomas Wemyss Fulton, *The Sovereignty of the Sea: An Historical Account of the Claims of England to the Dominion of the British Seas and of the Evolution of the Territorial Waters: With Special Reference to the Rights of Fishing and the Naval Salute* (Edinburgh and London: William Blackwood & Sons, 1911; facsimile reprint, New York: Kraus Reprint, 1976), 4–5.

19. Ibid., 538.

20. Grover Clark, "The English Practice with Regard to Reprisals by Private Persons," *American Journal of International Law* 27 (1933): 694–723; Richard Pares, *War and Trade in the West Indies* (London: Macmillan, 1936), 46–49.

21. Kenneth R. Andrews, *Elizabethan Privateering: English Privateering during the Spanish War, 1585–1603* (Cambridge: Cambridge University Press, 1966), 15–21.

22. Ibid., 30.

23. Ibid., 226–35.

24. Julian S. Corbett, ed., *Papers Relating to the Navy during the Spanish War, 1585–1587,* Publications of the Navy Records Society, vol. 11 (London, 1898), 36; Marsden, *Law and Custom of the Sea,* 252.

25. Proclamation, March 1, 1605, in Marsden, *Law and Custom of the Sea,* 353–58.

26. For example, the Swedish-built, high-speed motorboats used in the Gulf War, or the similar craft used by pirates in the Singapore Straits during the 1980s.

27. Philip C. Jessup and Francis Deák, *Neutrality: Its History, Economics and Law* (New York: Columbia University Press, 1935), vol. 1, *The Origins,* 12–16.

28. Quoted in Mahan, *Influence of Sea Power upon History,* 107.

29. Article XII of the Anglo-Swedish Treaty of 1661, quoted in D. J. Llewelyn Davies, "Enemy Property and Ultimate Destination during the Anglo-Dutch Wars, 1664–7 and 1672–4," in *The British Year Book of International Law* (London: Hodder & Stoughton, 1934), 24.

30. Ibid., 138.

31. Richard Pares, *Colonial Blockade and Neutral Rights, 1739–1763* (Oxford: Clarendon Press, 1938), 173.

32. Ibid., 50–104.

33. Ibid., 116.

34. Geoffrey Symcox, *The Crisis of French Sea Power, 1688–1697: From the Guerre d'Escadre to the Guerre de Course* (The Hague: Martinus Nijhoff, 1974), 221–33.

35. George N. Clark, "War Trade and Trade War," *Economic History Review* 1 (1929): 262–80; "Neutral Commerce in the War of the Spanish Succession and the Treaty of Utrecht," in *The British Year Book of International Relations* (London: Oxford University Press, 1928), 69–83.

36. Pares, *Colonial Blockade,* 180–204; James W. Gantenbein, *The Doctrine of Continuous Voyage, Particularly As Applied to Contraband and to Blockade* (Portland, Oreg.: Keystone Press, 1929), 1–10.

37. W. Alison Phillips and Arthur H. Reede, *Neutrality: Its History, Economics and*

Law (New York: Columbia University Press, 1936), vol. 2, *The Napoleonic Period,* 17, 300–303.

38. John W. Coogan, *The End of Neutrality: The United States, Britain and Maritime Rights, 1899–1915* (Ithaca, N.Y.: Cornell University Press, 1981), 18–21.

39. Act to Punish the Crime of Piracy, May 15, 1820, *U.S. Statutes at Large,* vol. 3, 600; Act for a More Effectual Suppression of the African Slave Trade, March 31, 1824, *British Statutes, 5 George IV, ch. 17;* U.S. Congress, Resolution on the Slave Trade, 1823, *Annals of Congress,* 17th Cong., 2d sess., 928, 1147.

40. Louis B. Sohn, "Peacetime Use of Force on the High Seas," in Horace B. Robertson, Jr., *The Law of Naval Operations,* Naval War College International Law Studies, vol. 64 (Newport, R.I.: Naval War College Press, 1991), 38–90; Christopher Lloyd, *The Navy and the Slave Trade: The Suppression of the African Slave Trade in the Nineteenth Century* (London: Longmans, Green, 1949), 39–60; Raymond C. Howell, *The Royal Navy and the Slave Trade* (New York: St. Martin's Press, 1979), 216–22.

41. Coogan, *End of Neutrality,* 23–24; Warren F. Spencer, "The Mason Memorandum and the Diplomatic Origins of the Declaration of Paris," in *Diplomacy in an Age of Nationalism: Essays in Honor of Lynn Marshall Case,* ed. Nancy N. Barker and Marvin L. Brown, Jr. (The Hague: Martinus Nijhoff, n.d.), 64–65; Francis R. Stark, *The Abolition of Privateering and the Declaration of Paris* (New York: Columbia University, 1897).

42. The U.S. Constitution, art. I, sec. 8, par. 11, gives Congress the right to grant letters of marque and reprisal. The United States could not have agreed to the Declaration of Paris without first amending the Constitution.

43. Stuart Bernarth, *Squall Across the Atlantic* (Berkeley: University of California Press, 1970), 2–14, 27–33.

44. See Norman B. Ferris, *The Trent Affair: A Diplomatic Crisis* (Knoxville: University of Tennessee Press, 1977).

45. Coogan, *End of Neutrality,* 28.

46. Naval War College, *International Law Discussions, 1903: The United States Naval War Code of 1900* (Washington, D.C.: Government Printing Office, 1904).

47. Mahan to Theodore Roosevelt, December 27, 1904, in Richard W. Turk, *The Ambiguous Relationship: Theodore Roosevelt and Alfred Thayer Mahan* (Westport, Conn.: Greenwood Press, 1987), 135–36.

48. Coogan, *End of Neutrality,* 90, 124, 125, 238–39.

49. Avner Offner, "Morality and Admiralty: 'Jacky' Fisher, Economic Warfare and the Laws of War," *Journal of Contemporary History* 23 (1988): 99–118.

50. Letter of British foreign office to British ambassador in Washington, November 3, 1914, in Naval War College, *International Law Documents* (Washington, D.C.: Government Printing Office, 1945), 52.

51. German ambassador to the secretary of state, February 15, 1915, in ibid., 54–55.

52. German ambassador to the secretary of state, January 31, 1917, in ibid., 55.

53. Quoted in Offner, "Morality and Admiralty," 114.

54. Ibid., 114–15.

55. Stephen Roskill, *Naval Policy between the Wars* (London: Collins, 1976), vol. 2, *The Period of Reluctant Rearmament, 1930–1939,* 320.

56. William T. Mallison, Jr., *Submarines in General and Limited Wars,* Naval War College International Law Studies, vol. 58 (Washington, D.C.: Government Printing Office, 1968), 91.

57. Ludovic Kennedy, "War Crimes of the Ocean," *Telegraph Magazine* [London], June 16, 1991, 16–21, 55–58. For *U-86* and the sinking of *Llandovery Castle*, see Walter Schwengler, *Völkerrecht, versailler Vertrag und Auslieferungsfrage: Die Strafverfolgung wegen Kriegsverbrechen als Problem des Freidensschlusses 1919/20* (Stuttgart: Deutsche Verlags-Anstalt, 1982), 348. For World War II actions, see John Cameron, ed., *The Peleus Trial: The Trial of Kapitänleutnant Eck and Four Others* (London: W. Hodge, 1948); Kurt Assmann, "Der Deutsche U-Boot-Krieg (1939–45) und die Nürnberger Rechtsprechung," *Marine Rundschau* 50 (1953), 2–8; Heinrich Dietz, *Völkerrecht und deutsche Prisenrechtsprechung im Zweiten Weltkrieg* (Frankfurt am Main: Metzner, 1979).

58. J. G. Merrills, *Anatomy of International Law* (London: Sweet & Maxwell, 1976), 77.

59. Burdick H. Brittin, *International Law for Seagoing Officers*, 5th ed. (Annapolis, Md.: Naval Institute Press, 1986), 226.

60. Article 0605 of *United States Naval Regulations, 1973*, and article 0705, *United States Naval Regulations, 1990*. Compare with article 0505, *United States Naval Regulations, 1948*, to see this change.

61. Naval Warfare Publication 9 (Revision A) [NWP 9 (rev. A)] and Fleet Marine Force Manual 1–10 [FMFM 1–10] is published as an appendix to Horace B. Robertson, Jr., ed., *The Law of Naval Operations*, U.S. Naval War College International Law Studies, vol. 64 (Newport, R.I.: Naval War College Press, [1991]), 385–508. A further revision to NWP 9 was in progress in 1992.

62. W. Michael Reisman and William K. Leitzau, "Moving International Law from Theory to Practice: The Role of Military Manuals in Effectuating the Law of Armed Conflict," in Robertson, *Law of Naval Operations*, 12.

63. Adm. Carlisle A. H. Trost, USN, "Alliances Work," in *Tenth International Sea Power Symposium: Report of the Conference, 22–25 October 1989* (Newport, R.I.: Naval War College Press, 1989), 36.

8. Land Warfare: From Hague to Nuremberg

1. A. Jurist, [pseudonym for F. J. P. Veale], *Advance to Barbarism* (London: Thomson & Smith, 1948), 7. This edition had 182 pp. Later editions, under the author's name, were published by C. C. Nelson, Appleton, 1953, 305 pp.; and Mitre Press, London, [1968], 363 pp. The author also wrote lives of Lenin (1932) and Frederick the Great (1935).

2. Veale, *Advance to Barbarism*, 8. On von Keitel's part in the policy of ignoring international legal constraints in occupied Poland, see below, text at note 46.

3. Veale, *Advance to Barbarism*, 9.

4. Veale, *Advance to Barbarism*, 60. His assertion that 1940 is the year when the decline really took hold follows on from his claim on 59 that, up to 1940, the war had the character of a European civil war: "It is submitted, therefore, that the war 1914–18 should be labelled European Civil War No. 8a, and the war 1939–40 European Civil War No. 8b."

5. This had been widely anticipated, as the circumstances of my birth testified. I was born in late August 1940 in Penrith, in Cumbria, where my family had moved (along with the Newcastle Royal Grammar School at which my father taught) in perfectly correct

anticipation that the Luftwaffe would shortly be expressing a considerable interest in Newcastle-upon-Tyne, but would be less interested in the Lake District.

6. As of November 15, 1991, there were 167 states parties to the four 1949 Geneva Conventions, compared with 166 member states of the United Nations. Information supplied by International Committee of the Red Cross (ICRC), Geneva, November 19, 1991.

7. Also known as Jean de Bloch and Ivan Bliokh, his study *The Future of War* was published in 1898–99 in 6 volumes and in three languages. In English there is only a one-volume version, first published in London in 1899.

8. From the text of the Rescript in Frederick W. Holls, *The Peace Conference at The Hague and Its Bearings on International Law and Policy* (New York: Macmillan, 1900), 9. Dr. Holls was Secretary and Counsel of the American Commission at the 1899 Hague Peace Conference.

9. Holls, *Peace Conference at The Hague,* 15.

10. Holls, *Peace Conference at The Hague,* 26.

11. Holls, *Peace Conference at The Hague,* 63, 93.

12. Holls, *Peace Conference at The Hague,* ix–x.

13. James Brown Scott, ed., *The Hague Conventions and Declarations of 1899 and 1907,* 2d ed. (New York: Oxford University Press, 1915), 101–2.

14. For example, J. M. Spaight, *War Rights on Land* (London: Macmillan, 1911).

15. See, e.g., Col. J. E. Edmonds and L. Oppenheim, *Land Warfare: An Exposition of the Laws and Usages of War on Land for the Guidance of Officers of His Majesty's Army* (London: His Majesty's Stationery Office, [1912]). This became chap. 14 of the 1914 British manual of military law.

16. Belgium's status of permanent neutrality had been established by treaties in 1831 and 1839, and confirmed by treaties in 1870. On the problems of neutrality in two world wars, see Nils Ørvik, *The Decline of Neutrality, 1914–1941: With Special Reference to the United States and the Northern Neutrals,* 2d ed. (London: Cass, 1971).

17. Two interesting examples of this genre are Coleman Phillipson, *International Law and the Great War* (London: T. Fisher Unwin, 1915); and Charles Andler, *"Frightfulness" in Theory and Practice: As Compared with Franco-British War Usages* (London: T. Fisher Unwin, 1916).

18. B. H. Liddell Hart, *The Revolution in Warfare* (London: Faber, 1946), 63–64.

19. For a view that Kitchener had been too sweeping in his statements condemning the German use of gas, see C. R. M. F. Cruttwell, *A History of the Great War, 1914–1918* (Oxford: Oxford University Press, 1934), 153.

20. This is the conclusion of Edward M. Spiers in his *Chemical Warfare* (London: Macmillan, 1986), 32–33.

21. On the limited relevance of the existing rules and legal categories to maritime aspects of the First World War, see Cruttwell, *History of the Great War,* 187–203.

22. Liddell Hart, *Revolution in Warfare,* 60–61.

23. James Wilford Garner, *International Law and the World War,* 2 vols. (London: Longmans, Green, 1920), 2:463.

24. Lloyd George, memorandum of December 31, 1914, Asquith Papers, Bodleian Library, Oxford. I am grateful to Don Markwell for pointing this out to me.

25. Veale, *Advance to Barbarism,* 61 (italics in original).

26. "Logically, it is difficult to object to the use of gas while accepting high explosives, especially as the percentage of victims who died or were permanently disabled was much smaller. But Germany's innovation outraged the general feeling of mankind, for a momentary and limited military profit" (Liddell Hart, *Revolution in Warfare,* 62).

27. "Modern nations have reverted to a more primitive extreme—akin to the practices of warfare between barbaric hordes that were armed with spear and sword—at the same time as they have become possessed of science-given instruments for multiple destruction at long range" (Liddell Hart, *Revolution in Warfare,* 8); see also his references to barbarism on 31 and 68.

28. On the trials, see James F. Willis, *Prologue to Nuremberg: The Politics and Diplomacy of Punishing War Criminals of the First World War* (Westport, Conn.: Greenwood Press, 1982).

29. In the interwar years very few states acceded to the 1907 Hague Convention IV on land war. Poland did so in May 1925, Ethiopia in 1935. A few other states, for example in the former Austro-Hungarian and Russian empires, may have considered themselves bound by succession, but often the position of such states on this matter was obscure.

30. Adam Roberts and Richard Guelff, eds., *Documents on the Laws of War,* 2d ed. (Oxford: Oxford University Press, 1989), 144–45.

31. *What Would Be the Character of a New War? Enquiry Organised by the Inter-Parliamentary Union* (London: P. S. King & Son, 1931), 411.

32. One book arguing that war was inevitable because men are imperfect, but that it was always limited morally, politically, economically, and technically, was Hoffman Nickerson, *Can We Limit War?* (New York: Frederick A. Stokes, 1934).

33. Spiers, *Chemical Warfare,* 62.

34. Spiers, *Chemical Warfare,* 67.

35. Martin Gilbert, *Winston S. Churchill,* vol. 6, *Finest Hour, 1939–1941* (London: Heinemann, 1983), 618. Also Spiers, *Chemical Warfare,* 68.

36. Churchill to General Ismay, July 6, 1944, quoted in Gilbert, *Winston S. Churchill,* vol. 7, *Road to Victory, 1941–1945* (London: Heinemann, 1986), 841.

37. Spiers, *Chemical Warfare,* 88.

38. Japan signed the 1929 Prisoners of War Convention, but did not ratify it as it was considered "an ignomiy to surrender to the enemy" (International Military Tribunal for the Far East, 1946–48, duplicated version of proceedings, vol. 125, Judgment, 49720-2). See also United Nations War Crimes Commission, *History of the United Nations War Crimes Commission and the Development of the Laws of War* (London: His Majesty's Stationery Office, 1948), 382–90.

39. Alexander Dallin, *German Rule in Russia, 1941–45: A Study of Occupation Policies,* 2d ed. (London: Macmillan, 1981), 419–20.

In his note of April 27, 1942, on German atrocities, Soviet foreign minister Molotov declared that the "Soviet Government . . . continues as hitherto to observe the obligations undertaken by the Soviet Union with regard to the regime for war prisoners according to the Hague Convention of 1907" (Jacob Robinson, "Transfer of Property in Enemy Occupied Territory," *American Journal of International Law,* vol. 39, no. 2 [April 1945], 218).

In *United States* v. *Von Leeb* (the *High Command Case*), a U.S. military tribunal stated that many provisions of the 1929 Geneva Convention on Prisoners of War had passed into customary law before the outbreak of war between Germany and the Soviet Union in 1941, and the parties had therefore been obliged to observe them (*Trials of War Criminals Before the Nuremberg Military Tribunals Under Control Council Law No. 10, Nuremberg, October 1946—April 1949,* 15 vols. [Washington, D.C.: Government Printing Office, (1949–53)], vol. 11, 462).

40. Dallin suggests that about 5,754,000 Soviet soldiers fell into German hands in the course of the war. "Of these, less than one million were released, either to return home as civilians, or to serve with collaborator units established by the German armed forces" (Dallin, *German Rule in Russia,* 427; see also *The Trial of German Major War Criminals: Proceedings of the International Military Tribunal Sitting at Nuremberg Germany,* 23 vols. [London: His Majesty's Stationery Office, 1946–51], 22:452).

41. See especially Christiane Shields Delessert, *Release and Repatriation of Prisoners of War at the End of Active Hostilities* (Zurich: Schulthess Polygraphischer Verlag, 1977), 144–56.

42. Winston S. Churchill, *The Second World War,* vol. 6, *Triumph and Tragedy* (London: Cassell, 1954), 46–47.

43. Article 54(1) of 1977 Geneva Protocol I states: "Starvation of civilians as a method of warfare is prohibited."

44. Using both German and Soviet sources, Gouré concludes that over one million Leningraders perished during the siege, principally from starvation, cold, and illness (Leon Gouré, *The Siege of Leningrad* [New York: McGraw-Hill, 1964], 217–18).

Drawing on a broad range of sources, Salisbury suggests: "A total for Leningrad and vicinity of something over 1,000,000 deaths attributable to hunger, and an over-all total of deaths, civilian and military, on the order of 1,300,000 to 1,500,000, seems reasonable" (Harrison E. Salisbury, *The Siege of Leningrad* [London: Secker & Warburg, 1969], 516).

45. Wladyslaw Bartoszewski, *Warsaw Death Ring, 1939–1944* (Warsaw: Interpress, 1968), 15. For the German text, see *Trial of the Major War Criminals before the International Military Tribunal, Nuremberg, 14 November 1945–1 October 1946,* 42 vols. (Nuremberg: IMT Secretariat, 1947–49), 36:329.

46. Top secret memorandum of a conference between Hitler and the Chief of the Oberkommando der Wehrmacht (OKW), von Keitel, entitled "Regarding Future Relations of Poland to Germany," dated October 20, 1939, in *Trial of German Major War Criminals,* 4:143.

47. Based on detailed estimates given by J. K. Zawodny, *Nothing but Honour: The Story of the Warsaw Uprising, 1944* (London: Macmillan, 1978), 210. Bartoszewski gives a slightly lower figure: "some 180,000–200,000 men, women and children perished during the Rising" (*Warsaw Death Ring,* 352).

48. For a clear discussion in the light of the events of the Second World War, see Lester Nurick and Roger W. Barrett, "Questions of Guerrilla Forces under the Laws of War," *American Journal of International Law,* vol. 40, no. 3 (July 1946): 563–83.

49. Richard R. Baxter, "The Duty of Obedience to the Belligerent Occupant," *British Year Book of International Law, 1950* (London: Oxford University Press, 1951), 260.

50. 1907 Hague Convention IV, Article 2. In the Second World War, several of the belligerents were not parties to this convention (nor to the almost identical 1899 version): therefore, in narrow letter-of-the-law terms, some could argue that the convention was not applicable to this conflict.

51. *Trial of German Major War Criminals,* 22:467.

52. Geoffrey Best, *Humanity in Warfare: The Modern History of the International Law of Armed Conflicts* (London: Weidenfeld & Nicolson, 1980), 217–18.

53. Geoffrey Best, "Restraints on War by Land before 1945," in *Restraints on War: Studies in the Limitation of Armed Conflict,* ed. Michael Howard (Oxford University Press, 1979), 36.

54. For an account of German investigations of Allied war crimes in the Second World War (with some material also on the First World War), see Alfred M. de Zayas, *The Wehrmacht War Crimes Bureau, 1939–1945* (Lincoln: University of Nebraska Press, 1989).

9. Air Power

The author would like to thank Luke Arant, Stephen Biddle, Lynn Eden, Richard Hallion, Steve Harris, Richard Kohn, Richard Muller, John Nagl, Vincent Orange, W. Hays Parks, Alex Roland, Mark Shulman, Edward E. Thomas, Jacob Vander Meulen, and Herman Wolk for their assistance and/or comments on earlier drafts. Responsibility for any errors that may remain is mine alone.

1. *Discriminate* is of course a relative term. Other forms of warfare besides aerial bombardment caused high numbers of civilian casualties in World War II. My point, which will be elaborated below, is that aerial bombing was not a precision instrument and was responsible for the deaths of many civilians, many of whom were involved in the war effort in some way, and many of whom were not.

2. All important developments in the law of war as applied to air power are reviewed in W. Hays Parks, "Air War and the Law of War," *Air Force Law Review,* vol. 32, no. 1 (1990): 1–225. Parks's essay is the most complete and up-to-date survey of the topic available. On this point, see 11–12. On the period up to and including World War II, see also Donald Cameron Watt, "Restraints on War in the Air before 1945," in *Restraints on War: Studies in the Limitation of Armed Conflict,* ed. Michael Howard (New York: Oxford University Press, 1979), 57–77; and Geoffrey Best, *Humanity in Warfare* (New York: Columbia University Press, 1980), 262–85.

3. The relevant sections of the text of the 1899 Hague Conference can be found in Dietrich Schindler and Jiri Toman, *The Laws of Armed Conflicts,* 3d rev. ed. (Dordrecht: Martinus Nijhoff, 1988), 83–84.

4. Detailed, insightful accounts of both Hague conferences and their bearing on air power can be found in M. W. Royse, *Aerial Bombardment and the International Regulation of Warfare* (New York: Harold Vinal, 1928). On the environment preceding the 1907 conference, see chap. 3, 51–122.

5. Ibid., 119–20.

6. The text of Convention IX of 1907 (Concerning Bombardment by Naval Forces in Time of War) can be found in Schindler and Toman, *Laws of Armed Conflicts,* 811–17.

7. On the topic of unavoidable damage, see Schindler and Toman, *Laws of Armed Conflicts,* 812. For Article 15 of the Lieber instructions of 1863, from which the quote is drawn, see Schindler and Toman, *Laws of Armed Conflicts,* 6.

8. On 17 of "Air War," Parks suggests that the drafters of the Naval Convention may have been better qualified than their counterparts working on land warfare. For the

clarification by Col. Gross von Schwarzhoff, see *The Proceedings of the Hague Peace Conferences* (The Conference of 1899), prepared under the supervision of James Brown Scott (New York: Oxford University Press, 1920), 424. See also Parks, "Air War," 14–15 and notes 57–60. On the final point, see Percy Bordwell, *The Law of War between Belligerents* (Chicago: Callaghan, 1908), 287.

9. Christopher Cole and E. F. Cheesman, *The Air Defence of Britain, 1914–1918* (London: Bodley Head, 1984), 6.

10. See J. M. Spaight, *Air Power and War Rights* (London: Longmans, Green, 1924), 225, and F. W. Lanchester, *Aircraft in Warfare* (London: Constable, 1916), 120–22. On this point it might be noted as well that London also contained factories manufacturing weapons, and soldiers and sailors on leave or in training.

11. A useful survey of strategic bombing in World War I can be found in Lee Kennett, *A History of Strategic Bombing* (New York: Charles Scribner's Sons, 1982), chap. 2. Kennett takes a deeper look at the subject in his new book, *The First Air War, 1914–1918* (New York: Free Press, 1991), esp. chap. 3. An excellent chapter on strategic bombing in World War I can be found in S. F. Wise, *Canadian Airmen and the First World War* (Toronto: University of Toronto Press, 1980), 284–327. On the early raids see Sir Charles Webster and Noble Frankland, *The Strategic Air Offensive against Germany, 1939–1945*, vol. 1 (London: Her Majesty's Stationery Office, 1961), 34–35.

12. See Malcolm Smith, *British Air Strategy between the Wars* (Oxford: Clarendon Press, 1984), 21; and Andrew Boyle, *Trenchard* (London: Collins, 1962), 287.

13. From Trenchard's dispatch of January 1, 1919, reprinted in H. A. Jones, *The War in the Air,* vol. 6 (Oxford: Clarendon Press, 1937), 136.

14. Smith, *British Air Strategy,* 61.

15. Burrus M. Carnahan, "The Law of Air Bombardment in its Historical Context," *Air Force Law Review,* vol. 17, no. 2 (Summer 1975): 53; and Spaight, *Air Power,* 217–18.

16. Spaight, *Air Power,* 220.

17. See Spaight, *Air Power and War Rights* (1947 ed.), 7. On trends in doctrine at the end of the war and production problems during the war, see I. B. Holley, Jr., *Ideas and Weapons* (Washington, D.C.: Office of Air Force History, 1983). The volume was originally published by Yale University Press in 1953.

18. I. F. Clarke, *Voices Prophesying War* (New York: Oxford University Press, 1966), 100–101.

19. Brian Bond, *War and Society in Europe, 1870–1970* (London: Fontana, 1984), 151.

20. For some interesting commentary on this, see Sir John Slessor, *The Central Blue* (New York: Praeger, 1957), 14–15, 151–52.

21. For an explanation of these trends, see an enlightening paper by Joseph W. Konvitz, "Cities as Targets: Conceptions of Strategic Bombing, 1914–1945," Woodrow Wilson International Center for Scholars, Paper no. 85 (Washington, D.C., 1987).

22. Guilio Douhet, *The Command of the Air* (Washington, D.C.: Office of Air Force History, 1983), esp. 10–19. The volume was originally published in the United States in 1942 by Coward-McCann.

23. This idea crops up throughout the history of warfare. William Tecumseh Sherman practiced a form of it in the American Civil War, and the Royal Navy's Adm. Sir John

Fisher was almost certainly its most vocal and colorful proponent. On the latter, see Adm. Sir R. H. Bacon, *The Life of Lord Fisher of Kilverstone,* vol. 1 (Garden City, N.Y.: Doubleday Doran, 1929), 121.

24. See letter by Count von Moltke on the laws of warfare as adopted by the Institute of International Law at its 1880 Oxford session, cited in Royse, *Aerial Bombardment,* 134; Article 29 of the Lieber instructions, in Schindler and Toman, *Laws of Armed Conflicts,* 7–8; and Douhet, *Command of the Air,* 61. Douhet's statement was particularly influenced by the horrific consequences of trench stalemate from the end of 1914 to the spring of 1918. Interestingly, this strong reaction to the Great War lingered in the thinking of J. M. Spaight even after World War II. He wrote that even though terrible things had occurred in World War II, there had been "nothing so calamitous as the cutting off of the flower of a generation" (*Air Power and War Rights,* 3d ed. [London: Longmans, Green, 1947], 28).

25. The Hague Rules of Air Warfare, 1922–23, in Schindler and Toman, *Laws of Armed Conflicts,* 207–17. For articles 22–25, see 210–11.

26. See Parks, "Air War," 25–36; and Royse, *Aerial Bombardment,* 213–36.

27. On Britain's economic problems, see, for instance, Paul M. Kennedy, "The Contradiction between British Strategic Planning and Economic Requirements in the Era of the Two World Wars," The Woodrow Wilson International Center for Scholars, Paper no. 11 (Washington, D.C., 1979). Also see Smith, *British Air Strategy,* 22–34; for discussion of air control see 28–31. Book-length accounts of the practice have recently been produced by Philip Towle, *Pilots and Rebels* (London: Brasseys, 1989); and David E. Omissi, *Air Power and Colonial Control* (New York: St. Martin's Press, 1990).

28. On the Geneva Disarmament Conference, see Smith, *British Air Strategy,* 112–21, and Uri Bialer, *The Shadow of the Bomber* (London: Royal Historical Society, 1980), chaps. 1 and 2.

29. See Robert Paul Shay, Jr., *British Rearmament in the Thirties* (Princeton: Princeton University Press, 1977), 34–42. For another view of the problems faced by the British in these years, see Wesley K. Wark, *The Ultimate Enemy* (Ithaca, N.Y.: Cornell University Press, 1985), 35–58.

30. John Terraine, *A Time for Courage* (New York: Macmillan, 1985), 83–85. The quote from Ludlow-Hewitt is on p. 85.

31. Thomas H. Greer, *The Development of Doctrine in the Army Air Arm, 1917–1941* (Washington, D.C.: Office of Air Force History, 1985), 14–15; also Holley, *Ideas and Weapons,* 170–71.

32. This key node orientation is articulated repeatedly in the lectures delivered at ACTS in the 1930s, which may be examined at the Air Force Historical Research Center, Maxwell AFB, Alabama. Authors have offered different hypotheses as to the genesis of the American focus on precision targeting. Included among these are the moral tone set by Secretary Baker and its legacy; the defensive orientation of American strategy in this period, including the funding of bombers as weapons designed to defend American shores against hostile navies; and the general popularity of industrial-economic interpretations of warfare in the United States in this period. One should also take into account the geographical isolation of the United States, which afforded planners the luxury of taking a fairly analytical and economic approach to the problem of strategic targeting. On the development of interwar doctrine in the United States, see Greer, *Army Air Arm,* 44–106; David MacIsaac, *Strategic Bombing in World War II* (New York: Garland, 1976), chap. 1; Robert

Frank Futrell, *Ideas, Concepts, Doctrine: A History of Basic Thinking in the United States Air Force, 1907–1964* (Maxwell Air Force Base, Ala.: Air University, 1974), chap. 3; Haywood S. Hansell, *The Strategic Air War against Germany and Japan* (Washington, D.C.: Office of Air Force History, 1986); and Donald Wilson, "Origin of a Theory for Air Strategy," *Aerospace Historian,* vol. 18, no. 1 (March 1971), 19–25.

33. Parks, "Air War," 39.

34. See "Comparison of Courses," Air Corps Tactical School, July 1, 1934. Air Force Historical Research Center (AFHRC), Maxwell Air Force Base, Alabama, file no. 248.192. By comparison it might be noted that in the year 1933–34 students were required to take 100 hours of training in horsemanship.

35. Parks, "Air War," 38–39.

36. Williamson Murray, "A Tale of Two Doctrines: The Luftwaffe's 'Conduct of the Air War,' and the USAF's Manual 1-1," *Journal of Strategic Studies,* vol. 6, no. 4 (December 1983), 86. See also Parks, "Air War," 39. Further insight into German air doctrine can be found in Richard Muller, *The German Air War in Russia* (Annapolis, Md.: Nautical and Aviation Publishing Company of America, 1992), esp. chap. 1. A debate exists on the question of whether the Luftwaffe was actually oriented to terror bombing. For contrasting views, see Olaf Groehler, "The Strategic Air War and Its Impact on the German Civil Population," and Horst Boog, "The Luftwaffe and Indiscriminate Bombing up to 1942," both in *The Conduct of the Air War in the Second World War,* ed. Horst Boog (New York: Berg, 1992), 279–97 and 373–404.

37. See "International Aerial Regulations," Air Corps Tactical School, 1933–34. Air Force Historical Research Center, file no. 248.101–16.

38. Royse was a Marine aviator in World War I who received his Ph.D. from Columbia University and went on to a distinguished career of teaching and writing. British writer James Maloney Spaight's comprehensive volume appeared in three successive editions (1924, 1933, and 1947).

39. Royse, *Aerial Bombardment,* 147. On 216 Royse writes: "The doctrine of the military objective would tend to operate against terrorization as a means of moral pressure upon civilian populations, but perhaps the most effective deterrent will be that of the conservation of energy, a purely utilitarian check." This passage, which was quoted at the Air Corps Tactical School (see Air Force Historical Research Center, file no. 248.101–16), served to reinforce the sentiment of Maj. William C. Sherman, army aviation advisor on the U.S. delegation to the 1922–23 Hague air conference, who believed that randomly dispersed or indiscriminate bombing would result in the decreased effectiveness of bombing as a whole. See Sherman's *Air Warfare* (New York: Ronald Press, 1926), 217.

40. J. M. Spaight, "The Chaotic State of the International Law Governing Bombardment," *Royal Air Force Quarterly,* vol. 9, no. 1 (January 1938), 25.

41. On the Roosevelt plea, see Carnahan, "Law of Air Bombardment," 53. Damning commentary on the Luftwaffe bombing of Warsaw and Rotterdam can be found in Groehler, "Strategic Air War," 282–83. In the early years of the war, British policy was determined as much as anything by the weakness of their own position and a desire not to provoke the Germans under such circumstances. For an explanation of British policy through the war, see a confidential annex done by J. M. Spaight in 1947 titled "International Law of the Air, 1939–1945," in AIR 41/5, Public Record Office, London. A description of the events of August 24–25, 1940, can be found in Webster and Frankland, *Strategic Air Offensive,* vol. 1, 152.

42. For the text of the Butt Report, see Webster and Frankland, *Strategic Air Offensive,* vol. 4, 205–13. After providing his initial figures, the author makes clear that "all these figures relate only to aircraft recorded as attacking the target: the proportion of the total sorties which reached within five miles is less by one third."

43. Webster and Frankland, *Strategic Air Offensive,* vol. 1, 321–25, and (for the text of the directive of February 14, 1942), vol. 4, 143–45.

44. For an indication of Harris's dogged faith in area bombing, see, for instance, Webster and Frankland, *Strategic Air Offensive,* vol. 3, 65–67. His outspoken commitment to the city bombing campaign and his desire (indeed determination) to describe it in the most direct and unvarnished terms was a source of consternation to his colleagues in the Air Ministry. In December 1943 Harris was told that though Air Council members recognized that Bomber Command's campaign "is bound to destroy large areas of German cities," they preferred to emphasize the point that "widespread devastation is not an end in itself but the inevitable accompaniment of an all-out attack on the enemy's means and capacity to wage war." Harris was reminded, also, that it was desirable in any event "to present the bomber offensive in such a light as to provoke the minimum of public controversy and so far as possible to avoid conflict with religious and humanitarian opinion" (Air Ministry letter CS.21079/43 [to Air Officer Commanding-in-Chief, Bomber Command], December 15, 1943, in Air 14/843, Public Record Office, London).

45. For the text, see Webster and Frankland, *Strategic Air Offensive,* vol. 4, 153–54. See also Wesley Frank Craven and James Lea Cate, *The Army Air Forces in World War II,* vol. 2 (Chicago: University of Chicago Press, 1949), 300–307.

46. In heavy raids in July the Eighth Air Force lost nearly a third of its operational aircraft. Two raids deep into Germany against the ball bearing works at Schweinfurt (in August and again in October) proved disastrously costly. In the latter, 60 B-17s were lost, 17 were badly damaged, and 121 damaged, though reparably, out of a total of 291 dispatched. Such losses could not be sustained. See Craven and Cate, *Army Air Forces,* vol. 2, 704.

47. On Arnold's order see Ronald Schaffer, *Wings of Judgment* (New York: Oxford University Press, 1985), 67. For a sense of the accuracy levels achieved by the U.S. Eighth Air Force, see "AAF Bombing Accuracy, Report No. 2" by the Operational Analysis Section of the Eighth Air Force, in RG 18, Box 550, Air Adjutant General Files, 470 (Classified, Bulky File), National Archives and Records Administration, Washington, D.C. Between September and December of 1944, for instance, the Eighth Air Force dropped most of its tonnage using H2X radar. Of the 81,654 tons dropped in this way, only 674 tons got within 1,000 feet of the aiming point (less than 1 percent of bombs dropped). Report No. 2 is summarized in Charles W. McArthur, *Operations Analysis in the U.S. Army Eighth Air Force in World War II* (Providence, R.I.: American Mathematical Society, 1990), 287–98.

48. Edward E. Thomas, "World War II: Ultra and the Strategic Bombing Offensive," text of a lecture delivered at the Smithsonian Institution, June 14, 1990. See also chaps. 54 and 58 of F. H. Hinsley et al., *British Intelligence in the Second World War,* vol. 3, pt. 2 (London: Her Majesty's Stationery Office, 1988). On the Portal-Harris issue, see Webster and Frankland, *Strategic Air Offensive,* vol. 3, 80–90; and Denis Richards, *Portal of Hungerford* (London: Heinemann, 1987), chap. 26.

49. Kurt Vonnegut, speech at the National Air and Space Museum, Washington, D.C., May 3, 1990, reprinted in Vonnegut, *Fates Worse Than Death* (New York: Putnam's, 1991), 103.

50. See Webster and Frankland, *Strategic Air Offensive,* vol. 3, 103. Incisive commentary on Churchill's role in the Dresden raid can also be found in Max Hastings, *Bomber Command* (New York: Dial Press, 1979), 397–98.

51. Because the Dresden raid garnered so much postwar attention, American participation has been a focus for critics of World War II strategic bombing. What happened at Dresden was horrific, and the attention it has received has not been inappropriate. Nonetheless, there is little evidence that the Americans conceived of Dresden as a terror raid. It was another attack on marshaling yards, designed to disrupt German communications, only it happened to fall on the heels of a particularly devastating RAF incendiary raid on a city full of refugees. Ten days before the raid on Dresden, the USAAF had attacked the city of Berlin with an eye to affecting the German will to fight. In its planning stages at least, the Berlin raid (Operation Thunderclap) had been designed as a means of shattering German morale at a critical moment. Though the Thunderclap raid was sizable it did not bring capitulation. Thus, it convinced the Americans that it was not appropriate to put faith in the notion that one big raid might push the Germans over the edge. On the Berlin and Dresden raids, see Richard G. Davis's well-documented article, "Operation, 'Thunderclap': The US Army Air Forces and the Bombing of Berlin," *Journal of Strategic Studies,* vol. 14, no. 1 (March 1991), 90–111.

52. See "Narrative History of the Twentieth Air Force," Headquarters XXI Bomber Command (Analysis of the Incendiary Phase of Operations, March 9–19, 1945), Air Force Historical Research Center, Maxwell Air Force Base, file no. 760.01. For further background, see Conrad Charles Crane, *Bombs, Cities, and Civilians* (Lawrence: University of Kansas Press, 1993), esp. 120–42. On the relationship between Arnold and LeMay, see Michael Sherry, *The Rise of American Air Power* (New Haven: Yale University Press, 1987), 264–73. It is worth noting too that Arnold felt pressure on this issue from the commander in chief, Franklin D. Roosevelt.

53. Carnahan, "Law of Air Bombardment," 54–55.

54. See G. Brand, "The War Crimes Trials and the Laws of War," in *British Year Book of International Law* (London: Oxford University Press, 1949). He wrote (419): "No records of trials concerning the illegal conduct of air warfare were ever brought to the notice of the United Nations War Crimes Commission. Although in the Charter of the Nuremberg International Military Tribunal indiscriminate bombardment was apparently made a crime cognizable by the Tribunal, the Judgment did not contain any definite reference to the subject." See also 419, n.1.

55. Telford Taylor, "Final Report to the Secretary of the Army on the Nuremberg War Crimes Trials under Control Council Law no. 10" (Washington, D.C.: Government Printing Office, 1949), 65. Also cited in Parks, "Air War," 37–38.

56. Michael Walzer, *Just and Unjust Wars* (New York: Basic Books, 1977), 251–63.

57. One can calculate, based on loss rates published in the official histories, that those flying with Bomber Command or the U.S. Army Air Forces in 1943 had only about a one in three chance of completing their required number of missions. Allied pilots endured horrendous conditions in World War II, and in any discussion of strategic bombing we must not forget their singular courage, loyalty, and patriotism.

58. Paul Fussell, *Thank God for the Atom Bomb and Other Essays* (New York: Ballantine, 1988), 1–35.

59. A useful overview of the literature on the Hiroshima decision can be found in J. Samuel Walker, "The Decision to Use the Bomb: A Historiographical Update," *Diplomatic History,* vol. 14, no. 1 (Winter 1990), 97–114.

60. Prior to the Japanese surrender the United States refused to explicitly guarantee the retention of the emperor as part of the postwar Japanese state. In the event, however, the emperor was allowed to stay on as a democratic and constitutional monarch. Whether an earlier moderation of the terms might have changed the timing of surrender in the Far East has been the subject of debate among historians. It is impossible to know the answer to such a hypothetical question, but it is one that seems worth asking. For an enlightening examination of the bureaucratic politics of unconditional surrender, see Brian L. Villa, "The U.S. Army, Unconditional Surrender, and the Potsdam Proclamation," *Journal of American History,* vol. 63, no. 1 (June 1976), 66–92.

61. Walzer, *Wars,* 263–68.

62. Thirty-one key reports of the USSBS are reprinted in David MacIsaac, ed., *The United States Strategic Bombing Survey* (New York: Garland, 1976). See the United States Strategic Bombing Survey, Over-all Report (European War), in MacIsaac, vol. I, 96–97. On the British side see the report of the BBSU (a confidential Air Ministry paper published in 1946, but not released to the general public) entitled "The Strategic Air War against Germany, 1939–1945" (London: Air Ministry, [1946]), 79; and Webster and Frankland, *Strategic Air Offensive,* vol. 3, 89, 288, and vol. 4, 54.

63. See Alfred C. Mierzejewski, *The Collapse of the German War Economy, 1944–1945* (Chapel Hill: University of North Carolina Press, 1988), 185. Also see Stephen L. McFarland and Wesley Phillips Newton, *To Command the Sky* (Washington, D.C.: Smithsonian Institution Press, 1991).

64. Sensitivity to collateral civilian casualties was in fact a planning factor for the coalition air forces. See "Conduct of the Persian Gulf War," Final Report to Congress by the United States Department of Defense (Washington, D.C.: Government Printing Office, 1992), 98, which states: "A key principle underlying Coalition strategy was the need to minimize casualties and damage, both to the Coalition and to Iraqi civilians"; see also 100. Appendix O of this document is titled "The Role of the Law of War" and contains a section devoted to "Targeting, Collateral Damage and Civilian Casualties" (611–17).

65. Anthony H. Cordesman and Abraham R. Wagner suggest that Saddam's use of SCUD missiles against Iran may have worked synergistically with other factors to force Iranian exhaustion. See *The Lessons of Modern War, Vol. II: The Iran-Iraq War* (Boulder, Colo.: Westview Press, 1990), 495–506.

66. Sherman, *Air Warfare,* 213–14.

67. On these modern developments, see Parks, "Air War," 70–225. This section of his essay is both a historical review and a critical analysis reflecting his role as a participant in the U.S. military review of Protocol I.

10. Nuclear War Planning

The author gratefully acknowledges the financial assistance of the Ford Foundation and the John D. and Catherine T. MacArthur Foundation in funding his research into the development of post-World War II American military strategy. He also acknowledges the excellent critiques of an earlier draft of this chapter by Michael Altfeld, special assistant to the director of the strategy, plans, and policy division of the Office of the Chief of Naval Operations, U.S. Navy Department, and by his Temple University colleague Richard H. Immerman. The views expressed in this chapter are the author's own.

1. Critical visual expositions of thermonuclear war include the motion pictures *On*

the Beach (1959), *Dr. Strangelove: Or How I Learned to Stop Worrying and Love the Bomb* (1963), and *War Games* (1986); the Public Broadcasting System special *Nuclear Nightmares* (1980) and its associated book by Nigel Calder, *Nuclear Nightmares: An Investigation into Possible Wars* (New York: Viking Press, 1979); and the controversial television movie *The Day After* (1983). Among important 1980s works on the anticipated causes and results of nuclear war are Jonathan Schell, *The Fate of the Earth* (New York: Alfred A. Knopf, 1982), and Thomas Powers, *Thinking About the Next War* (New York: Alfred A. Knopf, 1982). Nuclear winter is summarized in Carl Sagan and Richard Turco, *A Path Here No Man Thought: Nuclear Winter and the End of the Arms Race* (New York: Random House, 1990). Scholarly analyses of these images include Spencer R. Weart, *Nuclear Fear: A History of Images* (Cambridge: Harvard University Press, 1988), and Jack G. Shaheen, ed., *Nuclear War Films* (Carbondale: Southern Illinois University Press, 1978).

2. Nuclear weapons and their effects are described in Samuel Glasstone and Philip J. Dolan, *The Effects of Nuclear Weapons* (Washington, D.C.: Department of Defense and Energy Research and Development Administration, 1977); U.S. Office of Technology Assessment, *The Effects of Nuclear War* (Washington, D.C.: Government Printing Office, 1979); Kevin N. Lewis, "The Prompt and Delayed Effects of Nuclear War," *Scientific American* 241 (July 1979): 35–47; Paul R. Ehrlich, Carl Sagan, Donald Kennedy, and Walter Orr Roberts, *The Cold and the Dark: The World after Nuclear War* (New York: W. W. Norton, 1984); Thomas B. Cochran, William M. Arkin, and Milton M. Hoenig, *Nuclear Weapons Databook, Volume I: U.S. Nuclear Forces and Capabilities* (Cambridge, Mass.: Ballinger Publishing, 1984); Theodore Postol, "Targeting," in *Managing Nuclear Operations,* ed. Ashton B. Carter, John D. Steinbruner, and Charles Zraket (Washington, D.C.: Brookings Institution, 1987), 373–406; and Chuck Hansen, *U.S. Nuclear Weapons: The Secret History* (Arlington, Tex.: Aerofax Publishers, 1988).

3. On the development of nuclear forces, see Ernest R. May, John D. Steinbruner, and Thomas Wolfe, *History of the Strategic Arms Competition, 1945–1972* (Washington, D.C.: Historical Office, Office of the Secretary of Defense, March 1981; Top Secret history, declassified with deletions, December 1990); Lawrence Freedman, *The Evolution of Nuclear Strategy,* 2d ed. (New York: St. Martin's Press, 1989); Thomas B. Cochran, William M. Arkin, Robert S. Norris, and Jeffrey I. Sands, *Nuclear Weapons Databook, Volume 4: Soviet Nuclear Weapons* (New York: Harper & Row, 1989); and Cochran et al., *Nuclear Weapons Databook, Volume I.*

4. Carl von Clausewitz, *On War,* trans. and ed. Michael Howard and Peter Paret (Princeton: Princeton University Press, 1976), 579–81.

5. There is no standard text on the history of arms control. The most useful overviews are Albert Carnesale and Richard N. Haass, eds., *Superpower Arms Control: Setting the Record Straight* (Cambridge, Mass.: Ballinger Publishing, 1987); April Carter, *Success and Failure in Arms Control Negotiations* (New York: Oxford University Press, 1989); Alexander L. George, Philip J. Farley, and Alexander Dallin, eds., *U.S.-Soviet Security Cooperation: Achievements, Failures, Lessons* (New York: Oxford University Press, 1988); and Steve Weber, *Cooperation and Discord in U.S.-Soviet Arms Control* (Princeton: Princeton University Press, 1991). For START I and START II, the most comprehensive contemporary analyses are in the periodical *Arms Control Today,* published by the Arms Control Association.

6. Ivo Daalder, "The Limited Test Ban Treaty," in *Superpower Arms Control,* 9–39;

Alan Neidle, "Nuclear Test Bans: History and Future Prospects," in *U.S.-Soviet Cooperation*, 175–214; and George Bunn, "U.S. Law of Nuclear Weapons," *Naval War College Review* 32 (July–August 1984): 46–62.

7. Bunn, "U.S. Law of Nuclear Weapons," 48–51; Joseph S. Nye, Jr., "The Superpower and the Non-Proliferation Treaty," in *Superpower Arms Control,* 165–90; and Joseph S. Nye, Jr., "U.S.-Soviet Cooperation in a Nonproliferation Regime," in *U.S.-Soviet Cooperation,* 336–52. In 1978 the United States undertook to guarantee that it would not use nuclear weapons against any nonnuclear state party to the nonproliferation treaty except in case of attack on the United States, its allies, or military forces by a state allied or associated with a nuclear state carrying out the attack. U.S. Arms Control and Disarmament Agency, *Arms Control and Disarmament Agreements* (Washington, D.C.: Government Printing Office, 1982), 87.

8. Bunn, "U.S. Law of Nuclear Weapons," 52–55; Richard N. Haass, "Verification and Compliance," in *Superpower Arms Control,* 303–28; John Lewis Gaddis, "The Evolution of a Reconnaissance Satellite Regime," and Philip J. Farley, "Arms Control and U.S.-Soviet Security Cooperation," both in *U.S.-Soviet Cooperation,* 353–74, 618–40; Curtis Peebles, *Guardians: Strategic Reconnaissance Satellites* (London: Ian Allen, 1987); and Jeffrey Richelson, *America's Secret Eyes in Space: The U.S. Keyhole Spy Satellite Program* (New York: Harper & Row, 1990).

9. Albert Carnesale and Richard Haass, "Afterword: The INF Treaty," in *Superpower Arms Control,* 357–69; Carter, *Success and Failure in Arms Control Negotiations,* 172–229; and Dunbar Lockwood, "Strategic Nuclear Forces under START II," *Arms Control Today* 22 (December 1992): 10–14.

10. On U.S. and Soviet stockpiles and megatonnage, see Cochran et al., *Soviet Nuclear Weapons,* 22–43, and their "Nuclear Notebook" charts of "U.S., Soviet Nuclear Weapons Stockpile, 1945–1989" on number of weapons and megatonnage in, respectively, *Bulletin of the Atomic Scientists* (November 1989): 53, and (December 1989): 52.

11. Cochran et al., *Soviet Nuclear Weapons,* 25.

12. Ingrid Detter De Lupis, *The Law of War* (New York: Cambridge University Press, 1987), 203; see also Bunn, "U.S. Law of Nuclear Weapons," 57; and Elliott L. Meyrowitz, "The Laws of War and Nuclear Weapons," and Burns H. Weston, "Nuclear Weapons versus International Law: A Contextual Reassessment," in *Nuclear Weapons and Law,* ed. Arthur Selwyn Miller and Martin Feinrider (Westport, Conn.: Greenwood Press, 1984), 19–50, 133–80.

13. United Nations General Assembly Resolution 1653 (XVI), 1063d Plenary Meeting, November 24, 1961, in Dusan J. Djonovich, ed., *United Nations Resolutions, Series I, Resolutions Adopted by the General Assembly, Volume VIII, 1960–1962* (Dobbs Ferry, N.Y.: Oceana Publications, 1974), 236–37; Detter De Lupis, *Law of War,* 204–7.

14. United States Arms Control and Disarmament Agency, *Documents on Disarmament, 1961* (Washington, D.C.: Government Printing Office, 1962), 587–92, 648–50.

15. Bunn, "U.S. Law of Nuclear Weapons," 56; Detter De Lupis, *Law of War,* 204–7.

16. Bunn, "U.S. Law of Nuclear Weapons," 57–59; Detter De Lupis, *Law of War,* 232–44.

17. Bunn, "U.S. Law of Nuclear Weapons," 58.

18. Detter De Lupis, *Law of War,* 232–52; Meyrowitz, "Laws of War and Nuclear Weapons," 42–45.

19. Meyrowitz, "Laws of War and Nuclear Weapons," 42; Detter De Lupis, *Law of War*, 200–201, 207–9.

20. Meyrowitz, "Laws of War and Nuclear Weapons," 45n.

21. Bunn, "U.S. Law of Nuclear Weapons," 55–57.

22. Desmond Ball and Jeffrey Richelson, eds., *Strategic Nuclear Targeting* (Ithaca, N.Y.: Cornell University Press, 1986) provides an overview of national practices. NATO controls are discussed in Catherine Kelleher, "NATO Nuclear Operations," in *Managing Nuclear Operations*, 445–69. Soviet nuclear strategy is described in Stephen M. Meyer, "Soviet Nuclear Operations," ibid., 470–531; Desmond Ball, "Soviet Strategic Planning and the Control of Nuclear War," in *The Soviet Calculus of Nuclear War*, ed. Roman Kolkowicz and Ellen Proper Mickiewicz (New York: D. C. Heath, 1986), 49–67; and Robert P. Berman and John C. Baker, *Soviet Strategic Forces: Requirements and Responses* (Washington, D.C.: Brookings Institution, 1982).

23. The Atomic Energy Act of 1946, sec. 6(a), par. 2, in James R. Newman and Byron S. Miller, *The Control of Atomic Energy* (New York: McGraw-Hill, 1948), 298–99.

24. On congressional involvement in nuclear policy making, see Congressional Quarterly Service, *Congress and the Nation, 1945–1964* (Washington, D.C.: Congressional Quarterly Service, 1965), 233–333; Edward A. Kolodziej, *The Uncommon Defense and Congress, 1945–1963* (Columbus: Ohio State University Press, 1966); Alton Frye, *A Responsible Congress: The Politics of National Security* (New York: McGraw-Hill, 1975); Douglas Waller, *Congress and the Nuclear Freeze* (Amherst: University of Massachusetts Press, 1987); and James M. Lindsay, *Congress and Nuclear Weapons* (Baltimore: Johns Hopkins University Press, 1991).

25. Frye, *A Responsible Congress*, 15–83; Waller, *Congress and the Nuclear Freeze*, 101–285; and Lindsay, *Congress and Nuclear Weapons*, 55–61, 145–51.

26. Diary entry by the president, January 23, 1956, in U.S. Department of State, *Foreign Relations of the United States, 1955–1957, Vol. XIX, National Security Policy* (Washington, D.C.: Government Printing Office, 1990), 186–87 (hereafter *FRUS*).

27. Public Law 93–148, 93rd Congress, House Joint Resolution 542, November 7, 1973, secs. 4 and 5.

28. The structure of nuclear policy making is described in David Alan Rosenberg, "Reality and Responsibility: Power and Process in the Making of United States Nuclear Strategy," *Journal of Strategic Studies* 9 (March 1986): 35–51; and Michael David Yaffe, "Origins of the Tactical Nuclear Weapons Modernization Program, 1969–1979" (Ph.D. diss., University of Pennsylvania, 1991), 28–40, 642–54, 582–699. An overview of presidential concerns about nuclear weapons may be found in McGeorge Bundy, *Danger and Survival: Choices about the Bomb in the First Fifty Years* (New York: Random House, 1988).

29. David Alan Rosenberg, "American Atomic Strategy and the Hydrogen Bomb Decision," *Journal of American History* 66 (June 1979): 70–73; Briefing of WSEG [Weapons Systems Evaluation Group] Report No. 12, "Evaluation of an Atomic Offensive in Support of the Joint Strategic Capabilities Plan," April 8, 1955, Document Two in David Alan Rosenberg, "'A Smoking Radiating Ruin at the End of Two Hours': Documents on American Plans for Nuclear War with the Soviet Union, 1954–1955," *International Security* 6 (Winter 1981/1982): 29–38; and Fred Kaplan, *The Wizards of Armageddon* (New York: Simon and Schuster, 1983), 268–70.

30. NSC 30, United States Policy on Atomic Warfare, September 10, 1948, in *FRUS*,

Vol. I, Part 2, General; The United Nations (Washington, D.C.: Government Printing Office, 1976), 624–28.

31. David Alan Rosenberg, "The Origins of Overkill: Nuclear Weapons and American Strategy, 1945–1960," *International Security* 7 (Spring 1983): 16–39.

32. Draft Memorandum by N. Gordon Arneson, Special Assistant to the Secretary of State, April 24, 1951, Memorandum by Mr. Carleton Savage, Member of the Policy Planning Staff, May 23, 1951, Possibilities of War with the Soviet Union: Use of Nuclear Weapons, and Paper Prepared by the Joint Strategic Survey Committee and Representatives of the Department of State, August 3, 1951, United States Position on Considerations under Which the United States Will Accept War and on Atomic Warfare, *FRUS, 1951, Vol. I, National Security Affairs; Foreign Economic Policy* (Washington, D.C.: Government Printing Office, 1979), 820–26, 834–40, 866–74; Staff Study Prepared by Representatives of the Special Committee of the National Security Council on Atomic Energy, June 11, 1952, and Paper Prepared by R. R. Bowie, the Director of the Policy Planning Staff to the Secretary of State, *FRUS, 1952–1954, Vol. II, National Security Affairs* (Washington, D.C.: Government Printing Office, 1984), 973–79, 565–76; Leonard Wainstein, C. D. Cremeans, J. K. Moriarty, and J. Ponturo, *The Evolution of U.S. Strategic Command and Control and Warning, 1945–1972* (Arlington, Va.: Institute for Defense Analyses Study S-467, June 1975; Top Secret study, declassified September 15, 1992), 40–43.

33. Minutes of the Meeting of the Combined Policy Committee, at Blair House, Washington, D.C., January 7, 1948, with Draft Agreement between the Governments of the United States, the United Kingdom, and Canada, Annexes A, B, and C Appended, *FRUS, 1948, Vol. I*, 679–87.

34. Wainstein et al., *Evolution of Strategic Command and Control and Warning*, 40–43; Staff Study Prepared by Representatives of the Special Committee of the National Security Council on Atomic Energy, June 11, 1952, *FRUS, 1952–1954*, Vol. II, 973–79; NSC 162/2, Report to the National Security Council on Basic National Security Policy, October 30, 1953, *FRUS, 1952–1954, Vol. II*, 593.

35. Adm. Arthur W. Radford, Memorandum for Mr. John Foster Dulles, October 13, 1953, CJCS 040 Atomic Energy Commission, Records of the United States Joint Chiefs of Staff, Record Group 218, U.S. National Archives (hereafter JCS).

36. Memorandum of Discussion at the 166th Meeting of the National Security Council, Tuesday, October 13, 1953, and NSC 162/2, October 30, 1953, *FRUS, 1952–1954, Vol. II*, 546–47, 593; James S. Lay, Jr., Memorandum for the Secretary of State, Secretary of Defense, and Chairman, Atomic Energy Commission, Subject: Policy Regarding Use of Atomic Weapons, March 14, 1955, reaffirming (and reproducing) policy statement of January 4, 1954, Atomic Weapons, Correspondence and Background for Presidential Approval and Instructions for Use, Box 1, NSC Series, Subject Subseries, Dwight D. Eisenhower Library (hereafter DDEL).

37. Robert A. Wampler, *NATO Strategic Planning and Nuclear Weapons, 1950–1957*, Occasional Paper 6 (College Park, Md.: Nuclear History Program and University of Maryland Center for International Studies, 1990), 2, 40–41, 52; see also Robert A. Wampler, "Ambiguous Legacy: The United States, Great Britain and the Foundations of NATO Strategy, 1948–1957" (Ph.D. diss., Harvard University, 1991).

38. Par. 11, NSC 5602/1, Basic National Security Policy, March 15, 1956, *FRUS, 1955–1957, Vol. XIX*, 246; the displacement of NSC 30 by par. 11 of NSC 5602/1 is noted

in James S. Lay, Memorandum for the National Security Council, February 17, 1959, enclosing Annotated List of Serially Numbered National Security Council Documents (updated to December 30, 1960), Subject Filing of NSC Papers Folder, Box 20, Subject Series, Alphabetical Subseries, White House Office, Staff Secretary Papers, DDEL.

39. Kenneth W. Condit, *History of the Joint Chiefs of Staff: The Joint Chiefs of Staff and National Policy, Vol. VI, 1955–1956* (Washington, D.C.: Historical Office, Joint Staff, 1992), 12–21, 30–38.

40. Rosenberg, "Origins of Overkill," 48–49, esp. note 163; Daniel Schuchman, "Nuclear Strategy and the Problem of Command and Control," *Survival* 29 (July–August 1987): 336–59. Such authorization was recently reconfirmed with the April 1993 declassification of Brig. Gen. Andrew Goodpaster, Memorandum of Conference with the President, January 16, 1961, dated January 18, 1961, Staff Notes, January 1961, Box 55, Dwight D. Eisenhower Diaries, DDEL. It describes Gen. Lyman Lemnitzer's discussion with President Eisenhower of his briefing of incoming Defense Secretary McNamara "on the emergency action plan, as well as on the subject of authorizations by the President for employment of nuclear weapons." A 1964 Furtherance paper extended these authorizations. See Maj. Gen. C. V. Clifton, Memorandum for the Record, March 14, 1964, Meetings with the President, Vol. 1, National Security Files, C. V. Clifton Papers, Lyndon B. Johnson Library (hereafter LBJL).

41. Daniel Ellsberg, "Stranger Than Strangelove," *Win* (a short-lived antinuclear activist magazine), November 17, 1977, 4–8, 15, 21; Schuchman, "Nuclear Strategy and the Problem of Command and Control," 344–50.

42. NSC 20/4, Note by the Executive Secretary on U.S. Objectives with Respect to the USSR to Counter Soviet Threats to U.S. Security, November 23, 1948, *FRUS, 1948, Vol. 1,* 662–69.

43. NSC 5410/1, Note by the Executive Secretary to the National Security Council on U.S. Objectives in the Event of General War with the Soviet Bloc, March 29, 1954, and Memorandum of Discussion at the 190th Meeting of the National Security Council, Thursday, March 25, 1954, *FRUS, 1952–1954, Vol. II,* 637–46.

44. NSC 5904/1, March 17, 1959, remains classified. This information is based on the draft paper, NSC 5904, U.S. Policy in the Event of War, February 19, 1959, and S. Everett Gleason, Memoranda of Discussion at the 398th and 399th Meetings of the National Security Council, Thursday, March 5, and Thursday, March 12, 1959, in 398th and 399th Meeting Folders, Box 11, NSC Papers, Ann Whitman File, DDEL.

45. Brig. Gen. H. L. Hillyard, Memorandum for Gen. Twining, Adm. Burke, Gen. White, Gen. Lemnitzer, Gen. Shoup, Subject: Definitions for Use in U.S. Military Planning, SM 185-60, February 26, 1960, and CSAFM 84-60, February 29, 1960, both in CCS 3120, JSCP (August 24, 1959), JCS. JCS 1844/321, September 22, 1960, CCS 3120, JSCP (August 24, 1960), sec. 1, ibid., notes Gates's decision on April 15, 1960.

46. This view is based on discussions with Prof. Robert R. Bowie, former director of the State Department Policy Planning Staff, 1953–57, and Prof. Richard H. Immerman, who are collaborating on a book on national security strategy making in the first year of the Eisenhower administration. See also Richard H. Immerman, "Confessions of an Eisenhower Revisionist: An Agonizing Reappraisal," *Diplomatic History* 14 (Summer 1990): 319–42, and John Lewis Gaddis, "The Origins of Self-Deterrence," in *The Long Peace, Inquiries into the History of the Cold War* (New York: Oxford University Press, 1987), 104–46.

47. Wainstein et al., *Evolution of Strategic Command and Control and Warning*, 34, and "Nuclear Notebook," *Bulletin of the Atomic Scientists* (November 1989): 53.

48. Vice Adm. R. E. Libby, Memorandum for Op-00 (Chief of Naval Operations), Subject: Proposals Relative to Atomic Operation Concept, Serial BM00043-57, May 1, 1957, File A16-10, Atomic Warfare Operations, Box 8, Op-00 Files, 1957, Operational Archives, Naval Historical Center, Washington, D.C.

49. Rosenberg, "Origins of Overkill," 50–54.

50. Adm. Arleigh Burke, CNO Personal Letter No. 5 to Retired Flag Officers, Subject: Pertinent Information, Summary of Major Strategic Considerations for the 1960–1970 Era, July 30, 1958, Navy Folder, Box 28, Gen. Thomas D. White Papers, Library of Congress.

51. Herbert Goldhamer and Andrew W. Marshall, with the assistance of Nathan Leites, *The Deterrence and Strategy of Total War, 1959–1961: A Method for Analysis*, RM 2301 (Santa Monica, Calif., Rand Corporation, U.S. Air Force Project Rand, April 30, 1959), 191.

52. Kaplan, *Wizards of Armageddon*, 201–19, 238–47; Rosenberg, "Origins of Overkill," 57–60.

53. Rosenberg, "Origins of Overkill," 4–8, 61–65; Scott D. Sagan, "SIOP-62: The Nuclear War Plan Briefing to President Kennedy," *International Security* 12 (Summer 1987): 22–51; Kaplan, *Wizards of Armageddon*, 266–72; May et al., *History of the Strategic Arms Competition*, 592–97.

54. Sagan, "SIOP-62," 49–51.

55. Information on the leveling off of the nuclear weapons stockpile and JCS requirements is contained in "Nuclear Notebook," *Bulletin of the Atomic Scientists* (November 1989): 53; and Deputy Secretary of Defense Roswell Gilpatric, Memorandum for Mr. McGeorge Bundy, Subject: Nuclear Weapons, March 3, 1961, Nuclear Test Ban, April 1959–June 1961 Folder, Box 49–56, Theodore Sorenson Papers, John F. Kennedy Library (hereafter JFKL). McNamara's role in addressing the stockpile is indicated in Robert S. McNamara, Memorandum for the Secretaries of the Military Departments et al., March 1, 1961, enclosing list of 96 projects, Defense, January–March 1961 Folder, President's Official File, Box 77, JFKL; the JCS reply on Project 5, Gen. L. L. Lemnitzer, Memorandum for the Secretary of Defense, Subject: Reexamination of the Current and Long-Range Department of Defense Requirements for Production of Nuclear Weapons and Fissionable Material, JCSM 241-61, April 18, 1961, Directorate of Freedom of Information and Security Review, Office of the Secretary of Defense (hereafter OSDFOI); and Gen. Maxwell Taylor, Memorandum for the Secretary of Defense, Subject: Nuclear Weapons Production and Study Guidelines, JCSM 1028-62, Dec. 27, 1962, Tactical Nuclear Weapons Study Folder, Box 33, Maxwell Taylor Papers, National Defense University (hereafter MDT-NDU). According to a list of Draft Presidential and Tentative Record of Decision Memos at the Office of Program Analysis and Evaluation, Office of the Secretary of Defense, McNamara provided the president with annual statements outlining nuclear materials production schedules through fiscal year 1973 (1964), a ten-year nuclear weapons program (1965), and nuclear weapons stockpile and fissionable materials requirements (1966, 1967, and 1968); these memoranda remain classified. On Kennedy's White House National Security organization and McNamara's style of management, see Deborah Shapley, *Promise and Power: The Life and Times of Robert McNamara* (Boston: Little, Brown, 1993), 94–146; W. W. Rostow, *The Diffusion of Power* (New York: Macmillan, 1972), 160–84; and Rosenberg, "Reality and Responsibility," 35–38, 43–44.

56. Kaplan, *Wizards of Armageddon,* 252–83; Shapley, *Promise and Power,* 104–11.

57. Historical Studies Division, Historical Office, Bureau of Public Affairs, U.S. Department of State, *Crisis over Berlin: American Policy concerning the Soviet Threats to Berlin, November 1958–December 1962* (Unpublished Top Secret Research Project No. 614-A, October 1966; declassified with deletions, July 1987), pts. I–IV, November 1959–January 1961; Marc Trachtenberg, *History and Strategy* (Princeton: Princeton University Press, 1991), 169–234.

58. Jane Stromseth, *The Origins of Flexible Response* (New York: St. Martin's Press, 1988), 30–41; McGeorge Bundy, National Security Action Memorandum No. 40, for Members of the NSC, enclosing Policy Directive on NATO and the Atlantic Nations, April 24, 1961, NSC 1961 Folder, Box 4, Vice Presidential Security File, LBJL; Adm. Arleigh Burke, Memorandum for the Secretary of Defense, Subject: NATO Force Requirements Study (Project 106C), JCSM 306-61, May 5, 1961, CCS 9050/3410 NATO (April 29, 1961), Sec. 3, JCS; and Transcript of Nuclear History Program Oral History Interview on Contingency Planning in the Kennedy Administration with Brig. Gen. DeWitt Armstrong, USA (Ret.), Vice Adm. John M. Lee, USN (Ret.), Col. Lawrence Legere, USA (Ret.), and Amb. Seymour Weiss, June 7, 1991. It was then-Colonel Armstrong's "horse blanket" paper that was boiled down to a "pony blanket" and then "poodle blanket" of preferred options as the basis of NSAM 109.

59. McGeorge Bundy, National Security Action Memorandum 109 to the Secretaries of State and Defense, Subject: U.S. Policy on Military Actions in a Berlin Conflict, October 23, 1961, and letter, President Kennedy to General Norstad, with Enclosure, October 20, 1961, declassified in August and October 1992, respectively, National Security Archive, Washington, D.C. (hereafter NSA).

60. The above is based on an interview with Prof. Carl Kaysen, Deputy National Security Adviser to President Kennedy in 1961 (conducted with Marc Trachtenberg), Cambridge, Mass., August 3, 1988, and with Dr. Henry Rowen, Deputy Assistant Secretary of Defense for International Security Affairs in 1961, Washington, D.C., March 20, 1991; Gen. Maxwell Taylor, Memo for General Lemnitzer, Subject: Attached Memorandum on Strategic Air Planning and Berlin, September 6, 1961, Berlin Planning Folder, Box 34, MDT-NDU; Trachtenberg, *History and Strategy,* 224–25; and Kaplan, *Wizards of Armageddon,* 296–303.

61. No copy of the actual limited counterforce strike paper has yet been found in government archives, although it is likely that a copy exists in Carl Kaysen's still unprocessed files at the Kennedy Library. This description is based on a Draft Memorandum for the President, Subject: Consequences of Thermonuclear War under Various Conditions of Outbreak, October 28, 1961, unclassified paper in the mailroom rotary historical file in the Office of Program Analysis and Evaluation, Office of the Secretary of Defense. This document was discussed in person with McGeorge Bundy, Robert McNamara, Carl Kaysen, Henry Rowen (who in his capacity in March 1991 as assistant secretary of defense for international security affairs cleared the document for public discussion with this explanation), Marcus Raskin of the 1961 NSC staff, and in telephone interviews with Frank Trinkl and W. W. Kaufmann, both consultants to the OSD, and Fred Kaplan. None of them could identify the document itself. Kaufmann could not reliably recall the work in question. Rowen noted that while it looked like a "competent calculation," it was "not in any way, shape, or form a planning document" he recalled being associated with, and further emphasized that it was a "non-paper" that "never went anywhere." Kaysen and

Trinkl agreed that it represented something of the analyses they had been engaged in, but the draft memorandum was not written the way they would have written it. Kaplan recalled that Gen. David Burchinal, USAF, then director of the Joint Staff, indicated in an interview that work on the limited strike plan went forward in a secret cell under Burchinal's direct control, progressing to the point where actual units had been identified for participation, but its ultimate fate was uncertain. This document leaves no doubt that some off-line nuclear planning was conducted in the summer and fall of 1961. In the absence of any more concrete data, its contents are offered here as representing the constraints being considered at that time.

62. Draft Memorandum, October 28, 1961.

63. History and Research Division, Headquarters, Strategic Air Command, *History of the Joint Strategic Planning Staff, Preparation of SIOP-63* (prepared January 1964; partially declassified under appeal, 1992), 7–13; Rear Adm. F. J. Blouin, Note to Control Division, Subject: Guidance for the Preparation of SIOP-63, October 23, 1961, and Rear Admiral Blouin, Decision on JCS 2056/285 (Guidance for Preparation of SIOP-63), October 25, 1961, CCS 3105 (Joint Planning) (March 8, 1961) (3) Sec. 2, JCS.

64. Wainstein et al., *Evolution of Strategic Command and Control and Warning*, 357, n.13; Henry S. Rowen, "Formulating Strategic Doctrine," pt. III of vol. 4, app. K to *The Report of the Commission on the Organization of the Government for the Conduct of Foreign Policy* (Washington, D.C.: Government Printing Office, 1975), 220–34.

65. *SIOP Decision Handbook*, ca. 1971, quoted in Wainstein et al., *Evolution of Strategic Command and Control and Warning*, 346–47, 357, n.13; see also 290–91.

66. Ibid., 290.

67. McGeorge Bundy, National Security Action Memorandum No. 122 to the Secretaries of State and Defense, January 16, 1962, and Acting Secretary of State George Ball, Memorandum for the President, Subject: SACEUR's Command and Control Procedures for Use of Nuclear Weapons (NSAM 122), January 24, 1962 (both documents declassified April 1993), Folder 110, Box 37, MDT-NDU.

68. McNamara was briefed on SIOP 63 on June 20, 1962; he gave his famous Top Secret speech to NATO on counterforce strategy on May 5, and his public speech on the same subject at the University of Michigan on June 16. *History of JSTPS: Preparation of SIOP-62*, 25–26; David N. Schwartz, *NATO's Nuclear Dilemmas* (Washington, D.C.: Brookings Institution, 1983), 156–65.

69. John C. Ausland, Memorandum for Mr. Hillenbrand, Subject: Briefing for President on Berlin, August 2, 1962, with enclosed Top Secret briefing, Berlin Contingency Planning, declassified January 29, 1993, NSA. See also DEFE 4/142, COS(62) 7th Meeting, January 23, 1962, Minute 4, Confidential Annex, attachment: JP(62) 6 (Final), Berlin Contingency Planning—Phasing of Military Operations, Report by the Joint Planning Staff, January 19, 1962, Top Secret paper released to the public January 1993, Public Record Office, London.

70. John C. Ausland, "A Nuclear War to Keep Berlin Open?" *International Herald Tribune*, June 19, 1991; transcript of Nuclear History Program Oral History, interview with John C. Ausland, October 8, 1991.

71. History and Research Division, Headquarters Strategic Command, *History of the Joint Strategic Target Planning Staff: Preparation of SIOP-64* (Top Secret History prepared August 1964, declassified with deletions following appeal, 1992), 13–15.

72. Bromley Smith, Summary Record of National Security Council Meeting, September 12, 1963, 11:00 A.M.—Report of Net Evaluation Subcommittee, NSC Meetings

1963, No. 517, 9/12/63, Box 314, National Security File: Meetings and Memoranda, JFKL. See also Resume of Discussion during NESC Meeting of September 12, 1963, same file.

73. Secretary of Defense Draft Memorandum for the President, Subject: Recommended FY1965–FY1969 Strategic Retaliatory Forces, December 6, 1963, OSDFOI 10, 14, 19, 21.

74. Kaplan, *Wizards of Armageddon,* 315–27; Shapley, *Promise and Power,* 191–201.

75. Rowen, "Formulating Strategic Doctrine," 220–32.

76. Summary Record of National Security Council Meeting, December 5, 1963, 3:00 P.M.—Subject: Soviet Military Capabilities, vol. 1, 12/5/63 Meeting, NSC Meetings File, Box 1, National Security File; Maj. Gen. C. V. Clifton, Memorandum for Record, December 9, 1963, Meetings with the President, vol. 1, National Security Files, Box 2; and James V. Cornell for C. V. Clifton, Memorandum for Mr. Bromley Smith, August 17, 1964, SIOP Folder, Box 2, both C. V. Clifton Papers, all LBJL. Robert S. McNamara, "The Military Role of Nuclear Weapons: Perceptions and Misperceptions," *Foreign Affairs* 62 (October 1983): 59–80.

77. Scott Sagan, *Moving Targets, Nuclear Strategy and National Security* (Princeton: Princeton University Press, 1989), 31–37; Rowen, "Formulating Strategic Doctrine," 229–33; Berman and Baker, *Soviet Strategic Forces,* 18, 90–93.

78. May et al., *History of the Strategic Arms Competition,* 602–4.

79. Ibid., 596–608. See also Bruce G. Blair, *Strategic Nuclear Command and Control, Redefining the Nuclear Threat* (Washington, D.C.: Brookings Institution, 1985), 79–181.

80. Draft Presidential Memorandum, Subject: Fiscal Year 1969–1973 Strategic Offensive and Defensive Forces, January 5, 1968, OSDFOI.

81. McNamara's last Draft Presidential Memorandum called for 5,943 independently targeted missile warheads. DPM, January 5, 1968. U.S. warhead yields in the late 1960s are discussed in Cochran et al., *U.S. Nuclear Forces and Capabilities,* 10–11, 39; estimated U.S. missile accuracies are provided by Donald MacKenzie, *Inventing Accuracy: A Historical Sociology of Nuclear Missile Guidance* (Cambridge: MIT Press, 1990), 427–35.

82. Wainstein et al., *Evolution of Strategic Command and Control and Warning,* 292.

83. Ibid., 345–46.

84. "Targeting Flexibility Emphasized by SAC," *Aviation Week and Space Technology,* May 10, 1976: 29–34; David A. Anderton, *Strategic Air Command* (New York: Charles Scribner's Sons, 1977), 138–39.

85. Wainstein et al., *Evolution of Strategic Command and Control and Warning,* 292–94.

86. Blair, *Strategic Command and Control,* 239–40. See also Desmond Ball, *Can Nuclear War Be Controlled* (London: International Institute for Strategic Studies, 1981), 35–38; and Paul Bracken, *The Command and Control of Nuclear Forces* (New Haven: Yale University Press, 1983).

87. Brigitte Sauerwein, "SACEUR Sees the End of Flexible Response," *International Defense Review,* no. 3, 1991: 190–91. See also J. Michael Legge, *Theater Nuclear Weapons and the NATO Strategy of Flexible Response* (Santa Monica, Calif.: Rand Corporation, R-2964-FF, April 1983), 9–10.

88. Peter Douglas Feaver, *Guarding the Guardians: Civilian Control of Nuclear*

Weapons in the United States (Ithaca, N.Y.: Cornell University Press, 1992), 183–98; Robert S. Norris and William Arkin, "Nuclear Notebook: U.S. Nuclear Weapons Safety and Control Features," *Bulletin of the Atomic Scientists* (October 1991): 48.

89. Ivo Daalder, *The Nature and Practice of Flexible Response: NATO Strategy and Theater Nuclear Forces since 1967* (New York: Columbia University Press, 1991), 97.

90. Ibid., 98. See also Daniel Charles, *Nuclear Planning in NATO: Pitfalls of First Use* (Cambridge, Mass.: Ballinger Publishing, 1987).

91. Daalder, *Nature and Practice of Flexible Response,* 72–79; Legge, *Theater Nuclear Weapons,* 17–23.

92. Daalder, ibid., 87–93.

93. The best overview is ibid., 106–286; and Yaffe, "Origins of the Tactical Nuclear Weapons Modernization Program, 1969–1979," 415–641.

94. In addition to Daalder and Yaffe, see also Sherri L. Wasserman, *The Neutron Bomb Controversy: A Study in Alliance Politics* (New York: Praeger, 1983), and Samuel T. Cohen, *The Truth about the Neutron Bomb* (New York: William Morrow, 1983).

95. Daalder, *Nature and Practice of Flexible Response,* 158–286; see also the innovative interpretations of Jeffrey Herf, *War by Other Means: Soviet Power, West German Resistance, and the Battle of the Euromissiles* (New York: Free Press, 1991).

96. The most insightful analysis of U.S. nuclear strategy in the 1970s and 1980s is Leon Sloss and Marc Dean Millot, "U.S. Nuclear Strategy in Evolution," *Strategic Review* 12 (Winter 1984): 19–28. See also Janne E. Nolan, *Guardians of the Arsenal: The Politics of Nuclear Strategy* (New York: Basic Books, 1989), 89–139; Desmond Ball, "The Development of the SIOP, 1960–1983," in *Strategic Nuclear Targeting,* 57–83, 322–26; Sagan, *Moving Targets,* 39–57; and Col. Richard Lee Walker, USAF, *Strategic Target Planning: Bridging the Gap between Theory and Practice* (Washington, D.C.: National Defense University Press, 1983).

97. Rowen, "Formulating Strategic Doctrine," 221.

98. The Team B analysis was declassified with deletions in September 1992: Intelligence Community Experiment in Competitive Analysis, Soviet Strategic Objectives, An Alternative View, Report of Team B, December 1976. See also the Team A report, NIE 11-3/8-76, National Intelligence Estimate, Soviet Forces for Intercontinental Conflict through the Mid-1980s, December 21, 1976. A more recent analysis that combines both approaches was declassified in February 1993: NIE 11-3/8-82, National Intelligence Estimate, Soviet Capabilities for Strategic Nuclear Conflict, 1982–92. All available at NSA.

99. Sagan, *Moving Targets,* 53.

100. Ibid., 48–57; Ball, "The Development of the SIOP," 78–82. See also Col. Christopher I. Branch, USAF, *Fighting a Long Nuclear War: A Strategy, Force, Policy Mismatch* (Washington, D.C.: National Defense University Press, 1984); and Desmond Ball and Robert C. Toth, "Revising the SIOP: Taking War-Fighting to Dangerous Extremes," *International Security* 14 (Spring 1990): 65–92.

101. Sloss and Millot, "U.S. Nuclear Strategy in Evolution," 25; Nolan, *Guardians of the Arsenal,* 236–70. See also Gen. Russell M. Dougherty, USAF (Ret.), "The Psychological Climate of Nuclear Command," in *Managing Nuclear Operations,* 407–25; Robert Jervis, *The Illogic of American Nuclear Strategy* (Ithaca, N.Y.: Cornell University Press, 1984), 37–46, 54–85, 109–11; and Steven Kull, *Minds at War: Nuclear Reality and the Inner Conflicts of Defense Policymakers* (New York: Basic Books, 1988), 72–207.

102. This is based on discussions with a former presidential military aide who carried the nuclear football containing the SIOP codes in the first Reagan administration. See also Nolan, *Guardians of the Arsenal,* 269–70; Donald R. Baucom, *The Origins of SDI, 1944–1983* (Lawrence: University Press of Kansas, 1992), 140–96; and George P. Shultz, *Turmoil and Triumph: My Years as Secretary of State* (New York: Charles Scribner's Sons, 1993), 246–64.

103. The requirement for a protracted conventional war capability and the nonnuclear origins of the Maritime Strategy are discussed in Capt. Linton F. Brooks, "Naval Power and National Security: The Case for the Maritime Strategy," *International Security* 11 (Fall 1986): 58–88; and David Alan Rosenberg, "Process: The Realities of Formulating Modern Naval Strategy," in James Goldvick and John B. Hattendorf, eds., *Mahan Is Not Enough: The Proceedings of a Conference on the Works of Sir Julian Corbett and Admiral Sir Herbert Richmond* (Newport, R.I.: Naval War College Press, 1993), 141–75. On Air-Land Battle Doctrine, see Robert A. Doughty, *The Evolution of U.S. Army Tactical Doctrine, 1946–1976* (Fort Leavenworth, Kans.: U.S. Army Combat Studies Institute, August 1979), 42–50; and Colin McInnes, *NATO's Changing Strategic Agenda: The Conventional Defence of Central Europe* (London: Unwin Hyman, 1990), 116–62.

104. Robert C. Toth, "U.S. Scratches Nuclear Targets in Soviet Bloc," *Los Angeles Times,* April 19, 1991: 1.

105. Freeman Dyson, *Weapons and Hope* (New York: Harper and Row, 1984), 275–76. Dyson was talking about not targeting missiles while "negotiating their disappearance"; here it is anticipated that missiles remaining after START II will not disappear for a number of years.

11. The Age of National Liberation Movements

I would like to thank Dr. Fatsah Ouguergouz of the U.N. Office of Legal Affairs for his helpful comments on earlier drafts of this chapter.

1. Although *national liberation movements* has been used to describe entities in the pre-1945 period, particularly certain resistance movements in Occupied Europe, it really became a widely used term only after the Second World War, when most of these movements aspired to international legal status claiming that their struggles for self-determination are of an international rather than of an internal character. It should be noted, however, that the first three Geneva Conventions of 1949 reflecting the Second World War experience did grant combatant status to resistance movements in occupied territories provided that they fulfilled the conditions outlined in their common articles 13 §2, 13 §2, and 4A §2. J. Pictet, ed., *Commentary of the Geneva Conventions of 1949,* vol. 3 (Geneva: International Committee of the Red Cross, 1960), 56.

2. On the notion of territorially oriented nationalism, see Eric Hobsbawm, *Nations and Nationalism since 1780* (Cambridge: Cambridge University Press, 1990), 136–38.

3. Adam Roberts and Richard Guelff, eds., *Documents on the Laws of War* (Oxford: Clarendon Press, 1989), 390; see also article 96 §3 of Protocol I concerning its application and that of the 1949 Conventions to such a conflict, ibid., 443–44.

4. On the evolution of the juridical bases for the use of force by states, see Ian Brownlie, *International Law and the Use of Force by States* (Oxford: Clarendon Press, 1963), esp. 19–122; on United Nations practice, see Rosalyn Higgins, "The Legal Limits to the Use of Force by Sovereign States: United Nations Practice," *British Year Book of International Law* 37 (1961): 269–319.

5. See in this volume Howard, "Constraints on Warfare."

6. What follows are observations first outlined in G. Andreopoulos, "Studying American Grand Strategy: Facets in an Exceptionalist Tradition," *Diplomacy and State-craft* 2 (1991): 211–35.

7. Richard Falk, ed., "Introduction," in *The International Law of Civil War* (Baltimore: Johns Hopkins University Press, 1971), 14; see also his typology of civil wars on 18–19.

8. The term *guerrilla* appeared for the first time during the Spanish resistance to the Napoleonic invasion (1808–13); however, *irregular warfare* (a term used interchangeably with guerrilla warfare), which basically means the mobilization of civilians to fight as irregulars, has been recorded in ancient Egypt and China and in the works of classical historians such as Polybius, Plutarch, Herodotus, and Tacitus; see Peter Paret and John Shy, *Guerrillas in the 1960's* (New York: Praeger, 1962), 6; and Gérard Chaliand, ed., *Guerrilla Strategies: An Historical Anthology from the Long March to Afghanistan* (Berkeley: University of California Press, 1982), 1.

9. See relevant remarks in Michael Walzer, *Just and Unjust Wars* (New York: Basic Books, 1992), 180. There has been an extensive literature on guerrilla warfare and its counterpart, counterinsurgency warfare. Among the numerous writings see Walter Laqueur, ed., *The Guerrilla Reader* (Philadelphia: Temple University Press, 1977); Mao Tse-Tung, *On Guerrilla Warfare*, translated with an introduction by Brig. Gen. Samuel B. Griffith (New York: Praeger, 1961); Sam Sarkesian, ed., *Revolutionary Guerrilla Warfare* (Chicago: Precedent Publishing, 1975); William J. Pomeroy, ed., *Guerrilla Warfare and Marxism* (New York: International Publishers, 1968); Douglas Blaufarb, *The Counterinsurgency Era: U.S. Doctrine and Performance* (New York: Free Press, 1977); and D. Michael Shafer, *Deadly Paradigms: The Failure of U.S. Counterinsurgency Policy* (Princeton: Princeton University Press, 1988).

10. It is chapter twenty-six of book six and is entitled "The People in Arms"; see Michael Howard and Peter Paret, eds., Carl von Clausewitz, *On War* (Princeton: Princeton University Press, 1984), 479–83.

11. *On War*, 480.

12. Clausewitz uses the analogy of evaporation. The greater the surface exposed, the greater the effect. "The greater the surface and the area of contact between it [i.e., the resistance] and the enemy forces, the thinner the latter have to be spread, the greater the effect of a general uprising. Like smoldering embers, it consumes the basic foundations of the enemy forces" (*On War*, 480).

13. Ibid., 482; see also relevant observations in Paret and Shy, *Guerrillas*, 12–15.

14. I do not know how familiar Mao was with Clausewitz's work. However, he was aware of Lenin's high regard for the Prussian military thinker. To avoid any misunderstanding, let me clarify that Clausewitz was very much concerned with the political dimension of the war which, as we will see below, takes precedence over the military dimension. Thus, his comments on irregular warfare must be viewed within this context. Irregular warfare was a new form of warfare for him and what we have on record are his preliminary thoughts on this subject.

15. In discussing Mao's strategy, I follow Chalmers Johnson, "The Third Generation of Guerrilla Warfare," in Sarkesian, *Guerrilla Warfare*, 359.

16. During the Vietnam War, an Office of Systems Analysis study of five fights in 1966 showed that "the enemy could control his losses within a wide range" since "correla-

tions between enemy attacks and enemy losses were very high; similar correlations between friendly force activity and enemy losses were close to zero. In other words, regardless of the level of allied activity, the VC/NVA lost a significant number of men *only when they decided to stand and fight*" (author's emphasis). Alain C. Enthoven and K. Wayne Smith, *How Much Is Enough? Shaping the Defense Program, 1961–1964* (New York: Harper and Row, 1971), 297.

17. Johnson, "Third Generation of Guerrilla Warfare," 359.

18. Ibid.

19. Ibid.

20. Mao Tse-Tung, *On Guerrilla Warfare*, 88.

21. Likewise, *Preparation for the Insurrection*, instructions issued by the Viet Minh in May 1944 against the French and the Japanese, stress the need to "always be on the alert to feel the pulse of the movement and know the mood of the masses, estimate . . . the situation in each period in order to seize the right opportunity and lead the masses of people to rise up in time" (Vo Nguyen Giap, "The General Insurrection of August 1945," in Pomeroy, *Guerrilla Warfare*, 205.

22. See also relevant remarks by Giap in Russell Stetler, ed., *The Military Art of People's War: Selected Writings of General Vo-Nguyen-Giap* (New York: Monthly Review Press, 1980), esp. 163–84. This important aspect of the primacy of the political over the military was lost to the theorists of the Latin American variant of guerrilla warfare, in particular Che Guevara and Regis Debray. The latter, by elevating the *foco* (small mobile force of dedicated guerrilla fighters) to the status of "party in embryo" which can launch armed struggle without preparatory political work among the people, clearly misread both the lessons of the past and the prospects for the successful conduct of guerrilla operations in Latin America. See Regis Debray, *Revolution in the Revolution?* (New York: Monthly Review Press, 1967), esp. 95–126; Che Guevara, "Guerrilla Warfare—A Method," in Laqueur's *Guerrilla Reader*, 203–11; and Leo Huberman and Paul Sweezy, eds., *Regis Debray and the Latin American Revolution* (New York: Monthly Review Press, 1968), esp. 1–11, 70–83, and 119–38, the articles by Huberman and Sweezy, Eqbal Ahmad, and Peter Worsley.

23. Walzer, *Just and Unjust Wars*, 181.

24. Ibid., 180.

25. Article 4A §2, which as noted in note 1 is common to the first three Geneva Conventions, provides that captured members must (*a*) be commanded by a person responsible for his subordinates, (*b*) have a fixed distinctive sign recognizable at a distance, (*c*) carry arms openly, and (*d*) conduct their operations in accordance with the laws and customs of war; Roberts and Guelff, *Documents*, 218.

26. During the Vietnam War "the distinction between a bunker or shelter constructed by a villager for the protection of his family and a Viet Cong fighting position was usually left entirely to the judgment of the angry, frightened, and tired GIs searching the hamlet"; Ronald H. Spector, *After Tet: The Bloodiest Year in Vietnam* (New York: Free Press, 1993), 197.

27. Arnold Fraleigh, "The Algerian Revolution as a Case Study in International Law," in *International Law of Civil War*, 202.

28. Mohammed Bedjaoui, *Law and the Algerian Revolution* (Brussels: Publications of the International Association of Democratic Lawyers, 1961), 210.

29. Fraleigh, "Algerian Revolution," 202; Bedjaoui, *Law*, 209.

30. Richard Lillich, *International Human Rights: Problems of Law, Policy, and Practice,* 2d ed. (Boston: Little, Brown, 1991), 794.

31. *United States* v. *William L. Calley, Jr.,* 22 U.S.C.M.A. 534; 48 C.M.R. 19 (1973). Of course, this was not the only line of defense. A very prominent part of Calley's defense strategy was that he was following the orders of Capt. Ernest R. Medina (the company commander).

32. Heather Wilson, *International Law and the Use of Force by National Liberation Movements* (Oxford: Clarendon Press, 1988), 105; and Georges Abi-Saab, "Wars of National Liberation in the Geneva Conventions and Protocols," *Recueil des Cours* 165 (1979–IV) (The Hague: Martinus Nijhoff Publishers, 1981), 367.

33. See G. H. Hackworth, *Digest of International Law* (Washington, D.C.: Government Printing Office, 1940), quoted in Wilson, *International Law,* 93; and Barbara Jelavich, *History of the Balkans,* vol. 2 (Cambridge: Cambridge University Press, 1991), 270. For a good treatment of recognition, see Ian Brownlie, "Recognition in Theory and Practice," *British Year Book of International Law* 53 (1982): 197–211.

34. See, for example, the Geneva Convention III provisions on Quarters, Food, and Clothing of Prisoners of War (articles 25–28), Hygiene and Medical Attention (articles 29–32), Medical Personnel and Chaplains (article 33), and Religious, Intellectual, and Physical Activities (articles 34–38); Roberts and Guelff, *Documents,* 227–32; the relevant provisions in the Department of the Army Field Manual FM 27-10 *The Law of Land Warfare* (Department of the Army, July 1956), 40–45; and William V. O'Brien, "The Jus in Bello in Revolutionary War and Counterinsurgency," *Virginia Journal of International Law* 18 (1978): 225.

35. Bedjaoui, *Law,* 17–37.

36. Quincy Wright, "The Goa Incident," *American Journal of International Law* 56 (1962): 622.

37. Wright, "Goa," 623–24.

38. C. J. R. Dugard, "The Organization of African Unity and Colonialism: An Enquiry into the Plea of Self-Defense as a Justification for the Use of Force in the Eradication of Colonialism," *International and Comparative Law Quarterly* 16 (1967): 168–70.

39. G. A. Resolution 2625 (XXV), October 24, 1970, U.N. General Assembly. Official Records: Twenty-fifth Session Supplement no. 28 (A/8028). An earlier resolution, the Declaration on the Granting of Independence to Colonial Countries and Peoples, 1514 (XV), December 14, 1960, recognized the right of all peoples to self-determination, but it did not authorize the use of force in implementing that right. In fact, the text of Resolution 1514 makes no reference whatsoever to the use of force. Resolution 1514 is discussed below.

40. Abi-Saab, "Wars of National Liberation," 370–72; Christopher Quaye, *Liberation Struggles in International Law* (Philadelphia: Temple University Press, 1991), 281–86.

41. Georges Abi-Saab, "Wars of National Liberation and the Laws of War," *Annales d'études internationales* 3 (1972), 100; quoted in Wilson, *International Law,* 98.

42. See relevant discussion in Wilson, *International Law,* 99; Stephen M. Schwebel, "Wars of Liberation as Fought in U.N. Organs," in *Law and Civil War in the Modern World,* ed. John Norton Moore (Baltimore: Johns Hopkins University Press, 1974), 453.

43. The continuing ambivalence on the legitimacy of the initiation of the use of force

by national liberation movements was reflected in General Assembly Resolution 3314 which adopted the Definition of Aggression; G. A. Resolution 3314 (XXIX), December 14, 1974, U.N. General Assembly. Official Records: Twenty-ninth Session. Supplement no. 31 (A/9631). Article 7 of the Definition stated, "Nothing in this definition . . . could in any way prejudice the right to self-determination . . . of peoples forcibly deprived of that right . . . nor the right of these peoples to struggle to that end and to seek and receive support, in accordance with the principles of the Charter. . . ." Thus, although peoples were entitled to struggle in order to achieve self-determination, their struggle was to be expressed through activities consistent with the purposes and principles of the U.N. Charter. This type of broad phrasing played a major role in the resolution's adoption by consensus.

44. *Universal Declaration of Human Rights,* G. A. Resolution 217A (III), December 10, 1948, U.N. General Assembly. Official Records: Third Session. Part I, Doc. A/810; *International Covenant on Civil and Political Rights,* G. A. Resolution 2200A (XXI), December 16, 1966, U. N. General Assembly Official Records: Twenty-first Session. Supplement no. 16 (A/6316); *International Covenant on Economic, Social and Cultural Rights,* G. A. Resolution 2200A (XXI), December 16, 1966, U.N. General Assembly Official Records: Twenty-first Session, Supplement no. 16 (A/6316). For the growing postwar concern about human rights, see Burns Weston, "Human Rights," in Richard Pierre Claude and Burns Weston, eds., *Human Rights in the World Community* (Philadelphia: University of Pennsylvania Press, 1992), 14–30.

45. G. A. Resolution 1514 (XV), December 14, 1960, U. N. General Assembly Official Records: Fifteenth Session. Supplement no. 16, Doc. A/4684.

46. For comprehensive treatments of the war and the issues at stake, see Alistair Horne, *A Savage War of Peace: "Algeria," 1954–1962* (London: Papermac, 1987); John Talbott, *The War Without a Name: France in Algeria* (New York: Knopf, 1980); and Tony Smith, *The French Stake in Algeria, 1945–1962* (Ithaca, N.Y.: Cornell University Press, 1978).

47. On the notion of *mission civilisatrice* and French colonial policy, see Raymond F. Betts, *Assimilation and Association in French Colonial Theory, 1890–1914* (New York: Columbia University Press, 1961), 10–32, 106–64.

48. For the text of the proclamation, see Horne, *Savage War,* 94–95; National Liberation Front, *Aspects of the Algerian Revolution* (New York: Algerian Front of National Liberation Delegation, 1957), 11.

49. Bedjaoui, *Law,* 87.

50. Fraleigh, "Algerian Revolution," 188–89; Bedjaoui, *Law,* 89–101; on the evolution of the FLN's conception of justice and its uses during the war, see Said Benabdellah, *La Justice du FLN Pendant la Lutte de Libération* (Algiers: Société Nationale d'Édition et de Diffusion, 1982). It is instructive to note that one of the ten commandments (the ten commandments constituted "the first legal text which was announced . . . with the launching of the revolution") was to "observe in the destruction of enemy forces the principles of Islam and the international laws" (author's translation), 64.

51. Fraleigh, "Algerian Revolution," 189.

52. Fraleigh, "Algerian Revolution," 189–90; during the debate concerning the competence of the U.N. General Assembly to consider the Algerian question, the French representative Pinay argued that if all territorial acquisitions resulting from the use of force were to be taken up by the U.N., then the security of member states would be undermined;

see Mohammed Alwan, *Algeria Before the United Nations* (New York: Robert Speller & Sons, 1959), 19.

53. Fraleigh, "Algerian Revolution," 190.

54. Ibid.

55. Horne, *Savage War*, 98.

56. Shafer, *Deadly Paradigms*, 145.

57. The doctrine of *guerre révolutionnaire* includes both an analysis of the nature and processes of modern revolution and the principles and techniques of waging war against the revolution. The perception of counterinsurgency warfare is simply to reverse the sequence of strategies and tactics that presumably constitute the insurgents' mode of operation; see Roger Trinquier, *La guerre moderne* (Paris: La Table Ronde, 1961); for critical assessments see Peter Paret, *French Revolutionary Warfare from Indochina to Algeria* (New York: Praeger, 1964), 20–79, 98–122; and Shafer, *Deadly Paradigms*, 138–65.

58. The Algerian Communist party gave very little assistance to the FLN and they were marginal throughout the conflict. In addition, the Eastern bloc's support was, as Douglas Porch correctly points out, "largely rhetorical." And the French Communist party supported the government and some of the harshest measures including the Special Powers Law which lifted restrictions on police power; see Douglas Porch, *The French Foreign Legion* (New York: Harper Collins, 1991), 570; on the French Communist party (PCF), see Danièle Joly, *The French Communist Party and the Algerian War* (London: Macmillan, 1991), esp. 100–129.

59. Martin Alexander and Philip Bankwitz, *From Politiques en Képi to Military Technocrats: De Gaulle and the Recovery of the French Army after Indochina and Algeria* (unpublished manuscript, 15–16).

60. Alexander and Bankwitz, *Politiques en Képi*, 15.

61. ALN forces were composed of three categories of combatants: the *moudjahidines*, who were the uniformed combatants, and two categories of nonuniformed combatants, the *moussabilines* and the *fidaiyines*. The moussabilines were recruited and operated locally. Their duties included both sabotage activities and intelligence. They were the "eyes and ears" of the ALN and constituted a formidable intelligence network. The fidaiyines operated in towns and villages, and carried out attacks against installations and the gendarmerie. They were the dispensers of what may be called revolutionary justice since their duties included, in the words of Bedjaoui, "the killing of French torturers and traitors to the national cause" (*Law*, 50). The fidaiyines and their activities were often romanticized in the writings of supportive French intellectuals such as Jean-Paul Sartre.

62. Porch, *French Foreign Legion*, 570.

63. Alexander and Bankwitz, *Politiques en Képi*, 18.

64. For the Battle of Algiers, see Horne, *Savage War*, 183–207; Porch, *French Foreign Legion*, 580–97; Alexander and Bankwitz, *Politiques en Képi*, 17.

65. The arrival of such an elite division constituted France's admission that the FLN challenge necessitated a major military engagement; Talbott, *The War Without a Name*, 83; for Massu's version of events, see Jacques Massu, *La Vraie Bataille d'Alger* (Paris: Plon, 1972), esp. 87–328; for an indictment of Massu's methods, see Mohammed Lebjaoui, *Bataille d'Alger ou Bataille d'Algérie?* (Paris: Gallimard, 1972), esp. 83–206.

66. Porch, *French Foreign Legion*, 585.

67. PierNico Solinas, ed., *Gillo Pontecorvo's The Battle of Algiers. A Film Written by Franco Salinas* (New York: Charles Scribner's Sons, 1973).

68. Roberts and Guelff, *Documents,* 43–59, 169–337.

69. Fraleigh, "Algerian Revolution," 201.

70. Bedjaoui, *Law,* 211.

71. Bedjaoui, *Law,* 216; and Michel Veuthey, *Guérilla et Droit Humanitaire* (Genève: Comité International de la Croix-Rouge, 1983), 49.

72. For the FLN's account of France's violations of the basic humanitarian provisions of the Geneva Conventions, see Algerian Office, New York, *White Paper on the Application of the Geneva Conventions of 1949 to the French-Algerian Conflict* (New York, 1960), 26–58.

73. Veuthey, *Guérilla et Droit Humanitaire,* 49; Joan Gillespie, *Algeria: Rebellion and Revolution* (London: Ernest Benn, 1960), 167. By the time of the accession, twenty governments had recognized the GPRA as the legitimate government of Algeria.

74. G.I.A.D. Draper, *The Red Cross Conventions* (London: Stevens & Sons, 1958), 15, n. 47. Draper is also critical of the British government's similar reaction to the Mau Mau struggle in Kenya and to that of EOKA in Cyprus.

75. Here I follow Fraleigh, "Algerian Revolution," 196–97.

76. Comité International de la Croix-Rouge, *Le CICR et le conflit algérien* (Genève, 1963), 5.

77. *Le Monde,* January 5, 1960; cited in Fraleigh, "Algerian Revolution," 197; the summary of the ICRC report as it appeared in *Le Monde* can be found in *White Paper,* 74–84.

78. Pierre Vidal-Naquet, *La Raison d'État* (Paris: Les Éditions de Minuit, 1962), 60. The whole report can be found in 57–68.

79. Naquet, *La Raison d'État,* 58.

80. Naquet, *La Raison d'État,* 67. Author's translation.

81. The electrical method could adversely affect detainees with heart problems; Naquet, *La Raison d'État,* 65.

82. Author's translation; Naquet, *La Raison d'État,* 66.

83. According to Massu, the use of torture "was never institutionalized or codified." In addition, he claimed that in their use of torture to defeat terrorism, the French military proved to be "choir boys" compared to the corresponding use of terror by the fellaghas (Arab guerrillas): "the extreme savagery of the latter (i.e., fellaghas) led us, to be sure, to a certain ferocity. We remained well within the boundaries of the Leviticus Law of 'an eye for an eye, a tooth for a tooth'" (author's translation) (*La Vraie Bataille,* 167–68). For a critical perspective from a fellow officer, see Général de Bollardière, *Bataille d'Alger, Bataille de l'homme* (Paris: Desclée de Brouwer, 1972), esp. 131–53; and the penetrating essays of Pierre Vidal-Naquet, *Face à la raison d'État* (Paris: Éditions La Découverte, 1989), 115–204.

84. Trinquier, *La guerre moderne,* 73–87; Shafer, *Deadly Paradigms,* 155–59; and Rita Maran, *Torture: The Role of Ideology in the French-Algerian War* (New York: Praeger, 1989), 81–83, 98–100.

85. *White Paper,* 19–22; Fraleigh, "Algerian Revolution," 201; and see discussion in Maran, *Torture,* 5–11, 38–43.

86. Massu, *La Vraie Bataille;* Maran, *Torture,* 100.

87. Porch, *French Foreign Legion,* 588.

88. The argument is that the indiscriminate use of violence will alienate the very people on whose behalf the struggle is being waged.

89. See discussion in Walzer, *Just and Unjust Wars,* 197–98.

90. Porch, *French Foreign Legion,* 581.

91. Veuthey, *Guérilla et Droit Humanitaire,* 103–4. For a discussion of "free-fire" zones in Vietnam (which after 1965 were designated as "specified strike" zones), see Spector, *After Tet,* 198–99; and Guenter Lewy, *America in Vietnam* (New York: Oxford University Press, 1978), 105–7.

92. *White Paper,* 44.

93. *White Paper,* 44–45.

94. *White Paper,* 45. Article II (c) defines genocide as "acts . . . deliberately inflicting on the group conditions of life calculated to bring about its physical destruction in whole or in part." France had ratified the Genocide Convention on October 14, 1950.

95. Jean-Jacques Servan-Schreiber, *Lieutenant in Algeria,* trans. Ronald Matthews (London: Hutchinson, 1958), 39–40.

96. Walzer, *Just and Unjust Wars,* 195.

97. Alwan, *Algeria Before the United Nations,* 14–32. The vote on draft resolution A/L.276 was 39 in favor, 22 against, with 20 abstentions; U.N. General Assembly. Official Records: Fourteenth Session, 856th plenary meeting, December 12, 1959, 735–51.

98. The draft resolution was adopted by 89 votes in favor, 0 against, with 9 abstentions; U.N. General Assembly. Official Records: Fifteenth Session, 947th plenary meeting, December 14, 1960.

99. See, for example, the statement made by Krishna Menon (India), U.N. General Assembly. Official Records: Fifteenth Session, 944th plenary meeting, December 13, 1960; and the statements made by Omar (Somalia) and Boucetta (Morocco), U.N. General Assembly. Official Records: Fifteenth Session, 945th plenary meeting, December 13, 1960.

100. General Assembly Resolution 1573 (XV), December 19, 1960; in Dusan J. Djonovich, ed., *United Nations Resolutions,* ser. 1, vol. 8, 1960–62 (New York: Oceana Publications, 1974), 129. The resolution was adopted by 63 votes to 8, with 27 abstentions. For the discussion relating to the resolution, U.N. General Assembly. Official Records: Fifteenth Session, 956th plenary meeting, December 19, 1960, 1415–1431.

101. Edwin Brown Firmage, "The 'War of National Liberation' and the Third World," in *Law and Civil War in the Modern World,* 340–41.

102. This must be emphasized. Despite the general phrasing of U.N. resolutions, in practice states are prepared to consider self-determination almost exclusively in colonial situations. The attitude of African states and the OAU are indicative of this tendency. Although very supportive of colonial struggles, they have refused to apply the principle in secessionist struggles, as the case of the Ibos in Nigeria was to demonstrate; see Michael Reisman, "Humanitarian Intervention to Protect the Ibos," in Richard Lillich, ed., *Humanitarian Intervention and the United Nations* (Charlottesville: University Press of Virginia, 1973), 167–95.

103. This was one of the main criticisms leveled at the 1977 Geneva Protocol I by Western governments in their refusal to ratify it. The 1977 Protocol will be discussed in the concluding chapter of this volume.

104. The FLN's eagerness to declare its adherence to the provisions of the Geneva Conventions was by no means unique among national liberation movements; see, for example, similar statements by representatives of SWAPO and FRELIMO in Centre de droit international de l'Institut de Sociologie de l'Université Libre de Bruxelles, *Droit*

humanitaire et conflits armés (Bruxelles: Editions de l'Université de Bruxelles, 1976), 251–52, 285–87.

105. See note 25 and *White Paper*, 23–25.

106. See note 61.

107. Walzer, *Just and Unjust Wars*, 196.

12. The Laws of War: Some Concluding Reflections

1. Since 1945 we have paradoxically striven to codify more detailed and more humanitarian provisions for the conduct of warfare while at the same time creating impressive stockpiles of the most indiscriminate weapon that the world has ever known. It is a matter of intriguing speculation what the legal status of nuclear weapons would be today, if those weapons had first been used by the losing side during World War II. The only precedent we have is the use of asphyxiating gases by Germany during World War I, which resulted in the 1925 Geneva Protocol for the Prohibition of the Use in War of Asphyxiating, Poisonous or Other Gases, and of Bacteriological Methods of Warfare. While the language of the protocol points to the absolute prohibition of their use, many signatory states have ratified it with the reservation that its validity hinges on the mutual observance of its provisions; thus, an argument can be made that the 1925 Protocol should be viewed as a no-first-use instrument and we may have possibly ended up with a similar type of agreement on nuclear weapons.

2. Message from the President [Ronald Reagan] Transmitting Protocol II Additional to the 1949 Geneva Conventions, and Relating to the Protection of Victims of Non-international Armed Conflicts, in Richard Lillich, ed., *International Human Rights: Problems of Law, Policy, and Practice* (Boston: Little, Brown, 1991), 823.

3. Guy B. Roberts, "The New Rules for Waging War: The Case against Ratification of Additional Protocol I," *Virginia Journal of International Law* 26 (1985): 125–26.

4. Heather Wilson, *International Law and the Use of Force by National Liberation Movements* (Oxford: Clarendon Press, 1988), 172.

5. George H. Aldrich, "Progressive Development of the Laws of War: A Reply to Criticisms of the 1977 Geneva Protocol I," *Virginia Journal of International Law* 26 (1986): 702; see also his comments on 700–703.

6. Wilson, *International Law*, 168.

7. R. R. Baxter, "Modernizing the Laws of War," *Military Law Review* 78 (Fall 1977): 169.

8. Adam Roberts and Richard Guelff, eds., *Documents on the Laws of War* (Oxford: Clarendon Press, 1989), 388.

9. United Nations Department of Public Information, *United Nations Security Council Resolutions Relating to the Situation between Iraq and Kuwait* (n.d.), 9–19. However, the extent to which China's abstention in resolution 678 satisfies the provisions of article 27 §3 of the U.N. Charter concerning the concurring votes of all permanent members on nonprocedural matters is debatable.

10. *United Nations Security Council Resolutions*, 16.

11. Richard Falk, *Reflections on the Gulf War Experience: Force and War in the United Nations System* (unpublished paper), 20. See Falk's discussion in 15–22.

12. For a discussion of the air campaign, see Lawrence Freedman and Efraim Karsh, *The Gulf Conflict, 1990–1991: Diplomacy and War in the New World Order* (Princeton:

Princeton University Press, 1993), 312–30. Troubling questions about possible violations of the laws of war have been raised in Middle East Watch, *Needless Deaths in the Gulf War* (New York: Human Rights Watch, 1991). According to General McPeak, precision-guided bombs constituted a mere 8.8 percent of all munitions dropped by the allied forces during the Gulf War; *Needless Deaths,* 6.

13. Adam Roberts, "Humanitarian War: Military Intervention and Human Rights," John Vincent Memorial Lecture, Keele University (February 26, 1993), 12.

14. Francis M. Deng and Larry Minear, *The Challenges of Famine Relief: Emergency Operations in the Sudan* (Washington, D.C.: Brookings Institution, 1992), 8.

15. Roberts, "Humanitarian War," 12–13.

16. U.N. Security Council, *Report of the Secretary-General pursuant to Paragraph 2 of Security Council Resolution 808 (1993),* U.N. Doc. S/25704, May 3, 1993, 36. The Statute of the International Tribunal is in 36–48.

17. U.N. Security Council, Resolution 827 (1993), S/RES/827, May 25, 1993; and U.N. Security Council, Resolution 808 (1993), S/RES/808, February 22, 1993.

18. The secretary-general's report also included the 1948 Convention on the Prevention and Punishment of the Crime of Genocide and the 1945 Charter of the International Military Tribunal as part of the law applicable in this conflict; U.N. Doc. S/25704, May 3, 1993, 9.

19. Principle vii of the Statement of Principles guarantees "compliance by all persons with their obligations under international humanitarian law and in particular the Geneva Conventions of 12 August 1949, and the personal responsibility of those who commit or order grave breaches of the Conventions." *The London Conference: Statement of Principles Approved by the Conference on 26 August,* LC/C2 (Final), August 26, 1992, 3.

20. See, for example, Theodor Meron, "The Case for War Crimes Trials in Yugoslavia," *Foreign Affairs* 72 (1993): 132–33.

21. U.N. Doc. S/25704, May 3, 1993, 6–7.

22. Ibid., 7.

23. The Chinese ambassador to the U.N. expressed his delegation's strong reservations concerning the procedure used for the adoption of the Statute of the International Tribunal. Although China joined the other members of the Security Council in the unanimous approval of resolution 827, the Chinese ambassador stated, in his declaration after the vote, that China considers the international tribunal as an ad hoc arrangement applicable to the particular circumstances of former Yugoslavia, an arrangement that should not constitute a precedent; Nations Unies Conseil de Sécurité, *Procès-Verbal Provisoire de la 3217e Séance,* U.N. Doc. S/PV. 3217, May 25, 1993, 32–33.

24. U.N. Doc. S/25704, May 3, 1993, 8.

25. Given the international community's unsatisfactory record in cases where the linkages are obvious, one can hardly be optimistic for those situations in which the linkages are nonexistent.

26. U.N. General Assembly, Report of the Secretary-General on the Work of the Organization, *An Agenda for Peace: Preventive Diplomacy, Peacemaking and Peace-keeping,* U.N. Doc. A/47/277/S/24111, June 17, 1992, 3 and 5.

27. Ibid., 9.

28. Ibid., 3. According to Boutros-Ghali's report, the number of refugees has risen to 17 million, that of displaced persons to 20 million.

Acknowledgments

This book is the revised version of a series of public lectures delivered each Monday afternoon in the fall 1991 semester at Yale University under the auspices of the university's International Security Program. Every year these lectures, which are funded through the generous assistance of the Lynde and Harry Bradley Foundation, deal with a particular theme in military and strategic history. On this occasion the speakers were asked to focus upon the subject of constraints on warfare.

This volume could not have come into being without the aid of a number of people. In particular, we would like to thank our colleague Paul Kennedy, Dilworth Professor of History and director of the International Security Program, for his encouragement and support throughout this project. Ann Bitetti of the International Security Program gave invaluable help in the preparation of the lecture series and Marge Camera in the preparation of the finished manuscript. At Yale University Press it was a great pleasure to work with Charles Grench, executive editor, and Otto Bohlmann, assistant editor of the press; we owe them a lot for their strong interest in the project and their indispensable advice. In addition, we would like to thank Faith Short, production editor, and Thomas Rejensek, copy editor.

Above all, our thanks go to the contributors to this volume who made the whole thing possible. We sincerely hope that the end result lives up to their endorsement.

Contributors

George J. Andreopoulos is lecturer in the Department of History at Yale University. Until recently, he was also associate director of the Schell Center for International Human Rights at Yale Law School. Forthcoming books include *Genocide* and *The Aftermath of Defeat,* edited with Harold E. Selesky.

Tami Davis Biddle is lecturer in the Department of History at Duke University. She is currently editing a book based on a sixteen-month lecture series on the history of strategic bombing she ran in Washington, D.C. She has written several articles on air power and American foreign policy.

John B. Hattendorf is Ernest J. King Professor of Maritime History and director of the Advanced Research Department at the Naval War College, Newport, Rhode Island. He has recently coedited *Maritime Strategy and the Balance of Power, The Limitations of Military Power,* and *British Naval Documents, 1204–1960.*

Michael Howard is Robert A. Lovett Professor Emeritus of Military and Naval History at Yale University. His many books and articles include *War and the Liberal Conscience* and *The Causes of Wars.* His latest book of essays is *The Lessons of History.*

Paul Kennedy is J. Richardson Dilworth Professor of History and director of the International Security Program at Yale University. He is the author or editor of *The Rise and Fall of Great Powers, Grand Strategies in War and Peace,* and *Preparing for the Twenty-first Century,* among others.

Josiah Ober is professor of Greek history in the Department of Classics at Princeton University. He is the author of *Fortress Attica, Mass and Elite in Democratic Athens,* and (with Barry Strauss) *The Anatomy of Error.*

Geoffrey Parker is Robert A. Lovett Professor of Military and Naval History at Yale University. He has written *The Thirty Years' War* and *The Military Revolution,* among others.

Adam Roberts is Montague Burton Professor of International Relations at Oxford University and fellow of Balliol College. His main academic interests are centered on various limitations on the use of force. His latest book is *United Nations, Divided World,* edited with Benedict Kingsbury.

David Alan Rosenberg is associate professor of history at Temple University. He has published widely on the history of nuclear strategy and recent naval history and is completing a biography of Admiral Arleigh Burke.

Gunther E. Rothenberg is professor of military history at Purdue University. His writings on the Revolutionary and Napoleonic period include *The Art of Warfare in the Age of Napoleon* and *Napoleon's Great Adversaries.*

Harold E. Selesky is associate professor of history at the University of Alabama, Tuscaloosa, and director of the Master of Arts in Military History Degree Program at the Air University, Maxwell Air Force Base, Montgomery. His publications include *War and Society in Colonial Connecticut* and *The Aftermath of Defeat,* edited with George J. Andreopoulos.

Mark R. Shulman is lecturer in the Department of History at Yale University. He is the author or editor of several studies of naval and military history, including an upcoming book on navalism and the origins of American sea power.

Robert C. Stacey is associate professor of history at the University of Washington in Seattle. He is the author of *Politics, Policy, and Finance under Henry III,* and he is currently working on a history of the Jews in medieval England.

Suggested Readings

Chapter 2. Classical Greek Times

Connor, W. Robert. "Early Greek Land Warfare as Symbolic Expression." *Past and Present* 119 (1988): 3–27.

Ducrey, Pierre. *Warfare in Ancient Greece*. New York: Schocken Books, 1986.

Garlan, Yvon. *War in the Ancient World*. New York: W. W. Norton, 1975.

Goodman, M. G., and Holladay, A. J. "Religious Scruples in Ancient Warfare." *Classical Quarterly* 36 (1986): 151–71.

Hanson, Victor D. *The Western Way of War*. New York: Alfred A. Knopf, 1989.

———, ed. *Hoplites: The Classical Greek Battle Experience*. London: Routledge, 1991.

Ober, Josiah. *Fortress Attica: Defense of the Athenian Land Frontier, 404–322 B.C.* Mnemosyne Supplement 84. Leiden: E. J. Brill, 1985.

Pritchett, W. Kendrick. *The Greek State at War*. 5 vols. to date. Berkeley: University of California Press, 1971–.

Chapter 3. The Age of Chivalry

Allmand, Christopher T. *The Hundred Years War: England and France at War, c. 1300–c. 1450*. Cambridge Medieval Textbooks. Cambridge: Cambridge University Press, 1988.

Contamine, Philippe. *War in the Middle Ages*. Translated by Michael Jones. Oxford: Basil Blackwell, 1984.

Cowdrey, H. E. J. "The Peace and the Truce of God in the Eleventh Century." *Past and Present* 46 (1970): 47–67.

Erdmann, Carl. *The Origin of the Idea of Crusade*. Translated by Marshall W. Baldwin and Walter Goffart. Princeton: Princeton University Press, 1977, orig. ed., 1935.

Gillingham, John. *The Wars of the Roses: Peace and Conflict in Fifteenth-Century England*. London: Weidenfeld and Nicolson, 1981.

Johnson, James T. *Ideology, Reason, and the Limitation of War: Religious and Secular Concepts, 1200–1740*. Princeton: Princeton University Press, 1975.

Keen, Maurice H. *The Laws of War in the Late Middle Ages*. London: Routledge & Kegan Paul, 1965.

————. *Chivalry*. New Haven: Yale University Press, 1984.

Leyser, Karl. "Early Medieval Canon Law and the Beginnings of Knighthood." In *Institutionen, Kulture und Gesellschaft im Mittelalter: Festschrift für Josef Fleckenstein zu seinem 65. Geburtstag*. Edited by Lutz Fenske, Werner Rösener, and Thomas Zotz. Sigmaringen: Jan Thorbecke Verlag, 1984.

Russell, Frederick H. *The Just War in the Middle Ages*. Cambridge: Cambridge University Press, 1975.

Vale, Malcolm. *War and Chivalry: Warfare and Aristocratic Culture in England, France and Burgundy at the End of the Middle Ages*. London: Duckworth, 1981.

Wallace-Hadrill, John Michael. "War and Peace in the Early Middle Ages." *Transactions of the Royal Historical Society*, 5th ser., 25 (1975). Reprinted in his collected *Essays in Early Medieval History*. Oxford: Basil Blackwell, 1975.

Chapter 4. Early Modern Europe

Burke, James. "The New Model Army and the Problems of Siege-Warfare, 1648–51." *Irish Historical Studies* 27 (1990): 1–29.

Donagan, Barbara. "Codes and Conduct in the English Civil War." *Past and Present* 118 (1988): 65–95.

Hale, John R. *Renaissance War Studies*. London: Hambledon Press, 1983.

Johnson, James T. *Ideology, Reason and the Limitation of War: Religious and Secular Concepts, 1200–1740*. Princeton: Princeton University Press, 1975.

————. *The Just War Tradition and the Restraint of War: A Moral and Historical Inquiry*. Princeton: Princeton University Press, 1984.

Lynn, John A. "How War Fed War: The Tax of Violence and Contributions during the *Grand Siècle*." *Journal of Modern History* 65 (1993), forthcoming.

Redlich, Fritz. *De praeda militaris: Looting and Booty, 1500–1815*. Vierteljahrschrift für Sozial- und Wirtschaftsgeschichte, Beiheft 39. Wiesbaden: Steiner, 1956.

Soldi-Rondinini, G. "Il diritto di guerra in Italia nel secolo XV." *Nuova rivista storica* 48 (1964): 275–306.

Van der Essen, Léon. "Kritisch onderzoek betreffende de oorlogvoering van het Spaans leger in de Nederlanden in de XVIe eeuw, namelijk de bestraffing von opstandige steden." *Mededelingen van de Koninklijke Vlaamse Academie van Wetenschappen, Letteren en Schone Kunsten van België: Klasse der Letteren* 12 (1950)–22 (1960).

Chapter 5. Colonial America

Canny, Nicholas P. "The Ideology of English Colonization: From Ireland to America." *William and Mary Quarterly*, 3d ser., vol. 30, no. 4 (October 1973).

Higginbotham, Don. "Reflections on the War of Independence, Modern Guerrilla Warfare, and the War in Vietnam." In *Arms and Independence: The Military Character of the American Revolution*. Edited by Ronald Hoffman and Peter J. Albert. Charlottesville: University Press of Virginia, 1984.

Leiby, Adrian C. *The Revolutionary War in the Hackensack Valley: The Jersey Dutch and the Neutral Ground, 1775–1783.* Reprint ed., New Brunswick, N.J.: Rutgers University Press, 1980.

Shy, John. "The American Military Experience: History and Learning." In John Shy, *A People Numerous and Armed: Reflections on the Military Struggle for American Independence.* New York: Oxford University Press, 1976.

————. "Armed Loyalism: The Case of the Lower Hudson Valley." In John Shy, *A People Numerous and Armed: Reflections on the Military Struggle for American Independence.* New York: Oxford University Press, 1976.

Steele, Ian. *Betrayals: Fort William Henry and the "Massacre."* New York: Oxford University Press, 1990.

Vaughn, Alden T. "'Expulsion of the Salvages': English Policy and the Virginia Massacre of 1622." *William and Mary Quarterly,* 3d ser., vol. 35, no. 1 (January 1978).

Chapter 6. The Age of Napoleon

Bertaud, Jean-Paul. *The Army of the French Revolution: From Citizen Soldier to Instrument of Power.* Translated by R. R. Palmer. Princeton: Princeton University Press, 1988.

Chandler, David G. *The Campaigns of Napoleon.* New York: Macmillan, 1966.

Gates, David. *The Spanish Ulcer: A History of the Peninsular War.* New York: W. W. Norton, 1986.

Glover, Richard G. *Peninsular Preparation: The Reform of the British Army, 1795–1809.* Cambridge: Cambridge University Press, 1963.

Halleck, Henry W. *Halleck's International Law.* 2 vols. 3d ed. London: K. Paul, Trench, Trubner, 1893.

Lynn, John A. *Bayonets of the Republic: Motivation and Tactics in the Army of Revolutionary France, 1791–94.* Urbana: University of Illinois Press, 1984.

Paret, Peter. *Yorck and the Era of Prussian Reform, 1807–1815.* Princeton: Princeton University Press, 1966.

————, ed. *Makers of Modern Strategy: Military Thought from Machiavelli to the Nuclear Age.* Princeton: Princeton University Press, 1986.

Rothenberg, Gunther E. *The Art of Warfare in the Age of Napoleon.* London: Batsford, 1977.

————. *Napoleon's Great Adversaries: The Archduke Charles and the Austrian Army, 1792–1814.* Bloomington: Indiana University Press, 1982.

Chapter 7. Maritime Conflict

Colombos, Christopher John. *International Law of the Sea.* 6th ed. London: Longmans, Green, 1967.

Fischer, Horst, and Von Heinegg, Wolff H. *The Law of Naval Warfare: A Select Bibliography.* Bochumer Schriften zur Friedenssicherung und zum humanitären Völkerrecht, edited by N. Brockmeyer, vol. 3. Bochum: UVB Universitätsverlag, 1989.

Levie, Howard S. *The Law of War and Neutrality: A Selective English-Language Bibliography.* Dobbs Ferry, N.Y.: Ocean Publications, 1988.

O'Connell, D. P. *The Influence of the Law on Sea Power.* Manchester: Manchester University Press, 1975.

———. "Limited War at Sea." In *Restraints on War: Studies in the Limitation of Armed Conflict.* Edited by Michael Howard. Oxford: Oxford University Press, 1979.

———. *The International Law of the Sea.* Vol. I. Edited by I. A. Shearer. Oxford: Clarendon Press, 1982.

Oppenheim, F. L. F. *International Law.* Edited by Hersch Lauterpacht. 2 vols. 7th ed. London: Longmans, Green, 1952.

Ranft, Brian. "Restraints on War at Sea before 1945." In *Restraints on War: Studies in the Limitation of Armed Conflict.* Edited by Michael Howard. Oxford: Oxford University Press, 1979.

Restatement of the Law (Third). The Foreign Relations Law of the United States. St. Paul: American Law Institute Publishers, 1990.

Robertson, Horace B., ed. *The Law of Naval Operations.* Naval War College International Law Studies, vol. 64. Newport, R.I.: Naval War College Press, 1991.

Tucker, Robert W. *The Law of War and Neutrality at Sea.* U.S. Naval War College International Law Studies, 1955. Washington, D.C.: Government Printing Office, 1957.

Chapter 8. Land Warfare: From Hague to Nuremberg

Bailey, Sydney. *Prohibitions and Restraints in War.* Oxford: Oxford University Press, 1972.

Best, Geoffrey. *Humanity in Warfare: The Modern History of the International Law of Armed Conflicts.* London: Methuen, 1983 (orig. pub. 1980).

Greenspan, Morris. *The Modern Law of Land Warfare.* Berkeley: University of California Press, 1959.

Howard, Michael, ed. *Restraints on War: Studies in the Limitation of Armed Conflict.* Oxford: Oxford University Press, 1979.

Johnson, James Turner. *The Just War Tradition and the Restraint of War: A Moral and Historical Inquiry.* Princeton: Princeton University Press, 1981.

———. *Can Modern War Be Just?* New Haven: Yale University Press, 1984.

Kalshoven, Frits. *Belligerent Reprisals.* Leiden: Sijthoff, 1971.

McCoubrey, Hilaire. *International Humanitarian Law: The Regulation of Armed Conflicts.* Aldershot: Dartmouth Publishing, 1990.

O'Brien, William V. *The Conduct of Just and Limited War.* New York: Praeger, 1981.

Oppenheim, F. L. F. *International Law: A Treatise.* Vol. 2, *Disputes, War and Neutrality.* Edited by H. Lauterpacht. 7th ed. London: Longmans, Green, 1952.

Roberts, Adam, and Guelff, Richard eds. *Documents on the Laws of War.* 2d ed. Oxford: Oxford University Press, 1989.

Roberts, Adam, and Kingsbury, Benedict. *United Nations, Divided World: The U.N.'s Roles in International Relations,* 2d ed. rev. Oxford: Oxford University Press, 1993.

Schindler, Dietrich, and Toman, Jiri, eds. *The Laws of Armed Conflicts: A Collection of Conventions, Resolutions and Other Documents.* 3d ed. rev. Dordrecht: Martinus Nijhoff, and Geneva: Henry Dunant Institute, 1988.

Chapter 9. Air Power

Best, Geoffrey. *Humanity in Warfare.* New York: Columbia University Press, 1980.

Boog, Horst, ed. *The Conduct of the Air War in the Second World War.* New York: Berg, 1992.

Parks, W. Hays. "Air War and the Law of War." *Air Force Law Review,* vol. 32, no. 1 (1990): 1–225.

Royse, M. W. *Aerial Bombardment and the International Regulation of Warfare.* New York: Harold Vinal, 1928.

Schaffer, Ronald. *Wings of Judgment.* New York: Oxford University Press, 1985.

Sherry, Michael. *The Rise of American Air Power.* New Haven: Yale University Press, 1987.

Spaight, J. M. *Air Power and War Rights.* London: Longmans, Green, 1924.

Walzer, Michael. *Just and Unjust Wars.* New York: Basic Books, 1977.

Watt, Donald Cameron. "Restraints on War in the Air before 1945." In *Restraints on War: Studies in the Limitation of Armed Conflict.* Edited by Michael Howard. Oxford: Oxford University Press, 1979.

Chapter 10. Nuclear War Planning

Ball, Desmond, and Richelson, Jeffrey, eds. *Strategic Nuclear Targeting.* Ithaca, N.Y.: Cornell University Press, 1986.

Bunn, George. "U.S. Law of Nuclear Weapons." *Naval War College Review* 32 (July–August, 1984): 46–62.

Carnesale, Albert, and Haass, Richard N., eds. *Superpower Arms Control: Setting the Record Straight.* Cambridge, Mass.: Ballinger Publishing, 1987.

Carter, Ashton B.; Steinbruner, John D.; and Zraket, Charles, eds. *Managing Nuclear Operations.* Washington, D.C.: Brookings Institution, 1987.

Daalder, Ivo. *The Nature and Practice of Flexible Response: NATO Strategy and Theater Nuclear Weapons since 1967.* New York: Columbia University Press, 1991.

De Lupis, Ingrid Detter. *The Law of War.* New York: Cambridge University Press, 1987.

Feaver, Peter. *Guarding the Guardians: Civilian Control of Nuclear Weapons in the United States.* Ithaca, N.Y.: Cornell University Press, 1992.

Kaplan, Fred. *The Wizards of Armageddon.* New York: Simon and Schuster, 1983.

Lindsay, James M. *Congress and Nuclear Weapons.* Baltimore: Johns Hopkins University Press, 1991.

Miller, Arthur Selwyn, and Feinrider, Martin, eds. *Nuclear Weapons and Law.* Westport, Conn.: Greenwood Press, 1984.

Nolan, Janne. *Guardians of the Arsenal: The Politics of Nuclear Strategy.* New York: Basic Books, 1989.

Rosenberg, David Alan. "The Origins of Overkill, Nuclear Weapons and American Strategy, 1945–1960." *International Security* 7 (Spring 1983): 3–71.

———. "Reality and Responsibility: Power and Process in the Making of United States Nuclear Strategy." *Journal of Strategic Studies* 9 (March 1986): 35–51.

Sagan, Scott. *Moving Targets: Nuclear Strategy and National Security.* Princeton: Princeton University Press, 1989.

Sloss, Leon, and Millot, Marc Dean. "U.S. Nuclear Strategy in Evolution." *Strategic Review* 12 (Winter 1984): 19–28.

Chapter 11. The Age of National Liberation Movements

Abi-Saab, Georges. "Wars of National Liberation in the Geneva Conventions and Protocols." *Recueil des Cours* 165 (1979–IV): 353–445.

Draper, G. I. A. D. "Wars of National Liberation and War Criminality." In *Restraints on War: Studies in the Limitation of Armed Conflict.* Edited by Michael Howard. Oxford: Oxford University Press, 1979.

Firmage, Edwin. "The 'War of National Liberation' and the Third World." In *Law and Civil War in the Modern World.* Edited by J. N. Moore. Baltimore: Johns Hopkins University Press, 1974.

Fraleigh, Arnold. "The Algerian Revolution as a Case Study in International Law." In *The International Law of Civil War.* Edited by Richard Falk. Baltimore: Johns Hopkins University Press, 1971.

Maran, Rita. *Torture: The Role of Ideology in the French-Algerian War.* New York: Praeger, 1989.

O'Brien, William V. "The Jus in bello in Revolutionary War and Counterinsurgency." *Virginia Journal of International Law* 18 (1978): 193–242.

Pictet, Jean, ed. *The Geneva Conventions of 12 August 1949: Commentary.* 4 vols. Geneva: International Committee of the Red Cross, 1952.

Pomerance, Michla. *Self-Determination in Law and Practice: The New Doctrine in the United Nations.* London: Martinus Nijhoff, 1982.

Quaye, Christopher. *Liberation Struggles in International Law.* Philadelphia: Temple University Press, 1991.

Sarkesian, Sam, ed. *Revolutionary Guerrilla Warfare.* Chicago: Precedent Publishing, 1975.

Veuthey, Michel. *Guérilla et droit humanitaire.* Genève: Comité International de la Croix-Rouge, 1983.

Wilson, Heather. *International Law and the Use of Force by National Liberation Movements.* Oxford: Clarendon Press, 1988.

Index

ABM Treaty, 162
Absolute war, 161. *See also* Total war
Abyssinia, 9
Acheson, Dean, 177
ACTS. *See* Air Corps Tactical School (ACTS)
Adolphus, Gustavus, 50
Aerial bombing. *See* Air power
Aeschines, 12
Afghanistan, 9
Agenda for Peace, An (U.N.), 224
Agincourt, battle of, 36, 38, 58
Air Corps Tactical School (ACTS), 150–51, 257n39
Air power: in World War II, 118, 138, 140–41, 151–58, 217; in World War I, 124, 138, 144–46; and Hague Conference of *1899*, 141–42; and Hague Conference of *1907*, 142–44, 155; in interwar years, 146–51; Hague Aerial Bombardment Rules, 148; theories and capabilities of, 148–49; U.S. developments in, 149–50; and law of war on eve of World War II, 150–51; and Nuremberg tribunal, 155; and narrowly defined military targets, 157–59; in Gulf War, 158, 159, 221–22
Alba, duke of, 49–50, 52, 55
Alexander, Czar, 91
Alexander the Great, 25, 27
Alexander VI, Pope, 102
Algerian War, 193, 196, 198, 200–10, 212–13, 218, 275–76nn50–65
Alien peoples, 2, 3, 5, 18, 28, 43, 56–57, 60, 215–16. *See also* Native Americans
Alkmaar, siege of, 46
ALN. *See* Armée de Libération Nationale (ALN)
America. *See* Colonial America; United States

American Civil War, 5, 10, 57, 108, 109, 143, 243n38, 246n29, 255n23
American Indians. *See* Native Americans
American War of Independence, 5, 10, 44, 74–84, 243–44n43
Amphictyonic League, 12
Andreopoulos, George J., 10, 11, 191–225
Anglo-Dutch wars, 105
Angola, 210
Antiballistic missiles, 162, 163, 167
Antwerp, 52
ANZUS, 192
Apartheid, 220
Aquinas, Thomas, 2, 41
Aristotle, 56
Armée de Libération Nationale (ALN), 202–3, 276n61
Arms control. *See* Nuclear weapons
Army of Flanders, 47–48
Arnold, Gen. H. H., 153, 154
Asgill, Charles, 243–44n43
Assured Destruction concept, 180
Aston, Sir Arthur, 50–51
Athens. *See* Greece
Atomic bombs, 156–57, 160, 167, 169–70, 217. *See also* Nuclear weapons
Atomic Energy Act of *1946*, 167
Atomic Energy Commission, 167, 170, 176
Attack assessment networks, 182, 183
Augustine, St., 2, 28, 41
Austerlitz, 90
Avignon, 32
Ayala, Balthasar, 43, 44, 52
Aztecs, 56, 57

B-29s, 145, 154, 156
B-47s, 178
B-52s, 178

INDEX

Bacon, Francis, 43
Bader, Douglas, 214
Baghdad, 40
Bajadoz, 93
Baker, Newton, 149–50, 256n32
Balfour, Arthur, 111
Ballistic Missile Early Warning System, 182
Ballistic missiles, 174, 182–83, 188
Baralong, 113
Barbarians. *See* Alien peoples
Barbarossa, 56
Basic National Security Policy (U.S.), 171–72
Basing House, 47
Basra, 40
Battle of Algiers, 203, 206, 207, 208, 218
Battle of Britain, 151
Battle of the Cities, 159
Bavaria, 87
BBSU. *See* British Bombing Survey Unit (BBSU)
Belgium, 10, 123, 218, 251n16
Bellatores, 30
Belligerents versus neutrals, in maritime conflict, 105–8
Bellum hostile, 3, 34–38
Bellum Romanum (*guerre mortelle*), 3, 5, 27–28
Bentham, Jeremy, 126
Berlichingen, Götz von, 42
Berlin, bombing of, 118, 151, 259n51
Berlin crisis, 169, 176, 177, 192
Berlin Decree, 107
Bern agreements (*1917, 1918*), 124
Bernard, Richard, 43
Bertaud, Jean-Paul, 89
Best, Geoffrey, 92, 135–36
Biafra, 44
Bible, 41, 47, 54, 56, 58, 125
Biddle, Tami Davis, 7, 140–59
Biological warfare, 7, 127
Black Book of the Admiralty, The, 100
Black Prince, 37
Blake, Capt. Gen., 93
Blake, Robert, 101
Blitzkrieg, 130
Bloch, Jan, 120, 125, 137
Blockade, 106–8, 109, 111, 112, 131, 217
Bomber Command, 151–53, 156, 217, 259n57
Bombing. *See* Air power; *names of specific bombed cities*

Book of Chivalry, The, 27
Bordwell, Percy, 144
Borodino, 90, 91
Bosnia-Herzegovina, 40, 223
Bossu, count of, 55
Bougainville, Louis de, 71–73
Bouvet, Honoré, 31
Breed's Hill, battle of, 78
Briand, Aristide, 9
British Bombing Survey Unit (BBSU), 158
Brunswick, Duke of, 88
Bundy, McGeorge, 267n61
Burchinal, Gen. David, 268n61
Bush, George, 221

C3 systems, 182, 183
Caesar Augustus, 27
Calais, battle of, 38
Calley, Lt. William, 196, 213
Canada, 67, 70–71, 74, 85, 170
Carnot, Lazare-Nicolas-Marguerite, 88, 95
Carter, Jimmy, 185–87
Carthaginian wars, 228n5
Casablanca Conference, 152
Catapults, 25
Cavalry, 29, 39, 90, 229n11
CENTO, 192
Chamberlain, Neville, 149
Chandler, David G., 90
Chansons de geste, 27
Charlemagne, 28
Charles, Archduke, 89, 94, 95
Charles I, king of England, 42–43, 53, 101
Charles V, Emperor, 36
Chemical warfare, 7, 123–24, 127, 128–30, 252n26, 279n1
Chevaliers, 27
Chevauchées, 9
China, 9, 119, 128, 163, 169, 172, 173, 179, 192, 194–95, 235n20, 272n8, 279n9, 280n23
Chivalry, Age of: fighting on horseback in, 29; Peace and Truce of God movements in, 29, 30–31; standards of honorable conduct on battlefield, 30; basis of laws of war in, 31–32, 214; war-making power during, 32, 42; *guerre mortelle* in, 33–34; *bellum hostile* in, 34–38; *guerre couverte* in, 38–39; siege warfare in, 38; revenge in, 55
Churchill, Winston S., 86, 129, 131, 151–52, 154, 170
Churchyard, Thomas, 61–62